SIGNS GROW:
SEMIOSIS AND LIFE PROCESSES

This is the third volume in Floyd Merrell's trilogy on semiotics focusing on Peirce's categories of Firstness, Secondness, and Thirdness. In this book the author argues that there are passageways linking the social sciences with the physical sciences, and signs with life processes. This is not a study of the semiotics of life, but rather of semiosis as a living process. Merrell attempts to articulate the links between thought that is rooted in that which can be quantified and thought that resists quantification, namely that of consciousness. As he writes in his preface, he is intent on 'fusing the customary distinctions between life and non-life, mind and matter, self and other, appearance (fiction) and "reality" ... to reveal *that everything that is is a sign.*' In order to accomplish this goal, Peirce's tertiary concept of the sign is crucial.

Merrell begins by asking, 'What are signs that they may take on lifelike processes, and what is life that it may know the sign processes that brought it – themselves – into existence?' In order to answer this question he examines semiotic theory. He offers an original reading of Peirce's thought along with that of Prigogine and many others. Following Sebeok, Merrell reminds us that 'any and all investigation of nature and of the nature of signs and life must ultimately be semiotic in nature.'

(Toronto Studies in Semiotics)

FLOYD MERRELL is a professor in the Department of Foreign Languages and Literatures at Purdue University. He is the author of several books, including *Signs Becoming Signs: Our Perfusive, Pervasive Universe*; *Semiosis in the Postmodern Age*; and *Peirce's Semiotics Now.*

FLOYD MERRELL

Signs Grow:
Semiosis and Life Processes

UNIVERSITY OF TORONTO PRESS
Toronto Buffalo London

© University of Toronto Press Incorporated 1996
Toronto Buffalo London
Printed in Canada

ISBN 0-8020-0778-3 (cloth)
ISBN 0-8020-7142-2 (paper)

Toronto Studies in Semiotics
Editors: Marcel Danesi, Umberto Eco, Paul Perron, and Thomas A. Sebeok

∞

Printed on acid-free paper

Canadian Cataloguing in Publication Data

Merrell, Floyd, 1937–
    Signs grow : semiosis and life processes

(Toronto studies in semiotics)
ISBN 0-8020-0778-3 (bound) ISBN 0-8020-7142-2 (pbk.)

1. Semantics (Philosophy). I. Title. II. Series.
B840.M48 1996   121'.68   C96-930014-X

University of Toronto Press acknowledges the financial assistance to
its publishing program of the Canada Council and the Ontario Arts
Council.

Contents

Preface

Upon completion of the present enquiry, a twisting, whorling spiral doubles back upon itself. This volume, following on the heels of *Signs Becoming Signs: Our Perfusive, Pervasive Universe* (1991b), and *Semiosis in the Postmodern Age* (1995), ending with the beginning, beginning with the ending, evinces, in composite form, an image of the perpetual becoming of all thought-signs and sign-events, and the apparent signlessness – the absence of form and substance – of becoming.

The first book casts a very general spotlight, admittedly at times somewhat darkly – for, alas, we can hardly expect clear and distinct exposition of the matter – on Firstness, the very conditions for sign possibility. Within this unencompassed domain, this undemarcated space, this horizonless field, *what is is simply what it is*, without there yet existing any distinction regarding anything else. The second book plays somewhat the devil's advocate with the Faustian individual willing to settle for nothing less than absolute knowledge (episteme) of *what is, in so far as it is something other than the knowing self*, which implies a hopeful – though ultimately impossible – ingestion of the totality of the semiosic fabric. Our Faustian hero demands indication (indexing) of what has come into being with nary a nod to the beinglessness of becoming and the incessant becomingness of being. He prefers to deny the tenuous, fallible, ephemeral, and to all appearances unruly, nature of what he thinks is lying in mute expectancy of his all-knowing cognitive grasp. He wishes to ignore the perpetual give-and-take with otherness, that inevitable dialogue (*agonistics, doxa*) revealing that he is actually no more than a rather helpless bundle of feeble and fallible conjectures – arrived at during certain fleeting moments in the living process – and their negations (or in Peirce's terms, refutations), which entails the process by which he should become aware of the error of his ways. By and large this second study outlines in general terms the way of a sign's actualization, its coming into existence as a this-hereness, its ephemeral thingness as a fleeting haecceity. This view entails the sign as a mere surfacing, a baring of itself to whatever audience might happen to be passing by; and then, it almost immediately re-submerges into the semiosic flow. That is to say, focus in the second volume rests most generally on Peirce's category of Secondness.

The third and present book will most likely appear even more pretentious: it is an attempt to spread an umbrella over life processes and sign processes in general, placing them in the same ballpark while at the same time fusing the customary distinctions between life and non-life, mind and matter, self and other, appearance (fiction) and 'reality,' order and disorder, being and becoming, and the discrete and the continuous, ultimately to reveal that *everything that is is sign*, that whatever anything is other than its being a sign, it is also a sign. This places us squarely within the domain of mediation, 'tertiation,' the eternal semiosic push of successive 'nows' along the knife-edge race of time from past to future. In other words, the spotlight attempts an apparently impossible illumination both of what just happened to pass away, though leaving a trace of its having been, and of what happens to be coming into view, at this stage revealing no more than a vague, nebulous countenance. These are the conditions of sign potentiality, of the sign's offering itself up *to* some semiotic agent *for* some purpose *in* some respect or capacity. In other words, my concern now rests in general terms on the Thirdness of the sign.

Progression of the three volumes in question – if I dare evoke the term 'progression' in this context – is from oneness to duplexity to multiplicity, aleatory possibility to duality-actuality to potentiality-probability, or in short, as I have suggested, from Firstness to Secondness to Thirdness. The initial stage is the bare suggestion of distinction, the second entails indication, and the third opens the door *to* the possibility of meaning. First is the sign and nothing but the sign. Then the sign's 'delineation' – I tentatively say 'delineation' here in order to avoid the 'representation' trap – *of* some 'semiotic object' or other. And finally, the sign's mediary translation – that is, interpretation (via the interpretant) – *into* another sign, and that sign into another interpretant, ad infinitum. The sign of Firstness implies resemblance, since everything is in some form or fashion similar to everything else; that of Secondness evokes what is generally presumed to exist 'out there,' though it cannot be known absolutely; that of Thirdness, however, remains rather aloof, mediating between the others without getting its hands too dirty in the process. This third category is street-wise, yet it continues to dwell in its partly arbitrarily edified house on the hill; it enters the scene, meddling with everything, yet it is somehow able to maintain a relative degree of autonomy.

Admittedly, I began this trilogy on a perplexing – and what might appear to smack of a blatantly logocentric – cosmological note (*kosmogonia*, creation of the totality). Soon, however, in the second volume I set the props for the play of the world, that is, for the interaction between semiotic agents and their world, prototypical of which is Shakespeare's depiction of Macbeth and his dagger in chapter 8. And finally, in the pages that follow I built up an image of the ongoing recursive, self-organizing semiosic flow. In the beginning is the self-reflexive cosmological paradox, then the mode of sign production, followed by the mode of information-meaning, this latter characterized as a push toward self-sufficiency, toward recursive, self-reflexive, completion: the ultimate sign of unity. In other words, at the extremes, beginning and ending finally meet. The circle is closed.

Or in another manner of articulating the process, after their birth, signs begin growth in a twisting, turning world of ordered complexity, of chaotic harmony, and, in spite of any and all impediments, life somehow manages to get on: all signs in the semiosic river emerge, grow through puberty and mature, usually survive mid-life crisis, then enter into senescence and fade away. The process inexorably continues. It cannot do otherwise, for no sign is capable simply of standing still.

I cannot ignore those who have contributed to my exploratory incursions over the past decade or so. The list is inexhaustible; only a small portion of it can be included in the printed page. My hope is that I may be able to do justice to those most deserving of acknowledgments; regarding any unwitting omissions, *mea culpa*.

Close to home base, I have appreciated the input, the scrutiny, the support, the suggestions and criticism afforded me, by Djelal Kadir (now at the University of Oklahoma), Myrdene Anderson (our indomitable transdisciplinary spirit at Purdue), Virgil Lokke (whose absence occasionally provided motivation), Calvin O. Schrag (for his patience with my ignorance regarding certain procedural matters), and, rather surprisingly, Howard Mancing (ironically, and though he remains unaware of the fact, he was a catalyst instilling in me an obstinate determination I had never before experienced). I owe my warmest thanks to Marcel Danesi, Ron Schoeffel of University of Toronto Press, and my copyeditor Darlene Money. And most certainly, I wish to thank Thomas A. Sebeok for his continuing encouragement and support, without which this and the other books of this trilogy would never have seen the light of day.

I have cherished the academic camaraderie and the personal contacts – though they have been much too sparing due to the distances that separate us – with Fernando Andacht, Eugen Baer, John Deely, Dinda Gorlée, Claudio Guerri, Jørgen Dines Johansen, Helena Katz, Solomon Marcus, María Nélida de Juano, Irmengaard Rauch, Rosa María Ravera, Francisco Romera Castillo, Maria Lucia Santaella Braga, Elizabeth Saporiti, Paula Siganevich, Bill Spinks, and Jean Umiker-Sebeok. In so far as dialogue with the printed word goes, I must acknowledge my interaction over the years with a host of scholars too numerous to cite here: let the reference list at the tail end of this book speak for them. I also wish to extend my appreciation to Mouton de Gruyter for permission to publish material from an article, 'Of Signs and Life' (*Semiotica* 101 [3/4], 1994, 175–240) that makes up the major portion of chapters 1 and 2.

Of course, the dialogue making up my modest trilogy, which can by no means be brought to a close with the present volume, is dedicated, most appropriately, to Araceli, whose own spirit has, as far as I can recall, also vehemently resisted closure.

SIGNS GROW:
SEMIOSIS AND LIFE PROCESSES

1

Of Life and Signs

A few aphorisms, then, to set the tone of this enquiry. 'Life is produced by life' (Chicago Natural Museum of History); the 'dream of a bacterium is to become another bacteria' (Jacob 1982:72); 'people, animals, plants, bacteria, and viruses – are only a sign's way of making another sign' (Sebeok 1979:xii); 'life is but a sequence of inferences or a train of thought' (Peirce *CP*:7.583); a physicist is 'made of a conglomeration of the very particles he describes ... Thus ... the world we know is constructed in order ... to see itself' (Spencer-Brown 1979:105).

I offer these citations as a point of departure, for they hint at the complexity of both sign processes and life processes. Signs and life have no inherent need of any domain more complex than they for their self-perpetuation: as we shall note, they are, in so far as they are turned within themselves, recursive, self-sufficient systems; they are, regarding their self-referential nature, self-organizing. The question, then, is: What are signs that they may take on lifelike processes, and what is life that it may know the sign processes that brought it – themselves – into existence? What I am after in this and the following chapters is not a semiotics of life, which has been the focus of a number of recent studies, but rather, *semiosis as a living process*. Upon embarking on this exploratory venture, I shall call upon numerous current topics, including the 'hypercycle' idea, 'dissipative structures,' 'autopoiesis,' and some late work on time and space, in addition to Peirce on signs. Such digressive navigation may lead some readers into hitherto unknown and somewhat strange waters, though, I trust, a general cartographic scheme of the entire journey will eventually come into view.

After this brief preamble, I now offer a nutshell outline of the present enquiry's trajectory in order to establish the proper mood.

1. SELF-REFERRING SIGNS

Systems theorist Erich Jantsch (1980:97–156) takes pains to illustrate how biologist Manfred Eigen's concept of 'hypercycle' is the key to explaining the universe's grand bootstrap operation of self-organization. A hypercycle, in brief, is a closed catalytic process involving the intermediate production of chemicals one or more of which acts as an autocatalyst. According to this story, by means of hypercyclic activity, first, prokaryotic (nucleus-free) cells appeared, followed by eukaryotic (nucleus-possessing) cells, then cells that spontaneously organized themselves into colonies such as sponges and slime moulds arrived on the scene, and finally, primitive sentient organisms emerged. Consciousness as we know it eventually came into existence. And now, conscious 'man,' proud 'man,' that recent 'invention' according to Foucault (1970), that 'glassy essence' in Peirce's (CP:5:317) conception, has presumed, during the heyday of modernity, to take her/his place at the apex of the massive biological pyramid, from which vantage s/he will ultimately be able imperiously to survey all that *has been, is,* and *will be.*

But a problem rests in the notion of a discontinuous cosmic leap into consciousness. If we are to take Charles S. Peirce's concept of the sign seriously, and, in fact, if we dare swim against the current by heeding a certain aspect of ancient Eastern traditions, we must eventually confront the rather uneasy premonition that mind and consciousness are not independent and autonomous as we have traditionally held. Rather, like Peircean signs, they tend to merge into one another and into the world, ultimately forming in the process a continuous whole (Schrödinger 1967; also Merrell 1991b). Consciousness – that is, self-awareness or I-awareness – and mind itself, are no more than signs in the sense of Peirce. But they are not complete and self-contained signs. On the contrary. They have emerged from their predecessor-sign(s), and they will give rise to their successor-sign(s), all in a continuous process of signs incessantly becoming signs along the stream of semiosis.

Indeed, signs and consciousness cannot but be inextricably linked – however problematic the very idea remains. All signs strive for fulfilment by way of other signs, though *for* each and every particular semiotic agent the trail can never reach its end-point. As a sign passes over into its *other*, into what it *is not*, it has already begun the process of giving rise to something *other* than that *other*. That is, neither signs nor consciousness-as-sign can stand alone. If I may at this preliminary stage evoke Peirce's categories – to be discussed *et passim* – signs, as Firsts, are already passing into their Secondness, in order that they may give a nod to their respective *others* now entering the scene, which is made possible solely by the existence of Thirdness. During this process, signs engage in a perpetual endeavour to organize the/a 'semiotic world' in their own image, and if successful, they may be capable of patterning some aspect of a 'semiotically real' domain (not the 'real' *an sich* as we shall observe) *for* their respective semiotic agents. In comparable fashion, by the successive generation of what Peirce called 'thought-signs' (signs of the mind), consciousness tends to construct a world according to its own image, for, 'everything which is present to us is a phenomenal manifestation of ourselves' (*CP*:5.283).

Neither signs nor consciousness can hope to arrest the semiosic flow within which they are caught. They are swept along by the current, in spite of their feeble and futile efforts to bring permanence to the hustle-bustle of signs incessantly becoming other signs. Yet the intriguing and rather paradoxical enigma persists that, ultimately, a sign and its particular *other*, as well as thought-signs and the signs thought, reflect themselves and nothing but themselves. From the corporate view, they make up a self-organizing, self-contained sphere engaged in a breathtaking flurry of activity. The only possible key to an understanding of this riddle, Peirce tells us, lies in the fact that in thinking we become part of this very activity. 'What we think of,' he writes, 'cannot possibly be of a different nature from thought itself. For the thought thinking and the immediate thought-object are the very same *thing regarded* from different points of view' (*CP*:6.339). Ultimately, the mind is, itself, a sign.

Now these are strange words, enough to set even the most tenacious 'textual idealist' – to use Richard Rorty's (1982) phrase – back on her heels. This concept, nevertheless, must engage us repeatedly in the pages that follow. Before we enter into Peirce's enigmatic 'Mind ≈ Sign' dictum, however, I suggest we turn briefly to his most primitive of stages, the notion of 'nothingness' preceding all Firstness, Secondness, and Thirdness (for greater detail, see Merrell 1991b). As Peirce (*CP*:6.217) puts it:

We start … with nothing, pure zero. But this is not the nothing of negation. For *not* means *other than*, and *other* is merely a synonym of the ordinal numeral *second*. As such it implies a first; while the present pure zero is prior to every first. The nothing of negation is the nothing of death, which comes *second* to, or after, everything. But this pure zero is the nothing of not having been born. There is no individual thing, no compulsion, outward nor inward, no law. It is the germinal nothing, in which the whole universe is involved and foreshadowed. As such, it is absolutely undefined and unlimited possibility – boundless possibility.

From this 'absolute nothingness,' this *zero degree*, Firstness arises as if out of nowhere. It is a bound from sheer possibility (Firstness) to actuality (Secondness) – somewhat reminiscent of the quantum transition from 'waves' to 'particles'

– which is now capable of becoming an actual ('real,' detectable) sign-event *for* someone *in* some respect or capacity (Thirdness). In this coming into being of 'somethingness' from the domain of 'nothingness,' Peirce tells us that a space was severed to produce a 'cut' (potentially an icon as such), which could then give rise to a sign of indication (index), the combination of both creating the ground for an entity and an attribute – a subject and an object (or predicate) – each of which in the best of all worlds reflects the other.[1] And from that point onward, signs begin their arduous road toward development within what eventually becomes the flow of signs Peirce dubbed *semiosis* – which at times twists and turns into whitewater, and on occasion even appears chaotic, an infinitely complex maelstrom.

This formulation enjoys, I would submit, broad universal implications. From microsign levels to exceedingly complex macrosign levels to semiotic agents themselves, recursively dissonant sign generacy patterns at one and the same time the self-referential, recursive process being played out: the observer (a sign herself) engages in perpetual interaction with the semiosic process emerging from Peirce's 'nothingness.' This process, by a route complementary with that of the observer, eventually makes way for irreversible, asymmetrical, development – rather commensurate with Eigen 'hypercycles,' as we shall note – and finally, to the very evolution of the observer herself. In this manner, signs, like the evolution and development of biological organisms, 'grow,' ultimately giving rise both to observer and observed, knower and known, sign-thoughts and the signs thought, consciousness and self-consciousness: the universe of signs dialogues with itself.

2. A VERTIGINOUS WHORL

But I am getting ahead of myself. In order more properly to unfold this theme, let me return, at the most basic of levels, to the Eastern tradition I mentioned in passing above.

According to many ancient Chinese views, somewhat the equivalent of the space-time continuum was organized recursively according to a numerical pattern, from 1 to 9 and then to 10 – or if you wish, to 1 again – thus completing a cycle and beginning a new one. The operations of addition and subtraction, multiplication and division, were generated from these same number combinations, which eventually gravitated westward to become the cornerstone of our science and thought in general. In terms of Western mathematics, these ancient Chinese patterns can be regarded as 'square matrices' of the sort introduced by Cayley's matrix algebra whose range of applications has included quantum theory and contemporary technology (Noble 1969). The difference

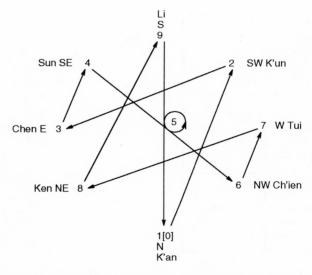

Li
S
9

Sun SE   4   2   SW K'un

Chen E   3   5   7   W Tui

Ken NE   8   6   NW Ch'ien

1[0]
N
K'an

FIGURE 1

between the Chinese system and Western mathematics lies in the former's matrices considered as qualities of a 'field' rather than pure sets (von Franz 1974:25–26).

Take, for example, the *Ho-t'u* model (Granet 1968:156) as interpreted by Marie Luise von Franz (1974:235–41) (figure 1). The order of the trigrams of the *I Ching* as a grouping of pairs of opposites is altered in such a way that it corresponds to the temporal progression of the phenomenal world in terms of annual cycles. The timeless order is temporalized. Stasis becomes movement. And feminine signs (*Sun, Li, K'un, Tui*) stand against masculine signs (*Ch'ien, K'an, Ken, Chen*) to retain a polarization of opposites as the unidirectional progression advances (see Wilhelm 1967 I:285–6).

The *Ho-t'u* spiral dovetails quite nicely with table 1, consisting of Peirce's nine categories combining to form his ten basic signs, and some common examples of them as depicted in table 2. The first cycle of signs is chiefly iconic: *qualisigns* (1), *iconic sinsigns* (2), and *iconic legisigns* (5). The second cycle is indexical: *rhematic indexical sinsigns* (3), *dicent sinsigns* (4), *rhematic indexical legisigns* (6), and *dicent indexical legisigns* (7). And the third cycle is symbolic: *rhematic symbols* (8), *dicent symbols* (9), and *arguments* (10).[2] Peirce's nine categories interact at three fundamentally distinct levels, each according to its own signifying mode, with two-way feedback between all levels and with no level or category necessarily prioritized over any other. Specifically – and if you will bear with me while I divulge some Peircean basics – the root modes are *monadic, dyadic,* and *triadic.*

TABLE 1

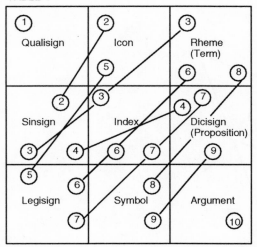

A monad (iconic relation) manifests some parallel with something else, but in order to do so it must be distinguished from it, such distinction existing as a potential to be realized by some semiotic agent in terms of Secondness. A dyad (indexical relation) consists of something in interaction with something else potentially for the semiotic agent. Typical of dyadic *relata* are A then B, A opposed to B, A greater than B, A higher than B, and so on. A triad (symbolic relation) includes the semiotic agent in the equation, such as the case, A gives B to C, which also necessarily involves some intention, purpose, or goal, whether explicit or tacit, in the sense of the agent's interpreting a triadic relation between exclusively phenomenal entities.

The upper integers in the categories in the table 1 grid evince discontinuous progression the gaps between which are 'smoothed over' by the intermingling integers below to produce ten signs from nine categories. In the *Ho-t'u* system viewed as a totality, there is no apparent cyclicality in terms of linear movement, but rather, an ordering of powers that stands as a vibrating, scintillating whole, much like standing waves in an atemporal state of orderliness (or like a hummingbird whose flight is arrested by adjusting the camber of her rapidly oscillating wings in order to maintain a dynamic yet fixed position while she inspects the flower before her).[3] However, the apparently static image actually contains an inner dynamism serving to generate time and change. In another way of putting it, the static image as a potential *description* of all signs that can spin out of the matrix calls for its complementary *interpretation*, a proper

TABLE 2

$R_1 O_1 I_1$	(1)	Qualisign	A sensation of 'blue'
$R_2 O_1 I_1$	(2)	Iconic sinsign	A self-contained diagram
$R_2 O_2 I_1$	(3)	Rhematic indexical sinsign	A spontaneous cry
$R_2 O_2 I_2$	(4)	Dicent sinsign	A weather-vane
$R_3 O_1 I_1$	(5)	Iconic legisign	A diagram apart from its self-containment
$R_3 O_2 I_1$	(6)	Rhematic indexical legisign	A demonstrative pronoun
$R_3 O_2 I_2$	(7)	Dicent indexical legisign	A commonplace evocation or expression
$R_3 O_3 I_1$	(8)	Rhematic symbol	A term
$R_3 O_3 I_2$	(9)	Dicent symbol	A proposition
$R_3 O_3 I_3$	(10)	Argument	Text

Where:
R = Representamen; O = semiotic object; I = interpretant
1 = Category of Firstness, 2 = Secondness, 3 = Thirdness
The arrow 'upward' represents semiosis (sign-event and thought-sign processes) and the arrow 'downward' represents phaneroscopy (thought-sign processes) (see glossary).

qualification of the attributes being described. And the very act of *interpretation* gives rise to the description's meaning in order to bring its cyclical, or better, spiraloidal, dynamism into proper focus.

Regarding Peircean symbols – or natural language in this case – every *descriptive* domain (as black marks on white), in so far as it is changeless once the phenomenon in question is described, requires an *interpretation* (signs arising out of the description in its interaction with a semiotic agent). The *interpretative process* is not incompatible, but *complementary*, with the description, and unlike the description, it must forever remain open and incomplete for any finite community of semiotic agents. The *descriptive process*, coupled with its corresponding interpretation, in this sense, is comparable to the dynamic *unfolding*, potentially to infinity, of numbers (signs) from the static matrix.[4] In similar fashion, Peirce's 'field' of ten signs and their matrical relations can be looked upon as a dynamic yet static set giving promise to recursively infinite sign generation, which, like the *Ho-t'u* matrix, would thus follow an *aperiodic spiral* rather than mere self-returning cycles.

Now, aperiodicity is made possible by occasional 'symmetry breaks' – in the order of Prigogine, as we shall observe – that serve to disrupt the otherwise monotonous cycles, and as a consequence, spiraloids emerge. Such spiraloids spring up most notably (1) at sign 5, the pivotal sign and first legisign to give an initial glimpse of authentic signs to come, and (2) at sign 10, the argument. Since the argument's concluding signs tie in with the initial premise signs, it can, in the eye of its beholder at least, come to be self-confirmatory and self-sufficient, ideally a self-referentially closed system (a sign of itself). In this manner, sign 10, like sign 1, is a recursive, self-reentering entity potentially evincing monadic – that is, autonomous – properties. As a totality comparable to the mandala, it is not governed by linear movement, but rather, it composes a matrix, an ordering of powers in timeless equilibrium. However, an argument, like all closed systems short of the universe as a whole, must exist within some context or other. As its context, like all contexts, undergoes incessant change, the argument, like all arguments, will eventually be 'opened,' subjected to re-interpretation, and ultimately revision or rejection. An alternate argument can then be generated: thus the combination of, and tension between, continuity and discontinuity, process and structure, change and stasis.

Sign 5, the iconic legisign, is the first sign of *law*, that is, of the sign's generation and processing by way of *convention, habit*, along *embedded* and *entrenched* pathways of least semiotic resistance – to be the focus of discussion below. *Tokens* at this point begin their long trek toward becoming *types*, association is in the process of forming habit, and regularity can now be at least provisionally acknowledged. With the emergence of sign 5, what *is*, is, paradoxically, the member of a class to which it belongs. Yet over time, it fortunately becomes something *other than* what it *was*, for every exemplification of a general type cannot but be transitory in the twisting, shifting world of semiosis. Sign 5 is in this manner a most tentative conjunction, and fusion, of stasis and dynamism, timelessness and temporality, continuity and discontinuity.

Following Niels Bohr's profound logical, scientific, and metaphysical notion of *complementarity* in quantum theory, what might be called in this context 'standing wave' functions are to their collapse into 'particles' as the sign matrix is to actualized signs, and as descriptions are to their respective interpretations – or, by extension, as genotype is to phenotype (Löfgren 1981a, 1981b). The first terms of these pairs correspond to Firstness, while the second terms pertain to a combination of Secondness and Thirdness. The first consist merely of what there is, without the existence of conscious participating agents, while the second involve 'realities' *put to use for* some specific purpose *by* someone *in* his/her participatory universe.[5] The first is the realm of chance, a matrix of possibilities; the second consist of the pragmatic give-and-take of life. Without any time-bound semiotic agent interacting with signs, the 1-10 recursive scheme remains atemporal, a mere oscillation between the either and the or. It remains unfulfilled: a field of somewhat less than genuine signs awaiting the intervention, collaboration, and corroboration, of some participatory agent.

After these necessary preliminaries, I now turn more specifically to the task at hand.

3. SIGNS OF LIFE

From the most general standpoint, the emergence and unfolding of life has often been compared to the emergence and unfolding of language,[6] and Peirce reiterates much the same of life and of the life of signs, especially regarding symbols.[7]

However, though there is to date no universally accepted model for this evolutionary process, at micro- and macrolevels Manfred Eigen's *hypercycle* idea, coupled with Ilya Prigogine's *symmetry breaks* and *dissipative structures*, appears to be a promising candidate for life modelling and sign modelling (see the glossary for definitions of terms). *En passant*, the hypercycle is purely biological; it moves 'upward' only. It consists of a coupling between nucleic acids and proteins, the former, as 'information components,' specifying the latter, as 'structural components,' within a cell. The entire process is closed, since not only do nucleic acids code for proteins, but some of the proteins are needed to produce the nucleic acid reactions in the first place. In this manner, the components making up the hypercycle, as a group, are self-sufficient and self-organizing: they raise themselves up by their own bootstraps (Eigen 1971).

In contrast, dissipative structures are inorganic as well as organic, and they maintain openness to their environment. Moreover, they swim against the current of classical physics. The classical interpretation of entropy calls for closed systems, although it is difficult to find one in nature. Prigogine argues that, on the contrary, some of the most simple open systems, when exchanging energy and material with their environment, enter stable states that are not merely chaotic – the end product of entropy – but represent organized complexity. Dissipative structures entail far-from-equilibrium conditions that reach branch points (bifurcations) from which the system is free to 'choose' particular paths. Since this 'choice' is not predictable, dissipative structures involve both determinism (between bifurcations) and unpredictable chaos (at bifurcations). A dissipative structure passes through bifurcations in response to energy and material input from its environment, and on so doing, enters successive stages of increased complexity and increased order (for further, see the appendix).

This pathway to higher complexity is irreversible, except by sudden collapse in response to inordinately high energy and material input. A system may thus respond to increased input by collapsing back to a more disordered state as well as by passing through a bifurcation point to greater order (Prigogine 1980). As we shall observe, dissipative structures evince counterparts both to sign growth 'upward' (see table 2), from signs of lesser complexity to greater complexity, from Firstness to Thirdness, from iconicity to symbolicity), and 'downward,' from greater to lesser complexity (though, as we shall note, the parameters may be expanded in the process).

Regarding our physical universe, an originary symmetry break, following the mould of Prigogine, might have occurred during the condensation and cooling of gases into stars, planets, and other celestial bodies later to become structured into equilibrium systems such as crystals. The Second Law of Thermodynamics, dictating the irreversible trend toward increasing entropy, usually leads to the destruction of structures, to disorder. But this tendency does not always hold. Under certain conditions, binding forces between atoms and molecules at low temperatures can give rise to symmetrically ordered structures. Crystals are a good case in point. They obviously manifest greater 'order.' At the same time, they may be – though not necessarily – of higher entropy than the liquid state from which they were formed, depending on whether or not they now have less available energy. This emergence of *form* as increased rather than decreased entropy – that is, decreased rather than increased available energy – may also help explain condensation models of the universe (Jantsch 1980:chap. 5). But ideally crystals are closed, autonomous systems, whose tedious replication is of little interest regarding our present concerns. In search of a more captivating example, let us shift focus to new and different structures that can come about by the spontaneous formation of open systems in constant exchange of energy and matter with their environment. At their highest levels of development, these open systems constitute life-forms generally characterized by a tendency toward asymmetry, irreversibility, and nonequilibrium, in contrast to the closed, symmetry-increasing equilibrium structures typical of the inorganic realm.

Of recent it has been speculated that life came about precisely from crystal forms, which represent the highest degree of organization found in the inorganic realm. J.D. Bernal (1967) believes crystallography is the key to molecular biology, and Graham Cairns-Smith (1982) argues that the origins of life can be located in primitive genes that are not merely crystal-like; they *are* crystals. Living organisms, according to Cairns-Smith, evolved from asymmetrical, aperiodic, self-replicating metallic minerals in clay deposits. The necessary information was coded in a crystalline structure that was eventually transferred to what later in the process became nucleic acids. For sure, crystalline matter was in abundance during the Precambrian period when life is believed to have emerged. It is not amiss to assume that, washed about by the primordial broth, and undergoing chemical evolution, they eventually developed certain molecular preferences. In this manner, a crystalline biochemistry could finally give way to a biochemistry controlled by organic compounds of no more than quasicrystalline form.

Perhaps the most imaginative leap along these lines was exercised earlier, by Erwin Schrödinger (1967). In a penetrating series of lectures delivered in 1943, he speculated that what was at the time considered the essence of life, a chromosome fibre, could suitably be called an *aperiodic crystal*. Aperiodic crystals grow by ions attaching themselves to the surface of the seed crystal, but attachment to the surface is weaker than attachment to indentations or 'flaws' that eventually appear somewhere in the process. As the crystal grows, the indentations spread trigonometrically – somewhat akin to what have been called 'strange attractors' in chaos physics (Gleick 1987). Ions recursively continue to pile upon ions, and gradual rotation, initially caused by the indentations, produces a spiraloid succession of layers ideally following the lines of a Fibonacci curve, as depicted in nature most notably by ram and narwhal horns, sea shells, and sea horses.[8] Schrödinger went on to suggest that in life processes at the molecular level regularities and irregularities are found in one and the same structure: an algorithm dictates successive reiterations, each of which, on completion, leaves conditions slightly different than what they were.

In certain ways quite true to Schrödinger's prediction, it was discovered that the DNA double helix consists of a regular arrangement of atoms along the outside of the two helix chains, but that inside there is an irregular arrangement of four chemical groups joining one chain to the other, each with a different shape and size (see the glossary for further). This tightly packed structure evincing regularity on the outside but irregularity on the inside was resolved by Watson and Crick in terms of what can be labelled, to re-evoke the term, *complementarity* (Wilkins 1987). The four different groups in DNA join together to form two pairs combining in such a way that their exterior dimensions are the same. There is difference within sameness, or, so to speak, difference that makes a difference and simultaneously sameness that erases trivial differences: the opposites of irregularity and regularity form a complementary whole, which, it is now generally believed, constitutes the essence of life.

However, in certain respects Schrödinger neatly missed the mark. He believed chromosomes were almost literally the molecular secret of life, writing that they 'represent the highest degree of well-ordered atomic association we know of – much higher than the ordinary periodic crystal – in virtue of the individual role every atom and every radical is playing there' (Schrödinger 1967:196). He envisioned a mechanical order-out-of-disorder principle that was capable of eluding the entropic push toward chaos. It is now known via dissipative structure investigations, however, that self-organizing systems, living and nonliving alike, create order out of chaos. Nothing is gained from nothing, nor do living systems play a trick on Mother Nature. Rather, they are able to capitalize on the natural tendency toward entropy production or equilibrium by maintaining remote-from-equilibrium conditions between themselves and their environment through metabolic pathways of dissipative activity. It is precisely a combination of order and chaos, equilibrium and disequilibrium, and closure and openness, within which the vital properties of life are able to reside.

Be that as it may, the fact remains that just as irregular aperiodic crystals, in contrast to the pristine purity of periodic crystals, suggest the possibility of life processes, so also life processes, consisting of unruly sloughs, sumps, slush, and sludge, find themselves patterned in the inorganic realm in the form of Prigogine symmetry breaking and dissipative structures, phenomena now believed by many to be prevalent in microscopic and macroscopic inorganic reactions as well as in life itself.[9] Symmetry breaking bears on a tension between order and chaos, or better, between apparent disorder and supervening order.

This tension is also geometrically illustrated by what have been dubbed *quasicrystals*, close cousins to Schrödinger's aperiodic crystals. The geometry of three-dimensional space exacts stringent limitations on the nature of crystal symmetries. A floor (planar surface) can be tiled following twofold, threefold, fourfold, or sixfold, but never fivefold, symmetry. Nevertheless, some strange crystal forms, *quasicrystals*, exist that violate this principle, as depicted by 'Penrose tiles,' named after physicist Roger Penrose (1989). Penrose tiles evince complexity (apparent disorder) at local levels, but apparent order when one considers the whole, and from the perspective of a third dimension. Nature ordinarily seeks out crystal configuration at the lowest possible energy levels. In the case of quasicrystals, the lowest energy is more difficult to discover: the most suitable, orderly, and symmetrical arrangement exists only at global, and never local, levels. Penrose argues that such global order arises out of cooperation between myriad entities at the quantum or microlevel to produce what we want to perceive and conceive as our relatively ordered macrolevel of 'reality' (Penrose 1989:chap. 10).

From a local perspective, this switch from fourfold to fivefold to sixfold symmetry, that is, from symmetry to asymmetry and back again, is comparable to what physicists call *phase transitions*, also germane to Prigogine's dissipative structures. A simple example of phase transition within a Prigogine system is experienced in the water issuing from a faucet. Turn the knob slightly and a steady stream is produced, which, with another turn, becomes turbulent upon entering a new phase, and then, with yet another turn, it stabilizes into an orderly flow that is nevertheless different in form from the first one. In Prigogine's (1980) terminology, the initial symmetry is ruptured at some bifurcation point by a symmetry break producing far-from-equilibrium conditions representing a more complex phase, which eventually settles down to a 'higher' form of order – and, as the complexity of these orders continues to increase, life eventually emerges. A well-documented practical example of this process is found in dissipative hydrodynamics, commonly referred to as *Bénard cells*. If a shallow pan of water is heated, at first the molecules at the bottom with higher kinetic energy are prevented from rising freely by the layers of molecules above, and a chaotic give-and-take ensues. Then, at some critical point, macroscopic molecular streams combine into hexagonal cells allowing the faster-moving molecules to rise while others replace them toward the bottom of the pan. A new macroscopic order has emerged from cooperation between countless molecules at the microscopic level.

Classical thermodynamics is predicated on the idea of equilibrium structures, such as periodic crystals. Bénard cells are structures as well, but of a different order: there is structure and order on one side of the equation but dissipation and waste on the other. That is, the system maintains a degree of autonomy at one level while at another it engages in constant interaction with the outside world. The parameters describing ordinary crystals are derivable from the properties of the molecules of which they are composed. In contrast, Bénard cells, like dissipative structures – and Penrose's quasicrystals – are 'a reflection of the global situation of nonequilibrium producing them. The parameters describing them are macroscopic; they are not of the order of 10^{-8} cm, like the distance between the molecules of a crystal, but of the order of centimeters. Similarly, the time scales are different – they correspond not to molecular times (such as periods of vibration of individual molecules, which may correspond to about 10^{-15} sec) but to macroscopic times: seconds, minutes, or hours' (Prigogine and Stengers 1984:144).

Another of Prigogine's favourite case studies of dissipative structures is the Belousov-Zhabotinsky reaction consisting of a mixture of cerium sulphate, malonic acid, and potassium bromate dissolved in sulphuric acid to produce a dramatic pulsating, fluctuation effect consisting of outward-moving concentric circles of Ce^{+3} and Ce^{+4} ions. The Belousov-Zhabotinsky reaction provides the first real chemical reaction that supports the notion of self-organization in much the sense of Eigen's hypercycles, and at more complex levels, of cell growth and replication. In Prigogine terms, it patterns self-organizing, via order (complexity) arising out of chaos (by way of symmetry breaks), and vice versa. The reaction appears to suffer no effects of the Second Law of Thermodynamics; it does not merely move irreversibly toward a chaotic, disordered state but remains self-perpetuating as long as optimal conditions inhere. On so doing, it seems to possess 'memory' and 'a will of its own,' as if it had been injected with a dose of life processes, as if it were organic rather than inorganic matter. Indeed, for Prigogine, ultimately the only difference between a hurricane and an amoeba is of magnitude and complexity. Both processes are not-quite-periodic, they evince far-from-equilibrium conditions, and they suffer occasional symmetry breaks.

In fact, it is becoming increasingly evident that binary distinctions regarding the empirical world are ludicrous at their worst and strained at their best. In mathematics, sharp lines of demarcation can usually be established between pairs of classes: asymmetrical structures are either left-handed or right-handed, every integer is either odd or even, a series is either discrete or continuous and countable or uncountable, geometric structures are either superposable into their mirror images or they are not. Regarding physical 'reality,' in contrast, divisions become fuzzy, from the quantum level up. No matter how the world is bifurcated, arbitrariness inevitably raises its ugly head, for (1) the two consequent domains could always have been subdivided in another way, and (2) near the dividing line, things inexorably become vague and ambiguous. The life/nonlife distinction suffers the same fate, especially following Prigogine's seminal work. Viruses perhaps most effectively illustrate the demise of our coveted life/nonlife dichotomy. Though considerably smaller than bacteria, they have the power to absorb material from their environment, grow, and make replicas of themselves, all properties of life. Yet when removed from living tissues, they crystallize, taking on the beauty of regular and semiregular polyhedrons and evincing no sign whatsoever of life. They are as 'dead' as a block of salt. But when placed once again into the life-forms they are designed to infect, they come back to 'life.' Just as the life/nonlife bifurcation is fuzzy, so are most other divisions, no matter how venerable their standing or how passionately they are coveted, from the quantum level to macrocosmic domains. The universe is radically asymmetrical, in spite of our wishes to the contrary.

An overriding problem is that the Western tradition in general, including classical logic, has been plagued by 'prejudice in favour of symmetry' (Hartshorne 1970:chap. 7). Even in classical logic – and especially classical logic, that bastion of Western thought – ideal symmetry is found in equivalence, self-identity, and monism (Peirce's Firstness). Negation, opposition, and inversion usher in otherness (Secondness) to generate two-way or binary symmetry, which is over the long haul every bit as directionless as monadic symmetry. But such symmetry is '*a special case*, not the general principle' (Hartshorne 1970:205). A more general principle is, precisely, one-way, time-dependent asymmetry. There exist, to be sure, one-way relations of Secondness (cause-effect, greater than, subservient to) that afford at least a glimpse into temporal and dynamic rather than static connectedness. Yet they still miss the mark. At a more sophisticated level, relations of *equivalence* and *either this or that* partake of Firstness and Secondness respectively. Still, there is no legitimate asymmetry. However, when negation is inscribed into the formula, conjunction of the two terms or entities in question can be mediated by a third to yield *neither this nor that*, or *not both this and that*, which revs up the engine of Peirce's process philosophy perpetually pushing signs irreversibly – generating asymmetry and aperiodicity as a by-product – toward their completion, their *ultimate interpretant*.

The catchword is unmistakably *negation*. Peirce (*CP*:203–6) was the first to conceive, and Henry Sheffer (1913) to publish, what became known as the 'Sheffer stroke function,' by which, from a primitive notion of negation, the propositional functions of classical logic can be generated (see Berry 1952; Merrell 1991b, 1995).[10] The 'stroke function' demonstrates that negation, used reflexively, can yield asymmetrical results, forcing the conclusion that asymmetry is more general and more fundamental than symmetry: triadicity, which is asymmetrical, encompasses dyadic symmetry. Hartshorne (1970:210) writes in this respect that '*symmetry within asymmetry*, we meet again and again. I see in it a paradigm for metaphysics. What we are to look for in basic concepts is comprehensive asymmetry or directional order embracing a subordinate aspect of symmetry.'

In another way of putting it, in the beginning was symmetry of the purest sort: the 'nothingness' of Peirce and the ancient traditions. But this creates a problem. For something to emerge from nothing, a 'distinction,' a Peirce 'cut,' must be made between that which *is* and that which it *is not*. This results in asymmetry of some sort or other, which at the molecular level may be simply the initiation of levorotary or dextrorotary movement – that is, Pasteur's 'stereoasymmetry,' the asymmetrical arrangement of atoms in complex molecules (recall note 8) – which may be viewed as the organic counterpart to aperiodic crystals. Such initiation of asymmetry is like the squirrel entering its squirrel cage: if it turns to its left, it will put its playground in counter-clockwise motion, and vice versa. Such asymmetry at this most basic level marks the beginning either of the left-handedness or right-handedness of the biological world (Gardner 1964). As Heinz Pagels (1985:246) puts it, 'the solution to a symmetrical configuration breaks the symmetry.' And from that point the resulting spiraloid pushes toward ever-higher levels of organizational complexity.

In a comparable vein attuned to life processes – and, as we shall observe, to sign processes – Prigogine (1983:122) tells us that the axiom 'Life springs forth from life' can be recast in more general terms: 'Irreversibility (asymmetry) engenders irreversibility (asymmetry).' The equation seems to be: 'Life $\approx$ Irreversibility (asymmetry-aperiodicity).' Prigogine believes he has found the secret of life not simply in the generation of asymmetry, but in more general irreversible processes. Biological order has been most often conceived to be physical states created and maintained by enzymes resembling Maxwell's Demon that miraculously bring about negentropic pushes and shoves against the grain of thermodynamics. Prigogine irreversible processes have an entirely different meaning. The biosphere as a global domain and its myriad components alike, living or dead, exist in far-from-equilibrium conditions all of which composes the supreme expression of self-organization. Prigogine and Stengers (1984:176) declare they are tempted 'to go so far as to say that once the conditions for self-organization are satisfied, life becomes as predictable as the Bénard instability or a falling stone.'

Thus, life is not merely like an autonomous, frictionless pendulum. It is precisely because of 'friction' – the agonistics inherent in all self-organizing processes – and exchanges of energy between a system and its environment – aperiodic vortices of diverse forms, from whirlpools to hurricanes to rhythmic biological phases – that new structural forms, and eventually life itself, can arise. In other words, life structures are dissipative: to stay 'alive' they must constantly dissipate entropy in order that it not be allowed to build up inside them and 'kill' them by reducing them to a relatively static state of equilibrium. For such equilibrium – maximum entropy – consists of no more than sporadic jerks and kicks, pure Brownian movement, with no overall change, or change of change. From this view, equilibrium systems simply *are* (Firstness and Secondness, devoid of the mediary force of Thirdness).

4. THE MERRY-GO-ROUND OF LIFE

To repeat, strictly within the biological realm of dissipative structures, open systems are capable of continuously assimilating free energy and expelling energy into their environment. But the flow from system to environment and vice versa must be largely irreversible, and a state of nonequilibrium must be in effect. Such irreversibility demands three basic modes of interpretation: (1) *classical Cartesian-Newtonian dynamics* (reversible, symmetrical) (2) *thermodynamics* (inorganic and nonliving, irreversible, asymmetrical), and (3) *dissipative structures* (organic and living as well as inorganic, irreversible, asymmetrical).

With regards to (1), it is irrelevant whether the moon revolves around the earth in one direction or the other – the equation remains the same. The implications of (2) include a statistically determinable push toward universal decay, heat death, irrespective of the apparently spontaneous surge of life-forms. But (3), a perpetual move toward higher forms of complexity via self-organization, offers the picture of islands of order punctuating the overriding current moving toward disorder, entropic decay. The distinction between these modes – by and large irreducible one to another – is discontinuous, not continuous; one is accessible from another solely by catastrophic shifts. For example, transition from classical mechanics to thermodynamics is quite apparent, since, as Jantsch puts it:

Irreversibility implies a *break of the time symmetry* between past and future, a symmetry which is still conserved in the equations for the evolution of a classical mechanical system. ... The direction of time cannot be reversed. Never will a non-uniform distribution result from a more uniform one if the system is left alone. If we pour hot water from one side and cold water from the other into a bowl, the result will be lukewarm water; but lukewarm water can never separate by itself into hot and cold water.

The symmetry break between past and future, or between the 'before' and the 'after', results in temporal order, or *causality* in a strict sense. Since a process which is described at the thermodynamic level can only run in the direction of uniformity and equilibrium, any non-uniform initial condition (such as the non-uniform temperature distribution in our example) is introduced as random fluctuation. There is no ordering principle at this levelwhich would be able to account for it. (1980:27–8)

However, Jantsch continues, a new ordering principle is imperative when attempting 'to account for the self-organizing of evolving systems at the third level [of interpretation]. It requires instability of the thermodynamic order which leads to a *break in time and space symmetry*' (Jantsch 1980:28; brackets added). According to a long-held belief, nonequilibrium conditions did not offer anything worthy of serious investigation. Thermodynamic nonequilibrium, often producing intellectual *Angst* in the face of an imminent 'heat death,' was generally treated as no more than a temporary disruption of a more normal state of equilibrium rather than as a source of something generative, something new. Prigogine argues that non-equilibrium, or more specifically, far-from-equilibrium conditions, can be a source of order, the most meaningful form of order. Such far-from-equilibrium conditions and their accompanying dissipative structures eventually evolve into a nonlinear thermodynamics of irreversible processes affording a glimpse into the inner workings of spontaneous generation, of *order through fluctuations* – that is, *order out of chaos*, all of which, Jantsch demonstrates, falls in line with the concept of biological self-organization.

For a most basic example of the life process, RNA and DNA depend for their existence upon a special form of catalysis resulting in the polymeriza-

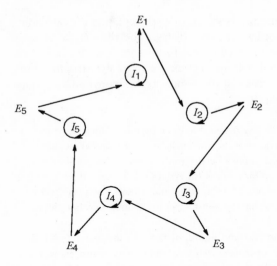

FIGURE 2

tion of polynucleotides – nucleotides combining to form polynucleotides or conglomerate nucleotides consisting of recursively repeating structural units of the original molecules. This involves molecules duplicating themselves over and over again until eventually they meet with some halting procedure. Such polymerization comes in two forms: (1) linear growth culminating in a stationary condition of equilibrium, and (2) cooperative polymerization arising out of complementary molecular templates following Watson and Crick's so-called 'pairing rule' according to which the four elementary bases join up in construction of the double helix (Eigen 1971).

For linear chain growth, a catalyst can consist of a relatively primitive medium of clay with traces of metals or silicates. More complex nonequilibrium polymerization, in contrast, requires autocatalytic processes, which lead to dissipative structures. These latter processes intensify as they proceed, in their own turn leading to exponential growth in contrast to the linear growth of ordinary catalytic processes. Dissipative structures are able to maintain their openness and selective interchangeability with their environment. They do not require any outside motivating force to perpetuate their self-organizing activity: they lift themselves up by their own bootstraps. This is quite unlike traditional theories specifying change in terms of outside agents (God as prime mover, cosmic rays causing genetic mutations, etc.) or mysterious intervenors (Newtonian force at a distance, the aether as medium for light rays, etc.).

Catalysts, in short, are enablers. They allow reactions to proceed under different conditions than otherwise possible, though they do not themselves enter into the equation. Quite significantly, for the purpose of this study, they also provide the basis for Manfred Eigen's (1971) provocative hypercycle hypothesis. After the formation of sufficiently complex protein molecules and polynucleotides, collections of both enter into a dynamic phase in which they interact in increasingly more complex steps. This interaction constitutes what Eigen calls a *self-reproducing autocatalytic hypercycle*, a minimal example of which is depicted in figure 2. The polynucleotides (I_i) are information carriers (1) for their own autocatalytic self-reproduction, and (2) for using the preceding protein or enzyme (E_{i-1}) to synthesize a new one (E_i) at the next step of the cycle. Eigen and Schuster (1979) call reaction chains with such dual functions *hypercycles of the second degree*. The total system is closed in so far as the last enzyme (E_n) becomes a catalyst for the formation of the first polynucleotide (I_i), thus rendering the circle autocatalytic. This interweaving and development of two molecular species, Jantsch (1980:102) remarks, 'may be viewed as a first expression of *symbiosis*. Each molecular species has to offer something which the other does not have: polynucleotides are, because of their molecular structure in long strands, the best available information carriers and proteins are excellent catalysts; both capabilities together make self-reproduction possible.'

A novel synthesis is not made possible merely by errors in information transcription from one molecule template to the next, bringing nonlinear development into play and pushing the system over the threshold, thus producing instability, dissipative structuration, and a new and higher order. Rather, the process may occur time and again. Entropy production rises during the transition phase between orders, when a system breaks rank and erupts into a violent discharge of apparently chaotic activity to produce radically distinct structures. Production can also rise when the system is in a relatively stationary stage, yet it engages in a fluctuation between a pair or more of possibilities due to errors in information transcription (comparable to the function of $\sqrt{-1}$ in computations used to describe physical world phenomena [see Pattee 1979]). In such case, entropy production is at a minimum, and reproduction results in virtual simulacra. Copies resulting from autocatalytic self-production can thus be both quasi-identical and nonidentical, stable and fluctuating. It is precisely this unstable, fluctuating characteristic of systems that demands our attention.

5. ORDER FROM CHAOS: THE MERRY-GO-ROUND OF SEMIOSIS

The water gushing from the kitchen faucet in a smooth, round, and transparent stream consists of a laminar flow, a sheaf of countless layers of molecules projecting downward at different velocities in harmony with one another. When increased water pressure causes the jet to form turbulent strands, the regularity of the laminar flow is destroyed, and disorder seems to rule, though it is actually a new form of order. On the other hand, while movement of the molecules follows a random statistical law in the laminar flow, the turbulent flow groups them together into powerful streams, which in their overall effect permit an increased volume of water to rush out of the faucet. Both flows, however, are forms of structure in their own right, but what is here termed 'structure' is not schematic, determinable, or rigid. Rather, it is a dynamic, ever-changing regime regulating the varying levels of flow. It is *process structure*, another name for dissipative structures (Jantsch 1980:21).

Such dissipative structures are marked by dynamic interconnectedness and nonlinearity. They generate relative order – that is, order at more complex levels – from 'chaos.' These processes are irreversible and time-dependent, at micro- as well as macrolevels, due to breaks of both time symmetry and space symmetry, in contrast to reversible classical mechanics coupled with, at the exclusive macrolevel, irreversible thermodynamics. Above all, to repeat, they are *self-organizing*. Life is no longer considered a thin superstructure over the lifeless inorganic world – recall the above on aperiodic and quasicrystals. Rather, as I suggested in the previous section, in the principle of self-organization lies the common ground between life and nonlife.

As I have intimated, the classical mechanical universe is incapable of describing the nonclassical universe of dissipative structures, which calls for another, complementary, language for its description. It requires a *describing process*, a language of ongoing change, of perpetual mutability – a sort of Shiva's dance of signs in pursuit of elusive and fugitive interpretants. Indeed, the very evolution of dissipative structures demands use of two complementary languages, a microscopic-stochastic one and a macroscopic-deterministic-but-unpredictable one. The complex levels making up this dynamic system, separated from one another by past symmetry breaks, cannot be described as such. Only the web of interrelations between them lends itself to any form of relatively unchanging description. As Prigogine has often put it, the universe is far too rich to be expressed in a single language. Just as neither music, painting, nor poetry can exhaust itself in a sequence of styles, so also our experience, intuition, contemplation, and intellection regarding the universe are irreducible to a single descriptive mode. We need a set of mutually exclusive, though at a closer look complementary, languages, with no precise rules of translation between them – in fact, any and all translations are rendered radically indeterminate.

TABLE 3

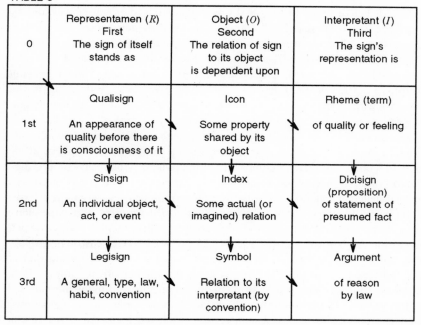

0	Representamen (R) First The sign of itself stands as	Object (O) Second The relation of sign to its object is dependent upon	Interpretant (I) Third The sign's representation is
1st	Qualisign An appearance of quality before there is consciousness of it	Icon Some property shared by its object	Rheme (term) of quality or feeling
2nd	Sinsign An individual object, act, or event	Index Some actual (or imagined) relation	Dicisign (proposition) of statement of presumed fact
3rd	Legisign A general, type, law, habit, convention	Symbol Relation to its interpretant (by convention)	Argument of reason by law

In this light, focus your attention on the general drift of Peirce's categories in table 3 while remaining mindful of the connections in table 1 that provide for the ten basic signs in table 2. Rows represent sign generation, from monadic to triadic. Columns depict an order of 'crosscatalysis,' from signs of Firstness to signs of Thirdness. And diagonals entail (cyclical) 'auto-catalysis' generating complexity out of simplicity from within a given category. Notice that sign fluctuation generally proceeds 'downward' with respect to sign *generacy*, but it can also be 'upward' moving, in the case of what Peirce calls *de-generacy*.[11] Steps 'downward' are accompanied by a greater propensity for far-from-equilibrium conditions, symmetry breaking, dissipative structures, and hence by open flows of signification between signs leading to new orders of signification out of the relative chaos: signs in the process escape into a 'higher' form of 'order.'

'How can this be?' one protests. 'Tough-minded rational arguments are certainly more stable than signs of "lower" order, subject as they are to ephemeral collective fads and individual fancies.' For sure, our need to believe in clear and distinct linguistic atoms making up molecular propositions that in turn offer themselves up as links in an ironclad argument at the molar level is a comforting pillow upon which to lay our weary minds. It can also be deceptive. Granted, Peirce's sign 10 may be by and large arrived at consciously and by cognitive means (Nesher 1983, 1990). As such it is the temporary end-product of a sustained process of mediative, inferential reasoning. In contrast, signs 1, 2, and 5, icons through and through, are relatively immediate, non-consciously perceived and processed, and tacitly related to other signs. Their evoking well-nigh – though never exactly – immediate responses puts them in the ballpark with qualitative, that is, emotional, sentimental, jaded, or merely gut, responses.

However, if one contemplates Peirce's sign *generacy-degeneracy* sufficiently, one is led to the notion that just as signs can develop from relative simplicity at the pole of iconicity to relative complexity at the pole of symbolicity, so also they can become, by convention and repetition (for example, Peirce's habit taking), so channelled in general sign use that they function *as if* they were signs of lesser complexity. Their use becomes *habituated* (*embedded, automatized*), thus compelling their makers and interpreters to process them in rather mindless fashion. Such is knowledge that, having been learned by explicit verbal instruction or by example, becomes implicit, tacit knowing – that is, one's achieving skill at playing tennis or a piano, driving a car, doing mathematical computations, learning a foreign language.[12] In this sense, sign processes following habitual pathways tend to become relatively stable. And the signs, initially generated by well-reasoned and explicit, consciously employed methods, now function along the lines of implicit, *nonconscious inferences* and thought processes.[13] They are now simply and tacitly taken to be *the way things are*, mindlessly, in the order of *de-generate* symbols having become self-contained icons. Subsequently, if subjected once again to consciously generated alternatives, rejoinders, rebuttals, and refutations, that is, if opened to their environment and to the gaze of the critical eye, these habitually, soporifically generated signs sooner or later risk losing face. Their balance may become precarious, and, deprived of equilibrium, dissipation can erupt, which then makes them likely candidates for a new form of order.

Indeed, if as Nietzsche made quite explicit – and as suggested by, among a host of others, Blaise Pascal, Nicholas of Cusa, Xenophanes of old, and in a more limited mode, Karl Popper – since we cannot embrace the Truth in its totality, what few bits and pieces of it we happen to stumble upon cannot but be in part erroneous and subject to alteration. Hence regarding this totality, there is no knowing with certainty any beginning, ending, or centre. Commensurately, in the Peircean decalogue of signs there is no necessary ascending order of value and importance, from sign 1 to sign 10. All signs are intimately related to all other signs in the vast semiotic web. They are used and abused, and they use and occasionally abuse their respective semiotic agents, at tacit and conscious levels and within individual and social spheres of semiosis.

This depiction of sign processes is quite commensurate, I would submit, with Prigogine's theory regarding natural phenomena. Prigogine did not appear out of nowhere nor does he exist in a vacuum. Like most creative giants, he should be viewed against the background of the entire Western tradition. Classical science was engaged in a search for the ultimate building blocks with which the whole edifice is constructed. In physics there were particles that combined to form atoms; in chemistry atoms made molecules; in biology molecules became supermolecules, and finally, life emerged, with humans standing magisterially at the apex of the massive pyramid. This grand design is now viewed, by Prigogine and others, as a mistake. Prigogine argues that no level of description is necessarily any more fundamental than any other; all levels are dependent upon all others in a vastly complex, interacting system. The universe simply cannot be disassembled into a fundamental set of Tinkertoys with which it was put together. From slime moulds to Einstein's brain to the complexities of human societies, it is an ongoing web of *process structures*.

Quite significantly, Prigogine characteristics are found in the monadic, dyadic, and triadic nature of Peirce's ten sign types. The monadic level is highlighted by *symmetry, reflexivity, nontransitivity, equilibrium, self-sufficiency,* and *self-reference.* At the 'lower' levels of the dyadic realm, symmetry and equilibrium rule, though at the 'higher' levels harmony wanes, transitivity enters the scene, and equilibrium tends to break down. Triadicity is marked by increasing *dissymmetry* (symmetry breaking), *disequilibrium* (and at the outer stretch, far-from-equilibrium conditions), and *transitivity,* all characterized by Peirce's nonlinear, aperiodic *generacy-de-generacy* cycle. At the extreme of triadic activity evolution begins: the translation of signs into signs, the spreading of signs throughout the semiotic web, thus bringing about a general growth or development of individual signs at local levels and a general evolution of the whole. From monad to triad we have the semiotic counterpart to biological progression, from genetic phenomena to epigenetic phenomena, nervous activity, and finally, cerebral activity and mind. The whole system is, in fact, *autosemeiopoietic.*

I write 'auto-,' for each local domain is in the sense of Peirce's sign decalogue a self-contained, self-returning monad, though in another sense it remains open to its environment. Either of its own accord or as a consequence of outside causes, it becomes subject to perturbations, symmetry breaks, and finally dissipation. And a new order of complexity can then arise. The same inheres regarding global systems up to the entire semiotic web as a whole – the set of all sets paradoxically containing itself. Newtonian wisdom held that perturbations in a system dragging it toward chaos must be the effect of outside causes. For example, using classical equations the movement of the moon about the earth could be easily computed using a few handy terms. Slight perturbations, such as the dragging effect of tides, were conveniently pushed under the rug, and the two-body system was viewed as a Newtonian ideal. If three, four, and many other bodies were injected into the equation, the system became even less precise. Yet with hedgehog obstinacy the same basic formulas and calculations were applied, though they were now considered to be no more than greater or lesser approximations to the ideal. And business usually went on, apparently without unbearable complications.

At about the turn of the century Henri Poincaré threw a monkey wrench in this apparently harmonious machinery. He demonstrated that when the number of terms in a system is multiplied manyfold and they become smaller and smaller with respect to the whole, minute perturbations are quickly amplified trigonometrically along nonlinear paths, eventually causing the system to break down of its own accord (that is, the way of 'strange attractors'). In such cases, we are suddenly taken to n-adic levels that are radically indeterminate, undecidable, and asymmetrical. Apparently insignificant perturbations within the phase space of a closed system thus cause it to behave erratically, and finally to self-destruct (dissipate in the Prigogine sense). It is mind-boggling to contemplate the many instances of turbulence in air currents, rapidly coursing rivers, lava flows from volcanoes, typhoons, and tidal waves. And it is daunting to think these disturbances had their beginning as microlevel perturbations that rapidly became magnified at macrolevels. It is like a young man who, from a bridge overlooking a flooding river, tosses his beer can into the water. This causes a slight perturbation, the ripples of which bring about a degree of turbulence some yards downstream, and as the turbulence is gradually increased a threshold is reached, then crossed. A dike gives slightly, then disintegrates. And a town is devastated.

It is in this manner that signs of 'higher' form and complexity – having been bred by asymmetry, aperiodicity – are generally less stable than signs of 'lower' form. Take, for instance, signs 8, 9, and 10, or *terms, propositions (descriptions)*, and *arguments (interpretations)*. In ordered, linear, chiefly binary (dyadic) systems – that is, in systems of interaction at the 'descriptive' level – the interpretation (interpretant) dominates whatever descriptions are generated. At more complex levels, however, descriptions become problematic. Interpretations (interpretants), rather than relating to the 'semiotically real' phenomena at hand or to their respective descriptions, begin, so to speak, interpreting themselves (translating themselves into themselves) (see Savan 1987–8).

During this process, the semiotic *object* becomes the sign being signed (it is never the 'actually real' *an sich*), the sign or *representamen* becomes the sign of that signed and hence the sign of a sign, and the *interpretant* serves to integrate the signing process into the stream of semiosis. The representamen-object-interpretant (*R-O-I*) relationship can in this manner be viewed as a *complementary* set of signing and signed entities whose roles are constantly changing. The sign signs the already signed while the signing process signs sign and signed at a spot slightly farther down the stream, and in this act, the signing process is always already becoming sign and signed. Signs change; they grow; they evolve. But they also inexorably lag behind themselves; they are always in the act of signing themselves.

Upon so signing (interpreting) themselves, signs tend to become, from the perspective of their reiterative reentry into themselves, self-referentially autonomous. Notorious self-referential sign strings include the likes of (1) 'This sentence contains precisely forty-five letters,' (2) 'This sentence is false,' and (3) Epimenides's paradox, 'I am lying,' which injects the sign generator into the formula. Automata theory, pioneered by Alan Turing, John von Neumann, and Norbert Wiener, entails a machine completely capable of describing itself, of reprogramming, and therefore of duplicating itself. Such an imaginary machine gives rise to the question 'Could it be consistent, like sentence (1), or would it inevitably fall into paradox and self destruct?' which has been the subject of heated debates that show little sign of abating.

Whatever the answer might ultimately be, evidence at present points to the self-referential paradox at the core of life itself (Pattee 1979). If this is so, the bad news is that the brain as a largely autonomous system cannot hope to construct a language with which to define itself. There is good news, however: the mind-brain enjoys open-ended and ongoing *unfolding* (into Seconds) of the indefinite, and potentially infinite, realm of *enfolded* possibilities (Firsts) toward perpetual interpretation (Thirds) of the universe of *unfolded* signs without the possibility of arriving at the finish line where Truth, in all its plenitude, lies in wait – which is still a rather frightening conclusion for those who continue to nurture modernity's dream of closure.

In order somehow to cope with these Peircean infinite regress tactics, I now focus more specifically on the sign.

6. THE TURN OF THE SCEW

In spite of Peirce's notion that there is neither any original sign nor final sign, *for* us mere mortals at least, and furthermore, that we cannot know precisely where

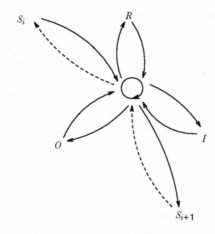

FIGURE 3

we are in the semiosic stream, assume the existence of some unfathomable sign somewhere, sometime. Let us call it S_i (that is, $R_1 O_1 I_1$). S_i engenders another sign consisting of, say, $R_2 O_1 I_1$, from the 'nucleus' outward in terms of the triadic relations between the three semiotic components as depicted in figure 3.[14]

This sign can then generate any number of combinations of Peirce's basic ten sign types according to what he calls 'valency' – that is, relations between components, from 1 to 3 (for example, figure 4, and in general, table 3). The connectors between the sign components can be classified as 'single-,' 'double-,' and 'triple-bonds,' the equivalent of chemical valency.[15] Assuming *generacy* from sign 1 to sign 10 and *de-generacy* in the other direction, we have an image of sign *development* and its obverse. But how, precisely, do signs *evolve*? How does the whole evolve? If a given sign's *potentia* is genotypical, and if it phenotypically develops within its environment by unfolding part of that *potentia* to the best of its capacity, then how is it that that very *potentia* can undergo change?

Signs possess the capacity to *grow* into symbols, from raw sensation to volition to cognition, from sentiment to desire to intellection, and from spontaneity to reaction to habit: that is, a sign can potentially run the gamut from Firsts to Thirds. Moreover, according to Peirce's 'objective idealism,' just as mind sublimates from matter and matter contains the stuff of mind, so also ideas, interpretants that they are, can, if they win the game of survival, evolve and grow like mind – and all symbols for that matter (*CP*: 6.289).[16] Indeed, mind-symbols are not simply opposed to matter, as classical thought has had it. They are *complementary* with it. Mind-signs or symbols can, as a result of *embedment, automatization*, gravitate by successive stages of de-generacy

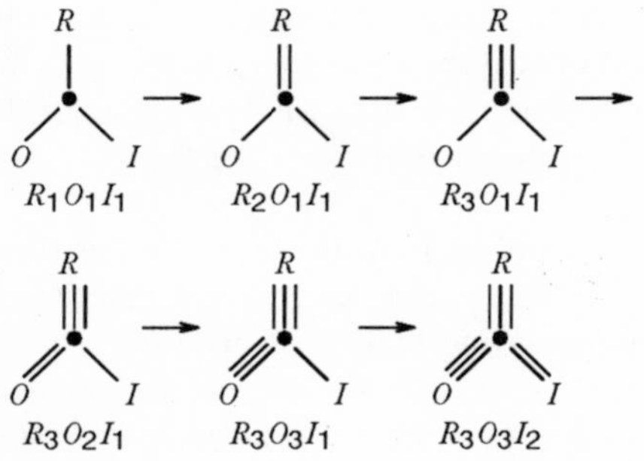

$$R_1O_1I_1 \quad R_2O_1I_1 \quad R_3O_1I_1$$

$$R_3O_2I_1 \quad R_3O_3I_1 \quad R_3O_3I_2$$

FIGURE 4

to the level of mindlessness such that they are processed and received with inertlike passivity; yet they do not necessarily disappear altogether, but remain as 'memory,' or 'trace,' possibly to be raised from the depths to energetic conscious levels at some time or other. But mind, especially that of the human variety, is also capable of generating such elaborate and complex systems of symbols that they tend to become labyrinthine in their countenance and numbing in their effect. Nevertheless, the essence of the problem rests at the very initial lurch of the life process itself: mind constantly perpetuates life processes, and life processes constantly exude mind sublimates as a necessary act of semiosis.

When a sign develops from 1 to 10, it has reached the pinnacle of success, we would suppose. But this is by no means the end of the line. There is no ultimate sign (R), just as there is no ultimate object (O), or interpretant (I). According to Tom Short (1982), the mature Peirce denied his earlier rather nominalist belief that interpretants were themselves signs in an unending regress, conceding that habits can be the ultimate Is. However, in the first place, if a particular I is somehow conceived to be ultimate, it is so merely *for* someone somewhere, not necessarily *for* anyone and everyone anywhere and everywhere. In the second place, sign 10, as a self-contained argument, can now reenter its own space as a sign of itself (that is, potentially as a monad). As such it has become tantamount to Firstness, like a smoke ring turning in on itself, a torus: equilibrium, balance, and harmony rule. Even though there is a hyperactive Brownian movement of smoke particles in the ring, the overall product of this movement is null. But this is a somewhat false image, for no sign can actually stand alone. Like a smoke ring, it soon dissipates due to its interaction with its environment. But unlike a smoke ring, it can then re-emerge as a sign of a slightly to radically distinct order. This dynamics within stasis and dissipation or development toward something else is prevalent in Peirce's remark that the universe is a vast representamen, an argument, a poem, a symphony (*CP*:5.119). It is a self-reentering whole. The problem is that this very universe, and indeed even the laws governing it, are perpetually metamorphosing into something other than what they are, for the very laws of nature are the result of an evolutionary process (*CP*:6.101, 7.512; see Turley 1977).

Consider, for example, this general semiosic transition process regarding a human language, English, and the obvious perils and pitfalls inherent in ordinary language use. A linguistic sign, having built itself up from 1 to 10, can then either (1) de-generate back to one of its 'lower' stages, (2) remain at square 10 for a while, felicitously gyrating about itself, or (3) dissipate and move (unfold, *generate*) to a 'higher' semiosic form, thus reenacting the formation of sign 1 at a more complex level and commencing the process anew (that is, in the order of the *Ho-t'u* model). As a self-reentering, self-referential sign it begins to manifest what may be termed *autosemeiopoietic* behaviour (*poiesis*: creation, production, formation). In contrast, a sign relating to its 'semiotic object' as something *other* is *allosemeiopoietic* (*allo*: production of a group the combination of which forms a whole, a sentence, dependent upon and related to something other than itself). A sign translated (transformed) into another sign – the interpretant of one sign becoming the representamen of its successor – is *heterosemeiopoietic* (*hetero*: production of entities of different classes or kinds, such as words from letters). And finally, a sign caught up in a contradiction is *parasemeiopoietic* (*para*: production of signs different from or even diametrically opposed to, and in conflict with themselves).

Now suppose we draw up (1) a list of *autoheterosemeiopoietic* sentences such as 'This sentence is in English,' and 'This sentence has five words,' and (2) a list of *alloheterosemeiopoietic* sentences such as 'All organisms are mortal,' and 'All men are either bald or not bald.' And suppose we construct the *descriptive* sentence 'This sentence is *alloheterosemeiopoietic*.' Now the question arises: Is the sentence *autoheterosemeiopoietic* or *alloheterosemeiopoietic*? It is quite obviously neither, strictly speaking. One might declare that it is apparently *autoheterosemeiopoietic*, but given its self-contradictory nature, it must be *parasemeiopoietic*. In other words, if we take it to be true, then what it says of itself is false, for it does not relate to something other than itself, so it is parasemeiopoietic. On the other hand, if we construe it to be false, then it must be an autoheterosemeiopoietic sentence, for it talks about itself, true enough, though what it says of itself is false. So on this count also it must be parasemeiopoietic. The sentence can do no more than oscillate until it finally vibrates to pieces, so to speak.[17]

In a real physical system, say, a computer, a programmed contradiction of this sort will produce a series of binary-Boolean yes-no answers (that is, a computer glitch). Of course, logical paradoxes are time-independent, as are computers, presumably silicon-based brutes rather than time-bound living organisms. In contrast, living physical systems, existing within the topology of space and time, are generally capable of resolving paradoxes – for example, the above case of 'This sentence is undecidable,' or Escher's visual paradoxes. They are resolved by softening them and breaking them up into their constituent parts, which can then be analyzed within broader contexts (Pattee 1979:105–23). For example, the liar paradox could refer to a previous sentence, to the author's ulterior motives, to the mere exemplification of a paradox for pedagogical purposes, and so on. Regarding such makeshift solutions to quandaries, from the closed chamber of staccato oscillations the door may be opened to reveal the light of day once again. The paradox seems to have disappeared – though it may have merely slithered under the rug – and life can go on.

But, alas, the doorway inevitably leads only to yet another domain that must be either *incomplete* – for questions remain unanswered – or *inconsistent* – there is an answer to all possible questions, though at the expense of internal contradictions. In the first case the system must be alloheterosemeiopoietic; in the second case it must be autoheterosemeiopoietic. If the second case inheres, then parasemeiopoiesis eventually raises its ugly head, and the system either self-destructs or there is dissipation to a new form of order. If the first case is in effect, then development may proceed along orderly lines until smug self-sufficiency is reached, and eventually catastrophe once again threatens.

Ultimately, what we have here, I would submit, is sign processes patterning lifelike autocatalytic, dissipative, hypercyclical processes. Signs develop and evolve, as the universe engages in its maddening apparently eternal cycles, and somehow, they all get on with their game of becoming.

7. THE LIFE OF SIGNS

One must be mindful, however – and this is not insignificant – that the evolutionary semiosic process (or by extension dissipative structures) to which I have referred involves not merely transfer of matter ('semiotically real' objects) but also, transfer of *information (signs) for the organization of matter (signs)*.

This opens up an entire new horizon – or, some will be prone to say, a can of worms – since the philosophy of openness and information transfer implies memory and memory transfer: the assimilation of information and thereby the acquisition of 'experience' can be passed on from generation to generation – whether speaking of biological or inorganic systems – along the nonlinear upwardly generated spiral. In Jantsch's (1980:103) words, 'whereas a chemical dissipative structure is merely capable of ontogeny, of the evolution of its own individuality, and its memory is limited to the experience accrued in the course of its existence, phylogeny (the history of an entire phylum) may now become effective.' Time and time-binding consequently become a factor. At first, generation in the sense of chemical dissipative structures is along a one-dimensional line, irreversible and either 'upward' moving, moving not at all, or moving irreversibly 'downward.' Biological evolution, in contrast, entails generation of increasingly 'higher' levels of complexity rather than mere reduplication of what there is.

Furthermore, commensurate with Peirce's process philosophy, there is *generacy*, but also *de-generacy*. Information carriers have, recorded within themselves, the rise and fall, the birth and death, of myriad systems before them. The paths branch out in multiple dimensions; there are many possibilities, potentially an infinity of them. Thus the 'experience' of earlier generations as well as fluctuations (rises and falls) and evolution are transferred vertically along the time axis. Simple structures and their corresponding cycles generally balance generation and de-generation without the capacity for change. In contrast, complex self-organizing autocatalytic hypercyclical systems are capable of net increase through order from chaos when thresholds are surmounted. As I pointed out above, simple catalysis allows for linear growth and autocatalysis for exponential growth, but with hypercycles growth becomes hyperbolic – comparable to Peirce's asymptote model. That is, at the outset hyperbolic growth increases much more rapidly than exponential growth, but in the latter the rate of increase remains constant while in the former it decreases as the upper limit is approximated asymptotically – an image also recalling Peirce.

Various aspects of hypercycles can be highlighted. An isolated system cannot undergo evolution (generacy) but devolves (de-generates) in the direction of equilibrium (homeostasis). When this state is reached, the dynamic, morphogenetic process ceases. In contrast, dissipative self-organization involves exchange with the environment, from cyclical or closed organization to open systems. During cosmic evolution, when hydrogen is transformed into helium, organization is cyclical and closed. Eigen (1971) has demonstrated that chemical evolution, through comparable dissipative systems is typical of precellular hypercycles. At higher levels, cyclical organization is characteristic of dissipative, self-organizing structures, and especially of life systems. In fact, the entire earth as Gaia can be characterized in terms of hypercyclical organization (Lovelock 1979; Jantsch 1980:185).[18]

Eigen and Schuster (1977, 1978a, 1978b) develop a hierarchy of cyclical reactions at the precellular level: (1) transformatory reactions acting as catalysts, (2) catalytic reactions acting as autocatalysts, and (3) catalytic autocatalysts acting as hypercycles. Types 1 and 2 take in and dissipate energy (signs) and material (semiotic objects). Reactions of type 1 are chiefly chemical and nuclear

TABLE 4

$A \longleftrightarrow B \longleftrightarrow C \longleftrightarrow C_{a\to1,2,3\ldots n}$			
First	Second (→ Haecceities)	Third (Non-haecceities)	Third (→ Quiddities)
Representation	Objects	Immediate and dynamical interpretant	→ Final interpretant
(Icon)	(Index)	(Symbol)	(Symbol)
Monadic	Dyadic	Dyadic → Triadic	Triadic
Quasi-identity	Sameness	Difference	Novelty
Quasi-closed	Self-replicating	Self-reproducing	Self-organizing (Selective)
→ Equilibrium	Linear generacy	Nonlinear generacy (Disequilibrium)	Nonlinear generacy (Far-from-equilibrium)
→ Stasis	→ Catalysis (Linear 'growth')	→ Autocatalysis (Exponential growth)	→ Hypercycle (Dissipative structures)

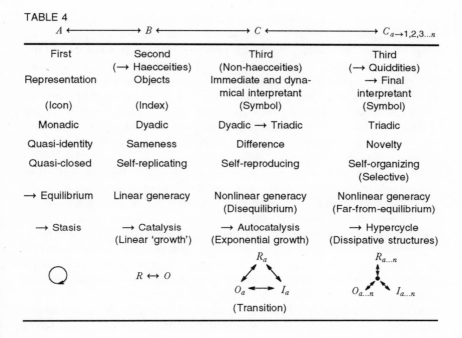

in nature, while type 2 reactions are either chemical or biological in the sense of information carriers. In contrast, reactions of type 3, involving autocatalysis, provide the most dramatic form of movement, of growth (Jantsch 1980:186).

Translating this aspect of the hypercycle concept to the realm of signs according to their development in the preceding sections, we have table 4. In general, from the self-sufficient, reiterative monad, $\mathcal{Q}$, sign generacy proceeds to the particularity, singularity, of dyadic relatedness, $R \leftrightarrow O$, *from whence* catalytic processes commence. Then, doors open to the first stage of Thirdness marked by three-way dyadic relata between R, O, and I, without there (yet) existing genuine triadicity: at least a glimpse of the tap root of Thirdness has been afforded by a triad of dyads. That is to say, the three dyadic relata, R_a–O_a, R_a–I_a, and O_a–I_a of column C_a become legitimate triadicity in the next column, with each sign component enjoying relations with the other two by way of a 'node,' a sort of 'empty set,' or $\mathcal{Q}$, constituting the nonessential 'ground' for all semiosis. Yet, the C_a stage is crucial in order for self-replication to become self-reproduction, linearity to become nonlinearity, and for autocatalysis to leap onto the scene.

The genuinely triadic R–O–I relata of $C_{a\to1,2,3\ldots n}$ maintain a level of dynamic urgency hitherto unknown: there is a scintillating oscillatory to-and-fro quivering between sign components enabling the I, while intimately tied both to R and O, to become translated, to translate itself, into another sign: and semiosis flows on. This last stage, or more adequately stated, progression toward the final interpretant (I_f), is accompanied by full-fledged novelty, self-organization, radical nonlinearity, and the semiosic counterpart to hypercycles (*generacy*) and dissipative structures (*generacy* and *de-generacy*). In this state of affairs, sign 10 becomes capable of doubling back upon itself and grabbing sign 1 by the tail – thus completing the self-returning spiraloid process discussed in previous sections – while engaged in the process of enveloping its interpreter in an oceanic embrace.

More specifically regarding table 4, systems gravitating from 'higher' types toward type A devolve (de-generate) in the direction of equilibrium, at which point sign interaction becomes well-nigh reversible; that is, with each recursive reentry signs remain practically the same as they were and are perceived and conceived as such. This is not to say that mere stasis results, but rather, there is *de-generation toward stasis*. Signs continue to oscillate or vibrate around their respective equilibrium state, yet they are poised and ready for action. Such signs are typical of the dance of grains of sand on a metal plate when a vibrator is attached to it and a magnet is placed underneath it. A pattern of sand grains, organized according to the field force, is established, and the vibrations merely cause the grains to dance about, incessantly changing places with one another, though the overall pattern remains constant – recall, once again, the *Ho-t'u* model. A systems are monadic and closed, characteristic of iconicity, or from another vantage, of the representamen (R), which is the information carrier for 'higher,' more complex, systems, though it does not itself enter into the overall reaction.

The next level, B, characterizes autopoiesis in its simplest state: pure self-replication, the production of haecceities proper to the indexical or dyadic sign, and to the 'semiotically real' object (O). This process entails reiteration or replication of the same sign within contexts that none the less never remain the same, though the difference from one sign instantiation to the next might be so minuscule as to go undetected. At this stage signs are generally taken as tokens without there being any conscious and intentionally established relation to the type of which they are an indication. The sign is simply an indication (index) in contiguity with its respective representamen. The first stage of Thirdness, category C_a, entails nonlinear, exponential, autocatalytic movement toward triadicity, without Thirdness – or symbolicity – yet enjoying full realization. Here, there are no haecceities in the pure sense, nor is there legitimate novelty, only difference that makes a difference. In other words, C_a cycles involve change without there being any serious change of change – which is typical in the physical world of the cosmic process by which hydrogen is transformed into helium in stellar evolution, and in simple dissipative structures of the Bénard cell sort (Prigogine 1980).

Thirdness of the $C_{a \to 1,2,3...n}$ sort introduces dissipative structures in the most radical sense. The sign as interpretant (I), at the level of symbolicity, implies typization of the token. We are now submerged directly into the stream of semiosis wherein interpretants are incessantly transmuted into their successor signs in a constant swim toward their chimerical final or ultimate incarnation. In the Peircean sense, triadicity enters full force here: self-organization perpetually results in novelty in various guises and in perpetually differentiating contexts, which patterns life systems. And indeed, it patterns the entire self-organizing universe, itself in constant evolution regarding its nature as icon, as 'semiotically real' manifestation, and as symbol.

A distinction remains to be made between proper autopoietic entities and the interacting elements of hypercycles and dissipative structures. A entities as closed systems enjoying no connectivity with any other entities in the environment are destined either to stasis or decay. B is proper to autopoietic entities only in the sense that there is quasi-self-identity through sameness via self-replication by indefinite recursion – hence a relative degree of stability and closure is maintained. At the same time, connectivity is established among entities in the environment, with the resultant interaction bringing about perturbations and compensations – requiring a marked element of resilience – in order to swing the process toward its former equilibrium, though that state of affairs cannot be recapitulated in its entirety.

C_a is still in part allopoietic rather than exclusively autopoietic. In light of the discussion ending section 6, allopoietic entities or signs (word processors, bicycles, tractors, video games) require outside agents for their proper functioning. The relation is one-way, between the operator as doer and the machine as recipient of the doing. The machine is incapable of countering the operator's actions with its own self-generated attack as a result of its continuing effort to cope with its environment by altering its own plan of action. C_a signs, in so far as they are partly autopoietic yet remain tied to their allopoietic origins, are quasi-species, quasi-sign-types; in Peirce's words, they are tantamount to 'quasi-mind.' They have not yet attained full self-organizing capacity, though their self-reproduction is nonlinear, generating differences that make a semiosic difference.

Allopoietic entities falling within category C_a are most properly classified as self-regenerative and self-reproducing, with little or no active selection from their environment for the purpose of re-constructing themselves and in the process altering their context and general surroundings. As a result, these signs are ordinarily short-lived. They potentially give way to signs of $C_{a \to 1,2,3...n}$, which are properly autopoietic in the hypercyclical sense. But, to repeat, they are not entirely autonomous; autopoiesis is only one of their two characteristic traits. Autopoietic entities or signs generated by $C_{a \to 1,2,3...n}$ in contrast to the products of C_a, also engage with their environment in constant give-and-take, accompanied by intake and expulsion of energy (information) and matter (semiotic objects). As a result they are capable of self-organization, of lifting themselves up by their own boot-straps. They are self-organizing by way of their active interaction with their environment, such self-organization accompanied by passage from dyadic to full-blown triadic relations, and from hypercycles to dissipative structures, the former characterized by relative closure and the latter by relative openness.

Self-organization finally becomes possible by selection from the environment of that which can enable such self-organization to occur in the most expedient manner. Consequently, dissipative structures entail hierarchical levels, with coordination and constant input-output of parts between levels (Pattee 1972, 1977). And they also inevitably include a semiosic counterpart to the parase-meiopoietic and heterosemeiopoietic sentences described above, inevitably snagged, somewhere along the stream, by self-referential paradoxes common to the 'limitative theorems' of Gödel and others (Pattee 1979). The watchword regarding such hierarchical systems, once again, is *complementarity* between coupled entities and between levels.

One must bear in mind, however, that just as the molecules of life systems do not merely reproduce themselves, so also signs of $C_{a \to 1,2,3...n}$ are not only self-reproductive and self-organizing, but participate in organized wholes: translation and reproduction are consequences of the total functioning of those wholes. Thus signs of $C_{a \to 1,2,3...n}$ depend upon a host of other signs of the same class, just as all those signs depend on their counterparts in C_a, B, and A. Semiosis is a holistic affair; no sign is an island unto itself.[19]

In sum, sign generation and interaction, like molecular and biological evolution, involves more than mere matter and energy for the organization of matter. Information, it is now acknowledged, is the necessary companion to signs and their semiotic objects. Without it there is no meaning to be had; with it, transformations along multiply varied lines is facilitated, from *linear* to *tree* to *rhizomic* relations (Deleuze and Guattari 1987; Jantsch 1980). A new dimension of openness is thus introduced since, through information, the cumulative 'memory' (of molecular and biological entities, of signs) may be passed on. Chemical dissipative structures are merely capable of ontogeny, of the evolution of a system's own individuality, and its memory is limited to the 'habit' resulting from the course of its existence. Phylogeny (the history of an entire phylum), as a mere collection of ontogenies (that is, B in table 4), stands hardly a chance of becoming much more effective. Its ancestral trees can be no more than thin, one-dimensional lines. Upon development into systems of higher complexity, however, branching trees can evolve (that is, C_a).

And finally, evolution of rhizome-relations characterized by space-binding as well as time-binding can occur (that is, $C_{a \rightarrow 1,2,3...n}$).[20] Concomitantly, growth passes through various stages, from linear, to exponential, to hyperbolic. Linear growth is arithmetic, exponential growth increases more rapidly, though the doubling of time – given by the value of the exponent – remains constant, and hyperbolic growth increases the value of the exponent at each step, but in somewhat Zenoesque – that is, asymptotic – fashion, it approximates the ultimate goal, becoming in the process more and more torpid. Self-organizing signs of Thirdness are thus willing candidates *par excellence* for Peirce's somewhat maligned convergence theory.

2

As Ongoing Semiosis

Lévi-Strauss's myths that speak themselves through man; Heidegger's language bringing about its self-realization through us; Derrida's we are always already in the text, wherever we are; Wittgenstein's the limits of my language are the limits of my world; and Peirce's I am the sum total of my thought-signs – all these indirectly testify in one form or another to the 'Language ≈ Life,' or better, the 'Signs ≈ Life,' equation. And they largely imply the self-organizing process under discussion. Creativity is crucial to an adequate – though inexorably partial at best – understanding of this process. Nature imitates art, Picasso once mused. And as the alchemists were wont to put it, what nature left imperfect, art perfects. But nature is more subtle than we would like to admit. It might well be that our own creative endeavours are but a pale reflection of the self-organizing universe's creative impulse.

All of which bears on Peirce's notion of mind (consciousness) and its crucial role in the progression of the interpretant, as we shall observe, from *immediate*, to emotional-energetic-*dynamical*, and finally to logical-ultimate-*final*. What we have here are possible clues to the origins of irreversibility by way of sign emergence, as can be revealed through Peirce's obsessive, cantankerous refusal to concede to any absolute distinction between matter and mind, and between the/a 'semiotically real world' and the entire realm of signs, both 'inner and 'outer.' In order to address these issues adequately, I return to the two-way directions of sign movement: *generacy* and *de-generacy*, *semiosis* and *phaneroscopy*.

1. VICIOUS OR VIRTUOUS CIRCLE?

Consider, for example, writing according to Jacques Lacan's topological model, which in turn is presumed to model the working order of the unconscious (Lacan 1975:118).

Specifically, Lacan uses knots, most typically the Borromean knot, to illustrate letters in a script. In the beginning, a form is brought into existence. This form can be thought of as a flattened knot drawn on the blackboard. Like the Möbius strip, this three-dimensional tangle is constructed on a two-dimensional surface such that, travelling along the curve, one is transposed from 'inside' to 'outside' without transcending the flat plane. When the knot-script is 'read,' according to Lacan, language is itself falsely injected into this extra dimension, thus allowing it to say what ordinarily exceeds it. The knot-script in this fashion goes beyond mere speech, hence its relevance also to Derrida's grammatology, as the following quotation reveals:

The telling, or re-telling, of stories in the time before writing was invented, was sometimes accomplished with the mnemonic device of knots tied on a string ... The device has lasted to the present, for example, among some Roman Catholics, who refer to their prayer beads as a 'rosary,' and some Buddhists. The next step probably was to have a particular knot, or combination of knots, represent a specific word, type of event, or quantity. When they were invaded by Europeans in the sixteenth century, the Inca Indians had a system for writing numbers and other information in knotted strings called *quipus*. The earliest forms of pictographic writing had the direction of reading signs ordered 'as if' on a string, in order to establish the proper sequence ... In a metaphoric sense, writing is the placing of alphabetic knots on a string. DNA and RNA, the chemical bases of life, use a similar method of amino acid 'knots' in a 'rope' of protein. (MacDermott 1974:58; in Ulmer 1985:215–16)

Placing this knot metaphor squarely within the domain of language, it is tantamount to our Cretan paradox, 'I am lying' – hence in light of the previous chapter it is *parasemeiopoietic*. Destined interminably to oscillate between 'true' and 'false' (that is, it is undecidable), it patterns the Möbius strip's switching, via dimensions, from 'inside' to 'outside' and back again. At each stage in this giddy seesaw activity, what the statement *is* ('I am lying'), it *is not* ('I am *not* lying'). In this sense, following Derrida, writing reveals more effectively than speech the undecidability of language in general: that which language *is*, it *is not*, and whatever it says a thing *is*, it *is not*.

This, we cannot help but note, is also the function *par excellence* of Peirce's symbolicity. The icon manifests similarity with the object of which it is an icon, though there must be some property of the icon that *is not* what its object *is*. The index indicates its object in positive fashion by virtue of its being a part of some whole, a cause for an effect, and so on, its contiguous relation to its object serving notice that, in space or time, it actually *is not* the object. The partly to wholly arbitrary nature of the symbol, in contrast, renders it a most likely candidate for undecidability of the Cretan (or Gödelian) sort. Here, most distinctly, the symbol *is not* what that of which it is a symbol *is* in so far as sign and object belong to entirely distinct signifying (perceptual and conceptual) domains. The interpretant of a symbol must translate the mind into another more abstract dimension in order that meaning may be forthcoming. This dimension demands conditionality, futurity, what *would be* the case if certain conditions were in effect, all of which is proper to Peirce's 'pragmatic maxim': symbolicity consists of mind-workings at their best.[1]

The written text is a likely candidate for revealing the self-organizing character of generacy, of semiosis, of the derivation of meaning. In current poststructuralist and postmodern parlance – and rather commensurate with Peirce (Merrell 1995) – it can no longer be assumed that meaning is simply present, which implies that it is not determined by the 'is.' The copula linking predicate (icon) to subject (index) reveals the tenuousness, the uncertainty, of the former, which, as a First, is radically indeterminate (*CP*:2.327). Meaning is neither itself a present form nor does it make present the form of an entity. It bears on the Peircean counterpart to Derrida's *différance* as self-productive, self-organizing, and therefore recursively hyperactive movement. *Différance* entails at one and the same time myriad 'differences' of which Saussure spoke in describing the possibility of meaning in general, and 'deferral' in that meaning is always 'put off,' displaced into the future, even dispersed, thus leaving open an indeterminate set of possibilities (Merrell 1985a). Meaning, in this sense, ultimately becomes that 'space' between signs in their relations and interrelations – Peirce's 'relational logic' – within an n-dimensional web of signification.

Meaning (order) is not established a priori. In the beginning, an initial, almost entirely freely selected, sentence is put down on paper. In view of initial observations in chapter 1, it can be said that the sentence is drawn from the zero-degree, nothingness, the pre-First domain prior to everything that is. But this initial sentence, as a First, implies a myriad and for practical purposes infinite number of possibilities that with greater or lesser degrees of freedom offer themselves up to the thought and compulsion, the sentiment and intuition, the whims and fancies, of its author. In other words, the author puts down the initial word or representamen (R_3) as a set of marks, which potentially refers to its 'semiotic' object (O_3), and relates to an intended but as yet implicit, and unfolded, interpretant (I_1) (cf. table 2). From this initial word, a sentence ($R_3 O_3 I_2$) is written, and ultimately, an entire argument or text ($R_3 O_3 I_3$) representing a potential for the perpetual generation of future interpretants (meanings) by an indeterminate number of semiotic agents (readers) comes into existence. Subsequently, a given reader, on approaching the initial word, the sentence, the text, brings her own form of semiotic freedom in her bag of tricks and generates her own initial textual interpretant $(R_3^1 O_3^1 I_3^1)$, which, given a sufficient temporal increment, and/or with successive readings, undergoes sequential, and even n-dimensional, development or 'growth' $(R_3^1 O_3^1 I_3^1 \rightarrow R_3^2 O_3^2 I_3^2 \rightarrow R_3^3 O_3^3 I_3^3 \ldots n)$ (cf. figure 3).

And thus we have gravitated from A to a relatively full displayal of $C_{a \rightarrow 1,2,3 \ldots n}$ in table 4. From a humble, rather simple, self-contained representamen with no relation to any *other*, a complex text consisting of symbols evincing an indefinite range of potential interpretants has been engendered. And now, the entire system is poised and ready for the possibility of eruption into semiosic chaos via dissipative structures from whence can arise ever-more-novel forms of order.

The originary sentence, in and of itself, does not embody meaning in the quasimystical or romantic sense, nor does it cry out to be heard over the clamour of the universe of competing meanings 'out there.' Any meaning to be had emerges in/by/through exchanges between the sentence and its textual context, its social context, and above all, between the reader as contemplator of its possibilities as a *might be* (Firstness), a *this-hereness* (Secondness), and its potential or conditional *would be* (Thirdness) – following, once again, Peirce's 'pragmatic maxim.' Meaning in wait of an interpreter is vibrant, a trembling, indecisive (and at its roots, undecidable) fluctuation between *either/or*, *this/other*, *now/then*. It can never be fixed. Derrida's notion of textuality and reading, via Gregory Ulmer's (1985) interpretation – that is, the op art moiré effect – is relevant here, as is the *Ho-t'u* model (see also Gombrich 1979). Textuality in the sense of Firstness consists of surface level kinetics, without embodied meaning or ultimate truth, in hopeful anticipation that it will soon be disembodied by a cadre of potential interpeters. With a given reading, the two-dimensional surface seems to erupt into three-dimensional pulsation: it comes 'alive.' The 'op' phenomenon – creation of optical effects through manipulation of geometric forms, color dissonance, and the kinetics of vision – serves to exploit the limits of perception, whether through illusions or 'real' phenomena. Regarding textuality, this phenomenon as metaphor affords the image of an *enfolded* domain of *possibilia* promising a potentially infinite array of dissipative *unfolding*.[2]

Consider the role of the writer-reader to be that of a collaborator as interpreter with an interpretant in conjunction with the above on hypercycles and dissipative structures. In the first place, representamen, object, and interpretant constitute a triad of signs whose definitions are self-referential, circular: each one is defined in terms of the other two. Of the three signs, the interpretant is most pre-eminent. Following Savan (1987–8), every *interpretant is a sign* in so far as it stands for its object in the manner that some antecedent sign does; it is a substitute for some other sign of the same object. Moreover, *every sign is over the long haul an interpretant*: it is related to its corresponding object through the sign it interprets. And if that sign it interprets is in the same relation to its respective object, it must likewise be related to another sign it is in the process of interpreting. That is, for every sign, there is an antecedent sign for which it is an interpretant and a consequent sign that in turn interprets that interpretant. And thus we have Peirce's notorious infinite regress of signification, of indefinite semiosis.

The terms 'sign' and 'interpretant' are distinguishable by virtue of the fact that interpretants follow from or, in what in our day and age appear to be Peirce's admittedly rather embarrassing, and even 'logocentric,' terms, 'are determined by,' signs – though, as is now well known, ultimate determination for Peirce is, and will remain, a pipedream. This is the 'push' factor of signs: the sign as motivator, as prime mover bringing about a perpetual thrust into futurity, which implies Thirdness, the conditional *would be*. The supreme example of such Thirdness, to repeat, is mind. In an 1868 paper Peirce argued that the content of consciousness, the entire phenomenal manifestation of mind, is a sign resulting from inference, concluding that the mind must be a sign developing according to the classical *laws* of inference (*CP*:5.462). And in his later years he wrote that 'any set of signs which are so connected that a complex of two of them can have one interpretant, must be determinations of one sign which is a Quasi-mind' (*CP*:4.550). The interpretant, or a set of interconnected interpretants, is not merely an idea produced in the mind of the knower; the mind *is* itself an interpretant. It follows, Peirce believes, that since the mind is an interpretant, or a network of interpretants, development and growth of the mind can occur solely by way of dialogic exchange – like a Maturana-Varela autopoietic entity or recursive self in interaction with its environment. In this sense, the utterance of one voice consists of signs that become the interpretants of other voices (interpreters). These interpreters exercise a 'pull' effect on the interpretant, which tends to counterbalance the above mentioned 'push' effect. 'Pull' entails the motivator, the mover or enabler, whose function is 'catalytic': it is instrumental in bringing about sign transformation under conditions that would otherwise be unfeasible.

Reconsider, in this light, the hypercycle idea embodied in figure 3. The representamen (*R*) is a sort of 'categorial skeleton' of the sign (Savan 1987–8:10). Signs of the genetic code, for example, are not signs in the full sense (discussed in chapter 9). They are the rough equivalent of the initial information carriers in the hypercycle; that is, they are not (yet) mental in nature but merely porters of signs from an established code capable of bringing about some change in the material world – which, interpreted *as* the genetic *mode of signification* by mental intervention, becomes a particular aspect of our 'semiotically real' world. Consequently, a sign is something that when we, as mind, (think we) know it, we also (think we) know more about something else (that is, what it *is not*). This 'projection forward' makes for the very possibility of semiosis. And semiosis is what makes the semiotic hypercycle possible in the first place. For when an information carrier (*R*) in the hypercycle is such that if its information is processed (by a 'catalyst') it becomes more than it was or would otherwise have been, it paves the way for an emergence of the 'semiotic object' (*O*) of signification. And while playing out its own role, the 'semiotic object,' in collaboration and corroboration with the representamen, determines, through interaction with some participatory mind, an interpretant (*I*).

Now, the object as a sign in the 'semiotically real' can be either *passive* and *immediate*, or *active* and *dynamic*. The immediate object is roughly the equivalent of raw experience. Peirce once cited the case of an observer commenting on a ship at sea that is not seen by her addressee, who must use his immediate object, the sea, with which he is familiar, as a point of departure actively to infer a possible ship; that is, to experience the sea *as* bearing a ship in the distance. The familiar Necker cube offers another effective example of this bare, passive *seeing* in contrast to actively *seeing as* and *seeing that* such-and-such is the case – that is, automatized knowing *how* in contrast to knowing *that* (Merrell 1995). Seeing the drawing as immediacy entails a feeling or sensing of nothing more than a *quality* (Firstness): whiteness punctuated with thin intermittent blackness. A split moment later it is *seen* in terms of some *existent* entity 'out there' in the 'semiotically real' merely as a set of interconnected lines. But it is not (yet) actively *seen* as a cube, or anything else for that matter. The set of twelve straight lines, eight of them of equal length and the other four slightly shorter, and all of them connected at various angles, are at this point simply *seen*, without there (yet) being any awareness on the part of the observer *of* the cube *as* a cube. It is at this point no more than an impact or effect on the mind (Secondness) by virtue of its very existence. (An imaginary Martian from a culture not accustomed to our mental projection of three-dimensionality onto two-dimensional planes, however, would *see* it *as* nothing more than lines, clearly and simply.)

Then, after approximately 1/10 second, the cube's observer identifies it *as* a cube.[3] The object of the sign has become *dynamical*. This is indeed a remarkable feat of abstraction, this act of projecting three-dimensionality onto a two-dimensional plane. Now the maze of lines is *seen as* such-and-such: it is distinguished from all things it *is not* and indicated (indexed) to be a token of a particular type. This is *active* Secondness, which includes a second order interpretant, a *dynamic interpretant*, during the process of our cube-observer's consciousness flowing further down the stream of semiosis. However, such indication (indexing) in the full sense would not be possible were the observer to possess no conception of a type of which that particular token is itself an indication (index). That is to say, in order to *see* the cube and indicate (index) it *as* such, she must be in possession of a storehouse of background knowledge of cubes – that is, *that* they are twelve-lined and six-sided, that eight sets of three lines meet at ninety-degree angles, and so on. This seeing *that* the drawing is a cube with certain properties pertains to the domain of Thirdness, and requires, for its proper execution, generation of a third-level interpretant, a *logical interpretant*. Moreover, our observer must have been in a state of anticipating readiness, of expectation, with an elaborate set of dispositions and proclivities for *seeing* drawings on pages, for *seeing* them *as* drawings of such-and-such types, and for *seeing that* they evince specific characteristics requiring her going 'beyond the information given' in order properly to identify them (Bruner 1957).

Thus the interpretant (I), as mediacy, synthesis, provider of *relata*, rounds out the semiosic process. Representamen and object are meat and potatoes, but the interpretant is the dessert hopefully followed by an elegant liqueur. Every sign, to repeat, is potentially an interpretant. Its significance is inherited from all predecessor signs by virtue of which it is able to stand for its object. The interpretant (I_i *immediate interpretant*) as a First, a qualitative possibility, entails a feeling of familiarity, the absence of hesitancy, a sense of security, and an animal or instinctive sort of confidence. For example, the experience of a falling stone without there being any action on or contemplation of the event is such an automatized, 'objective' construal of the immediate interpretant. This level of perception corresponds to Peirce's *abduction* or *hypothesis*. It approaches the second-level interpretant (I_d, *dynamical interpretant*), the significant information carried by the sign, but as yet it remains a mere possibility, to be further determined by future signification. The dynamical interpretant consists of (1) the *qualitative* or *emotional* effect on the mind of, say, a falling stone, (2) an *energetic* or actual muscular encounter with the world or an active manipulation or exploration of images in the mind's inner world, and (3) the *logical* consequence of such action (a thought, concept, or general understanding of, for instance, the effect of the falling stone on the mind's processing of its 'semiotically real' world, which Peirce likens unto a 'thread of melody running through our sensations'). This experience of the 'semiotically real' coupled with action and reaction to it corresponds to *induction*.

What Peirce calls the *final interpretant* (I_f) – the ultimate extrapolation of the third order *logical interpretant* in the service of an entire community of semiotic agents – involves legisigns (symbols) in so far as they constitute ephemeral islands of 'living habit' in the ongoing stream of sign evolution. If, according to Peirce, the immediate interpretant is linked to *rhemes* (*terms*), and dynamic interpretants to *dicisigns* (*propositions*), the final interpretant is, ideally, a complete and consistent *argument* generated by way of *deduction*, as the product of a serial inner struggle of conjectures and refutations.[4]

A dictionary provides a concrete illustration of my point. The dictionary, of course, is roughly, and from a holistic grasp, tautological: a word's definition is available by means of other words, whose definitions are in turn by others, until finally, the entire fabric doubles back onto itself. Savan (1987–8:41–2) suggests that if someone does not know the meaning of *homme* but is aware that it is a French word, she can look it up in a dictionary, thus learning that it means *man*. *Man* somewhat closely approximates, she now assumes, a 'replica' of *homme* regarding meaning, and hence its interpretant. The problem here is that word meanings are themselves subject to the semiosic flow of things. Savan's own example of the change history has wrought on the scientific definition of 'atom' belies the possible implication that '*homme* = *man*.' We are speaking of two different cultures and a word in each culture that can never attain the status of immutability. *Replicas* (column *B* in table 4), as tokens in the sense of Peirce, can be re-iterated, potentially to infinity, but with each new instantiation, given incessantly changing contexts, frail memories, and in general, human fallibility, the word is never-quite-exactly what it was. There is always a *difference*, though ever so slight, from one reiteration to the next.

2. THE BIRTH OF IRREVERSIBILITY

'Fine and dandy, but what,' the reader has surely asked at this point, 'is the relation between *R–O–I* in figure 3, on the one hand, and all the palaver that followed on the other?'

Admittedly, I have exercised a not-quite-exact replication of Peirce's terminology. *R* as a bare category is simply a sign function in terms of its qualitative character; it has the makings of a *qualisign*. *O* as an instantiation of Secondness is tantamount to a *sinsign*, and *I*, of Thirdness, evinces the essence of a *legisign*. For example, a red patch appears as qualisign, which, when translated into a sinsign, may be *seen as* a particular flat object of a specific color containing letters from the English language. The prefix 'sin' refers to the sign's character as singularity, unicity, haecceity. As such it entails ritualized sign use, much like a signal in animal communication (Leach 1964; Sebeok 1976a:83–93). Every sinsign must contain as a subordinate part of itself a qualisign, for, without qualisigns there can be no sinsigns. A stop sign at the side of a street *seen as* an object of such-and-such characteristics transformed into the mode of *seeing that* it is a red hexagonal object used for the purpose of a traffic warning to which a certain response must be forthcoming is a legisign. Legisigns involve repeated and hence generalized use of particular signs. With each repetition there is a certain sinking into consciousness (habituation) of the sign and its use, and its *differences* come to be more and more tacitly assimilated as *identity*. Sign use in this manner leads to *embedment, automatization* (recall note 12 of chapter 1). In this fashion, reaction to the interpretant of the stop sign on the part of the experienced driver tends to become *as if* mindless, *as if* it were the information carrier of a rigidly encoded RNA molecule in a hypercycle. It becomes *as if* the mind *qua* mind were nonexistent; or better, the mind has itself properly become an automatized sign (interpretant) rather than a somewhat artificial interpreter *of* signs from some outside domain. Referring back to figure 3, the solid arrows can be labeled *sign generacy* and the broken arrows *sign de-generacy* (entailing *embedment, automatization*), a contrast that must now be further specified.

As suggested above, R–O–I, in terms of the subscripted values evolving from 1 to 3, represents sign *generacy* according to the range of an ordered series of generations – semiosis: self-reproduction, re-duplication, self-organization (as depicted in tables 2 and 4). In contrast, I–O–R, the inverse order, counter-balances semiosis with *de-generative phanerosis* (but recall note 11 of chapter 1). From the parent 3, or Thirdness, the system de-generates 'downward,' and sign activity tends toward increasing sameness, equilibrium, stasis – that is, toward B and A in table 4. It entails almost faithful – but not quite exact – reiteration, comparable to mindless responses to the stop sign example. This mode of sign activity corresponds to what I have termed *embedment, automatization,* and *habitual sign use,* which follow pathways of least resistance. Sign de-generacy is quite obviously entropic: it corresponds to the ordinary arrow of time, unlike sign generacy exercising a swim against the current – but bear in mind that de-generacy can be negentropic when signification is boosted to higher levels of organization involving composite signs, via dissipative structures.[5]

One might be attracted toward the notion of something akin to an entropic birth, life, and death of signs, from growth to the robust effervescence of youth, mid-life crisis, senility and decay, and finally death. After all, it is common knowledge that neologisms, especially metaphors, overflow with vibrant activity in the beginning, ultimately to sink into oblivion – as so-called 'dead metaphors.' But this image is somewhat false to itself (as we observe further in chapters 8 and 9). Recall, for instance, that according to figure 3, generacy entails the sequence $R \rightarrow O \rightarrow I$ while de-generacy proceeds either along $I \rightarrow O \rightarrow R$ in both *linear* and *nonlinear* fashion.[6] This is indeed significant. We live in a pluralistic universe – whether speaking of it in terms of signs or of empirical entities – in which reversible and irreversible processes coexist, all embedded in a monstrously complex expanding system. Classical mechanics dealt largely with reversible processes (that is, the movements of planets around the sun, swinging pendulums, colliding billiard balls, vectorial forces) for which the time element can be either -1 or $+1$ without altering the equation. In contrast, linear thermodynamic processes at the macromolecular level are irreversible.

Ludwig Boltzmann's studies with the Second Law of Thermodynamics at the micromolecular level, such as the collison of gas molecules, were partly correct: at the macromolecular level, there is an irreversible aspect proceeding toward equilibrium, entropic decay, chaos. Prigogine, on the other hand, argues that this macrolevel affords another, complementary interpretation, of irreversibility: that is, there is a push from chaos to order, by way of *nonlinear* dissipative structures that have their roots firmly planted in microlevel phenomena (Nicolis and Prigogine 1989). His Bénard cell example is a good case in point. When the liquid is heated, a dissipative structure takes effect, and an orderly spatial pattern of convection cells results at the upper layers of the liquid. That is to say, entropy or disorder is produced and exported in such a manner that it generates a relatively improbable, negentropic state of affairs. Classical thermodynamics dictates static equilibrium structures such as two-way chemical equations, with a corresponding increase of entropy in the system. Bénard cells are also structures, but of a quite different, dynamic sort. The result of dissipation, they appear at the outset paradoxical, for intuiton tells us that structure and order should exist on one side of the equation and dissipation or waste and disorder on the other side. However, heat transfer, considered a source of waste in classical thermodynamics, becomes a source of order in the Bénard cell.

The fluctuating, vibrating Bénard cell is thus a far-from-equilibrium condition oscillating between the either and the or, between disorder and order. Interestingly enough, Boltzmann would have assigned a near-zero probability to the occurrence of Bénard convection. But whenever new coherent states occur under far-from-equilibrium conditions, the relevance of probability theory, such as the collisions of gas molecules as if they were a collection of billiard balls, for example, breaks down. Prigogine in this regard tells us:

For Bénard convection, we may imagine that there are always small convection currents appearing as fluctuations from the average state, but below a certain critical value of the temperature gradient, these fluctuations are dampened and disappear. However, above this critical value, certain fluctuations are amplified and give rise to a macroscopic current. A new molecular order appears that basically corresponds to a giant fluctuation stabilized by the exchange of energy with the outside world. This is the order characterized by the occurrence of what are referred to as 'dissipative structures.' (1980:89–90)

In other words, Prigogine's microscopic theory of irreversibility of processes patterns, in a rather uncanny way, classical macroscopic theory.

This close relationship between microscopic irreversibility and traditional macroscopic theory apparently caught the scientific community off guard. Yet the concept has persisted in forcing its way into contemporary discourse. The important point is that in both macroscopic and microscopic processes, the distinction between what is permitted and what is prohibited is based on time by the laws of dynamics. The temporal nature of the macroscopic universe of our everyday living coincides with irreversibility. The systems of interest to Prigogine, whether chemical or biological, are also temporal on the macroscopic level, where time-asymmetry (anisotropy) reveals a broken time-symmetry (isotropy) at the microscopic level (such as the irreversible 'collapse' of a 'wave packet' to a 'particle-event'). Prigogine argues that irreversibility 'is either true on *all* levels or on none. It cannot emerge as if by a miracle, by going from one level to another' (Prigogine and Stengers 1984:285). This form of irreversibility, with its roots in symmetry breaking at microscopic levels that produce irreversible macroscopic order, is taking on increased importance. In this vein, Prigogine concludes: 'At all levels, be it the level of macroscopic physics, the level of fluctuations at the microscopic level, *nonequilibrium is the source of order. Nonequilibrium brings "order out of chaos."* ... [T]he concept of order (or disorder) is more complex than was thought. It is only in some limiting situations, such as with dilute [sic] gases, that it acquires a simple meaning in agreement with Boltzmann's pioneering work' (Prigogine and Stengers 1984:287) Matter, to repeat, seems to have a 'will of its own' (Davies 1988:87–8).

With this in mind, let us return to figure 3. Specifically, the obvious asymmetry between the solid and broken arrows is to be found in the I–R relation. According to Peirce, each interpretant is the outgrowth of a sign (S_i in terms of its representamen, R) and it becomes in turn another sign (S_{i+1}) by way of its interpretant, which is illustrated by an $I \rightarrow S_{i+1}$ transition. With regards to generacy, this indicates that the sign from which an I was derived and the sign into which it transmutes itself are not the same. The generative push, in line with Peirce's evolutionary hypotheses, is, both continuously and with fits and jerks, progression incessantly toward greater heights. For this reason the subscripted S is generally on the increase – and, I must repeat, neither a branching nor a linear series is implied here, but something akin to the Deleuze-Guattari (1987) *rhizome model*, which for obvious reasons defies graphic illustration. In this sense the $R \rightarrow I$ transition can also occur as the result of an S instantiation of lower subscript developing into one of higher subscript according to the above illustration of successive readings of a text.

That is to say, following table 2, a 'chair-support $\approx$ "leg"' image ($R_2 O_1 I_1$, iconic sinsign) can develop by means of a sense of commonality between 'legs' and 'chair supports' ($R_3 O_1 I_1$, iconic legisigns), and that into a sign relating one class of sign-objects to another ($R_3 O_2 I_1$, rhematic indexical legisign), and finally into the evocation 'leg' ($R_3 O_3 I_1$, rheme or term) as a metaphor with reference to a 'chair support.' On the other side of the coin, by habituation, use of this metaphor can sink into consciousness, thereby pulling it toward levels of greater simplicity, but heightened richness (vagueness), though that richness is implied rather than explicit. The metaphor, in other words, has suffered slow 'death,' it is now used without necessary awareness of the metaphor *qua* metaphor. Yet, at a moment's notice, the metaphor as embedded sign can be pulled up to conscious levels such that it can be imaged, indicated, cognized, and articulated.

Such a 'quantum leap' into consciousness of that which had become the product of habituation entails what I have termed semiosic de-embedment, or de-automatization, a generative process in contrast to the *phanerosic* de-generacy process (following the broken arrows in figure 3) (Merrell 1995). As I have argued, one can, by such de-embedment, become aware at various levels (1) of 'dead metaphors' *as* 'dead metaphors' (that is, the 'leg' of a chair, or the universe-as-machine metaphor-model, which ultimately became construed tacitly *as if* the universe, and all its parts, were *literally* machines), (2) of the ulterior messages underlying commercial hype and propaganda, or the fact that one has been deceived (say, by the simple words 'I love you,' whose false meaning at some point in the dialogical relations between two people comes through loud and clear), (3) of one's embedded and habitualized muscular activity (when explaining one's response to stop signs to a novice driver, when one has become partially paralyzed, or when one's respiratory function is impaired by an asthma attack), and so on. This sign activity is tantamount to a system, which, originally at some loose form of equilibrium, deviates from the norm until at some critical point a 'bifurcation' occurs in the direction of alternative pathways.

Such 'symmetry breaking' is the case of a René Thom-like 'catastrophe' from a 'lower' level R to a 'higher' level I to *generate* relative order from chaos, or conversely, from a 'higher' level I to a 'lower' level R in the case of *de-generacy*. This process is easily demonstrated by the model of a simple equilibrium reaction plotted on a graph (figure 5) where X represents transition from a 'higher' I to a 'lower' R, and Y from a 'lower' I to a 'higher' R, with E_1 and E_2

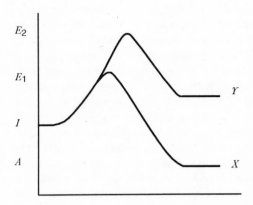

FIGURE 5

as their respective 'threshold' energies. The difference is that an equilibrium reaction reaches its respective E solely by heat transfer from outside, whereas a far-from-equilibrium reaction engaged in interaction with its environment spontaneously, of its own accord, and at some indeterminate point, undergoes a radical transition, completely 'flipping out' and entering into a new pattern of behaviour.

$S_i \ldots S_{i+1}$ in figure 3 must enter the picture as well, which relates once again to Peirce's notion of interpreters-interpretants (represented by the subscripts) pushing signs toward their completion. In other words, individual sign development and evolution of the process as a whole, along channels of *generacy* and *de-generacy*, and linearly as well as nonlinearly, depend upon interpreters (themselves sign-interpretants), whether of human or nonhuman variety. Peirce's remark in 1906 on the distinction between two classes of indeterminacy, indefiniteness (or vagueness) and *generality*, effectively conveys his thoughts on the matter. Vagueness 'consists in the sign's not sufficiently expressing itself to allow of an indubitable determinate interpretation,' while generality 'turns over to the interpreter the right to complete the determination as he pleases' (*CP*:5.448n). It is strange, 'when one comes to ponder over it,' Peirce continues, 'that a sign should leave its interpreter to supply a part of its meaning; but the explanation of the phenomenon lies in the fact that the entire universe – not merely the universe of existents, but all that wider universe, embracing the universe of existents as a part, the universe which we are all accustomed to refer to as "the truth" – that all this universe is perfused with signs, if it is not composed exclusively of signs' (*CP*:5.448n).

This quotation cries out for commentary, especially regarding what Peirce calls 'that wider universe,' which holds both signs and their interpreters as coterminous collaborators and corroborators in its tight embrace. As we shall note, the entire process involves sign *possibility-actuality-potentiality*.

3. EMERGENT SIGNS

In that same year, 1906, Peirce, on attempting to work out the idea of 'real possibility' as distinct from individual existence, referred to three 'modes of being' – which, in deference to current 'antilogocentrism,' I prefer to dub 'modes of signification' (Merrell 1991b) – and occasionally as 'modes of Reality,' though at other times he reserves 'reality' solely for 'existents' (*CP*:4.547).

With this broader use of the term 'reality' – that is, the range of all possible 'semiotically real worlds' according to the present enquiry – Peirce alludes to a sort of 'nondependence upon thought,' while existence is 'reaction with the environment, and so is a dynamic character' (*CP*:5.503). If *possibility* and *existence* belong to Firstness and Secondness respectively, then Thirdness is *potentiality*, that which is destined to occur at some indeterminate future point, though there is no absolute necessity that it will actually occur in a finite world (*CP*:4.547).

Though this third mode need not necessarily emerge into existence, it is nonetheless essential to the overall scheme of things. Without it, there would be no method for distinguishing mere possibilities – as fictive or imaginary constructs in so far as they can be available to thought – that may never be actualized from potentialities, law, or habit, themselves connected with actualized existents. The realm of *possibilia*, as opposed to *potentia*, constitutes 'that wider universe,' which, in much the sense of physicist David Bohm's (1980) *implicate order*, consists at most of mere ideas, mental constructs, or 'airy nothings to which the mind of poet, pure mathematician, or another *might* give local habitation and a name within that mind. Their very airy-nothingness, the fact that their Being consists in mere capability of getting thought, not in anybody's Actually thinking them, saves their Reality' (*CP*:6.455). This infinite extension of possiblities is potentially generated by an indefinite community of knowers to become brute actuality, a particular 'semiotically real world.' And it is precisely the third mode, that of *potentia*, that serves to connect *possibilia* with actualities.

An example. Sodium ions in solution are capable of producing an orange-yellow flame. This flame, as a mere signifying mode of quality or the possibility of a feeling, is not (yet) an actual, a Second. Its 'reality' is merely that of *implicitness* rather than *explicitness*. What is more, sodium can be said to possess this property as a secondary signifying mode of existence even though it never actually existed, or say, if it did not exist on earth but on the planet Krypton. Moreover, actual production of an orange-yellow flame as such would hold little relevance to the universe of signs and their meaning – interpretants – without the existence of Thirdness, the signifying mode of habit more or less determining how sodium would behave under such-and-such conditions. Even though sodium might have once existed on earth but was all destroyed before such a confirming test could have been conducted, its Thirdness would nevertheless have been 'real.' In this sense, Peirce's three modes bear rough comparison with Karl Popper's (1972) Worlds 1, 2, and 3. Ideas, at the outset 'airy nothings' (World 2, the domain of consciousness), can be put down on paper, say, as a political tract (World 1, physical existence), which, as part of another realm (World 3, the realm of arguments and counterarguments), can then elicit a reaction from a reader who sits down with his own 'airy nothings' to write a rebuttal, which then takes its rightful place as another World 3 object. Thus links are established between the marks on paper and the realm of possibilities, which contain both the initial argument and its counterargument – and hence the law of contradiction becomes of little consequence, if not simply inoperative.

The relationship between possibility and conditionality bears on Peirce's concept of 'modes of being' ('signification') in the sense that different 'modes' can be given a meaning with reference to some definite practical consequence, such as that which follows from a statement regarding a particular substance's not being scratched by certain objects. The statement is derived from a possibility, which, under certain conditions, specifies what would most probably be the case if the statement were put to the test – that is, the 'pragmatic maxim.' If true, the statement will stand up to the test of she who investigates the substance an indeterminate number of times over an indeterminate lapse of time. If in this manner 'mode of signification' implies whatever there is about any word that enables it to serve the ultimate goal of enquiry, it would also comprise different ways of performing the tests (*CP*:2.118). This 'signification' would hardly become part of the 'actual universe.' Rather, it must remain, more properly, 'semiotically real.' That is, an *interpreter* – which is/becomes over the long haul an interpretant – is absolutely essential in order to select, distinguish, indicate, and record 'natural events.' But, given Peirce's fallibility of any and all interpreters, those 'natural events,' are destined never to become more than 'semiotically real' events *for* an interpreter, and indeed, *for* the entire community within which she arrives at her interpretations.

For example, assume that the sodium flame as a possibility was somehow actualized during a holocaust consuming all available sodium on the earth, although this destruction was not actually witnessed by any surviving organism, human or otherwise. During the holocaust, sodium's particular spectral property would have been realized as a monstrous, totalizing existent or dynamical property capable of causing or determining other signs. As such, it would have represented a giant step along the evolutionary path of all signs. It would in a sense be superior to sodium's production of an orange-yellow flame as a mere possibility, or even as an immediate object, which would have had (as yet) no 'real' status, save its potentially being subject to determination by other signs. However, as brute existence, the actualized flame of a certain hue could not enjoy inclusion within the domain of 'semiotically real' entities in the general scheme of things in the universe *for* the surviving community of interpreters, for there was no interpreter who collaborated with this cosmic event without being consumed in the fireball. So no living interpreter could bear witness to the 'ultimate interpretant' of sodium in terms of its chemical behaviour.

To illustrate this deficiency of any and all signs as they can exist *for* our feeble, fallible minds, consider Mendeleyev's original construction of the periodic table of the elements, with its valencies-as-possibles subject to further investigation. On the basis of apparent periodicities revealed by the elements known at the time, Mendeleyev drew up a scheme remarkably close to the table used today, with empty slots for the absent elements as possibles rather than actuals. But more than mere possibles as Firsts, they were potentials in so far as their conditionality for becoming interpretants capable of determining the properties of these absent signs (that is, number of protons and electrons, relations to other elements, general reactivity, etc.) remained for future actualization. Without their interpretants having (yet) been actualized, these signs were 'real,' though not (yet) 'semiotically real' physical existents *acknowledged* and *recorded for* some semiotic agent or community of agents in some respect or capacity and *put to use* with some purpose or other in mind. The 'really real' itself – that is, the sodium holocaust without surviving observers – following Peirce, was 'real,' but it must always remain above and beyond whatever any particular semiotic agent may think it to be. *Our* world, whatever particular world it may be as a selection from the myriad, potentially infinite number of, possible worlds, can be no more than 'semiotically real.'

This idea, once again, bears on Peirce's 'Man ≈ Sign' equation, since an actualized 'semiotically real' sign is not the source of intelligibility except in so far as it is determined by a process of signification. For, if every sign 'has the unified living feeling of a person' (*CP*:6.270), and if the sign a 'man uses *is* the man himself' (*CP*:5.314), then both the sign and its user are equally signs, as well as the sign and its interpreter collaborating in the determination of the sign's interpretant – which becomes, in the process, yet another sign.[7] In other words, the sign can be construed as 'semiotically real' only in so far as it can be to a greater or lesser degree determined by other signs – users and interpreters included. Regarding users-interpreters, this sign as immediacy appears, spontaneously as it were, to the mind that can then determine it more or less as it pleases. The sign is in this sense tantamount to the emergence of an *abduction*, the result of passive musement, a free flight of fancy, intense concentration, or thinking about virtually nothing at all. It merely pops into the mind, so to speak. This might appear to be a spontaneous, unpredictable, chance affair (*pace* Popper), but it is not, in the sense of Peirce, since mind possesses a certain tendency to bring itself in tune with nature (more on this later).

Peirce occasionally used the term 'interpreter' in reference to something that is itself a sign (*CP*:1.553, 5.3; also Dewey 1946). Manley Thompson (1953:227–48), however, argues that this notion is shot full of holes. It apparently presupposes that signs in their function as interpretants include both sign users (utterers) and interpreters. In the first place, according to Peirce, an interpretant exercises a significate effect on the interpreter, and at the same time the interpreter, as a sign, affects the interpretant. Semiosis becomes circular, which is actually neither tragic nor vicious. Nor does it appear to be radically novel, given the current status of Peirce studies. But the point is at the outset well taken. First, the interpretant (as mind) is an interpreter, an architect of signs, of interpretants: the mind constructs a world, the 'semiotically real,' consisting wholly of signs, which, in their turn and when transmuted into interpretants, determine their own offspring. Second, an interpretant (mind), as listener, is capable of initiating the determination of an interpretant (mind) as utterer. Combining both activities, there seems to be, Thompson argues, a problem of distinction between the mind as architect of signs and as a sign to be investigated by another mind. How can the sign be both interpretant and interpreter, utterer and listener? This circularity, to which Thompson refers – and to which I have alluded repeatedly – is perhaps inevitable, and without it we, as largely autonomous, self-referential, autopoietic entities, could not exist.

But actually, Peirce does not attempt categorically to identify interpreter with interpretant, nor can the two coexist in absolute simultaneity: they are, more properly put in the terminology of chapter 1, *complementary*. As Peirce articulates it, the interpreter as sign is that which 'determines something else (its *interpretant*) to refer to an object to which itself refers (its object) in the same way, the interpretant becoming in turn a sign, and so on, *ad infinitum*'

(*CP*:2.303). That is, it can potentially reach termination, but this will never actually be the case in a finite world, hence it must remain general (incomplete in Gödelian terms, for it cannot be both complete and consistent).[8] Peirce continues: 'If, an interpretant idea having been determined in an individual consciousness, it determines no outward sign, but that consciousness becomes annihilated, or otherwise loses all memory or other significant effect of the sign, it becomes absolutely undiscoverable that there ever was such an idea in that consciousness; and in that case it is difficult to see how it could have any meaning to say that that consciousness ever had the idea, since the saying so would be an interpretant of that idea' (*CP*:2.303).

A sign, once determined by consciousness, remains as a future possibility even though, given human frailty and fallibility, at some future moment it may be lost to that particular consciousness. On the other hand, it will ordinarily not be lost if it has been *recorded*, as marks on paper, an inscription on computer software, a memory trace, or whatever. But as long as it remains merely in this state, it cannot interact with other signs, cannot interpret or determine other signs, that is, until it has been *put to use*, in the sense of John A. Wheeler's (1980a, 1980b, 1984) 'meaning physics.' In other words, if the sign has not been put to use, it has not (yet) pushed its way into the domain of 'semiotically real' objects *for* someone or something *in* some respect or capacity.[9]

Assume, however, that at some indeterminate future moment a particular sign pops into the consciousness in question. According to Peirce's dialogic this consciousness as interpreter determines the sign's meaning, and on so doing it addresses itself to its other self of the next moment, which, as interpreter, determines the first self. And that second self in turn moves on down the line to address itself to its own other, and so on. Thus Peirce's infinite series of interpretants and the mind's entry into it, his complementarity of interpreter and interpretant, of self and other, of one mind and another mind, of inner and outer (mind as sign and the 'semiotically real'). And thus the circularity:

$$\text{SELF}_1 \leftrightarrow \text{SELF}_2 \rightarrow \boxed{\text{SELF}}$$

which, in so far as it illustrates the *autosemeiopoietic* nature of the sign, serves as the fundamental model for semiosis.

4. SEMIOSIS AND AUTOPOIESIS

This circularity has further implications, including a transition from two-way symmetry to asymmetry, which bears on biophysicist Howard Pattee's (1970, 1972, 1986) concept of the *hierarchical organization* of living systems, in addition to the work of Eigen, Prigogine, and others.[10]

As we have noted, smaller units (atoms, molecules, cells) integrate and aggregate into larger units. This interaction gives rise to novel rules of organization that in their turn regulate and constrain the subsystems contained within them such that they conform to the behaviour of the system as a whole. In this sense, regarding the human semiotic agent, there is a hierarchical chain of command from brain levels to emergent mind levels, and back again, with all levels mutually influencing one another.[11] This-chain-of-command idea calls to mind the 'upward-downward' movement of signs described above. The capacity of 'higher' levels in a hierarchical chain influencing 'lower' levels in the same system – 'downward' causation – as well as the other way round, is not restricted to living organisms. A computer, for example, while obeying 'higher level' laws of mechanics and electricity, harnesses those very laws at the 'hardware' level in order to perform specific functions at a 'higher, emergent' level, that of the computer's 'software.'

Comparable phenomena have been observed in physical systems not ordinarily conceived to possess 'intelligence' in any form whatsoever. Bohm (1957) points out that a given collection of gas molecules never conforms to the letter of Boyle's laws of an ideal gas due to the fact that minute differences at the molecular level collude to cause slight deviations at the molar level. Norbert Wiener (1948) has observed much the same in simple feedback cybernetic systems such as governors and thermostats. At exceedingly more complex levels, E.M. Dewan (1976) writes on feedback mechanisms ranging from subcellular processes to social, economic, and political systems. The most simple generalization subsuming these types of mechanisms, he suggests, is the 'mutual entrainment of oscillations' – such as the dramatic case of a swarm of fireflies, whose on and off flashing becomes at some point synchronized. This phenomenon exercises a direct effect on emergent biological properties: the 'higher level' community of organisms influences the behaviour of each organism at the 'lower level.' But, Dewan observes, this is itself a phenomenon capable of even greater generalization, applicable to nonbiological as well as biological systems. He cites the familiar example of television (see also Hofstadter 1979). The electron beam scanning the screen is controlled by two oscillators, one for the vertical and one for the horizontal direction. When the oscillators are 'locked in' or entrained to pulses emitted from the transmitter, the picture remains stationary; when not, synchrony breaks down and the picture rotates. Readjusting the frequency of the oscillators at the 'higher level' to make them cohere with the input frequency entrains the oscillators at the 'lower level,' and the picture once again stabilizes.

Frequency coherence is also evident at other various and diverse levels of biological organization. The cardiac cell, for example, is its own autonomous oscillator as demonstrated by *in vitro* cultures. Each cell beats on its own if isolated, but when a group of them are allowed to mutually interact, they soon enter into a phase in which they beat as one organism (Winfree 1987). In a more general sense, circadian rhythms lock the day/night cycle of an organism into various periods that add up to twenty-four hours in a manner remarkably analogous to the mutually entrained oscillation phenomenon in television production. In both cases, by means of feedback loops, an oscillator sets itself in synchrony with an input channel, thus finding a stable phase. Any subsequent disturbance will be corrected such that the oscillator re-establishes its coherence with the input. In this sense the oscillation acts as a control system regarding its input frequency, and at the same time it is already a feedback control system with respect to its own internal working, since it possesses controlled amplitude manifesting a tendency toward a stable state.

These and a host of other case studies are relevant to Maturana and Varela's concept of dynamical, *autonomous* (*autopoietic*) entities. Such entities can be coupled with one another to bring about a harmonious, synchronic whole that can become *self-organizing*, thus regarded as a single unit in so far as its function is concerned. The system contains its own virtual governor governing the entire system by means of feedback loops (Wiener 1948). In other words, the governor is not local but pervades the entire system, as if it were a hologram (Pribram 1971, 1981, 1991; Bohm 1980). Or as if, given a sufficiently rich system, two otherwise incompatible perspectives were united into one complementary perspective evincing a Janus-faced countenance allowing for either one or the other to present itself, but not both in simultaneity. This is commensurate, it bears mentioning, not only with the 'complementary principle' as described in chapter 1, but also with the essence of Gödel's proof on formally undecidable propositions (Pattee 1979).

Gödel, it is now common knowledge, succeeded in constructing a self-referential statement within a (sufficiently rich) calculus that has, mirrored within itself, a metamathematical statement about that statement. The formula, F, asserting 'F is not formally demonstrable' is such a metastatement. It assumes an extrinsic perspective on a calculus while remaining intrinsic to that very calculus. Assuming a system, Z, labelled a 'human brain,' to be such a metastatement, then the brain would be incapable of demonstrating the rightness of any and all its assertions, and Gödel's proof would do a slam dunk in the physicalist's face. That is, the physicalist argument based on an identity between systems F and Z and between mind and brain as a solution to the age-old dualist problem would be seriously compromised. For according to the F–Z system, the 'governor' (mind, undecidable sentence) of the system could have no physical existence as such but, so to speak, it would be no more than an emergent property in the hierarchical chain of command comparable to Roger Sperry's (1966) emergent mind sublimated from brain matter, or Howard Pattee's (1970) upper levels somehow controlling the lower levels of the hierarchy.

This combination of hierarchical organization and mutual entrainment can be subsumed under Donald Campbell's (1974a, 1974b) interpretation of 'downward causation' according to which 'lower' level processes conform in one sense or another to the rules governing 'higher' level processes – for example, our computer above. Along these lines, Paul Davies (1988:172–4) discusses information systems, or in computer jargon, 'software,' in terms of 'downward causation.' He rather controversially brings quantum complementarity into the picture, relating the 'wave' aspect of an electron to 'software' and the particle aspect to 'hardware.' The wave function containing the physicist's knowledge of the quantum system represents information, or 'software'; it is a 'wave of software.' In contrast, the 'particle' manifestation of the electron is akin to computer 'hardware.' Using this language, Davies (1988:173) posits that: 'just as a computer has two complementary descriptions of the same set of events, or in terms of the program (e.g. the machine is working out somebody's tax bill) and another in terms of the electric circuitry, so the electron has two complementary descriptions – wave and particle.'

Admittedly, the normal behaviour of a computer does not provide an example of 'downward causation.' The computer-mongering human semiotic agent can hardly alter a computer's 'hardware' via information contained in its 'software.' If the computer is rapidly becoming our best friend – a user-friendly beast – it is without doubt the most obstinate house pet around: the best its user can do is 'cause' certain of its circuits to fire; and it will hardly suffer any alteration regarding its putative 'mental' characteristics in the process. In other words, there is no active give-and-take between the computer's 'software' and 'hardware' levels of organization, nor is its 'software' an epiphenomenal manifestation of the 'hardware,' but rather, parallelism exists in both the 'hardware' and 'software' descriptions of a given set of happenings. In contrast, with respect to a quantum measurement: 'what is apparently a closed quantum system (electron plus measuring apparatus plus experimenter) evolves in such a way that there is a change in the information or software, which in turn brings about a change in the hardware (the electron moves differently afterwards' (Davies 1988:173).

However, Davies extends his computer analogy to cover a most important difference. We are asked to visualize a computer equipped with a robot arm operated by the computer itself, comparable to the devices in automobile assembly lines. If the computer could somehow be programmed in such a manner that it is capable of modifying its own circuitry – for example, a self-replicating von Neumann automaton – then its 'software' would be able to bring about alterations in the workings of its 'hardware.' This is comparable, Davies suggests, to the information contained in a wave packet 'downwardly' causing change in the behaviour of an electron during a quantum measurement. Mere information ('software'), depending upon how it is put to use by the physicist, modifies the macroscopic state of affairs ('hardware').

The inevitable irreversibility inherent in such processes forces a return to Prigogine's contention over the years that processes of becoming are primary, while apparently reversible phenomena are secondary. The so-called elementary particles are not elementary at all, but the secondary product of what is really important: interrelations, brought about by interaction between inseparable observers and the observed, subjects and objects, knowers and the known, the ongoing, transitory effects of which are irreversible. 'Hardware' and 'software' levels are thus inextricably mixed; 'downward causation' competes with 'upward causation' in the Heraclitean flux and flow of things; both the grandest and the most insignificant domains are given a role and allowed entry onto the stage of becoming, of happenings. From this perspective, the Maturana-Varela autonomous autopoietic entity is not absolutely but at most chiefly autonomous, since there is perpetual give and take 'up' and 'down' the hierarchy. In other words, on the one hand the so-called autopoietic entity is autonomous in so far as it is a self-referential, self-sufficient, self-confirmatory system, but on the other hand, it is in constant 'dialogue' with its environment. Both exercise an influence on each other; both are altered, even though in infinitesimal degrees, in the process. This more general process is most appropriately labelled, as I suggested above, *autosemeiopoiesis*.

Now for a return to Peirce, with focus on the concept, briefly mentioned above, that a *relatively* autonomous, autopoietic system contains its own – nonlocal and 'holographic' – 'governor,' which in turn regulates the entire system.

5. CONGEALED MIND AND SUBLIMATED MATTER

If we replace 'system' by 'body' ('hardware') and 'governor' by 'mind' ('software'), we have something akin to Peirce's general view of things. And very significantly, this formulation centrally involves his 'Man ≈ Sign' equation. That is to say, sign is central, and 'man,' yet another sign, is placed at the centre of the – 'his' – universe.

Peirce's use of 'Man ≈ Sign' to fuse the mind/body dualism is intriguing. The move entails 'thought,' which is released from the dark recesses of its damp, mysterious dungeon into the light of day to take its place alongside the realm of external signs. To the question 'Can we think without signs?' Peirce points out that the most common argument in the affirmative is that a thought must precede every sign. Of course this notion presupposes an infinite regress, but it actually provokes no knee-jerk reaction on Peirce's part: Achilles, he states, 'as a fact, will overtake the tortoise' (*CP*:2.250). Like Bergson and Whitehead after him, Peirce learned to live quite comfortably with such apparent logical antinomies taunting us from the swamp of infinite regresses, since they are incapable of dictating the course of concrete, everyday existence. However, Peirce does assert, with respect to the age-old question, that 'if we seek the light of external facts, the only cases of thought which we can find are thought in signs. Plainly, no other thought can be evidenced by external facts. But we have seen that only by external facts can thought be known at all. The only thought, then, which can possibly be cognized does not exist. All thought, therefore, must necessarily be in signs' (*CP*:2.251).

In the conception of Sperry and other emergentists, it might be assumed that just as mind consists of emergent brain properties, so thoughts – that is, signs – are nothing more than emergent mind properties. But this is not what Peirce is all about. Mind itself *is* by its very nature sign. This concept bears on his 'pragmatic maxim' in so far as meaning is to be derived from one's thought-signs by measuring or otherwise verifying what one does with them; thought-signs, and mind itself, cannot be absolutely divorced from the give and take of everyday life activities. Thought-signs so externalized to become public, however, are not simply equivalent to 'operationalism' or 'logical behaviourism.'[12] Rather, thought-signs are understood in terms of their interaction with other thought-signs, which does not necessarily demand the existence of physically measurable or verifiable sign-data: the cognizable is not directly linked to what is 'out there.'

This is not to imply that there exists some sort of mysterious transcendental Supreme Signified beyond, yet within, the realm of signifiers – like the 'ghost in the machine' idea – that can somehow be knowable (that is, the ultimate import of the Saussurean framework as interpreted, critiqued, and extrapolated to the extreme by Derrida). What I have in mind, rather, is the notion that thought 'objectified' in/as signs among other signs is part and parcel of Peirce's 'objective idealism.' In a manner of speaking, thought externalized or objectified stipulates that meaning is tantamount to what is being communicated in the interaction between communicators and their signs. In other words, the *meaning of the sign is purely the conception it conveys*, no more, no less (*CP*:5.255, 5.310). In this sense, there simply is no separation between signs and their meanings. Peirce's 'man' – or any other semiotic agent for that matter – can thus be read also as a sign, for s/he *is* a sign, a process of knowing, the result of possessing knowledge, whether by instinct or learning. 'Man' and mind, or brain and mind, are thus inseparable. And '*cognizability*' (in its widest sense) and *being* are not merely metaphysically the same, but are synomymous terms' (*CP*:5.257). This apparently obscure remark calls for some elaboration.

In the first place, the immediate simply *is as it is*. It is 'unanalyzable, inexplicable, unintellectual,' it 'runs in a continuous stream through our lives; it is the sum total of consciousness, whose mediation, which is the continuity of it, is brought about by a real effective force behind consciousness' (*CP*:5.289). In the second place, both being and knowing are most adequately qualified as processes in a continuum comparable to the process of Achilles easily overtaking his torpid competitor without further ado, in spite of Zeno's placing the entire race within a digital framework of infinitely converging increments (*CP*:5.263). Since Peirce's thought-signs flow along in a continuum, there can be no first cognition nor is there a last one, nor any discernible mid-point: cognitions can themselves arise solely as part of a continuous process (*CP*:5.267). Moreover, given Peirce's idea that consciousness – hence cognition as well – is mediate rather than immediate, when one thinks, one has present to consciousness some feeling, image, concept, or other representation that serves as a sign. 'But,' Peirce goes on to say, 'it follows from our own existence ... that everything which is present to us is a phenomenal manifestation of ourselves. This does not prevent its being a phenomenon of something without us, just as a rainbow is at once a manifestation both of the sun and of the rain. When we think, then, we ourselves, as we are at that moment, appear as a sign' (*CP*:2.583).

If I understand Peirce correctly, the rainbow is a manifestation – reflection, icon – of the sun, and at the same time an indication – index – of the rain. By the same token, when we think, the object *of* our thought is not a 'real' object 'out there' but a 'semiotically real' object of thought. It is a manifestation of the thinker – a sign – as well as of the thought-sign that thinks it. After all, when one thinks, to what thought does that thought-sign, which is the self that thinks it, address itself? Here we have the human counterpart of Davies's self-reprogramming computer mentioned above. It may, via the medium of outward expression – which evolves only after considerable internal development – address itself to the thought-signs of someone else. But whether this is the case or not, it will certainly always be interpreted by another of one's own thought-signs. A current of ideas can thus flow freely, one into the other, though there can be interruptions or punctuations in the becomingness of the continuum of becoming, whether inferential and intentional or happenstance.

Peirce places almost overbearing stress that, following from his notion of there existing no thought-sign, cognition, or intuition undetermined by a previous thought-sign, cognition, or intuition, the striking in of a new experience, a new First, 'is never an instantaneous affair but an event occupying time and coming to pass by a continuous process' (*CP*:5.284). The prominence of one thought-sign in consciousness must be the consummation of an evolving process, and if so, there is no reason for a thought-sign to cease abruptly and instantaneously when another thought-sign emerges. On the contrary, Peirce argues. A train of thought 'ceases by gradually dying out, it freely follows its own law of association as long as it lasts, and there is no moment at which there is a thought belonging to this series, subsequently to which there is not a thought which interprets or repeats it' (*CP*:5.284).

Peirce then takes up the question 'Does the thought-sign stand for a "real" outward object?' When such an object is thought of, this might appear to be the case. But such is the stuff dreams are made of. For, once again, what is ordinarily construed to be 'real' can be no more than 'semiotically real.' Moreover, since a given thought-sign is determined by a previous thought-sign of the same object, it only refers to the thing through denoting the previous thought-sign. Peirce offers the example of Toussaint Louverture, the Haitian freedom-fighter. Toussaint 'is thought of, and first thought of as a *negro*, but not distinctly as a man. If this distinctness is afterward added, it is through the thought that a *negro/* is a *man*; that is to say, the subsequent thought, *man*, refers to the outward thing by being predicated of that previous thought, *negro*, which has been had of that thing. If we afterwards think of Toussaint as a general, then we think that this negro, this man, was a general. And so in every case the subsequent thought denotes what was thought in the previous thought' (*CP*:5.285). In other words, to reiterate our now common theme, the sign 'negro' breeds an interpretant, which in turn becomes another sign, 'man,' whose own interpretant is then engendered, and from whence yet another sign, 'general,' can arise, and the process goes on.

There is another interesting facet to this quote. Discounting Peirce's rather unfortunate choice of terms – after all, he remained, like all of us, partly a child of his times – here as well as elsewhere, he was quite perceptive to race-consciousness and sex-consciousness. In fact, we could in a roundabout manner relate his words to Roland Barthes's (1972) 'decoding' and 'demythifying' a photograph in *Paris-Match* of a young black soldier in a French uniform saluting the flag to demonstrate that 'patriotism' at one level is decadent 'colonialism' at another level. On the other hand, perhaps we should not be so presumptuous as to suppose – as apparently does Barthes – that we, Peirce, or anyone else, are capable of stepping outside our own 'bourgeois-academic' skins in order to see what we suppose ordinarily remained concealed to the mind-numbed readers of a magazine geared to popular consumption: in one form or another, we are all victims of sign *embedment* (*automatization, de-generacy*), whether we know it or not and whether we like it or not. In other words, much of what our 'hardware' is doing is not always available to, nor can it be controlled by, our 'software' process of consciousness and self-consciousness.

This problem aside – it warrants an entire study in itself – the point Peirce was making – and indeed, it is as far as we can expect to go – entailed the most cardinal nature of signhood: signs cannot but refer to other signs, even when that reference is directed toward the conscious mind itself, which is yet another sign. This compels us further to solidify the idea that signs do not refer to 'real' objects, acts, and events at all but to 'semiotically real' domains of the/our mind's own making, which bears, once again, on Peirce's 'objective idealism.' In this regard, and in a critique of his colleague William James, Peirce once pithily remarked that 'James wants to say *things*. I reply that *ideas* were always meant as *objects*, direct *objects*, not matters of psychology, by those who talked of them. When he says *things* he cannot mean the real external things; for they are beyond the power of thought. He can only mean the perceived *objects*, which are precisely what is meant by "ideas." What is *perceived* is an *idea*, in contradistinction to a raw sensation' (*CP*:7.408 n9). The object, acts, and events of perception are not directly available to us, only the signs perceived-conceived; there is no 'real' in terms of 'the way things are,' clearly and simply, but merely one of a myriad array of possible 'semiotic realities.'

Elsewhere we read that 'the reality of the external world means nothing except that real experience of duality' (*CP*:5.539). This 'duality,' this Secondness, is the 'hard fact' impinging upon one's consciousness to become a percept: not the thing-in-itself, but the interaction between one's mind and what is 'out there' (the 'actually real') only in so far as it is understood 'in here' (the 'semiotically real'). For one's existence consists in one's reaction with 'other things in the universe.' This 'does not in the least contradict idealism, or the doctrine that material bodies, when the whole phenomenon is considered, are seen to have a physical substratum' (*CP*:1.436). Rather, in another way of putting it, 'every sign stands for an object independent of itself; but it can only be a sign of that object in so far as that object is itself of the nature of a sign or thought' (*CP*:1.538).

Peirce's 'objective idealism,' rather than merely conceived to be the unhappy collusion of 'physical stuff' and 'semiotic stuff' – as has often unfortunately been the case – should imply that the mental and the material, mind and body, are fused into a blend of signs in such a way that one cannot definitely say here is a thought-sign and there is a sign-event. The human signifying animal does not simply consist of ideas imprisoned within a body, on the one hand, and the furniture of the world 'out there' on the other. Rather s/he is the very embodiment of this fusion of what there is into signs. Like all other 'semiotically real objects,' we are not best described as 'things' but more fruitfully construed as sign processes ourselves. Peirce refers to the 'miserable material and barbarian notion according to which man cannot be in two places at once.' On the contrary, Peirce asserts, he is like a sign (interpretant) which, as mind (interpretant), 'may be in several places at once' (*CP*:7.591). The formula can also be inverted: like the human sign, 'every symbol is a living thing, in a very strict sense ... it is no mere figure of speech' (*CP*:2.222). This is because, to repeat: 'Symbols grow. They come into being by developing out of other signs ... it is only out of symbols that a new symbol can grow' (*CP*:2.302).

In the final analysis, this fusion of 'physical stuff' with 'semiotic stuff,' 'brain stuff' with 'mind stuff,' and 'life-stuff' with the inorganic world, also amalgamates the 'semiotic object' with its respective thought-sign. For a thought-sign stands for its object according to how it is thought; that is to say, how it is thought is the immediate object of consciousness *in* the thought. This 'object' is the thought itself, or at least what the thought is thought to be in the subsequent thought of which it is a sign. Thus 'objective idealism' renders matter and mind continuous; they differ in degree rather than kind. Just as mind, sign, and physical existence are basically one, so also are living organisms, their 'semiotically real' spheres of existence, and the 'real world' (*CP*:5.257, 283, 313). As Peirce notoriously puts it, 'the one intelligible theory of the universe is that of objective idealism, that matter is effete mind, inveterate habits becoming physical laws' (*CP*:6.25). This quotation encapsulates the spirit of Peirce's entire philosophical vision. Mind and matter, like habit and law, or the 'semiotically real' and the 'real,' are in the final analysis made of the same 'stuff,' though, commensurate also with Peirce's view, the 'real,' given its myriad complexity, is destined to remain in its totality independent of whatever any collection of minds may think it to be. Thus in matter as crystallized mind, we find an analogue with the above pairs: 'hardware-software,' 'particle-wave,' and 'life-nonlife.' Neither can be separated from the other; they are *complementary*. There is an ongoing self-sufficient, self-confirmatory, self-organizing melting of two units into one; there can never again be any all-or-nothing slash between them.

The upshot is that mind is another phase of matter, and vice versa, in roughly the sense, one would conjecture, that steam is another phase of water, which is in turn another phase of ice. Gaseous molecules of H_2O inherently possess the capacity (habit) to crystallize into a hexagonal lattice structure when conditions are propitious. Comparably, 'matter is merely mind deadened by the development of habit' (*CP*:8.318 – as a matter of principle, commonplace dualisms were quite alien to Peirce). In passing, I might add that Peirce's notion recalls Schrödinger's (1967:104–5) timely remarks on actions, which, by repetition, gradually drop out of consciousness to become habitualized – an observation that conveniently brings us back to the signs-life theme winding its way throughout this enquiry. The *ontogeny* of our mental life, Schrödinger suggests, sheds light on the *phylogeny* of unconscious nervous processes, as in the heartbeat, the peristalsis of the bowels, and so on. Given a relatively constant train of events over many generations, such activities long ago dropped out of the sphere of consciousness; in the terms of this enquiry, they became *embedded, automatized*. There are intermediate grades of such habituation. For example, the movement of the diaphragm ordinarily occurs inadvertently. But on account of what Schrödinger calls *differentials* in an immediate context such as a smoke-filled room that in successive stages brings on an asthma attack – as mentioned above – the function of the diaphragm can suddenly push its way into consciousness. At yet a more immediate level, when one is balanced on a bicycle moving down the road, an unexpected flat tire can suddenly jerk one into consciousness *of* one's ordinarily non-conscious actions in an attempt to maintain the machine upright. Examples, of course, abound.[13]

Schrödinger (1967:105) concludes that 'consciousness is associated with the *learning* of the living substance; its *knowing how (Können)* is unconscious.' This activity bears on our distinction above between knowing *how* and knowing *that*, the implicit and the explicit, and seeing, on the one hand, and on the other, *embedded, automatized* seeing *as* and seeing *that*. To translate Schrödinger into Peircean terminology, *learning* and *knowing that* such-and-such is the case is 'conscious,' intentional, and reasoned 'mind-stuff.' *Knowing how* to do such-and-such without the necessity of thinking *about* it is 'unconscious,' *embedded* 'matter-stuff' (brain, body, the physical world). Combining the two, one might declare, 'I signify, therefore I am,' which could not be more un-Cartesian. The term 'signify' includes both thought-signs and their physical manifestations in one package, and, at the same time, it includes nonthought-signs (generated by 'unconscious' activity, *knowing how*) in their collaboration with consciously and intentionally generated thought-signs.

'Reality,' that is, 'semiotic reality,' is not fragmented, but a unified field, a 'language' in constant evolution, a monadic *uni*-verse made up of many *pluri*-verses, of many 'semiotically real' worlds – possible, actual, and potential – plus the 'real.' And 'objective idealism' presupposes a universe of physical-cognitive (material-mental) signs, all of which make up a given 'semiotically real' world for a particular community. In order that anything may be 'real' in this sense, it must be a sign system that is at once one and many, continuous yet allowing for particulars; it is objectivity conjoined with subjectivity (*CP*:6.203,

6.590). Peirce's philosophy 'can never abide by dualism,' for it does not allow a distinction between 'physical and psychical phenomena' (*CP*:7.570). The paramount centrality of the sign in Peirce's scheme of things is thus re-emphasized.

6. A ONE-WAY STREET DURING RUSH HOUR

Let us now exercise a convolution of figure 3. Notice, in the first place, that this figure is comparable to a Borromean knot, with Q as the nodal point or central axis about which a particular sign develops.

Like a mere haecceity (column *B* of table 4), the sign is of that incommunicable nature constituting individual differences – *difference* and *deferment*: Derrida's *différance* fused with Schrödinger's *differentials*. This demands a principle of individuation whereby singulars belonging to a general class stand straight and tall, though their instant of glory is ephemeral: they soon pass into oblivion, that is, into their respective other at the very moment they emerge and begin playing out their act of signification. Moreover, the sign's instant of dignity can *be* only with respect to something *other*: a given instantiation of a sign *is* only in so far as it *is not* what it *is not*; it *is*, only in relation to its *other*. This might seem to contradict my above assertions regarding figure 3 that S_i merges into S_{i+1} while it is emerging into the flow of semiosis. But not really. For S_i, in the now of its ephemeral existence, has not emerged *ex nihilo*; rather, it is in the process of emerging from S_{i-1}. Moreover, in the sense of Peirce, S_{i-1}, S_i, and S_{i+1} cannot be simultaneously present *to* consciousness. Granted, they are signs. But they are such only in regards to their being related *to* something *in* some respect or capacity, that relation remaining virtual until actualized *by* some semiotic agent, such actualization occurring in *mediate* rather than *immediate* fashion. Hence the reactions implicated in the above equation can occur only over that certain increment of time, approximately one-tenth of a second, the time Wiener attributes to the delay between the immediacy of perception (Firstness) and consciousness *of* the percept (Thirdness) (cf. note 3).

However, since no sign remains the same or identical after each successive temporal turn, each and every sign carries with it a tainted dash of what it *was*, and it is an anticipation of – that is, it is always already shaded with – what it most likely *will have been* at some future moment. Extrapolating from this focus on the fugitive haecceity of the sign, it can be said that each sign instantiation as a consequence of semiosis implied by figure 3 contains vestiges of its previous instantiation, and that vestiges of the present instantiation will be in turn contained in the next instantiation. This container-contained trope re-evokes the theory of knots, and especially, regarding mind and consciousness, Jacques Lacan's provocative formulation (Lacan 1982; Turkle 1978).

According to Lacan, mathematics is not merely disembodied knowledge. It is constantly in touch with its roots in the unconscious. This contact has two consequences: (1) mathematical creativity draws on the unconscious, and (2) mathematics repays its debt by giving us a window back to the unconsciousness. A topological form such as a knotted loop drawn on the blackboard could be a letter in an unknown script, for writing flattens three-dimensional knots onto a two-dimensional plane, the loops and overlaps becoming in the process concealed. The knot as a metaphor for writing – commensurate with an above quotation – reminds one once again of those knotted messages carried by Inca messengers (*quipus*), prayer beads used by Catholics and some Buddhists, medieval calligraphy, and DNA-RNA knots (the 'knot of life'). Knots, like topology in general, create the image of immanence but at the same time of unboundedness within a finite system where every act of limiting serves as a sort of 'transcendence' (Neuwirth 1975).

Recall the above formulation of a system containing its own 'governor' which in turn regulates the system. It becomes apparent, in light of the work of Eigen, Prigogine, and others, that the vocabulary this concept is dressed in is absolute, given its deterministic, mechanistic, cause-and-effect import. The quasi-self-returning 'strange loop,' Q, in figure 3 could be construed as the 'governor' regulating the $R–O–I$ system, the former corresponding to the 'semiotically real' constantly forcing itself into the consciousness of the interpreter, and the latter corresponding to 'mind-stuff.' One might surmise, in this respect, that Q not only owes its existence to $R–O–I$, but, in addition, it 'contains,' as *possibilia*, vestiges of its predecessor and projections into the next S – comparable to 'retention' and 'protention' in Husserl's terms. Thus $R–O–I$ also depends on, and owes its very existence to, Q. The problem is that we are still left with the image of linearity.

Significantly enough, both Eigen and Prigogine posit irreversible, asymmetrical, nonlinear processes – for example, catalysis, autocatalysis, and ultimately, far-from-equilibrium conditions, in which the presence of a product is required before it can be produced. In formal terms, to produce X the system must already contain X. But X does not merely produce more X in linear fashion. It uses another entity, A, which is converted into X by a 'reaction loop' describable as a nonlinear differential equation implying a temporal process. Thus, in formal terms: $A + 2X \rightarrow 3X$ (defined as $dX/dt = kAX^2$), where the rate of variation of the concentration of X is proportional to the square of its concentration. An excellent instance of this type of reaction is, once again,

Eigen's hypercycle, whereby a nucleic acid sequence contains the information for proteins, which are in turn in needed to generate that very sequence. When the system has reached a sufficient level of organization it is capable of stable survival; it is now relatively autonomous, autopoietic, to a degree sheltered from perturbations from outside. It can now grow on the stable foundation it has created for itself. This domain of spontaneous (re)productive activity is vastly distinct from the two-way, symmetrical, relatively ordered, and indifferent world of classical mechanics. Yet it emerged from a system that, to all appearances, might have been governed by dynamic classical laws; there appeared to be, a priori, virtually zero probability for the phenomenon of self-organization to occur. Yet it occurred.

Enzymes paving the way for such self-organization are not merely order generated from disorder by means of which they provide the role of a sort of Maxwell's Demon bringing about organization in a system that according to probability factors could not have been so organized. Enzymes do not alter the chemical differences in the same way the chimerical Demon alters temperature and pressure differences. On the contrary. The mechanistic interpretation of the Second Law of Thermodynamics dictates heat death, while the nonlinear, non-mechanistic interpretation permits perpetuation of life. As Prigogine puts it: 'In the context of the physics of irreversible processes, the results of biology obviously have a different meaning and different implications. We know today that both the biosphere as a whole as well as its components, living or dead, exist in far-from-equilibrium conditions. In this context life, far from being outside the natural order, appears as the supreme expression of the self-organizing processes that occur' (Prigogine and Stengers 1984:175).

Another point bears emphasis regarding the above comments on 'aperiodicity' as generation of asymmetry. Morphologically, the biological world is by and large organized in terms of bilateral symmetry. But, as I pointed out in chapter 1, there are obvious exceptions. Thousands of different fossil shells with right- or left-handed helices have been classified. The narwhal's horn is helicoidal, as are the tusks of most animals. Certain species of birds have bills that cross either on one side or the other. Many types of bacteria and the spermatazoa of all higher animals have helicoidal structures, and so on (see Gardner 1964).

Prigogine suggests that such asymmetry from random fluctuations culminating in bifurcations involves the system's 'choosing' a pathway for future development between or among the states around a bifurcation point. This seems to imply that the system behaves as a whole as if it were the focus of some outside controlling agent, but it is not. In spite of the fact that interactions between a given set of molecules do not exceed a range of some 10^{-8} cm, the system is structured as though each molecule were 'informed' about the overall state of the system (Prigogine and Stengers 1984:171) – which reminds us in an uncanny way of the double-slit phenomenon in quantum theory (Herbert 1985), or of biologist Rupert Sheldrake's (1988b) 'morphic fields.' It is commonplace that modern science was born when the Aristotelian concept of heterogeneous, hierarchical space, inspired by biological morphology, was discarded in favor of the homogeneous and isotropic space of Euclid, which attained its maximum expression with Newton's mechanics. The theory of dissipative structures, however, 'moves us closer to Aristotle's conception. Whether we are dealing with a chemical clock, concentration waves, or the inhomogeneous distribution of chemical products, instability has the effect of breaking symmetry, both temporal and spatial. In a limited cycle, no two instants are equivalent; the chemical reaction acquires a *phase* similar to that characterizing a light wave, for example. Again, when a favored direction results from an instability, space ceases to be isotropic. We move from Euclidean to Aristotelian space!' (Prigogine and Stengers 1984:171).

I have much to say on this theme in the chapters that follow. For the moment, it bears stating that, according to all indications, the 'semiotic triad' is radically dynamic, a 'form dynamics' of nonequilibrium fluctuations, which, like all such nonlinear processes, manifests feedback action on what in linear systems would be their 'cause' (Prigogine and Stengers 1984:153). This phenomenon, relatively rare in the inorganic domain, is *sine qua non* as far as living systems are concerned. Signs, like all living systems swimming against the dictates of classical equations, are 'alive.' In this sense, Q is not merely a 'governor' (the mechanistic image and terminology), but the embodiment of everything possible in so far as it is a superposition of all actualizable thought-signs and sign-events. We have observed how Peirce's collusion of continuity and discontinuity effectively conveys his elaborate notion of sign. Signs spread continuously in space as they grow through time. In this manner they are properly Aristotelian or non-Euclidean – as we shall note further in chapter 5. Though their passage into Secondness is realized in discontinuous or Euclidean space, in their composite, ideally they are continuous and anisotropic, or nonsymmetrical. Thus we are forced to concede that, in light of table 4, signs (1) are recursively self-sufficient (A), at the same time that, (2) upon replicating themselves, they relate to some other (B), (3) leave dyadicity in their wake to emerge into the level of self-reproductive triadicity (C_a), and (4) become, regarding their role within the whole of semiosis, self-organizing (as agents of *generacy* and *de-generacy*) and genuine signs ($C_{a \to 1,2,3...n}$).

In this manner, from the large view, the processes or 'reactions' made possible by the Eigen-Prigogine 'life triangle' are, as I see it, three in number:

(1) *autocatalytic* (X must be present in order that its own synthesis may be accelerated), (2) *autoinhibitive* (the presence of X blocks the catalytic action necessary to synthesize X), and (3) *cross catalytic* (two or more signs belonging to different reaction cycles aid and abet each other's synthesis). Injecting these three processes into the Peircean 'semiotic triad,' we have a spatially and temporally anisometric, asymmetrical, irreversible spiraloid. Interpretants incessantly spew forth mediately to become successive signs (as representamina) at 'higher,' more complex levels. On occasion, they give rise to vortices (symmetry breaking), and at certain unpredictable (bifurcation) points, they erupt (dissipate) temporarily into disorder, only to begin navigation once again toward more sophisticated levels of order.

The process incessantly begins its becoming; its becoming incessantly begins anew.

3

The Time of the Mind-Sign

Let us for the moment eschew the brain-mind problem, as did Peirce, and place his 'Man ≈ Sign' in the spotlight. Consideration of this equation will foreground the intrinsic/extrinsic, inner/outer, intensional/extensional dichotomies finally revealing, I will take pains to point out, a paradox. In fact, these binaries are not either/or affairs at all, but rather, there is, in light of Peirce's work, a 'middle ground' that lies at the paradoxical mainstream of the very semiosic process itself. This aspect of Peirce's thought, as I shall hammer out in subsequent chapters, is patterned in the tenor of our times in so far as it is at its very tap root a yield of that which also lies at the heart of quantum theory and relativity, the 'limitative theorems' in mathematical logic, avant-garde movements in the arts, and the recent shift in philosophical thought, all of which have radically altered our view of time and space. This altered view is indeed more than simply a tectonic shift. It places the very notion of mind in both a timeless and a time-bound framework, both as mere abstraction and as a living process.

(In good faith I should also mention that the reader may confront what he/she considers undue abstractions in this chapter, which, to make matters worse, at the outset even appear irrelevant to semiotics. The formalities are, I would submit, inevitable, for the content can hardly be presented otherwise; and the features of the content presented are self-referentially progressive as well as regressive, due to the very nature of their form. It is my hope, however, that this turn to quite formal concerns will prove timely, and that I shall eventually be able to bring the spaceship back to Earth in subsequent chapters, where, the ground having been tilled properly, the true relevance of Charles S. Peirce with respect to our contemporary milieu will spring forth.)

1. WHAT IS 'REAL'?

As suggested in the previous chapter, according to Peirce, in the process of generating thought-signs, or of conveying something to someone by signs that are in one form or another empirical, the 'man' becomes coterminous with the 'sign.' In this regard, each semiotic agent generating a stream of signs pointing toward some final but always indeterminate interpretant is ultimately limited by what I shall term the *intrinsic* perspective: in terms of its role as an autonomous entity the semiotic agent sees the physical world as thought-signs 'in here' mediating sign-events 'out there,' rather than there being a monopoly of external sign-events dictating – via the *external* perspective – the nature of what is considered 'real.' In this sense there is neither exclusively 'inner' nor 'outer' processing of signs, but an ongoing interaction between *intrinsic* and *extrinsic* perspectives.

This conclusion, of course, is on a collision course with our age-old hopeful imperative according to which the interpreter should ideally enjoy a detached, exclusively objective, *extrinsic* view of the world, and that knowledge (*episteme*) can thus be shorn of subjectivity and mere opinion (*doxa*) (Globus 1976). However, such an imperative is an illusion. In order to illustrate my point, allow me to outline a few dicta that are basically in line with Peirce's general thought, as I shall subsequently argue.

There is only one *intrinsic perspective* at a given moment *for* a particular interpreter existing in the 'now,' a knife-edge moving along the race of time. The same can be said regarding the *extrinsic perspective*, in light of psychological studies drawing from the Necker cube and other such phenomena. However, at any given moment the number of possible *extrinsic perspectives* available to us is, for practical purposes, unlimited; any one of them can be actualized at a given moment, but the range of all possible extrinsically 'real' worlds is timeless. In their composite, they exist, *en bloc*, as *potentia*. I suppose an ideal but impossible Laplacean supernatural Omniscient Observer would be able to see and know them all in simultaneity. The most we can do, however, is become aware of minute slices of the totality along successive time increments. But actually, much the same could be said of intrinsic perspectives: two of them cannot be effectively inhabited by the same person (or thought-sign) in simultaneity, for each person exists within her own mind for the moment, so to speak. Each moment, as far as her consciousness *of* it is concerned, is eternally separated from all other moments *of which* she is, or can become, conscious. All moments belong to a particular series of 'nows' along her 'world-line.'

In the final analysis, on the one hand it would appear that the intrinsic and extrinsic perspectives must be considered *complementary* (the dualist view), yet, on the other hand, consciousness is constructed in such a manner that the intrinsic and extrinsic perspectives become united, a harmonious whole (the monist view). Now, while I cannot be so presumptuous as to suppose I can dissolve this perennial dilemma, I wish to establish a distinction between the intrinsic and extrinsic in such a way that another set of conceptual terms – including their own form of fusion – is evoked: *continuous* and *discontinuous*. This formulation will prove quite Peircean in spirit.

We ordinarily believe our perceptual field to be 'grainy' (Sellars 1963). We categorize coloured patches 'out there' as objects of one sort or another and in terms of the relations between them; we differentiate continuous variations of a spoken language into discrete phonemes, and our olfactory, gustatory, and tactile sensations are generally broken down into sets and classes. But this picture of the world remains false to itself. Sensory experiences at their most basic level of 'quale,' Peirce's Firstness, are *continuous*, and since each First as such simply *is as it is*, without (yet) enjoying any mediated connection with anything else, its borders necessarily remain 'fuzzy.' It is by its very nature *unbounded*. Indeed, there is no definitely specifiable point where a given sensation begins and another leaves off; there is no clear-cut demarcation between *that* sensation and some other virtual sensation that is not experienced at that particular moment. Our visual field merely fades into a brownish or blackish zone – peripheral vision – which becomes increasingly vague. Depending on 'rods' rather than 'cones,' the acuity of peripheral vision is therefore poor. For this reason our sensory field must be considered, for practical purposes, unbounded and continuous.

During one of his many arguments that experience at the most fundamental level is continuous, Peirce alludes to our 'blind spot,' that place in the retina termed the 'optic disc' where there are no receptor cells since it is the exit point of the optic nerve. Closing one eye and sliding a coin along the table one can find the 'black hole' where the coin disappears from view entirely. Then, when one opens the other eye, it pops back into existence (*CP*:5.220). Peirce goes on to remark on the organism's capacity to see the otherwise discontinuous field 'out there' as if it were continuous, considering this phenomenon a practical demonstration of the continuity of experience. Gordon Globus (1976:282) uses the same strategy in emphasizing his point that visual (and all other) experience 'is unbounded; even with a defect in the center of the phenonenal field, there is no definite boundary where visual experience leaves off and something else begins.' Extrinisic stimuli as they impinge on the visual cortex, even after it has been for some reason or other damaged, can find no specifiable direct correspondence to the intrinsic mode of perception.

A fundamental distinction between the purely intrinsic and the extrinsic – though one must bear in mind that the 'distinction' is a sliding-scale ideal between two extreme ideals – consists in the latter's necessarily entailing the equivalent of a Spencer-Brownian (1979) *distinction* and *indication* of something as such-and-such (but not [yet] *with respect to* something else).[1] The *with respect to* essentially entails Secondness, which is of necessity discontinuous and 'grainy.' The difference between intrinsic and extrinsic perspectives is in this sense comparable to that between *seeing* and *seeing as-that* – as I outlined briefly in chapter 2. Seeing is merely receiving raw sensations without their (yet) being classified and described *as* so-and-so with such-and-such characteristics. To see a coloured patch *as* an orange *that* is spherical in shape is a far remove from raw seeing (Hanson 1958, 1969). Merely seeing what is 'out there' knows no bounds, while seeing *as-that* entails a contribution of preconceived categories (thought-signs) from the intrinsic perspective 'in here,' which are, over time, indefinitely variable regarding their numbers and qualities.

Thus the extrinsic perspective's property of unboundedness is quite unrelated to the unboundedness of the intrinsic perspective. It requires a subject *set apart* – albeit artificially – from the world, which is an objective stance, though it is destined to remain merely pseudo- or quasi-objective. Of course Thirdness, by means of an interpretant and an interpreter interpreting it, ties intrinsic and extrinsic seeing into a loosely bound package, but, *pace* Peirce, every interpretant, in the twinkling of an eye, is destined to pass on, thus making way for its successor sign. In this manner, consciousness is capable of attending to the interpretant not as it is, in its full presence, but only as it was in the past moment. So even here we have the permanence, yet transience, of Thirdness, of interpretants.

Now, what has all this to do with semiosis as a living process? The method to my frequent displays of digressive idiosyncrasy includes, as we shall note, not only the impossibility of distinguishing clearly and distinctly between intrinsic and extrinsic perspectives, and thought-signs and sign-events, but also, of demarcating the very boundary between semiotic agents and their signs.

2. SIGNS THAT SIGN THEMSELVES

However, what strikes a discordant note in the heartstrings of even the most stalwart of Peirceans is a paradox that lies at the very core of Peirce's 'Man ≈ Sign' equation. If 'man,' that is, mind, is in the act of thinking itself a sign, and if the mind is capable of becoming (mediately, not immediately) aware *of* itself, of its ongoing dialogue *with* itself, then it should be capable of time-dependent, intrinsic, self-referential – and above all, mediated – *self-awareness* (hereafter *SA*).

The view to be presented here in light of the preceding chapters, and following Peirce and Whitehead, holds that consciousness and self-consciousness are neither exclusively material nor ideal: they are not substance but movement, they are process. Yet consciousness and self-consciousness enjoy a marked element of autonomy – with a nod to Maturana and Varela – in so far as they do their thing *within* their 'semiotic world' only by virtue of their withdrawal *from* that world. The entire semiosic process, including that *self*, is 'a coherent whole' that is 'never static or complete' (Bohm 1980:ix). Within this whole, consciousness and self-consciousness, as 'idealists' so to speak, are in perpetual movement, constantly annihilating those moments when they lurch from their starting blocks in search of new interpretants. Yet at the same time, as 'materialist,' they pull themselves back toward where they were, toward the more comfortable furniture of their world. They are both 'idealists' – in terms of the continuity of becoming as quali- and legisigns – and 'materialists' – in terms of the discontinuous being of becoming, as sinsigns. *SA* perpetually strives to link these two tendencies.

If the general notion of *SA* presented here is valid, then it should also be capable of self-denial of the 'I am lying' sort, that apparently puts it in hot water. That is, *SA* implies the negating proposition, 'M at this instant has the property not P_1,' where M is the mind state of the utterer, which corresponds to *SA*, and P_1 is the property of existing in the mind at a particular instant and hence of being available to *SA* – though not in the immediate 'now' but only mediately, after one-tenth of a second or so. The problem is that the proposition in question, 'M at this instant has the property not P_1,' is not empirically demonstrable from within M. It is roughly equivalent to the Gödelian sentence 'This sentence is not decidable' generated from within the axioms and proofs of *Principia Mathematica* calculus. In this sense, if the negating proposition regarding M is true, then M cannot have the property P_1, clearly and simply. However, the self-referential trap remains. For, if M does not actually possess P_1 and hence the proposition is true, neither can *SA* possess P_1. Both M and *SA* are incompatible with the 'now' of any and all particular intrinsic states and their properties. Now assume the extrinsic perspective requires that *SA* become merely *awareness* (hereafter A). That is, it merely becomes aware *of* such-and-such *as* something or other 'out there' (the 'clash' of Secondness) after some intervening lapse of time. In this event, A implies the proposition 'B has at this instant the property P_2,' where B is the brain state corresponding to A and P_2 is the property of impingement on the brain of certain sensory stimuli. There seems to be no anomaly here, self-referentially or otherwise.

But the question that now surfaces is, 'How can SA actually jump out of its skin to become A, or vice versa?' – that is, Zeno in a new garment, which entails the impossibility of rendering discontinuity compatible with continuity, finitude with infinity. It must be by means of the self-negating proposition 'M has at this instant the property not-P_1.' But if this proposition is not demonstrable, then how can SA, which is invalid through its self-negation, validly be transferred – transfer itself – to A? By exercising a Tarski-like SA–A move, one might respond. With such an act of faith, we can presumably jump to a higher-level language in order to resolve the inconsistency. In other words, SA entails, at the first level, A of such-and-such 'out there,' and SA_1 at the second level entails SA entailing A, and so on. However, the second level introduces the same inconsistency inherent in the initial proposition, and in order provisionally to remedy this unfortunate state of affairs, another jump is necessary, and then another, and so on: the system is invariably either *inconsistent* or *incomplete*, or in Peircean terms, *vague* or *general*. This state of affairs, equivalent to the notion of an infinitely regressive consciousness, is reminiscent of Ignacio Matte Blanco (1975) and J.W. Dunne (1934), whose models of consciousness revel in paradoxical tactics – consciousness as infinite sets for the former, consciousness as an infinite Chinese box for the latter (see Comfort 1984). And, it bears mentioning, both models are comparable to Josiah Royce's map paradox to which Peirce occasionally made reference.

In fact, Peirce's concepts of *vagueness* and *generality* are, I believe, quite crucial to an understanding of his notion of the universe as a perfusion of signs. From a Peircean perspective, the equivalent of both SA and A can be subsumed within an alternative perspectival framework including (1) a *superposition* of incompatible (*inconsistent*) *views*, thus potentially violating the principle of noncontradiction, and/or (2) *open* or perpetually *incomplete* views capable indefinitely of taking in more and more within their purview, thus potentially violating the excluded-middle principle.[2] Not only that, but (2) also contravenes the principle of identity, since nothing remains absolutely identical with itself in terms of what it was, given Peirce's notion of haecceities regarding Secondness. This all-encompassing open perspectival framework of *inconsistency-complementarity-incompleteness* is quite anathema to the long tradition of Western thought: it appears to undermine the very idea of logic and reason as we know them.

But actually, it is not so unpalatable, once one has taken the necessary steps. A, pertaining to what is 'out there,' is *differential* and *deferential* (Derrida 1973). Hence it must be perpetually *incomplete*. In so far as it is incomplete, it remains

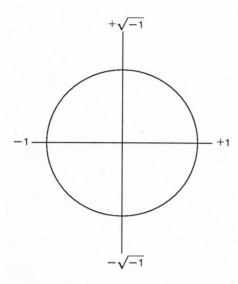

FIGURE 6

open to its 'outside' environment, to the interjection of additional 'axioms' or 'premises' regarding formal systems, or of 'energy' or 'information' regarding general semiotic and biological systems, in order to maintain its incessant push toward completion. And *SA*, implying the existence of the self, the 'I,' must be chiefly – though never wholly – an autonomous, autopoietic, self-referring and self-sufficient entity. As such, by the very nature of its self-referentiality, the constant risk exists of an *inconsistency* popping up sometime, somewhere. This inconsistency will be manifested in the form of a 'contradiction' or 'paradox' in formal systems, or 'ambiguity,' 'error,' 'dysfunction,' or 'mutation' in general semiotic and biological systems, demanding an opening out to the environment in order that the abnormality may be ameliorated.

My own formulation, admittedly, is not without its own inherent self-contradiction, and so it cannot help but fall into its own inconsistency. However, from a broad synthetic vantage, *SA* plus *A* rather paradoxically unite *inconsistency* and *incompleteness*, and *vagueness* and *generality*. In this sense, together they can most appropriately be termed *complementary*. *SA*, 'mind-stuff' (thought-signs), is for all intent and purposes unbounded. Since it tends to gravitate toward *generality* and *continuity*, it has no readily conceivable upper bound, given an indefinite range of contexts within which it can operate. In contrast, *A*, tied to 'thing-stuff' (sign-events), is, like Secondness, an ongoing parade of differentials, of particulars, *discontinuities* arising from the *continuum* of *vagueness*.

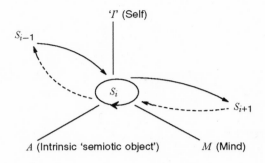

A (Intrinsic 'semiotic object') M (Mind)   FIGURE 7

In addition to the complementary pair, SA and A, there is, interestingly enough, a third perspective, a 'middle ground.' It involves, following physicist Arthur Eddington, what can be termed the *imaginary perspective* (also Globus 1976; Merrell 1983).[3] This perspective stems from the capacity of numbers to mirror-image themselves by a 180° rotation, thus producing an infinite series of negative integers as an antipode to the positive integers. The planes resting halfway between the series of positive and negative integers and orthogonal to them constitute what is called the *complex plane*. Illustrated graphically by an Argand diagram made up of *imaginary numbers*, $+i = +\sqrt{-1}$ and $-i = -\sqrt{-1}$, the complex plane engages in the process 'schizophrenically' of oscillating between a value and its contradiction (see figure 6). The plane is neither 'inside' nor 'outside' the system, nor does it entail a spatial dimension, for 'space' as such does not exist here. It merely represents a 'hole,' so to speak, allowing for accessibility to the series of integers. That this plane is essential for considerations of the quantum world as well as relativity testifies to its likely importance in any overarching scheme of things. Among other formal necessities in contemporary descriptions of quantum and relativity 'reality,' the complex plane also gives rise to the possibility of a space-time singularity, or a 'wormhole' in physicist John Archibald Wheeler's (1980a, 1980b) conception, where the usual notions of time and space are of no consequence.

Let us, as a sort of metaphorical exercise, transform the complex plane into a triadic framework, following Peirce. Figure 7 is roughly an extension of figure 3, where S_i, in place of the 'empty node,' represents a sign subject to the attention of some semiotic agent, M (mind) is the locus of intensional thought-signs, A is the moving force behind the interaction between M and 'semiotically real objects,' and 'I' is the the counterpart to SA, the self-referential self. M, A, and 'I' are, faithful to Peirce's ongoing semiosic vortex, in perpetual gyration about S_i, which activity brings about the continuous engenderment of signs. This scheme might at the outset appear to be unbearably Cartesian. M – thought

(thought-signs) – is separated from A and 'I' as that which thinks them, and it is therefore apparently aware of that which it thinks in simultaneity with its thinking. As such, it is presumably set apart from the 'semiotic object' and its own 'I,' a detached contemplator of the physical world. However, this is not the case when one considers Peirce's *mediacy*, rather than Cartesian *immediacy*, of consciousness according to which both M and 'I' as themselves signs are contiguous with and equal in status to their own thought-signs 'in here' and the sign-events of their 'semiotically real' world 'out there.' Just as no thought is directly observable, so no 'semiotic object' is directly accessible to the mind in its full-blown presence. In fact, the 'semiotic object,' given Peirce's fallibilistic asymptote model of knowledge, cannot be absolutely coterminous with the 'actually real,' which implies that the 'actually real' *as it is* in the *here and now* is not observable. Neither is the 'I,' or the thought thought by it, directly observable for that matter.

Furthermore, one could most likely explore the nooks and crannies of a brain during the lifetime of a given individual and never discover a thought-sign, a mind-state, or the 'I' in any form made intelligible in a tensed language of denotation or direct representation. Yet relatively few of us would extrapolate from this futile exploration to doubt that thought-signs, mind-states, and the 'I' exist. If they are not directly observable and cannot be dressed in denotative language, then one should at least be able to endow them with some sort of modelling or representation. Such modelling would most likely be none other than *imaginary*, though it 'refers' to nonobservables (Charon 1987). The *imaginary* rests in a netherworld, like the complex plane; it is neither in the realm of positive integers nor in that of their negation (falsification, refutation). It is, once again, a 'middle ground,' so to speak. Neither purely mental nor equivalent to the self or the semiotic object, it is simply imaginary, the stuff of mind. As such, this 'middle ground,' like the expression $\sqrt{-1}$ in the complex plane as well as in quantum and relativity computations, can none the less at least be put to work in describing relations between A, M, and 'I.'

That is to say, the source of signs from the 'middle ground' must be comparable to the metaphorical semiotic counterpart of a 'complex plane' resting orthogonal to the legs of the triadic relations depicted in figures 7 and 3. Purely *imaginary* constructs emanating from this 'complex plane' enjoy no direct relation to any 'semiotically real' world. They are in a sense nothing, no-*thing*; yet potentially they can be at least indirectly related to the thingness of things in terms of their becoming and to their becoming in terms of their thingness. They can become models (and metaphors) affording a better view of what appears to be, as facts of the matter. That is, models (and metaphors) from the 'complex plane' would render the apparently unintelligible and empirically unavailable a slight degree more intelligible (see Black 1962; Hesse 1966; Merrell 1991b).

This general concept must surely appear anathema to many bystanders. However, in the first place, I am using the *imaginary* and the 'complex plane' as metaphor, but, I would suggest, as quite faithful metaphor (especially in conjunction with Merrell 1991b, 1995). In the second place, both relativity and quantum theory use the 'complex plane' as a model (perhaps we could call it 'metaphor' also) (Penrose 1989). But the road leading to this use has been rocky. As a result of the at times devastating effects of nineteenth-century positivism and its twentieth-century outgrowth, logical empiricism, developed in the aftermath of Mach's macho phenomenalism, natural science has remained at times pathologically preoccupied with strictly observable phenomena, or at least phenomena that are only at most indirectly observable. It is common knowledge that Einstein indefatigably hammered away at the Copenhagen interpretation of quantum mechanics on the grounds that it was incomplete – since the whole of quantum phenomena was not accounted for in a consistent package nor could it be available to empirical scrutiny in one gulp. His counsel tended to fall on deaf ears for decades, however, for the general assumption was that quantum theory simply 'worked,' so it should not be tampered with. Finally, with the general – though still somewhat debated – acceptance of black holes, quarks, leptons, and so on, a populous set of imaginary 'objects' was ushered in. Though these 'objects' are not directly observable or denotative, they can at least be given various forms of 'representation' (or more properly anti-foundational, 'signification') within the purely imaginary sphere of 'complex numbers.' Consequently, to the question 'Are they real?' the answer must be an emphatic 'Yes!' They belong to a given 'semiotic reality,' which, if the physicists happen to be lucky enough to have hit the mark, is a collusion and collaboration with the 'actually real.'

And what motivates this semiosic generation of these *imaginary* non-things which none the less stand a chance of becoming full-blown things? In essence I would submit, the motivating force is equivalent to the central 'enzymatic' Q in figure 3. Q is, in a manner of speaking, the semiosic cascade taking sign component R to its respective O and then to I, which mediates between the prior two components and then back again to R, this time either at a 'higher' or 'lower' level – in this vein, once again contemplate the similarity between figure 7 and figure 3. Both the 'semiotically real' on the one hand and the domain of thought-signs and the *imaginary* on the other are modellable, the first corresponding to what is 'out there,' the second to the 'in here.' But by taking that ubiquitous crowd of imponderables – the unobservables 'out there' – and placing them in a historical framework, one is forced to conclude that one domain is hardly any less 'real' than the other. What for one generation is observable, hence 'real,' that is, 'semiotically real,' can be for another generation merely *imaginary*, and vice versa.

This question must be pursued further.

3. FACTS, FIGMENTS, FANTASIES

It might be contended that Q as a model-metaphor of the variables, R, O, and I, is extensional, therefore 'semiotically real,' while that which it models – that is, the variables themselves – must be perpetually relegated to nonexistence – or at best of 'subsistence' in the sense of that philosopher of 'mental objects,' Alexius Meinong.

On the contrary, however. R, O, and I as *imaginary* entities enjoy their own form of existence. If we follow current science, everything consists of one and only one sort of 'stuff': time-space, which is of *imaginary* 'stuff.' Actual 'things' are nothing more than 'knots' in this time-space continuum, and nothing is separable from anything else in the cosmic fabric of so-called 'existence.' The *imaginary* realm of possibilities, in contrast, is manyfold. It is outside actuals in time and space. The composite of all possible 'semiotic worlds,' it is the *enfolded* from which particular 'semiotic worlds' can be *unfolded* (Bohm 1980).

For example, the Necker cube as a mere set of lines on paper without its (yet) being actualized into one of a pair of possible cubes exists in the *imaginary* dimension. The unactualized cube is neither one nor the other of the two possibilities, yet it can be said that it is both one and the other (like the particle manifestation and wave manifestation of a subatomic entity). Such non-empty sets containing both what something *is* and *is not* are becoming more frequently employed in the physicist's 'semiotically real' representation of the 'real.' As an illustration, imagine we place the central 'flip-flop' portion of the Necker cube in the overlap of a Venn diagram (see figure 8). This central portion of the cube can be looked upon as merely a set of two-dimensional lines and incompatible with the 'three-dimensional' construction of each alternative cube. It is a non-empty set, yet, in terms of its two-dimensionality, it is not included within either cube A or cube B when perceived and conceived as purely 'three-dimensional' constructs. Consequently, the equivalent of 'AB-lessness' exists in the two-dimensional overlap. Yet 'AB-lessness' is non-empty when considered on its own terms.

In more formal jargon, A ∩ B, if isolated, evinces no necessary 'three-dimensional' properties before its viewer. Yet this very incommensurability between the totality of the diagram, A ∪ B (= 3-D), and part of what it contains, A ∩ B (= 2-D) renders the disjunction between the two cubes non-empty

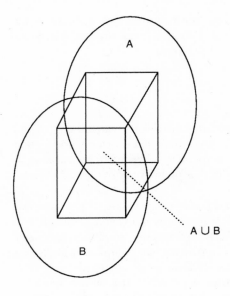

FIGURE 8

('cube up' ∩ 'cube down' ≠ Ø). The disjunction is 'AB-lessness,' yet it is non-empty. In this sense, the lines constituting A ∩ B on a two-dimensional sheet as a two-dimensional figure imply neither 'cube up' nor 'cube down,' but by 'burrowing' underneath the lines through 'wormholes' in an extra third-dimension – *pace* Wheeler and Spencer-Brown regarding the quantum world – they can be seen now as part of 'this cube,' now as the 'other cube.' Such 'burrowing' from within another dimension provides accessibility from one 'three-dimensional' domain to its incompatible *other* through 'AB-lessness,' which lies exclusively in a two-dimensional world.[4]

This apparently simple example is actually quite relevant to our own three-dimensional world embedded in the four-dimensional space-time continuum. Slightly before the turn of the present century, and significantly, prior to Einstein's theories of relativity, the idea of a fourth, fifth, and nth dimension fascinated scientists, scholars, and cranks of sundry sorts. In fact, there was a revival of mysticism during this period that led some to believe the fourth dimension was an ideal candidate for the source of otherworldly experience. Among the books to appear during those years was C. Howard Hinton's *The New Era of Thought* (1888). Hinton claimed it was possible to acquire a mental grasp of a dimension of space higher than that in which we work and play. He provided a series of mental exercises along with twenty-seven three-dimensional coloured cubes that fit together into a single cube, supposedly of four dimensions – that is, a 'hypercube.' If one could bring oneself to create a mental picture of the relations between all the cubes, it was claimed, then one could know this fourth dimension.

Hinton (1887) also developed the ingenious idea that in addition to the three dimensions of space and one of time, the mind somehow operates in a five-dimensional hyperspace orthogonal to the temporal dimension and of infinitesimal thickness. In such case the two-dimensional set of lines could represent the doorway through which the mind gains entry from one cube to its enantiomorphic other. H.A.C. Dobbs (1971) has experimented with the Necker cube from another angle, dividing time itself into two dimensions: (1) *real* or *experimental time*, the time of becoming, and (2) *mathematically imaginary* or *complex time*.[5] The first corresponds quite closely to Peirce's notion of concrete time, which is continuous in contrast to the timeless 'time' of abstract intellections such as those propagated by Zeno. It consists of events as they happen. The second is comparable to what Colin Cherry (1968:139) calls 'static' time, that is, events *as recorded* or *stored* on magnetic tape, a floppy disk, or whatever.[6]

In a formal sense, imaginary or complex time owes a debt to the seminal but bizarre work of mathematician William Rowe Hamilton, who once argued that just as geometry is the science of space, so there must be an equally pure mathematical science of time, which, he proposed, was algebra. Time in its algebraic formulation would be regarded as a one-dimensional continuum of point-instants. This put Hamilton in hot water when considering the roots of quadratic equations, which involve *imaginary numbers*: how can anything apparently as 'irreal' as $\sqrt{-1}$ be linked to the obviously 'real' passage of time? Hamilton's attempts to find an answer to this perplexity led him to the invention of 'quaternions,' the first example of a non-commutative algebra, which includes the 'complex plane' discussed above. And thus imaginary numbers took their place at an orthogonal plane with respect to the natural integers.

Interestingly enough, the second form of time, 'static' time, is rather compatible with Peirce's *expectation, belief, habit,* or *law,* which, after their formation, are simply *there,* quite irrespective of the flow of experiential time – though, one must bear in mind, there is never in Peirce's formulation any static state of affairs, but rather, with each sign reiteration a difference inheres. This distinction between experiential time and 'static' time differs somewhat from the dualistic conception of time held by, among other anthropologists, Clifford Geertz (1975) and Edmund Leach (1961). According to the terms as used here, both 'static' time and experiential time are imaginary in the most abstract sense. They are purely formal and biological, respectively; as formal, 'static' time is that of the complex plane, a paragon of abstraction, and as biological, experiential time is rooted so deeply in the life process itself that it cannot be cognized except along abstraction lines. That is to say, 'static' time and biological time correspond to Thirdness and Firstness. In contrast, the two times according to the anthropologist consist of (1) the experience of repetition (a tetronome, the ticking of a clock, the heartbeat, the recurrence of days, weeks, months), and (2) the experience of nonlinear, irreversible time (birth, growth, and death). Both anthropological times are experiential, while in the present formulation one time is abstract in terms of its being a purely intellectual construct while the other must be conceived in the abstract because it cannot exist in the immediate present *for* its respective semiotic agent.

These points aside, Peirce's *expectation, belief, habit,* and *law,* regarding time, bear on the problems of *tense* in language, a characteristic that, before we move on, calls for a brief detour through the category of Firstness. Firstness, for practical purposes tenseless, is the realm of *possibilities* or *might be's.* Various possibilities of Firstness exist for, say, a glass of milk sitting on the table. It can be overturned by a mischievous child, lapped up by the nearest cat, poured down the sink, placed in the refrigerator, or in time it can clabber. If, for example, it is spilled, that event is most properly qualified as Secondness. It becomes tensed. The event occurred in a particular *now,* afterward it became a *past* event, and as an actualized event it is future to every event preceding it. Thirdness, a conditional *would be* – and we can even say with some justification that it is hypothetical or contrary to any fact *now* occurring – is also tenseless. It entails something that would happen but is not (yet) determinately either a future, actual, or past event. None the less, when it happens to occur, it takes its place in contiguity with all other occurrences, those that preceded it and those that followed it.

The sentence (1) 'If the glass were overturned the milk would spill' applies yesterday, today, and tomorrow. It is potentially true irrespective of any temporal framework. The difference between (1) as applied *belief, habit,* or *law,* and the *expectations* it entails, on the one hand, and its actualization as (2) 'The milk was spilled,' on the other, lies in the fact that (2) is necessarily tensed, and it entails most properly a token-event rather than a token-thought. That is to say, (1), commensurate with Peirce's 'pragmatic maxim,' stipulates that if certain conditions were to inhere, then certain other consequences would follow: it is purely a *thought-sign,* a hypothetical conditional, a contrary-to-fact situation. If what is predicted comes to pass, then once the event transpires, it falls along the past-present-future stream of time as sentence (2) either preceding or following other events for the particular person involved. Sentence (2) is most adequately related to spoken language describing events – *sign-events* 'out there' – that become true at the particular moment they take place. In contrast, the element of Thirdness incorporated in the 'pragmatic maxim' as a thought-sign more closely approximates written language, much in the order of that which exists in a memory bank, on a punch card, or a magnetic tape. It is (potentially) true at all times and places, its actualization depending on a particular set of circumstances. That is, the Thirdness of the 'pragmatic maxim' sort entails, as a natural concomitant to *belief* derived from *habit,* a disposition or readiness for action in such-and-such a manner when certain conditions happen to come to pass. And such a disposition gives rise to the *expectation* that when these conditions are present, such-and-such will in all likelihood ensue.[7]

In short, regarding language, the Secondness of signification is relatively more attuned to 'sign-event-orientation,' while Thirdness is attuned to 'thought-sign-orientation,' in so far as the first correlates most closely with the dynamics of uttered sentences and the second with written sentences and the probable consequences of the range of all possible readings. The first promptly passes away along the time stream; the second is always already *there,* capable of exercising its influence on events that happen to emerge into its purview.

And once again Peirce's 'Man $\approx$ Sign' equation bounds onto the scene. Matter as effete mind is ordinarily taken to be a thing – or in the Peircean sense a crystallized thought, which is fundamentally to say the same – not an event. And mind, inasmuch as it thinks, availing itself as it must of Thirdness at each major step, is law-like, not event-like. 'Man' and 'mind' are one in this sense: they equally partake of *signness.* Unlike events, each of which occurs once and once alone and possesses truth value solely regarding its particular happening, thoughts are as they are – true, false, meaningless, or imaginary entities – at each instant, and can therefore change from one instant to the next. Of course the truth value of events is perpetually subject to change also, as historical revisions amply demonstrate. But such revisions necessarily become tensed in order for changing belief systems to maintain correspondence with what are taken to be the 'facts.'

Belief in certain characteristics of Napoleon as interpreted before a historical revision, X, of the French general, must be altered in light of his interpretation after revision X. Such change of belief is thought-like, not event-like. Napoleon after X simply is not the same person he was before X, which accounts for the change in interpretation of the events surrounding him. The belief regarding Napoleon changed, the belief itself being a changeable property of the believer, and the judgment of events suffered a change, though the actual ('real,' rather than 'semiotically real') events did not. Before X they were recorded as one thing and after X as another (Mellor 1981:73–102). In this sense, the chief difference between something as thought-like and as event-like is that things and thoughts have no temporal parts: they are wholly present during the span of their existence. Events, in contrast, are not: they occur once and once only. Apparent changes in events are merely differences between their temporal parts as reinterpreted from time to time. In contrast, things, lacking in temporal parts, can undergo change in their entirety.

But, it must be re-emphasized, the tenderly fallible human semiotic agent, even an entire community of them, cannot be in possession of 'truth' for all time, hence any particular conception of 'truth,' like all thought, must eventually suffer change of one sort or another. Peirce's doctrine of fallibilism and his theory of 'truth' as convergence – though successive steps toward the ideal cannot be guaranteed – are relevant to changing thoughts as opposed to presumably changeless events. And it bears on the impossibility of two token-events (that is, two spoken sentences) being absolutely identical, as well as the impossibility of exact translation. To translate a sentence in the target language, one must find a sentence in the home language with a comparable meaning. Assuming the target language sentence to exist on the printed page, it is thought-like. In order to match it with a home language sentence one must either utter or write a sentence in that language. This entails a contextualized act that is necessarily event-like at distinct temporal spatial coordinates, and hence by its very nature, as an event, it is different from the target language sentence. That is, the target sentence was an event written on a page as the event-like token of a type, and, in some future copy of the same or another edition of the sentence, one of its many types found its way into the hands of the translator.

Now, as a thought-token more properly of spatial than temporal characteristics, the target language sentence can coincide with the home language sentence consisting of an event-token hopefully conjured up as its equivalent. But temporally, this event-token stands hardly a chance of enjoying absolute identity with the original event-token when it was put on the page within a specific context. In other words, the thought-token, as tenseless, cannot mean the same as its corresponding tensed event-token (Mellor 1981:77–8). So, since 'truth' is ordinarily conceived as tenseless, it is simply incompatible with the finite human being immanently caught within her world of apparent becoming where things are perpetually undergoing change in terms of an incessant stream of events – that is, sign-events. 'Truth,' in the general sense of the term, and in contrast to this notion of the ongoing becoming of events for particular semiotic agents, implies *one* timeless Cosmic Event, not *many* little contextualized events.

And here we have Peirce's fallibility and hopeful *approximation* to 'truth' without the possibility of reaching the *final* destination. It all stems from the singularity of events – that is, sign-events. Thoughts, though believed to retain their self identity through the particular series of events (sign-events) involving them, are with each event something other than what they were. In this manner, rather than the thingness of a thing thought, a thing is more properly conceived as a series of contextualized thought-signs (sign-events 'in here'). If there is no absolute translatability between two languages regarding a particular thought-sign, this does not necessarily imply that the target language cannot be learned by comparison and contrast with the home language. Rather, the language is learned as a set of particular thought-signs both by comparison and contrast and on its own grounds. And discussibility is possible between the two languages, for, after all, they are about thought-signs in their respective worlds, the conjunction of which composes one world, elusive and slippery though it may be. That is to say, each language refers – if we can speak of reference at all in this setting – to a conjunction of contextualized thought-sign-events 'out there' and hence to a world. The things themselves play only a subsidiary role, and the world to which they belong, in 'fusion' with that of another language, makes up a larger, though invariably *vague*, set of thought-sign-events.

The upshot is that the 'fusion' (superposition) of all possible 'semiotic worlds' composes a completely *vague* – and thus continuous – domain, which might be termed *The World*. It would be the superposition of all possibilities with none of them necessarily actualized for any particular semiotic agent (see, in general, Goodman 1978). This World, for any set of finite, fallible semiotic agents, would actually be no world at all. It would be timeless, a set of myriad possibilities without the actualization of any concrete sign-event for someone in some respect or capacity, a World accessible solely to the consciousness of the above-mentioned Laplacean Omniscient Observer – to be the focus of future sections.

4. TIME *EN BLOC*?

The two types of 'time' I have spoken of – the tensed and tenseless varieties, which roughly correspond to our *imaginary* ('static') and *experienced* time – lie squarely within the corpus of literature regarding time in our contemporary milieu.

From Plato to Kant, and from Francis Bradley to J.M.E. McTaggart, Hermann Weyl, and Einstein, the argument that the temporal mode of our perception is of no ultimate significance has been reiterated. McTaggart's (1927) argument is especially germane to our present concerns (see also Merrell 1991b, 1995). He distinguishes between the changing A-series of *past, present*, and *future* and the static B-series in which events are simply recorded as *before* and *after*. The B-series is permanent in the sense that if the statement 'Event X preceded event Y' is true, then it is forever true. 'The American revolution occurred before the Cuban revolution' is true today, and it will be equally true to the end of time. This is the way we normally *contemplate* a sequence of events. Events are ordered like positive and negative numbers in a static series. If the series is subjected to alteration, for example in the historical revisionist interpretation of Napoleon, the equivalent of the 'complex plane' consisting of *imaginary* numbers is tapped. And whatever change is wrought, the series takes on a slightly new countenance, once again as a static state (remotely comparable to Saussure's 'block' domain of *langue*, which was the exclusive focus of his Copernican revolution in linguistics, while *parole*, counterpart to 'experienced time,' was conveniently pushed under the rug).

In contrast, the A-series consists of *experienced* events (that is, sign-events). It is an ever-changing series giving meaning to the *becoming* of the universe. However, since it is an infinitely pliable series of events whose nows were future and after their occurrence they were pushed into the past, false statements can and are often made. In addition, a vicious infinite regress is implied by the A-series. If one assumes a statement about event X is present, will be past, and will have been future, this implies that X is present at a moment of present time, past at a moment of future time and future at a moment of past time. The problem is that each of these moments is an event in time, hence it is at once past, present, and future all at once. McTaggart's experienced (A-series) time must in this sense be conceived as a process within one static cosmic instant of (B-series) 'time': the occurrence of an experienced event (that is, consciousness *of* the event) is itself another event, and the experience of that event is yet another event, and so on. We have here what appears to be the rough equivalent of Peirce's infinite *regressus* and infinite *progressus* of signs and of consciousness. A principal distinction between Peirce and McTaggart is that the former did not consider the infinite series to be vicious, but merely resolved by mediary Thirdness – by the becomingness of being and the beingness of becoming, or by the experience of intellection and the intellection of experience, so to speak. In other words, consciousness and self-consciousness are capable tacitly of overcoming the quandary as a matter of course, with no further ado.

Regarding the 'block' universe idea, variously interpreted in Einstein's relativity, one-dimensional time is given space-like meaning, and conversely, three-dimensional space can take on a time-like countenance. To know the time-events of Napoleon, one must plot the happenings during his lifetime along a singular 'world-line,' which is in essence a series of points (time-slices) within the 'block' universe. The rough equivalent of this 'world-line' is found in Napoleon's various spatial positions in B-series time: it is, conceived in its totality, static. Napoleon's spatial happenings, in contrast, could be specified as a myriad scattering of points in three-dimensional space on the earth's surface representing each spot Napoleon occupied during each instant of his life, which would, in its composite, make up a static set. His spatial happenings would engulf his time-line within a system of higher dimension by mapping his 'world-line,' regardless of time, onto the coordinates represented by the earth's surface. Conversely, his temporal happenings would project his spatial happenings, regardless of spatial location, onto the singular time-dimension. Of course the spatial happenings of an object ordinarily merit a plotting only when they closely approximate its temporal happenings, such as is the case of relatively immobile objects (trees, mountains, buildings, etc.). In such cases a plotting of their three-dimensional spatial coordinates does not vary appreciably from their one-dimensional 'world-line.'

The important point to be made here is that tenseless B-series happenings do not change with time as do tensed A-series happenings. Just as along the B-series 'Napoleon was defeated at Waterloo' is always the same in so far as it is merely plotted before some happings and after others, so 'Indiana is between Ohio and Illinois' is the same state of affairs no matter at which point along Indiana's 'world-line' it is plotted. The first sentence is the same regardless of *when* it is uttered, though it gives no indication as to how remote the happening is from *when* it is uttered; the second provides no information about how far the happening is from *where* it is uttered (see Mellor, 1981:58–72). Our spatial and temporal coordinates, like our experience, are always already *here* and *now*. The *present* of experience, however, is generally conceived to be that proverbial razor-edge moving along the time continuum and dividing past from future. Experience, unlike coordinates in the B-series, appears to be dynamic: it incorporates change. Yet the fact remains that in experience everything happens precisely *here* and *now*.

The contradiction between experience and the static B-series bears on indeterminism and the emergence of novelty proper to time as transitional. The indeterminism of future events, according to Peirce, and as revealed by Ilya Prigogine's dissipative structures as a result of far-from-equilibrium conditions, from molecular to molar levels and from inorganic to organic to biological systems, is associated with the *transitional nature of time*. This points to the plausibility of some deep connection between transitional or experienced time and the existence of an incalculable factor in the universe, in contrast to the predetermined 'block' model of the universe. Consequently, if, as Prigogine and Peirce before him have asserted, the universe is evolving in time and the future is never wholly determinable, since the present state of affairs does not contain the necessary information fully to determine future states, then the very notion of the 'block' must be subjected to close scrutiny.

5. THE 'IMAGINARY' AND THE 'REAL' FROM A DIFFERENT GLANCE

A point of departure for such scrutiny can be found in the above mentions of experience and interpretation, which re-introduce us to McTaggart's A-series with respect to the core of H.A.C. Dobbs's intriguing study of spatio-temporal perception.

Change in the B-series has hardly anything in common with the ordinary use of the term 'change.' Something is merely something at one happening (event) and something else at another, like two discrete events with no necessary indication of the transition from one to the other. The body of my new car is smooth, lustrous, and attractive; when old, it is pock-marked, with several dents and a few rust-outs. Of course the two spatial happenings from this view are mutually incompatible. Yet I continue to call the car my car as if it were the same, regardless of time and the changes it has suffered. It has retained a certain identity in spite of the changes. None the less, changes have been wrought. These changes are B-series changes across space and quite divorced from the ordinary conception of alterations through time. The smooth/nonsmooth happenings with respect to my car's body can hardly be accounted for by attending to each *here* and *now* of my experience as discrete packets, barring any radical transmutation such as a head-on collision. The car's identity through time, on the other hand, appears to be the natural product of my ongoing, processual experience *of* it from one moment to the next, when relatively few appreciable changes occur.

Experienced change, one might tend to assume, involves A-series time-dependent alterations in contrast to B-series alterations that are discrete spatial segments, time being nothing more than another dimension of space. That is, according to the B-series, before (in a *here-now*), the car had a smooth body, but later (in another *here-now*), it had a nonsmooth body, without any indication in terms of a transition, either temporally or spatially, from one happening to the other, the two *here-nows* being autonomous of each other. But this is somewhat misleading. There is actually no reason the properties of a given object cannot vary from place to place in the same way they do from time to time. If while being driven my car is in a head-on collision, it can be said that *here* its body is smooth and *here* (separated by fifty-five feet or so) it is nonsmooth. Or that *here* the entire body is smooth and *here* the front half is nonsmooth and the back half smooth. In comparable fashion, it can be said that at this *now-event* along the car's 'world-line' the body is smooth, and at that *now-event* it is not. There is no real need for movement *through* time, or the movement of time (Mellor 1981:89–118).

One might now object that this spatial, tenseless view reduces change to nothing more than a static series of changeless happenings, a system that would, by reason of Zeno, fall victim to an obvious paradox. The point is well taken in light of our experienced world, as Peirce indefatigably argued. In regard to experience presumably in the A-series, on the other hand, there is simply no real spatial analogue. Time is time and space is space, and never the twain shall meet, it appears, relativity theory notwithstanding. And the debate will most likely continue, ad infinitum.

What is at stake here, once again, is a split notion of time: *real* or *experienced time*, and imaginary ('static') or *complex time*. The first corresponds quite closely to the A-series and the second has the logical properties of spatial dimensions, that is, of the B-series. Dobbs points out that in spite of our penchant for regarding experienced time as a simple linear series, where everything is prior to or subsequent to something else, experience is best defined as a partial ordering of events. Experiments tend to bear this out. Upon perceiving a rapid succession of different sounds, two of them, A and B, may be reported either as simultaneous, as A followed by B, or B by A (Gibson 1966; Pöppel 1972, 1988). This inability to give such phenomena any form of reliable linear order is the result of our capturing percepts in *Gestalts* during what is commonly termed the 'specious present' – which Dobbs, by the way, calls the 'sensible present.' Rapidly succeeding auditory bursts, in experience lacking a determinate serial order, Dobbs argues, are characteristic of the time dimension discussed above, assimilated to space dimensions. An important feature of this *imaginary* or *complex time*, in contrast to 'real' time, is its reversibility, its symmetry, its lack of any indication of 'time's arrow.' It is a simple linear order, like that of the points along an undirected line in Euclidean space.[8]

Combining this *imaginary time* with 'real' *experienced time* produces a *complex* frame describable by the Argand diagram, constructed with complex numbers following the discoveries of Hamilton, as illustrated in figure 6. In this *complex* frame there is neither, properly speaking, the serial order of one-way experience nor the two-way simple linear order of *imaginary time*. Combination of the two orders itself forms a partially ordered set in the mathematical sense. There remains a fundamental distinction between the two orders, however. The experience of happenings in 'real' time is both of linear order and irreversible, while *imaginary time* is symmetrical and reversible. For example, a sentence is put down in a text in the process of being written. Assuming the text remains unaltered, the sentence is what is *now* written; it follows all sentences that *have been* written and it precedes all those that *will have been* written: it is like the

B-series. On the other hand, the author's experience of his writing process at this point can never duplicate that of the writing of all previous sentences, and the same can be said of all future sentences. In the act of writing there is an irreducible transitory process during which it is impossible for anything that occurred before to precede anything that occurred after, or for an effect to precede a cause.

This irreversible, transitory characteristic of writing has no bearing on the text once it is on the printed page for all time. As mere marks on paper there is no necessary linearity, no past-present-future, but only before/after.[9] Such transitoriness is also alien to the equations of motion in Newtonian physics, as it is in relativity, which generally ignores one-way dissipative forces. Here, all expressions are equally valid for $+t$ or $-t$. However, in many equations including a time, $t = 0$, separating positive from negative values, and future from past, there is an important feature regarding determinacy or prediction. All negative values are determinate, whereas positive values can be based on nothing more than statistical probabilities. This is analogous to the above-mentioned 'stored' or 'recorded' time in contrast to 'real' time.

Regarding our Necker cube, certain features of experience, given our perceptive faculties, are important, some of which Dobbs occasionally gives passing mention. Our conscious awareness of time depends on the fact that our minds operate by successive acts of attention: percepts come in packets, in quanta. On the other hand, experience appears to be in general linear. Only with difficulty can we attend simultaneously to a visual and aural piece of information, though attention can switch from one to the other in a fraction of a second. Granted, two distinct activities can sometimes be combined into a single performance. Playing a piano with both hands, playing the bass drum with one foot and snare drums and cymbals with the hands, juggling a few oranges while playing a harmonica, and playing a guitar while vocalizing a piece of music are prime examples. These are learned abilities, however. They become possible only when at least one of them has become *embedded*, *automatized* (that is, Polanyi's tacit knowing [1958]).

In light of these and other comparable activities, there is a diversity of opinion concerning whether or not we have a single, unified train of thought. To cite a scattering of cases, D.O. Hebb (1949) argues that two independent thought processes can run parallel to each other. John Z. Young (1978:216) points out that although many parts of the brain operate in simultaneity, the entire system is centrally controlled. And Colin Cherry (1953, 1954) has offered experimental evidence that when distinct signals are presented to each ear, only one message can be consciously processed at a time. Yet attention can tend to wander from one percept to another, which helps account for the oscillating transformations elicited by the Necker cube. In fact, contrary to the continuity of experienced time postulated by Peirce, Whitehead, and especially Bergson, there appears to be a discontinuity in our perception, given the discontinuity of our attention, which is generally smoothed out by experience. In other words, a brief moment of comparatively continuous perception is ruptured by the introduction of a new and slightly to radically distinct perception, the duration of these perceptions depending on the individual's mind-set, the context, and the conditions of perception. The upshot seems to be that if there were no sense of such discreteness, there would likely be no sense of 'real' time.

In short, when the spectator is experiencing the sudden transition from one (*superposed*) possibility represented by the Necker drawing to the other, she is merely acting out her natural perception of all phenomena in 'real' (*alternating*) time. *Imaginary* or *complex time*, in contrast, is a horse of a different colour. Dobbs (1971:118) suggests that there are several features in connection with the transformations between alternative perspectives – the Necker cube being his paradigm case – which place them closely in line with mathematical time:

(1) A transformation (from one superposed possibility to another) is *continuous*, it does not involve a *break* in the continuity of the lines joining the corner points of the skeletal cube.
(2) The transformation involves oscillation, alternation, a scintillating pulsation.
(3) Not only does the transformation apparently occur within a 'sensible present,' a mental 'now,' it also takes place in the same manner as the motion of the second hand of a watch. That is: 'One *can actually see* the skeletal cube swing some 30 degrees of arc from right to left (and *vice versa*) in azimuth; and also tilt by about the same angle in the vertical plane.'
(4) The transformation is an *Augenblick*, between two incompatible three-dimensional counterparts.

Dobbs then concludes that the transitions from one Necker cube to the other as actualizations (Seconds) from superposed possibilities (Firsts) cannot occur in three-dimensional space and linear 'real' and *experienced* time, but rather, they are folds, involutions in another dimension consisting of 'mathematical' or *imaginary time*. Thus the transformation from one cube to the other would be something like a magician turning a right-hand glove wrong side out to convert it into a left-hand glove in the blink of an instant such that the audience is unaware of the sleight-of-hand act. Indeed, it appears that not only time, but signs – our entire *Umwelt*-created semiotic universe – insist on playing such tricks on us, and, helplessly limited human beings that we are, we can hardly expect to catch them in their game.

6. 'DEAD TIME' AND STATIC MIND?

Dobbs concedes that in point of experimental evidence the subjective reports of observers vary. Nevertheless, he proceeds with the assumption that his thesis is correct, since it conforms to an important mathematical concept introduced by the nineteenth-century geometer, G. Möbius.

Möbius observed that continuous transformations between incompatible three-dimensional counterparts are mathematically impossible within a three-dimensional manifold. Such transformations demand rotation about a plane, not merely a single line, within a four-dimensional manifold. In other words, just as a two-dimensional glove cannot evolve into its enantiomorphic twin without being flipped over in three-dimensional space, so also a three-dimensional left-hand glove requires a fourth dimension – unless it is turned wrong side out – to be transformed into a right-hand glove. Dobbs extends this idea to postulate a fourth dimension for any phenomenon such as the Necker cube perceived as two different alternatives in an *Augenblick* (during a 'sensible present'), which he then conceives to be the static *imaginary time* dimension, as opposed to 'real' time. I must hasten to point out, as Dobbs is well aware, that the term *imaginary time* in this context does not imply any subjective or psychological meaning; rather, it is strictly mathematical. It enjoys a relationship to 'real' subjective or psychological time in a manner comparable to the relationship between the plane represeting the 'imaginary' or 'complex' numbers on the Argand diagram coupled with the axis of 'real' numbers.

Such an *imaginary time* is, rather commensurate with Arthur Eddington's (1946:125) remark regarding the equations of relativity theory, equivalent to a 'real' space dimension. Specifically, in his popularization of relativity, he assures us that 'the difficulty of thinking in terms of an unfamiliar geometry may be evaded by a dodge,' which he proceeds to bring about (Eddington 1959:48). He goes on to write – if you will once again bear with me during a moment of formality – that instead of 'real' time, t, we could consider imaginary time, γ, by letting $t = \gamma\sqrt{-1}$. Then the square of the difference between t_1 and t_2 becomes equal to the negative value of the square of γ_1 and γ_2: $(t_2 - t_1)^2 = -(\gamma_1 - \gamma_2)^2$. This 'imaginary plane,' when conjoined with our familiar three dimensions of space, renders everything symmetrical, with no distinction between γ and the spatial variables. Eddington goes on to suggest:

the continuum formed of space and imaginary time is completely isotropic for all measurements; no direction can be picked out in it as fundamentally distinct from any other.

The observer's separation of this continuum into space and time consists in slicing it in some direction, viz. that perpendicular to the path along which he is himself travelling. The section gives three-dimensional space at some moment, and the perpendicular dimension is (imaginary) time. Clearly the slice may be taken in any direction; there is no question of a true separation and a fictitious separation. There is no conspiracy of the forces of nature to conceal our absolute motion – because, looked at from this broader point of view, there is nothing to conceal. (1959:48)

In this sense, the observation in 'real' time of irreversibly directed successivities is, from the view of the entire 'block,' no more than a set of static spatial contiguities, with interpretation providing the successivities. Eddington warns that it would be unprofitable wildly to speculate on the implications of the mysterious factor, $\sqrt{-1}$, which is used in relativity and quantum theory alike. It can hardly be regarded as more than an analytical device. For Dobbs – who does not, I am assuming, commit Eddington's sin of unbridled speculation upon stressing the function of $\sqrt{-1}$ – the issue at hand involves neither formal mathematics nor its appropriation in contemporary physics. The point is, rather, that the *imaginary time* plane is purely mathematical – and, one must concede, *ipso facto* artificial – pertaining to the domain of pure thought-signs 'in here.' In contrast, 'real' *experienced time* is concrete, subjective, and phenomenological or psychological, by and large governing how we perceive sign-events 'out there.' The two perspectives are *complementary*. From a formal standpoint two different objects cannot occupy the same position in three-dimensional space; yet as far as experience is concerned, the two alternative Necker cubes *do* occupy the same *juxtaposed set of points* on a two-dimensional plane perceived as an object in three-dimensional space. They do not do so at the same *point* in time, however.

Experience of sign-events 'out there' normally involves movement sensed as if it were continuous: even though it may be discontinuous, it is made continuous, somewhat like the discontinuous flashes before our eyes in the movie theatre made continuous by experience. Paul Kolers' (1972) experiments demonstrate how almost-simultaneous flashes on a screen are perceived as a continuous 'stream' of light from the previous burst to its successor.[10] David Bohm's concept of consciousness constructing continuous movement from discrete emanations from the implicate order are apropos also. Such experience is quite different from that of Freud's dreams consisting of a disconnected set of 'stills' as if from a slide show (a discontinuous spatial rather than temporal series), comparable to the perception of patients suffering from certain mental disorders.[11]

Of course I am, I must again emphasize, speaking of two different sorts of phenomena: (1) the continuity of experience, which entails a certain duration or 'specious present' spreading an umbrella over transformations from one Necker cube alternative to the other, and (2) discontinuity, which accounts for the actual break between the two alternatives when one of them is suddenly and, it would seem, spontaneously actualized *for* its viewer. The construction in perception of continuous movement out of two discontinuous segments within a single 'specious present' in 'real' time requires, for its proper realization, the additional dimension as evidenced by the Necker cube transformation. This conjunction, as exercised by human perceptual faculties, of the continuous flow of experience and the discontinuity between the two Necker cube alternatives produces the 'semiotic' equivalent of a reversible *complex* or *imaginary time* variable.

Mathematically, the complex numbers, result of a collusion of imaginary numbers with real numbers, are devoid of serial order. Thus it cannot be said that complex numbers are definitely either positive or negative, or that they are ordered in terms of smaller-than and larger-than, or predecessor and successor. In other words, $\sqrt{-1}$ is not, as Leibniz trenchantly put it, that strange amphibian between being and nonbeing. It is certainly not *becoming*, but neither is it precisely *being*, though, as pure superposition, it might constitute something comparable to the driving force behind *becoming*. Yet it remains incommensurable with any notion of asymmetry, irreversibility, one-way evolution, history. 'Real' experience of the becoming of time, the successive happenings of events, in contrast, has a serial order and some sense of direction, like the order of positive numbers. But the order is only partial: there is no necessary greater than or lesser than relation, but rather, only relations of predecessor and successor.

Dobbs' associating a set of *imaginary times* with the set of 'real' times yields a complex variable in which the real numbers play the role that is ordinarily linked with the becoming of events (A-series) in contrast to the static collection of elapsed events (B-series) comparable to the whole numbers. What we have here is a conception of *temporal happenings* in contrast to an abstract conception of *history*. *Happenings* are given direction from past to present to future; history is simply either before or after. Historical time in the abstract, Dobbs points out, is that 'which engineers often call "dead time" or "elapsed time" or "recorded time," which is merely a variable used for the description of the extants of a fourth co-ordinate, required to specify one aspect of events that have happened in the past and are no longer happening. This "dead" or "elapsed" time of *recording* (rather than *happening*) is exactly analogous to a one-dimensional space component, as we can see very simply by noting that it is conveniently measured in terms of so many feet of film or inches of magnetic tape' (1971:123). It is precisely this 'dead' time Dobbs labels *imaginary*. And, he proposes, a conjunction of the two times is necessary in order to develop an adequate time analysis of what he calls the 'sensible' (that is, 'specious') present.

Such a creative conjunction bears on the quantum interpretation of John A. Wheeler, as I suggested in passing in chapter 2 and as I outlined it in the previous two volumes of this trilogy within a semiotic context. In Wheeler's conception of the world of quanta, a phenomenon is not 'real' (actualized *for* some semiotic agent) until it has been *distinguished, indicated, recorded,* and *put to use*, though it is always already *there* as a sign *in potentia*: it exists as a sign in so far as it exists *for* some possible future destination and recording. After it has been recorded and *put to use*, it can become a sign in the full sense of its being some-*thing* standing *for* some-*thing for* someone in some respect or capacity. In this sense, before it was *put to use*, the B-series had not yet been *opened to* it. That is, in the Wheeler respect, before event X was recorded, there was no relation between it and other recorded events. If undetected by a human ear, Napoleon's ability to call a young lad among his troops by his given name, 'Pierre,' after having heard it once among a hundred or so names a month before, was not properly registered by a human semiotic agent and could not have found its way into folklore, a history book, a novel, or whatever. Hence it could not have taken its place among the range of 'semiotically real' signs. It would have remained entirely outside the range of B-series events, properly conceived.

Nevertheless, in spite of Wheeler's evolutionary concept of physical law, and of his interactive mind collaborating in participatory fashion with the self-organizing universe, we have, when viewing his scheme of things *in toto* – that is, the range of all events, whether they have become 'semiotically real' or not – something reminiscent of the 'block' universe idea powerfully reinforced by the space-time interpretation of relativity. Within the 'block,' everything is always already *there*. The 'block' does not distinguish between what has been recorded and *put to use*, semiotically speaking, and what has not. As such, the 'objective world' of the 'block,' Hermann Weyl (1949:116) writes, 'simply *is*, it does not *happen*. Only to the gaze of my consciousness, crawling upward along the lifeline of my body, does a section of the world come to life as a fleeting image in space which continuously changes in time.' But this picture is severely limited. It recognizes only recorded differences between earlier and later (the B-series), not experienced events along past, present, and future (the A-series).

It ignores any and all possible events that remain unrecorded and outside the domain of 'semiotically real' worlds.

Eddington (1958b:75) argues that relativity does not offer an adequate account of time. In spite of Weyl's passage, the theory is not incompatible with the happening of events, though it appears to be entirely neutral toward them. That is to say, if a given observer is conceived as a recording instrument, time has a past, present, and future within that observer's particular 'light cone' ('semiotically real' world), but when all 'light cones' are considered as a totality, there is an objective order for all possible events within a timeless framework. In other words, one can consider either the set of all actualized 'semiotically real' events from within a B-series framework or the transition of an individual 'semiotically real' event, which does not invalidate the A-series framework, while the realm of all possible 'semiotically real' world events remains outside any conception of time whatsoever (Whitrow 1980:352–60). If for Wheeler there is no 'before' for an event until it is recorded *by* someone, that 'before' presumably became a past event *for* that someone at some particular *now*, which interjects it into the A-series from the B-series in which it previously dwelt. However, if cooler heads are to prevail, it would appear that the two series simply cannot – they should not – be mixed in this manner.

On the other hand, Kenneth G. Denbigh (1975:44–53) points out that if the 'block' universe is taken as deterministic, then nothing new could come into existence. That is, actualized 'semiotically real' world events are not the consequence of dice throws; from the very beginning they were actually preordained for all time, hence B-series 'semiotically real' events recorded and put to use could not have been other than what they are, and A-series events would be no more than figments, fabrications of the mind. In this sense, if (following Peirce, Bohm, Prigogine, and Wheeler, each from his own somewhat distinct perspective) the universe is construed to be creatively evolving in time and hence the future is not wholly predictable, then the B-series as an actualization of 'semiotically real' events, from within the 'block,' cannot provide a satisfactory concept of time. Specifically regarding Peirce's notion of becoming, it seems that his universe exists independently of any particular interpreter or community of interpreters – that is, it is what it is regardless of whatever interpretants may be derived from it for someone in some respect or capacity. Even though the physical universe remains what it is independently of any and all actualized 'semiotically real' worlds, still, a given sign-event could always have been something other, so variables always exist. The universe is a self-organizing, creative advance; any given B-series could always have been something else, the same as its A-series counterpart.[12]

The only possible account for such a cosmology might well be something comparable to Hugh Everett's 'many worlds interpretation' of the quantum world. Very generally, each community creatively realizes, *for* itself, one of the countless universes *there*, in the *bloc* for the taking, but at the same time all other possible universes exist, and the 'semiotically real' events actualized within them are as 'real' from within their respective domain as any other event (DeWitt 1973). This image dovetails in a bizarre sort of way with Bohm's timeless *implicate order* (the 'being of becoming') coupled with his time-bound *explicate order* (the 'becoming of being') (Griffin 1988). In this sense, the past would be 'now' determined, and the future would remain 'as yet' to be determined by the equivalent of Wheeler's observing subject in her participatory universe. The set of indeterminate future 'nows,' as B-series, would be constructed somehow, somewhere, and somewhen *for* some semiotic agent, so to speak. A particular 'semiotically real' universe would remain perpetually open *for* a given individual. And the universe as the possibility of all particular 'semiotically realities' would slowly realize its becoming, in minuscule bits and pieces, as a collection of sign-events *distinguished* and *put to use* by myriad communities of semiotic agents *collaborating with*, and thus *bringing about*, that universe's very becoming.[13]

In conjunction with this notion, Dobbs' work suggests that an individual's purely sensory output of 'semiotically real' events, ordered serially and irreversibly in the 'real,' 'live' time dimension, is associated – perhaps in the unconscious – with 'history,' 'memory,' and 'past experience,' that is, with the simple linear and reversibly ordered *imaginary time* dimension. This extra time dimension provides an additional degree of freedom, which is required for a reversal of perspective, as illustrated by the Necker cube phenomenon: a discontinuous transformation made continuous. The Necker cube manifests the case of a reversal from within the *imaginary time* dimension imposed on 'real' time. But, of course, such reversals or oscillations are not available to ordinary perception of the physical world, since 'real' time generally exercises its dominion over *imaginary*, or 'dead' time.

All in all, it appears that the days of empiricist innocence, of the neutral subject standing at a distant remove from, and imperiously viewing, his world, have drawn to a close. According to the perspective put forth here, the semiotic agent collaborates with, yet is inextricably a part of, the monstrously complex self-organizing universe. There is no absolutely separable intrinsic/extrinsic, self/other, inner/outer, mind/matter, or subject/object. As a consequence, the time has come, as Skolimowski puts it, much in a Peircean vein, 'to work out a theory of the mind that not only recognizes its active role but also shows how it contributes to the creation of knowledge; how its creative nature makes it the same agency both in science and in the arts ... how the early systems of knowledge and traditional cultures can be seen as products, extensions and manifestations of the same mind; and how different systems of knowledge can describe reality differently, although they are products of the same human mind [or collective communities of human minds]' (1987:78; brackets mine).

7. OR BEYOND REVERSIBILITY?

But what, actually, is this so-called 'real,' 'live' time from the viewpoint I have provisionally adopted here? More particularly, how can the distinction be specified between Eddington's serial time (t) and *imaginary time* (*i*), which possesses the same logical properties as a space dimension?

A possible response to this question has its roots, I believe, in the idea of *complementarity*. In light of the developments in chapter 1, and for the sake of illustration, I shall avail myself of the term according to its interpretation in quantum theory – while bearing in mind that *complementarity* as I use it is not enshrouded in formal garb, but rather, it takes on informal, and even metaphorical if you will, trappings. We begin with classical mechanics, where a single *function*, called the Hamiltonian, *H*, describes the dynamics of a system in terms of two variables: position and momentum. In quantum theory the Hamiltonian as well as the variables have *operators*. On the one hand, in the stock Copenhagen interpretation of the quantum world, operators play a fundamental role: their *eigenvalues* – a timeless, discrete set of numbers specifying a probability (in terms of wave amplitudes in the present case) – correspond to energy levels. On the other hand, operators also determine the temporal process taking place in the system.

The operators in Heisenberg uncertainty relations are anisotropic in the sense that a particle-event's happening to pop up is the *unpredictable*, and *irreversible*, actualization of one of a set of probabilities. In contrast, Schrödinger's equations express continuously evolving and *deterministic* changes brought about in particular domains of the system as a whole, a sort of hold-over from the classical view of things. Yet, put the incompatible Heisenberg and Schrödinger interpretations together, and you have the general quantum picture. This strange *coniunctionis oppositorum* went against the metaphysical grain of many physicists, as mentioned above most notably Einstein himself, who argued for a complete and deterministic account. Such a description at the outset seemed to exist when the superposition of possible states specified by Schrödinger's equations 'collapses' into a 'particle-event,' which could then theoretically be described with a degree of determinacy: it would exist in the *eigenstate* indicated by the resulting measurement. The problem is that in the first place, as Bohr elegantly argued, such a 'collapse' (that is, a sign's 'actualization') must integrate the observer ('semiotic agent') via her instruments into the system, thus demolishing the cherished classical notion of objectivity. And in the second place, each measurement must mark out an *irreversible* event of the sort Einstein and his allies found repugnant.

Therefore, in addition to particle/wave and position/momentum complementarity, we also have 'complementarity' between the two quantum interpretations, the one deterministic and classical – Schrödinger's wave mechanics – and the other probabilistic, indeterministic, and nonclassical – Heisenberg's matrix mechanics. Quantum theory is neither entirely out of the classical ballpark nor inside what it considers to be its own nonclassical game; nor does it straddle the fence, so to speak, but must oscillate between classical and nonclassical principles in an effort to paint the entire picture.

To date there appears to be no Ariadne's thread leading the physicist out of this quantum complementarity labyrinth. The common approach to the dilemma, as Prigogine bluntly puts it, is that 'quantum mechanics has no choice but to postulate the coexistence of two mutually irreversible processes, the reversible and continuous evolution described by Schrödinger's equations and the irreversible and discontinuous reduction of the wave function to one of its eigenfunctions at the time of measurement. Thus the paradox: the reversible Schrödinger equation can be tested only by irreversible measurements that the equation is *by definition* unable to describe. It is thus impossible for quantum mechanics to set up a closed structure' (Prigogine and Stengers 1984:228).

There have been diverse responses to this state of affairs. The Copenhagen solution is operationalistic: don't ask questions, just do the calculations, and if they work, don't tamper with them. Some, notably Eugene Wigner (1967), have taken refuge in a sometimes strident form of subjectivism with the proposal that mind or consciousness determines the evolution of the system, which breaks the natural or objective law of reversibility. Those following Einstein's reactionary view argue that the Copenhagen interpretation is 'incomplete': there are 'hidden variables' that must be ferreted out before adequate account of 'reality' can be possible. Other wilder solutions have cornered a few true believers as well (see Herbert 1985, for a lay person's summary).

Prigogine inclines toward the view that a not-too-peaceful coexistence in quantum theory of reversibility and irreversibility, of 'static' time and 'real' time is evidence that the classical idealization describing the universe as a self-contained, timeless whole is unfeasible at the microscopic level. The mathematical language used quite effectively to describe quantum events is incompatible with the language describing the macroscopic domain that includes the physicist and her instruments. Yet the two domains cannot be categorically separated: the quantum level description presupposes the physical world in which the physicist lives and breathes. It has precisely been Prigogine's argument that there is a close tie between the world described by Hamiltonian operators and Schrödinger's equations in conjunction with the macroscopic world of irreversible processes we ordinarily place in 'real' time. Irreversibility is not simply mind-dependent, Prigogine argues vehemently, but a very fundamental characteristic of the universe at all levels. Actually, the macroscopic or phenomenological theory of irreversibility is hardly up for serious questioning. The controversy surrounding Prigogine's enticing approach stems from his notion that microscopic processes are also irreversible, which flies in the face of those who nurture faith in some sort or other of an eternal Parmenidean cosmos.

Further to aggravate the problem, Prigogine's theory is also obviously antithetical to the 'reality' of 'static' or *imaginary time*. As I pointed out above, within the past century the 'static' notion of time has evolved in one direction from Bradley's idealistic philosophy, and in another direction following Hinton and other gurus of the fourth dimension such as P.D. Ouspensky. Moreover, Dunne's theory of 'serial' or multidimensional time in a attempt to account for the alleged phenomenon of precognition and Hinton's proposal that objects in the four-dimensional space-time manifold are like static 'threads' – 'world-lines' in relativity parlance – appear completely off-the-wall. Yet, after all is said and done, a perplexing question remains: If the *complex* or *imaginary* temporal counterpart to 'real' time really exists, what are its implications for the semiotic enterprise I have taken on in this enquiry? Were Peirce alive today, he would undoubtedly reject the likes of Dunne and Hinton out of hand. To make matters worse, there is also the question of Peirce's ongoing infatuation with (1) Zeno's paradoxes, even though he believes experience merely overcomes them as a matter of course, (2) the continuum and its implication of *generality* – which in the long run discounts the excluded-middle principle – and (3) infinite sets, which introduce *vagueness*, thus softening the impact of the principle of noncontradiction.

Peirce's hypothetical 'book of assertions' is prototypical of these uncertainties. The 'book' elicits the image of a static set of infinite possibilities all of which are *there*, *en bloc*, so to speak – from which, through time, finite conglomerations of signs can be engendered (*CP*:4.512). That is to say, this empty 'book,' the originary 'nothingness' to which I referred in chapter 1, gives rise to Firstness or quality, which holds the possibility for becoming *actuals* (Seconds). As such the 'book' incorporates Peirce's notion of utter *vagueness*, that domain tolerating the coexistence of contradictory sign sequences. We have the apparently incompatible concepts of static possibilities *en bloc* and dynamic actualities, of infinity and finity, continuity and discreteness. Peirce seems to be telling us that we can eat our cake and have it too. The nature of mental constructs, and hence of nature itself, is inherently paradoxical, but, fortunately for all of us, we have that marvellous handyman's tool, experience, capable of dissolving any and all quandaries.

In other words, we have the self-awareness (*SA*) paradox in a new set of threads: the 'semiotic agent' is aware of her world, and aware of her awareness of her world, and the infinite regress is up off its launching pad and into space.

8. AND SOMEHOW ALL THERE IN ONE FELL SWOOP?

In spite of the apparent incongruities evinced by this paradox and others of comparable ilk – which throughout history have provoked fits in the most robust thinkers – it bears on a fundamental distinction between Peircean semiotics and Saussure-based structuralism-semiology (Merrell 1992).

Take, for example, Saussure's (1966) chess-game metaphor of language. Having categorically separated synchrony from diachrony and *langue* from *parole* as virtually incommensurable domains, Saussure then proposed that in an atemporal sense a language is like a chess game. At a given point in the game there is a static set of relations between each of the arbitrarily sized, shaped, and coloured pieces and all the others, which serves to endow them with meaning in terms of their differences. Then, if a piece is moved, the relation between it and all the other pieces, and hence between each of those other pieces and all others, suffers an alteration such that an entirely new state of affairs is established. This, Saussure claims, is analogous to the switch from one state of a given language to another. By and large Saussure's hypothesis stipulates an immanent role for the speaker since she, as an individual, cannot bring about changes in a language state but must rather passively follow linguistic conventions set by the community at large.

However, the very fact that Saussure has developed his theory of immanence entails his own nostalgia for a quasi-Platonic transcendence – and in this respect the Genevan linguist is not unlike Einstein, who set the parameters of each observer's world from an otherworldly perspective, as if there were some absolutely self-aware being. Assuming that such a transcendental grasp, *sub specie aeternitatis*, were possible for some particular observer of a given *langue*, and that all language states existed *en bloc* as a set of chess-match states after each move, from beginning to end, we would in essence have Maxwell's Demon and Laplace's Superobserver wrapped and neatly tied into one package. That is to say, this venerable Maxwell-Laplacean Monster – let us call him Ludwig

– would have no *a prioris* and his/her perspective would be nonpositional, nonsingular. It would embrace all our possible perspectives, past, present, and future at once. Ludwig would be you, me, and everyone.

He/she would consequently despair when trying to comprehend language as we know it: he/she would see only a massive 'block' – all possible states of *langue* – sliced up into a virtual infinity of static sections certain points in each of which would be well-nigh incompatible with certain points in contiguous slices. Unlike you and me and everyone, he/she would be incapable of experiencing irreversible language changes – in time, our 'time' – along an anisotropic, unidirectional line describing our particular trajectory within the 'block' (that is, as if we were privy to the macroscopic manifestation of Heisenberg matrix mechanics in the Prigogine sense). Alterations from one slice to the next would be completely reversible, hence 'time,' whatever that might mean for him/her, would be thoroughly isotropic (that is, the Saussurean counterpart to Schrödinger's wave mechanics). Moreover, Ludwig could not discriminate between words in use along our singular 'time lines' within some sort of Saussurean semiological salami. Although he/she could distinguish an adjective from a noun, or one noun from another, he/she would be incapable of distinguishing between the same word used today and used again tomorrow except as a trace (vector) in the synchronic 'block,' represented by *langue*.

Consequently, Ludwig would perceive in one monolithic grasp not a language evolving through time but a superposition of the set of all imaginable permutations in that language from beginning to end, with each component of the superposition allowing for a limited number of possible states. In one state, 'pig' would be a fat quadruped. In another, metaphorically speaking, it could be a slovenly person, in another, it would be someone who eats too much, and in yet another, a person charged with upholding the law. But there is little probability that it would become, we might suppose, a 'cauliflower' or a 'rose.' In one state, 'amigdala' might have evolved into 'almond,' in another 'elmound,' and in still another 'ilmumb,' but most likely not 'xclargk.' In other words, Ludwig would identify the original Greek term with a matrix table specifying all probable permutations. But he would see the table as a set of operations by which something is timelessly transformed into something else, not as a sequence of changes from one day to the next, one year to the next, or from the beginning to the end of time. He would be naturally endowed with the instinctive capacity to analyse the lexical items of the language in question in terms of permutations, not 'things.'

On another note, and comparable to Peirce's game of infinities, our imageless image of Ludwig presents a situation not unlike that of Dunne's (1934) unimaginable consciousness generated from the infinite regress he constructs in his effort to account for precognition. Time, in this formulation, is itself a process in time. Therefore it can be eliminated only by evoking the notion of an infinite number of spatial dimensions and a hypothetical observer at infinity who would have to be the last term in the series – which is actually contradictory, for the series can have no last term. Nevertheless, assuming an observer the like of Ludwig to exist, it would be expected that for him/her our notion of time as a moving slit allowing us to scan the world in successive slices would be well-nigh incomprehensible. He/she would see slices out of the language 'block' merely in terms of a superposed set of *possibilia*; we would experience transitoriness, alternative, minuscule, serial grasps of the experienced world, be they dynamic or continuous. For him/her the 'block' would include a static sequence of *possibilities*; for us there would be only *actual* changes, which we could then analyse in terms of their discrete properties. So goes the Saussurean 'block' about which much controversial ink has been expended.

Peirce's image of items of Secondness spinning out of Firstness and those in turn being mediated by Thirdness offers a vast improvement over Saussurean structuralism-semiology. The image stems from a comparison between Peirce and physicist David Bohm (see Merrell 1992). In an effort to render our world a linearly developing domain of becoming along our 'world-line,' Bohm's (1980) notion of the *implicate* and *explicate* orders, the one existing as a range of possibilities, the other as a selective (abstracted) actualization of a minute portion of them into what *is* – as opposed to what *could have been* but *is not* – is quite effective. This notion is comparable, in mathematics, to the unwinding of a binomial equation $(x + y)^n$ or a real number such as π – in fact, Peirce sometimes likened the asymptotic process of a community of knowers arriving at a final opinion to the process of computing the value of π. Along the fastidious game of spinning out integers in order hopefully to reach the end-product, one would draw closer and closer to the finish line, but, though the ultimate value admits of indefinite refinement, there can be no end-point in a finite world (*CP*:5.565, 8.226, 7.78).

Moreover, further computation would not reveal that π is substantially anything more or less than, say, 3.14. As the computations increase, π would never turn out to be 3.13 or 3.15. So the moral to the story might well appear to be that we might as well quit while we are ahead, for the ultimate value of π (the totally unfolded, which is infinite and eternally beyond reach) is continuous, multidimensional, and unordered, while our particular finite computation (a finite unfolded section) is discontinuous and linear, and it can perhaps be partially ordered, or merely random. According to this story, though the infinite stretch of π is inaccessible, and though there can be no determining whether or not it is random, finite segments can be at least ordered *for* us. And, though there is no knowing when symmetry breaking, fluctuations, dissipation, and chaos will erupt, *pace* the Prigogine model, given the self-organizing universe, and as long as life goes on and living signs continue their swim, order, of some semblance or other, will continue to emerge from the unruly sea of disorder.

The ultimate mind-bender occurs, however, when Ludwig tells us – assuming that he could be in command of a language intelligible to mere mortals – that there is no reason for us to suppose the world to which our language refers is in any form or fashion 'real,' or singular, or even typical. Actually, as we use language along our series of *nows*, it should enjoy no priority over any other possible language. We could just as well say 'elmound' or 'olmund' instead of 'almond' – if it were tacitly agreed upon by the speech community – and our lines of communication would hardly be hindered. Or instead of 'Snow is white' we could say '*Schnee ist weiss*,' or '*La nieve es blanca*,' or we could divide 'snow' into some thirty odd categories, and it would make little difference. Given the superposition of every possible language there is no singularity by which to classify all languages and all worlds to which they presumably 'refer.' After all, 'atom' for Democritus, for Newton, for Mach, for Bohr, for Feynman, for Wheeler, and for the person in the street at this moment is merely a set of static trajectories (vectors) from one point to another in the 'block.'

Or what is more intriguing, 'quarks,' as the term occurs in *Finnegans Wake*, is no less 'real' for our venerable omniscient friend, Ludwig, than its instantiation in the *Physics Review* or in a science fiction piece. They all enjoy equal status in the semiological salami from a massive perceptual gulp *sub specie aeternitatis*. This, however, does not imply that Ludwig is a radical determinist. True, whenever a language change is recorded – as Seconds in brains, in dictionaries, in classrooms, at computer terminals, in subway stations, on rest room walls – it becomes 'real,' though for him/her there is nothing to get excited about, for the change was there all along. There simply is no temporal 'next.' There are merely possibilities (Firsts), tendencies to become – *potentia* as Heisenberg called unactualized quantum events – which are probabilistically defined. Our *langue* in the *now* is merely one among a spectrum of other languages that *could have been* actualized in our particular linguistic community at this point in time – which is minuscule in comparison with the whole picture Ludwig grasps in simultaneity – *but were not*. Besides, if we successively see our world as if through a slit, and if our language as we know it at each instant could be specified by a competent Saussurean linguist, a structuralist, or a semiologist – though artificially – by a moving point on a sequence of synchronic slices, then our experienced time, as well as the ongoing stream of language-in-use, would surely entail an *orthogonal dimension* (that is, a grasp from a ninety-degree angle of everything at once) with respect to our 'world-line.' And everything would be the equivalent of the Minkowski 'block.' However, *langue*, like the 'block,' fortunately for us all, is not of our world. And time, *our* time, is that of concrete experience, of Firstness in the act of becoming Secondness: it is not exclusively the imaginary, artificial product of pure intellect, of Thirdness.

In short, *langue*, as it has generally – though not always – been interpreted, is a hopeless Platonic ideal, and the signifier/signified dichotomy frequently suffers from severe relapses into psychological or mentalistic nominalism. *Langue* is overwhelmingly cumbersome; besides, it is totally beyond grasp. And the signifier/signified pair discounts 'semiotic objects' and semiotic agents, that which makes signs full-blown signs. *Our* time, the time of our 'semiotically real' world, I would submit, renders both *langue* and signifier/signified unviable candidates for a legitimate notion of the sign.

A further word, then, on the ramification of *our* time with respect to spatiality as discussed here.

4

A Pluralist Semiotic Universe

Chapter 3 set the stage for a dynamic typology of semiotic entities (sign-events and thought-signs), especially with respect to their temporal character. This chapter focuses primarily on what we might dub the 'dimensional nature' of signs.

Dimensionality, for obvious reasons, lends itself quite well to enticing graphic and diagrammatic representations of conceptual matter. Points, lines, planes, cubes, and even hypercubes and tessaracts can be handy tools for descriptive, explanatory, and didactic purposes. James Bunn (1981) makes ample use of spatial dimensions in constructing his unique 'polydimensional semiotics.' I shall juxtapose his attractive thesis with J.T. Fraser's (1979, 1982) correlation of Jakob von Uexküll's (1957) *Umwelt* idea of diverse levels of temporality with various existential realms, from that of photons to biological organisms to human societies. This juxtaposition will return us to McTaggart's A-series time in contrast to B-series time and Eddington's attempt to account for both from within the postclassical perspective, a problem, we shall note, that has actually been with the Western world since Parmenides and Heraclitus battered heads with each other. The spatio-temporal conceptual scheme developed in the present and preceding chapters can be looked upon as a preparatory stage for chapter 5, where Prigogine, and Peirce's notion of the sign, will be placed within an increasingly broad panorama.

1. TIME IN ALL DIRECTIONS SIMULTANEOUSLY?

With a combination of three dimensions and three variables, (1) 'highlighted' (foregrounded), (2) 'torqued' (brought into action), and (3) 'suppressed' (backgrounded), Bunn generates a set of six classes of semiotic instruments, tools, and media, which function much like a group of permutations (see table 5).

TABLE 5

(A)	3-D Highlighted	2-D Torqued	1-D Suppressed
(B)	2-D Highlighted	3-D Torqued	1-D Suppressed
(C)	1-D Highlighted	2-D Torqued	3-D Suppressed
(D)	3-D Highlighted	1-D Torqued	2-D Suppressed
(E)	2-D Highlighted	1-D Torqued	3-D Suppressed
(F)	1-D Highlighted	3-D Torqued	2-D Suppressed

'Utilitarian' semiotic units[1] can come in three forms: A: three-dimensionality 'highlighted,' two-dimensionality 'torqued,' and one-dimensionality 'suppressed' (neolithic pots, modern tools); B: two-dimensionality 'highlighted,' three-dimensionality 'torqued,' and one-dimensionality 'suppressed' (graphs, diagrams, video images, pictographs); and C: one-dimensionality 'highlighted,' two-dimensionality 'torqued,' and three-dimensionality 'suppressed' (writing, speech, number, logical and formal symbol strings). The complementary counterparts to these 'utilitarian' objects, that is, 'aesthetic' semiotic units, can have D: three-dimensionality 'highlighted,' one-dimensionality 'torqued,' and two-dimensionality 'suppressed' (ballet, theater, sculpture, architecture); E: two-dimensionality 'highlighted,' one-dimensionality 'torqued,' and three-dimensionality 'suppressed' (painting, lithography, silk screening), and F: one-dimensionality 'highlighted,' three-dimensionality 'torqued,' and two-dimensionality 'suppressed' (music, poetry). In each case, one dimensionality of each 'semiotic object' is 'highlighted' while the other two dimensionalities are either 'torqued' or 'suppressed' (Bunn 1981:38–46).

Bunn's trio of variables, 'highlighted,' 'torqued,' and 'suppressed,' meshes conveniently with Peirce's possibility-actuality-necessity, and Firstness-Second -ness-Thirdness triads. In three-dimensionality A units, for instance, a neolithic pot or a monkey wrench, one-dimensional characteristics are suppressed, while the pot's symmetry depends upon two-dimensional rotation of the potter's wheel as it is being formed, and the wrench's use entails twisting motion along a two-dimensional plane. A planar ('torqued') surface, then, is paramount in the unit's construction and use. B units illustrated on a flat surface, on the other hand, suppress the first dimensionality, for it is hardly any more functional than in A units, and that which they illustrate – or signify, as it were, in the Peircean sense – occupies three-dimensional space. Thus in Western societies the relatively simple Necker cube – like some of Escher's lithographs (E units) – is viewed in terms of the the ambiguity or visual paradox it evinces solely when the two-dimensional surface is projected onto an imaginary three-dimensional domain, with the inherent 'real' time/*imaginary time* problematics outlined in chapter 3. Displayal of C units is necessarily linear. Signs exist in relation of contiguity, but in their composite form, as a text, a mathematical or logical proof, a series of integers, or whatever, they occupy a plane, a page, while their third-dimensional manifestation is shoved under the rug as if it were inconsequential. Thus we have, in A, B, and C units, a foregrounding of iconicity, indexicality, and symbolicity respectively.

Units in category D must be unfolded in three dimensions. But in the process of this unfolding – for example, the rhythm of a ballerina, the contours of a statue, the baroque façade of a Spanish cathedral, the movements on stage playing out *Hamlet* – are brought about during the time of their creation or their performance along a one-dimensional and temporal 'world-line' in three-dimensional space. Two dimensions are highlighted on the painted canvas, an instantiation of E. Like D units, the painting is created along a one-dimensional 'world-line,' while the three-dimensionality of the item it represents is not of the same consequence as it is for category B entities, which must model their object of representation in terms of its three-dimensionality. Finally, music or poetry highlight the linear continuity of rhythm flowing out in n-directions in three-dimensional space, while the two-dimensional page upon which the lines or score are printed are suppressed, since the effect of the aesthetic piece depends upon a synthetic grasp, from beginning to end, of the relations of parts to parts and parts to whole. Once again we have a progressive foregrounding of iconicity, indexicality, and symbolicity, from semiotic objects D, E, and F.

That is to say, referring back to tables 2 and 3, if I may, chiefly iconic signs (1,3,5), most properly signs of themselves without their (yet) enjoying any definite reference or mediation by Thirdness, highlight three-dimensionality (the pot does not necessarily represent anything, the dance is a dance is a dance – like a rose is a rose is a rose as a representation of itself and nothing but itself). Chiefly indexical signs (2,4,6,7) highlight two-dimensionality (a diagram, graph, or video game picture 'point to' that of which they are models or simulacra). And chiefly symbolic signs (8,9,10), in their inception partly to wholly arbitrary, and generated in linear fashion, depend on, and are at the same time superordinate to, signs of relation of Secondness and of monadic Firstness (logic, mathematics, computer language). In short, iconicity as *possibility*, indexicality as *actuality*, and symbolicity as *probability* or *necessity*, tend respectively to highlight (1) self-referential, self-sufficient, three-dimensionality, (2) two-way, symmetrical, planar relationality, and (3) one-dimensional, linear development along n-tuple lines – as I shall argue in greater detail in this and the chapters that follow.

Before constructing a variation on Bunn's set of permutations that includes time as well as space, and, in addition, the notion of a four-dimensional space-time manifold,[2] I shall evoke J.T. Fraser's (1979, 1982) categories of temporality, couple them with the notion of 'real' and *imaginary time* (as presented in chapter 3), and integrate them with a generative model developed from Eigen's hypercycle idea and order out of chaos via Prigogine dissipative structures, as discussed in the first two chapters. Then, I shall attempt to demonstrate how Fraser's categories fit with Bunn's.[3]

Fraser takes his point of departure from German biologist Jakob von Uexküll's species-specific *Umwelt* concept, according to which an organism's receptors and effectors determine the nature of its world – all of which is now quite well known among Peircean semioticians (J. von Uexküll 1957, 1982; T. von Uexküll 1982). In semiotic terms, the organism does not live in actual 'reality' but in its particular 'semiotically real' world consisting of signs that have been filtered and formed according to its species-specific perceptual and conceptual capacities. A 'semiotic world,' in short, consists of that circumscribed portion of the whole of 'reality' made meaningful by a particular species (recall note 13 of chapter 3). Wittgenstein once mused that if a lion could speak, we humans would not understand it. We must assume that a lion's world is for it such that what is is simply the way things are: as far as it is concerned, its world is sufficient as it is and could not be other than what it is. Yet a lion lives in a three-dimensional world, the same as we. We would suppose, then, that there must be some overlap between his *Umwelt*-generated 'semiotic world' and our own, but that there is no determining, with any guarantee of success, where the lines of correspondence, if indeed there be any, are to be found.

For an even more extreme nonhominoid example, a spider's world consists essentially of polar coordinates specifying its two-dimensional web. Comfortably situated in its 'Planeland' of vectors and distances and awaiting an unwary fly, it has little use for Cartesian space of three dimensions. Like the lion's 'semiotic world,' its environment in so far as it senses it is what it is and could hardly be anything else. It is capable of coping quite effectively in the same physical world as ours, though we must suppose we hardly share any 'semiotically real' links with our tiny neighbours, the arachnids or 'octopeds.' The upshot is that from ticks to bats to elephants, porpoises, and simians, the *Umwelt*-generated 'semiotic world' of a particular species, as far as each member of that species is concerned, is *complete* and *consistent* – save for the human animal, which at some point began asking of him/herself and of nature what for the more practical nonhuman species were entirely unnecessary questions. But more on that later.

An attractive feature of Fraser's interpretation of the *Umwelt* thesis consists in his integrating it into distinct levels of temporality. These levels, five in number – though commensurate, I hope to demonstrate, with Bunn's six categories – comprise the *Umwelten* of (1) *atemporal* entities with zero rest mass travelling at

TABLE 6

4-D Free, none committed	Atemporality
3-D Free, one committed	Prototemporality
2-D Free, two committed	Eotemporality
1-D Free, three committed	Biotemporality
0-D Free, four committed	Nootemporality

the speed of light (photons, gravitons, neutrinos), (2) *prototemporal* elementary particles with nonzero rest mass moving at speeds somewhat less than that of light (microlevel subatomic particles), (3) *eotemporal* macrolevel entities generally subject to the laws of classical mechanics (from millet seeds to books, cars, mountains, planets, stars, and galaxies), (4) *biotemporal* living organisms, and (5) *nootemporal*, exclusively self-conscious organisms, and entire societies of such *nootemporal* self-conscious organisms (see table 6) (Fraser 1982:23–9).

Fraser's *atemporal* entities perpetually rushing about at the velocity of light are capable of 'seeing' nothing: since they themselves *are* light, there is nothing *else* to 'see.' Darkness prevails. Or 'nothingness' in the sense of Peirce's (*CP*:4.512) initial state prior to his three categories, a sort of 'pre-First.' But the atemporal is not to be mistaken for the ordinary philosophical concept of nothingness. It is more adequately associated with the pre-Socratic or Oriental notion of chaos – which was, as we observed above, Peirce's source of the term. It is entirely without law or connectedness – an intrinsically uncorrelated mess, pure chance. Fraser (1982:31) compares this state of affairs to a blank sheet of paper, which reminds us of Peirce's (*CP*:4.512) empty 'sheet of assertion' constituting the first page of his tropological 'book of assertions.' Time is, properly speaking, nonexistent in the realm of this blank sheet, that state prior to the primordial 'cut,' or 'mark of distinction.' From the vantage of a particular 'piece' of this 'sheet,' any notion of past, present, or future simply cannot exist as such.

This is much in line with the mind-set of our enigmatic Ludwig from chapter 3. Like his/her dwelling-place, the photon's atemporal 'reality' is a four-dimensional manifold, embodied in the static Minkowski 'block' interpretation of relativity theory where everything simply *is as it is*. There is no becoming. For the photon there is only what we most properly might call a *point universe*. Each photon exists snugly and smugly in its isolated, monadic, though infinitesimal, sphere (point), joyously vibrating away, oblivious to anything and everything outside its infinitely limited, yet at the same time infinitely unlimited, domain.

It would be incorrect, however, to consider the atemporal domain to be at absolute rest, as the Minkowski 'block' is often mistakenly interpreted. Rather, it is a hustle and bustle of activity, Heraclitean motion at its best. On the other hand, for the photon, from the vantage afforded it by its particular *Umwelt*, and travelling like all its kin at the speed of light, everything is frozen; all is there in simultaneity, a Parmenidean one. Einstein's special theory of relativity of 1905 dispenses with the idea of absolute rest – the frame of reference of a photon – and builds upon the idea of motion for a particular macrolevel observer with respect to a different absolute condition: constant unrest. Yet the fact remains that the 'block' can be conceived either as absolute rest (from the photon's *Umwelt*) or absolute change (from a temporal *Umwelt*) (Fraser 1982:29–37). It is strange that in the atemporal realm of pure oneness, from a photon's supposed *Umwelt* there is nothing that corresponds to *our* idea of absolute rest, but rather, all photons are equally hyperactive, in a state of pure *becoming* without *being*. This uncomfortable situation, which gave Nicholas of Cusa, Pascal, Nietzsche, and others fits, has become part and parcel of the contemporary relativity scientists's description of the universe (to be be placed in the spotlight during the unfolding of chapter 9).

The problem with any attempt to come to grips with the atemporal realm is, of course, that it is totally divorced from common sense assumptions and normal modes of perception. Textbooks and popular accounts of relativity theory customarily begin by relating to the experiential primacy of classical physics. The idea of a particular frame of reference is established, whether on earth, in a moving train, or in a spaceship. Then, arguments are generated regarding how items of experience would look from this 'stable' vantage. The universe of the photon, however, enjoys absolutely no stability or rest, and at the same time there is absolutely no time and hence no change. Past, present, and future simply bear no meaning; all instants are 'there,' in simultaneity. We would like to think that a photon leaves the nearest star and after its long journey enters the retina of a contemplative earthling astronomer. But this comfortable anthropocentric image could not be farther from the 'truth' – in so far as it is conceived in relativity theory. For the photon there is no departure, no travel, no arrival time. Everything is simply *there*. It resists description in tensed language, and any attempt to dress it in a tenseless language is awkward at best.

In the realm of primordial atemporal chaos, there is no comparison between states of affairs; in fact, there are no determinable states or degrees of ordering. Without comparison between different orders, there can be neither entropy nor information, properly speaking. A leap from chaos to the rudiments of prototemporal order is commensurate with physicist Niels Bohr's (1958) contention that the term 'physical reality' cannot be attached to the world 'out there' without conditions of measurement (interaction) between physicist and the nonphysical realm of wave functions. The physicist has no alternative but to 'think herself' – albeit with a degree of anthropomorphism – into the world of a particle. Since such 'thinking' cannot be launched into the stratosphere of community discourse without its being couched in natural language, it becomes over the long haul, in Werner Heisenberg's (1958) conception, more directly about language itself than about the wave-particle or event-thing – or 'wavicle-eventing,' if you wish – to which it hopefully refers. Furthermore, at this level, given the inevitability of language use, both mathematical and natural, and in view of the introduction of a 'before' and an 'after' regarding human perception, language use, and interaction with 'physical reality,' *time* and *space* now begin to make their presence felt – albeit vaguely, as it were. And thus we begin entry into prototemporality.

But in the prototemporal realm, time and space are still only vaguely distinguishable in the sense of a 'here-now' and a 'there-then.' They are as yet without a 'now' rushing along the rail from past to future. Events and positions are specifiable only statistically, and causality is no more than probabilistic; in fact, a state of probabilistic lawfulness – or lawlessness if you wish – reigns. Any *Umwelt*-generated perception and conception of the world from within the prototemporal realm is properly one-dimensional, and it is irreversible if only in the sense that with the collapse of each wave packet an event occurs once and for all. Of the total of four dimensions, in other words, one dimension is *Umwelt* committed and three remain free. For example, a prototemporal 'particle' (of three dimensions of space and one of time) in a three-dimensional box is free to move about at will, though its linear trajectory, like that of a hypothetical Linelander, will allow it solely a one-dimensional tunnel vision. If any sort of world-view is conceivable for a prototemporal entity it might be roughly comparable in our terms to that of an earthworm with no sense of anything around it, but merely whatever is subject to its receptors along the linear tunnel (Lineland) it is carving out of the earth at a given instant. Its awareness and description of its world, with no conception of time except that of the actualization of potentialities, might simply be: 'Now this, now this ...' There is merely a succession of 'points' coming into its purview with hardly any relation to anything else in its surroundings or of any temporal succession.

The probabilistic character of prototemporality appears to lie in a halfway house, the twilight zone, between delirious atemporal chaos and the stable, deterministic eotemporality of classical physics. The problem is that there apparently remains an unbridgeable gap between them. Regarding wave functions in the prototemporal realm, quantum theory can tell us nothing with certainty; there are only varying degrees of probability. In everyday (eotemporal) life, we can toss a coin, secure in our belief that with fifty/fifty probability heads will show. With each flip and flop the coin will be either heads-up or heads-down, but once the coin comes to a rest and an irreversible state of affairs has been established, uncertainty wanes, and determinacy enters. Events in quantum theory, in contrast, strangely remain forever probabilistic: there is never any absolute certainty, even after a measurement has been taken. Differences in quantum theory between prototemporal and eotemporal domains are in a certain manner of speaking accounted for with recognition of *pure* and *mixed states*, the first remaining exclusively wave functional and the second manifesting particulate as well as wave characteristics. That is to say, there are on the one hand self-propagating superposed probability waves, and on the other quantum averages that, through measurement (interaction with something, someone, the physicist's instruments), take on a determinate value. By piling mixed states upon mixed states, microlevel quantum phenomena become sufficiently populous to manifest macrolevel, eotemporal, and rather determinable (if only statistical) behaviour somewhat typical of our experienced world (Herbert 1985).

The problem – if we follow the Copenhagen interpretation of quantum mechanics – is that the physicist's measuring device cannot exist as such outside its interaction with its immediate environment, and that environment with some more encompassing environment, and so on. The physicist must take account not only of her pointer reading but also herself, the chair she sits in, the laboratory, the building, the grounds, the city, the surrounding countryside, and so on. An infinite regress appears to be the only logical by-product. One signpost promising a route out of this infinite morass has been proposed, as I mentioned in the previous chapter, by Eugene Wigner: consciousness, he argues, is responsible for drawing eotemporal events from prototemporal statistics. Semiotically speaking, this solution would not hold water, however, since for Peirce mind, self, and consciousness are merely signs among other signs, and hence should enjoy no such privilege. Another, all encompassing, map, to which I also referred above, comes in the form of Everett's 'many-worlds interpretation' of quantum mechanics, according to which the entire universe is a unique wave function of virtually infinite complexity. It is its own final referent; it refers to itself. This might appear *prima facie* comparable to Peirce's universe as a massive, unique sign, an argument, the cosmic poem, the ultimate interpretant. The problem here is that the many-worlds universe cannot accommodate the evolutionary complexification of Peirce's dynamic, ongoing cosmological view. It is completed and fixed for all time, unlike Peirce's universe of signs – as well as Prigogine's self-organizing universe – the very laws of which continue to undergo change. That much said, let us turn to the more familiar and comfortable domain of eotemporality.

The eotemporal is that time of classical mechanics represented by the physicist's *t* in his equations that is directionless and symmetrical: it is isotropic, the 'static' time of pure, directionless succession, as would be a digital watch with pulses but no numbers. And it is reversible. If a stone is dropped from the Tower of Pisa and a video camera traces its flight in mid-air, disregarding the movement of background objects, it will show no indication of direction, or even of movement. A movie could equally have been taken of the stone thrown from ground level and caught by someone at the top, and it would be merely the video in reverse. For another example, the air can be pumped out of a bell jar and the outlet connected to a bottle of perfume. A video can be taken of the perfume rushing into the vacuum in the jar. Then if the video is reversed and shown to a vacuum-system engineer he could explain that the molecules merely could have rushed out of the jar into another container with less pressure than that of the jar. Diffusion is not an irreversible process. The symmetrical, isotropic eotemporal realm in the sense just described gives the picture of a universe of *being* without any clear notion of *becoming*, typical of classical mechanics.

In the eotemporal realm, two spatial directions are committed while one spatial and the time dimension remain free. For example, the spider's two-dimensional 'web-universe' can be conceived as a coordinate extension of its receptors. From the vibrations of the web the spider can determine roughly the size and position of its prey. Its space is reversible, symmetrical, and any movement of the spider in it is pure succession, like any other eotemporal body. The spider's 'Flatland' is in this sense comparable to an event in our three dimensions of space and one of time mapped onto a Cartesian plane such that all is there all at once, in the order of two dimensions of space and a frozen dimension of time (by the same token, compare our view of the spider's universe to our own universe from the view of our venerable Ludwig). In short, the atemporal realm is without law or connectedness, the prototemporal implies indeterminate (that is, probabilistic) tendencies or potentialities for occurring – which is an intermediate step between lawlessness and classical determinacy – and the eotemporal is a world of reversible, yet largely deterministic, causation.

Toward the final gasp of classical mechanics a rather unexpected and often undesirable addendum to the Newtonian paradigm cropped up: the Second Law of Thermodynamics. When one considers a closed system, the tendency toward maximum entropy demands an irreversible, asymmetrical, and hence temporal process. Our imaginary 'web-universe' of the spider is two-dimensional. But, to repeat, the fact is, that the spider exists in a three-dimensional world, properly the biotemporal realm, with three dimensions committed, and only one, which for a few centuries gave quite adequate account of the eotemporal, remaining free: time. Presentness becomes definable from the biotemporal *Umwelt* in terms of the coordination necessary for a living organism to maintain a certain degree of autonomy *vis-à-vis* its environment (Maturana and Varela 1980, 1987). The organism is an entity *set apart*, it sets its-*self* apart, from the rest of the universe, which enables it to alter, as the species evolves, its 'time,' from a simple present to cyclicality, and finally, to complex orders increasingly polarizing past and future, beginnings and endings. In successively more complex *Umwelt*-generated 'semiotically real' worlds, time becomes progressively more asymmetrical and irreversible, as the notion of causality enters the scene. At the upper reaches, finally, conscious self-awareness and death-awareness enter into the equation, especially in the human semiotic animal (Dobzhansky 1962).

Regarding thermodynamics, a further dilemma raises its ugly head, however. The entropy principle is based on a probability factor – albeit classical rather than quantum theoretical. At the eotemporal level of thermodynamics, probabilistic equations are applied to aggregates as if the members of the aggregates were distinct, and hence countable, but also indistinguishable one from another with respect to their behaviour to which the probabilistic law applies. In classical mechanics, probability laws explain the transition from the chaotic atemporal sphere to the deterministic eotemporal sphere, while bypassing the prototemporal and giving no account of the biotemporal except as an extension of a mechanistic universe. The problem, upon jumping from atemporality to eotemporality, is fundamentally that of the contradiction between *ensemble* and *history* or *time* (comparable to the Saussurean semiological 'block' versus Peircean semiotic triadicity, with mediation ushering in time).

Taken as a whole, history and ensemble are coterminous: measurement of an *ensemble average* and its corresponding *history* or *time average* are theoretically identical. For example, take a pair of dice, throw them 10,000 times over a 50,000-second (roughly 12.5 hours) period, and record the results. Now take 10,000 pairs of dice, throw them simultaneously, and record the results. The two results will be very close, perhaps well-nigh identical. The question is: How is it possible to account for the identical behaviour of an aggregate spread out *en bloc* and surveyed at an instant, on the one hand, and as a series of moments spread out in time, on the other? It would appear that there is, rather paradoxically, some sort of free exchange between spatial and temporal distributions. One possible answer is that an aggregate governed by statistical laws pertains to the prototemporal sphere in which space and time are, for certain purposes, interchangeable (Fraser 1982:69–70). In other words, in this sphere the temporal arc of history and the behaviour of the ensemble are for practical purposes one. But they cannot be one, of course, for human self-aware and death-aware semiotic agents. Humans are cognizant of the fact of a beginning and ending of their very existence, which is understandably all-important, though epistemologically, the ensemble, as product and parcel of timeless intellectual grasps, is what matters most.

All this is confusing, to say the least. At the outset it gives the impression – contrary to the theses developed in the first two chapters – that time is merely subjective: it appears to do away with any distinction between the eotemporal and biotemporal realms. One is conceived merely in terms of ensemble, the other in terms of history. But it all reduces to the same parade, whether seen in some artificially contrived time-bound fashion from the perspective of the streetwise youth, or timelessly from the privileged vantage of the Goodyear blimp. It is much like the distinction between light as objective waves (primary qualities) and as subjective colour (secondary qualities). The waves are reality; the colour is mere mind-spinning. The colours of the world that please, excite, and inspire have no relevance to the objective world. However, when we interject time into our history-ensemble distinction, we seem to have another ball of wax altogether. It is rather easy to comprehend that the matter of a comfortable chair is no more than a curvature in space-time and its colour is nothing more than electromagnetic waves. But to say that our sensation of the movement of time is no more than an entropy-gradient is to stretch the imagination. It is as if becoming were passively spread out in the Minkowski 'block,' with one's consciousness inventing a serial order much like a three-dimensional 'worm' inching its way along a path in four-dimensional space-time. There would exist only the illusion that external events are 'taking place.'

This problem must engage us during the digressionary lapse of a brief subsection before we move on.

2. THE EYE ('I') CAN'T SEE ITSELF (AS ITS OWN ICON)

Arthur Eddington (1958b:99–100) offers the example of an extraterrestrial being who wishes to discover the temporal relation of two events in our world. He must use two different time meters. The first indicates the degree of disorder (entropy) of a system. This is 'time's arrow' determining which events are 'earlier' and which 'later.' But it does not indicate how much 'earlier' or 'later.' In order to determine the temporal spacing between events our cosmic traveller needs a reliable clock, which we happen to be able to provide him.

Now, the first instrument determines roughly the equivalent of McTaggart's B-series; the clock determines his A-series. The B-series needs an 'arrow' to give it direction; the A-series would be a meaningless succession in the eotemporal

Umwelt without the 'arrow.' The B-series is ensemble-like; the A-series is history-like. In concert they are capable – with the aid of a semiotic agent, of course – of fleshing out time, which would otherwise remain a mere skeleton in the space-time 'block.' In other words, time as we sense it is subjective, and the flow of events and the changes they bring about are what we experience as we trace out our particular 'world-line,' merely one trajectory among myriad other possible, actual, and potential trajectories in the cosmic salami.

As we noted in the previous chapter, Prigogine, in contrast to this conception of things, believes he brings these two 'times' together into one package, thus endowing irreversible time with objectivity. Irreversibility via Prigogine's dissipative structures pertains equally to the prototemporal, eotemporal, and biotemporal spheres. Irreversibility regarding the biotemporal realm is clear enough, whether we speak of living organisms or living signs. Encompassing autopoiesis, hypercycles, and dissipative structures arising out of far-from-equilibrium conditions, it entails, given its inclusion of life processes, the ebbs and flows of germination, life, and decay. Biological systems take in matter, energy, and information (signs all) from their environment, then return them in other, more highly entropic, forms – the Heraclitean give and take of semiosis. While organisms (or sign domains) are alive and well, they create increasing order ('up' the 'hypercycle' spiral: $1 \rightarrow 10$) at the expense of the world 'out there.' When order wanes, de-generacy threatens, the rate of outflow of organization having become greater than the inner production of organization, and if the direction of the arrow is not reversed, the grim reaper is sure to enter centre stage – a metaphor 'dies,' sign differences become sameness, the organism passes away (in such cases signs de-generate 'downward': $10 \rightarrow 1$).

But actually, it can be conceived that the roots of Prigogine's irreversible dissipative structures giving rise to the possibility of life-forms lie in what Eddington called the 'arrow of time.' Implied by the (eotemporal) Second Law of Thermodynamics, the 'arrow' expresses time's one-way property, which has no analogue in space (Eddington 1958b:69). This conception of time, it would appear, is close to 'real' time as I have discussed it above in so far as (1) it 'is vividly recognized by consciousness,' (2) it 'is equally insisted on by our reasoning faculty, which tells us that a reversal of the arrow would render the external world nonsensical,' and (3) it 'makes no appearance in physical science except in the study of organisation of a number of individuals' (Eddington 1958b:69). By individuals Eddington refers to the aggregate of elementary particles believed to exist in the past, present, and future states of the universe.

Granted, the classical laws governing a particular individual can be stated by reference to time. The sequence of states running from past to future can be considered the *becoming* of events; the sequence running from future to past is the *unbecoming* of events. But the classical (eotemporal) laws of nature are indifferent regarding direction. In algebraic symbolism there is no more of a distinction between past and future than between right and left. Left is $-x$ and right is $+x$, and past is $-t$ and future is $+t$. Over the long haul it's all the same. The exception to this rule is the Second Law, which recognizes a difference between past and future, if only in terms of statistical averages. Without any mystical appeal to consciousness, Eddington observes, it is possible to find a direction of time on the four-dimensional map of the universe by a study of organization. He explains: 'Let us draw an arrow arbitrarily. If as we follow the arrow we find more and more of the random element in the state of the world, then the arrow is pointing towards the future; if the random element decreases the arrow points towards the past. That is the only distinction known to physics. This follows at once if our fundamental contention is admitted that the introduction of randomness is the only thing which cannot be undone' (1958b:69).

Eddington speculates on the subjective nature of the Second Law and the notion of 'real' time, that is, of becoming, without arriving at a definite conclusion. He does concede that the entropy principle is of a more subjective nature than other physical laws; it is subjective much in the sense that the constellation Orion is subjective. That which is arranged in the firmament is objective, but its association into a cluster representing, in symbolic form, something not inherent in the cluster itself, is subjective. While a physicist would generally tell us that the chair is in reality a curvature of space and its colour a set of electromagnetic waves, she would be less prone to claim that it is an entropy-gradient, though she would most likely hold that there is some sort of connection between time and entropy. She would find herself compelled to admit that 'there is something as yet ungrasped behind the notion of entropy – some mystical interpretation, if you like – which is not apparent in the definition of [this connection] by which we introduce it into physics' (Eddington 1958b:95). Indeed, at the time of Eddington's writing it appeared that physicists had yet to resolve this problem entirely.

Almost two decades later, David Layzer (1975) went so far as to toss another time bomb in the works with the implication, following an elaborate thought experiment, that there is no way to determine whether randomness is on the increase or decrease and hence whether or not time has an 'arrow' moving in a particular direction.[4] Layzer's universe is incessantly in the process of generating semiosis as well as falling into entropy (disinformation, sign de-generacy), of creating order as well as becoming disordered. Sign generacy, and hence life, occurs whenever expansion of the whole of a semiosic system exceeds the composite rate of equilibration of all local domains. Although the incessant generation of new lines and domains of order (signs and their meanings) is characteristic of both biological and cosmic processes, the underlying causes are another story entirely. 'Cosmic evolution,' Layzer writes, 'is a consequence of the cosmic expansion; biological evolution and the phenomenon of life depend on the interaction between biological systems and their environment – in particular on the ability of biological systems to extract information [signs and their meanings] from their environment' (1972:286; brackets added). But that information, as well as those signs and meanings, were actually always already there in the first place, because they were generated by cosmic evolution. In contrast, for Peirce, cosmic evolution cannot be divorced from the emergence of life systems: in Fraser's terms, prototemporal events emerged from atemporality, then eotemporal events appeared, and finally, biotemporal and nootemporal organisms evolved. It is a matter of irreversible becoming.

Closely in line with Peirce, as I illustrated above, Prigogine presents a convincing argument to the effect that irreversibility, becoming, and the generation of order from disorder can all be generally attributed, if not exclusively at least primarily, to life processes. Such irreversibility pertains to the microscopic as well as the macroscopic domain, and both are parcel and product of cosmic evolution. In this sense, Prigogine's hypothesis includes at one and the same time the prototemporal and the classical aspects of eotemporality, as well as an overlapping of biotemporality and nootemporality, which embraces the Euclidean, vectorial description of events on a two-dimensional plane – inert reversible events – and the three-dimensional becoming of living organisms – irreversible dynamic processes.

An icon, index, or symbol, and from other various and sundry vantages, an electron, DNA molecule, amoeba, shark, or eagle, or a sprinter during a hundred-metre dash, a New York taxi, or a jumbo jet, all moving in a three-dimensional medium along a one-dimensional trajectory, give an approximate picture of this situation – a counterpart to Bunn's C and F units. Thought-signs and sign-events, sign-organisms and sign-consciousness, are all engaged in an effervescent swim along the semiosic stream. They incessantly submerge and resurface. They become embedded and automatized by Peircean habit, only at some other point along the stream to reemerge as signs that are wilfully engendered – that wilfully engender themselves – in a process of construction and deconstruction and reconstruction, within the whole perfusive gush. Each signifying entity, no matter how simple or how complex, enacts at each moment a minuscule portion of the entire 'world-line' it will describe during its lifetime. Each constitutes an integral part of the total interconnected fabric. Each is a necessary link playing out its role in the evolutionary whole, the great nonlinear chain of becoming.[5]

The transition from chaos to order in the creation of more developed signifying entities along their respective 'world-lines' proceeds from simplicity to organized complexity. To give a glimpse into this series of bounds toward complexity along the chain of this ever-changing process, the number of atemporal entities consists of a mere handful, while the prototemporal realm contains well over two hundred subatomic particles at a recent count. There are some 1,500,000 stable chemical compounds, 10^{30}–10^{40} biological structures, and 10^{10} (and that taken to the ninth power – that is, ten to the tenth to the ninth), number of nootemporal states (equal to the total number of possible states of a human brain!) (Fraser 1979:154–7). In spite of this numbing complexity at the upper level, each human organism persists in considering herself to be an individual, unique, one: she is in possession of an identity. This *one*, like Peirce's cosmic sign, is at once many and one, complex and simple. For if not one, an individual is indistinguishable from all other individuals; and if not many, the upper levels of temporality vanish in the shadows.

The becoming of living entities in a three-dimensional domain by means of continuous generation along the single free dimension, the 'time-' or 'world-line,' introduces us, finally, to the realm of four dimensions, accompanied – strangely enough, Fraser tells us – by zero-degree freedom. Fraser refers, of course, to the space-time continuum, the Minkowski 'block' in which all is there all at once. Time no longer appears to be of any consequence, for the system is once again reversible and symmetrical. Yet, given human semiotic experience (or consciousness, as Eddington uses the term), a sharp division between future and past is definitely established, as well as long-term expectation, habit, and memory, and of a present – though it be no more than mental – with continuously altered borders. These are the hallmarks of Fraser's nootemporal realm, coined from *noetic* (Nôus: mind, or thought). The features of the noetic *Umwelt* are generated by the human capacity as individuals, and especially as communities, to convert experience into signs of Thirdness, symbols, and then manipulate them as part and parcel of the inner world of the mind or of the 'semiotically real.' Beginnings and endings are more clearly defined, forming the bases of private world-images centred around self-identity and consciousness of the *other*. In addition to self-awareness and death-awareness, there is a delineated 'mental presence,' a mind-state lodged between future and past, in addition to the ever-moving linear stream of experience as a 'now' rendering future events past events.

This distinction between mind (nootemporal) and experience (biotem-porality) is that of description in contrast to interpretation-understanding-explanation in traditional hermeneutics, or of textuality in contrast to writing-reading in contemporary critical theory, and of memory-expectations-dispositions (themselves ever-changing) in contrast to linear mnemonic print-outs in cognitive psychology – recall also Löfgren's description-interpretation in chapter 1. The difference is also comparable to that between Borges' (1962) massive aetheneum, his 'Library of Babel,' on the one hand, and the myriad readings of largely unintelligible books by the pathetic seekers of truth contained within it on the other, or between his 'Immortal,' living in an eternal now, and that supernominalist, 'Funes the Memorious,' who was incapable of thinking in generalities, of abstracting, of conceiving the self-identity of things. It is Valéry's 'Monsieur Teste' (1947) as opposed to Beckett's (1955) cerebral rats, 'Molloy,' 'Malone,' and especially 'The Unnamable.'

Speaking of an entire civilization, the languages, arts, sciences, technologies, in sum, all the artefacts of human civilizations, are products of the nootemporal realm, which is vital and ongoing, not statically Platonic – much in the sense of Popper's (1972, 1974) World 3 – to be discussed further in chapter 9. This is a dynamic integrative realm consisting of individuals daily transforming experience into signs according to their inclinations, intuitions, desires, thoughts, beliefs, and even idiosyncrasies and eccentricities. All such signs are, by the very nature of the nootemporal *Umwelt*, sooner or later subjected to countersigns in the sense of censure, negations, refutations, replacement, displacement, and additions and deletions, and they are all-too-often relegated to oblivion or simply ignored. This 'mental presence' with continually changing borders corresponds quite closely to 'real' time as described above. Yet, within the 'block,' there is no 'real' time of experience but only 'static' or *imaginary time*, properly speaking.

Which presents us with the same ageless problem. To give the universe a temporal direction – the domains of entropy – dissipative structures and biology are necessary. To give it history, the human community (nootemporality) is necessary. Yet, in the final analysis, history, or ensemble – which is to say the same, depending upon whether it is viewed as experience or mind – exists in a four-dimensional framework as what appears to be an eternal 'now.' A question thus arises: Is there indeed a 'real' time or is it the figment of our imagination? Is the truly 'real' somehow that of the 'now' of the 'lower' animal and perhaps some sort of mystical state? Or, as Fraser (1982:46–51) argues, is the 'world-line' of the human observer not collapsed into a T-axis enabling it to construct a sharp polarization between past, future, and present, which is assumed or implied prior to the Minkowski construct having been made possible?[6]

Perhaps Jantsch's (1980:231–8) notion of time- and space-binding is apropos here, since quite obviously we are dealing with time, whether it be 'real' or contrived, playing out its role in/through space (see note 20, chapter 1). Such binding comes in three forms: (1) structure-oriented (various past configurations culminate in the same present configuration, and when futurity is added to the equation, it becomes possibly teleological), (2) process-oriented (a past configuration can bifurcate into various present configurations, with futurity introducing a note of teleonomy), and (3) space-oriented (everything is bound to everything else in the system). (1) and (2) are primarily temporal, while (3) can hardly be related to temporality at all; it is purely spatial. And (1) is arborescent, (2) is root-like, and (3) is rhizomic (in the sense of Deleuze and Guattari 1987). *Prima facie*, (3) appears to be the most likely candidate for nootemporality (it is hardly 'temporal' in the sense of biological time), while (2) coincides with biotemporality, and (1) with eotemporality in its thermodynamic incarnation. Appearances are deceiving, however. Microlevel prototemporality in the Prigogine interpretation merges with (1), as it also does with (2). And, in the Peircean sense, there is no distinction of kind but of degree between biotemporality (brain, experience) and nootemporality (mind, thought), which implies a certain modicum of temporality in the latter and spatiality in the former.

Prigogine bears witness to biology's resisting reduction to bare-bones physics in the classical mode, though regarding possible symbiotic relations between biology and twentieth-century physics, any demarcation remains fuzzy at best (Pattee 1970, 1977, 1986). In this light, time- and space-binding are germane to biotemporal *Umwelt*-generated 'semiotically real' worlds. Implying an intensification of life processes, they include the organism's experience of the past and anticipations of the future (that is, the 'real' time of becoming, where everything, including sign, semiotic agent, and the world, is considered in terms of 'organism').

In this light, contemplate figure 9. Here, we have the sphere of vagueness the ultimate extension of which is Peirce's *tychism* – that is, pure chance, and the sphere of *generality* the completion of which, were it possible *for* finite semiotic animal, would become *synechism* – the continuity of all things. The domains of Firstness, Secondness, and Thirdness are linked by the now familiar 'node' or 'empty set,' which would be the ultimate repository of nootemporality (reason, logic, intellect, cognition) and the companion of atemporality. Prototemporality corresponds to microcosmic uncertainty, complementarity, discharging into eotemporality at the mesocosmic level, for practical purposes governed by classical laws. Semiosis takes leave of the inorganic world upon entering biotemporality, where dissipative structures

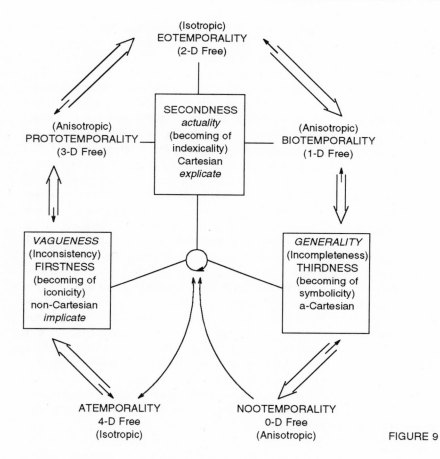

FIGURE 9

take on a more active and creative countenance expressed as a perpetual push toward the outer reach of nootemporality. The 'real' time of one-dimensional experience is contrasted with abstract ('static,' *imaginary*) time in the zone of Thirdness. Within this zone, the mind and its construct, 'mind-stuff,' as anisotropic, enjoys zero dimensions of freedom, but, in terms of its capacity for selection, it is free, exercising its choices as if it were coterminous with isotropy.

3. IS 'MIND-STUFF' RESTLESS OR MERELY LISTLESS?

One might conclude, then, that in the final analysis 'real' time and 'static' or *imaginary time* are all merely the spinning of 'mind-stuff,' another of Eddington's favourite terms. Yet, from a somewhat divergent vantage, they are part and product of a mind, which, if we follow Peirce at this juncture, is somehow in tune with the march of nature, which in turn fecundates the mind.

Mind in the Western tradition has generally been conceived as intellect, timelessness, permanence, that which *is*. Zeno's constructs bear ample witness to the fact that if we follow the logical pathways of the mind with sufficient tenacity we are destined finally to arrive at Parmenides' open arms. 'Achilles overtakes the tortoise' is, of course, false by Zeno's mighty logic. On the other hand, it is true according to experience, as Peirce often remarked – an alternative focus on the pathway of experience that drives us into Heraclitus' rampageous camp. While the intellect, product of the brain-mind, is capable of generating abstract constructs *as if* within the realm of 'static' time where all is eternally *there*, experience, also a product of the mind-brain, is never in the *here-now*; it is never stationary; in fact it is never any-*where* at all. Photons, in the atemporal, are likewise continually in motion; they are restless, chaotic, producing neither rest nor change. The prototemporal realm contains apparently changeless entities, but they are perpetually being transmuted one into another. And the eotemporal provides for permanence of structure, but its laws of motion defy stasis. Permanence is found, it appears, solely in the inner recesses of the mind and in its constructs. In other words, even though 'the arrow flies' is true to our senses but false to Zeno's logic, none the less, Zeno's mind-dependent permanence, or rest, is more basic to the world of the mind than is change. Only in the mind do we find pure examples of invariance and self-identity. Rather than the transient A-series as a mere figment of the mind, according to the nostalgic classical conception, perhaps it is, following Prigogine's advice, more properly the perpetually immutable, perdurable universe that is mind-dependent.

Mental constructs stipulating the primacy of permanence have abounded, of course, from Parmenides to Einstein, and, regarding the universe of signs, we have Saussure's 'block' conception of *langue*. Bunn (1981:138) goes so far as to suggest that 'to put Saussure in a historical context is to place his celebration of synchronic cross sections of the evolutionary tree within a movement that celebrates Einstein's presence' – which evokes reminiscences of Derrida's 'myth of presence.' Even Jakobson (1972) made an effort to demonstrate how structural linguistics and relativity are historically comparable, and perhaps even mutually influenced.[7] Be that as it may, such mental constructs arresting all change, even as it is subjectively experienced, are, if indeed 'mind-stuff,' at their best charged with Parmenidean permanence. That is to say, while mind, following the line of 'real' time, is pure movement, then, if we are to take Peirce seriously, that selfsame mind, while operating in 'static' time, must be in line with permanence. In this respect it cannot but understandably evince the nature of habit.

Now habit, upon becoming increasingly embedded, risks congealment into matter, which is none other than effete mind, Peirce tells us. Yet in light of the above discussions of the self and consciousness, the general consensus seems to have it that there is something, a human being in this case, retaining a certain sense of self-identity, though atoms and molecules are constantly being replaced in her body from birth to death. In this sense, it may be said that to think of a self – *one's* self – as a stable entity without considering its changes throughout this temporal duration is every bit as abstract as thinking of a human being in the *here-now* in terms of an empty surface devoid of viscera. Eddington (1958a:36–62) refers to this self's emergence, development, and decay as it creeps along its 'world-line' much like what we imagined above to be a 'worm-like' trajectory in the four-dimensional space-time continuum. The entire 'worm' projecting out in three-dimensional space and through seventy- or eighty-odd years of time as a function of c – the velocity of light – is a valid picture of the self inhabiting a living and breathing organism. In contrast, conception of this entity as a cross-section in a particular 'here-now' of the four-dimensional 'block' is radically abstractive – comparable, say, to a mere segment taken from an adult tapeworm. Yet, since the sections are abstracted somewhat differently by different observers, there is hardly even a self-identical self in a given '*here-now.*' Each space-time slice from an indefinite number of possible vantages is different with respect to all other space-time slices. Thus in spite of the relentless criticism by, among others, Milic Capek (1961, 1965), of what he conceives to be the Minkowski myth of a deep-frozen ice-cube universe, the 'block' idea is actually not static from the perspective of experienced time.

However, Capek's desires to the contrary, the problem remains. The space-bound nootemporal sphere within which mind operates persists in its appearance of incompatibility with the eo-biotemporality of the time-bound experiencing self. An example pitting our world against that of Ludwig can illustrate my point. Suppose a basketball star exclaims: 'I've improved my game considerably since the start of the season!' Ludwig, given his/her view *sub species aeternitatis*, might respond:

'There is no evidence to back up your assertion. I see you merely as a static four-dimensional entity extended along space-time. Granted, toward the upper extremity of your world-line you slam-dunk a basketball more "spectacularly" (as you put it, actually I have no value judgment to make concerning the issue), but I do not isolate this characteristic from any of your other attributes. As far as I'm concerned, nothing is any "better" than anything else – if, heaven forbid, I dare make even this value judgment, for it is not really within my province to do so – but your feeling, seeing, and thinking merely make it so. Every facet of you is simply *there*. Your conception of "becoming" a better slam-dunker, if not merely illusory, implies that you have some preconceived notion of up and down, development and decay, good and bad, and so on, which as far as I am concerned are non-existent.'

Of course, Ludwig dwells solely in what I have termed 'static' or *imaginary time*, or perhaps something roughly the equivalent thereof. For this reason, a serious difficulty seems to persist with respect to any attempt to link the world of contemporary physics – that of Ludwig – with our world of experience, which includes 'real' time, or for that matter, with respect to any attempt to link the world of deterministic classical mechanics and the statistical concept of entropy – as Peirce was well aware, hence his subtle critique of classical mechanics (Murphey 1961). Is the universe always already *here-now* and becoming a figment of our imagination, or is our linear experience commensurate with the universe's process? In spite of our intuitive conviction that the 'dynamic time' of our experience is 'real,' it would be possible, given either classical mechanics or relativity, to take the view that there is no becoming in the physical world. As Eddington puts it: 'My consciousness then invents its own serial order for the sense impressions belonging to the different view-points along the track in the external world, occupied by the four-dimensional worm who is in some mysterious way Myself; and in focussing the sensation of a particular view-point I get the illusion that the corresponding external events are "taking place"' (1958b:92).

Eddington's 'worm,' *prima facie*, evinces a rough parallel with our tropological earthworm in its prototemporal Lineland. But the analogy soon self-destructs. Our earthworm's 'Now this, now this' bears no indication of any form of consciousness 'higher' than one-dimensional. In contrast, the Eddington-'worm's' consciousness generating memory and anticipation is a *sine qua non* for our experience of 'real' time. That is, Eddington's 'worm' is quite properly eo-biotemporal, and in addition it falls into the domain of nootemporality, unlike our imaginary 'earthworm,' limited to prototemporality. Consequently, the 'world-line' of Eddington's individual making up her particular 'worm-self-identity' is one-dimensionality sensed as a flow, like a transient point along a line. Her 'past' has one kind of existence (constituting memory), her future another existential mode (bearing on anticipations) and her-self as a transient point along her 'world-line' yet another one (the 'now'). In other words, this individual's 'world-line' entails one-dimensional generativity within a three-dimensional domain – once again comparable to Bunn's C and F units.

One might baulk in the face of my positing the necessity of three dimensions, for after all, the 'worm-line' is merely a one-dimensional trajectory. However, if one considers the one-dimensional time-line as curving through space in partly arbitrary fashion, it should become clear that the domain within which the line is supposedly 'trapped' must consist of three-dimensions – as a matter of fact, as we shall observe below, it consists of n-dimensions. Experienced 'time,' prior to clocks and measure, and perhaps independently of the Second Law of Thermodynamics – though in this regard there has been speculation to the contrary – continues to elude analytical description. It cannot be subjected to analysis because its unidirectionality cancels the possibility of its having a contrary. It simply *is as it is*, somewhat in the manner of Peirce's Firstness.

The space-bound realm of intellect or the mind, in contrast, lends itself to timeless intellectual procedures. Here, relations of symmetry, (self-)reflexivity, and identity-similarity-difference prevail. For example, by way of intellect, a domain can be semiotically mapped, modelled, or diagrammed. The map is an icon that indicates (indexes) the mapped domain, and its meaning (the interpretant) by way of Thirdness, orchestrates both the map and its domain, ideally with the accompaniment of symbolicity, given a certain degree of arbitrariness inherent in a portion of the totality of the map (which is especially prominent in mathematical mapping and modelling). All always already exists, as an integrated whole, whether in the mind (space-binding, Fraser's nootemporality), or slapped down on a flat surface (Bunn's B, C, and E units, or A, D, and F units as products having been, or to be, performed).

This is rather a far cry from eo-biotemporal experience, which enjoys solely transient relations that can mutely be pointed to but not effectively described, mapped, or modelled (Bunn's time-bound A through F units as performances only). The situation regarding experience, significantly, is comparable to the Zen question 'What is the sound of one hand clapping?' and other such koans. No words can convey a particular experience or the apparent impossibility of any such experience. Words and analysis are an artificial sieve through which experience passes unmolested. The intrinsic order of experience is exclusively time-like and nonanalytical rather than space-like and describable by static Cartesian coordinates. Experienced time, it might be contended, falls in line with Kant's notion of space and time as a priori. However, space and time in separation are by no means a priori. Rather, the linear succession of events – occupying space – in time constitutes the a priori, if a priori there must be.[8]

In short, experience unidirectionally moves along a 'worm-line,' and thus senses 'real' time. Mind or intellect, in contrast, when putting on its best show is capable of halting the movement of the point, the 'now,' along the line as if it were a static trajectory in three-dimensional space. This is comparable to a

TABLE 7

EXPERIENCE One-dimensional (Domain of sign-events and perception)	INTELLECT Four-dimensional (Domain of thought-signs, conception, and memory)
1. Matrix of feeling.	1. Matrix of mind.
2. Provides movement, content, and value.	2. Provides measure, form, and concept.
3. Asymmetrical.	3. Symmetrical.
4. Ordering in one direction.	4. Ordering in any direction.
5. Ordering in time (A-series).	5. Ordering in space (B-series).
6. Sequentiality, irreversibility.	6. Simultaneity, reversibility.
7. Possibility $\rightarrow$ Actuality.	7. Potentiality-Necessity.
8. Firstness $\rightarrow$ Secondness.	8. Thirdness.
9. Might-be $\rightarrow$ Is.	9. Would-be.
10. Quality $\rightarrow$ Happens-to-be.	10. Habit, regularity.
11. Tone-*vagueness*, token.	11. Type-*generality*.

shark's pursuit of its prey in its three-dimensional H_2O medium. The pursuit is a temporal process when experienced. When analysed, in contrast, it is a static line defined at all points by three numbers along the $x, y,$ and z axes. Experience is one-dimensionally Heraclitean; intellect is n-dimensionally Parmenidean. The first is kinetic, providing for dynamic movement, content, and value; the second is static, lending itself to measure, form, and concept. The first is ordered temporally in one-direction in n-dimensional space; the second is ordered in many-directions timelessly, in an exclusively space-binding mode. The first is the possibility of Firstness coupled with the actuality of Secondness; the second is the potentiality-necessity of Thirdness (see table 7, which encapsulates many of the concepts discussed thus far and others to be discussed in more detail below.)[9]

It must be said, however – and with reference to figure 9 – that intellection cannot stand alone. Measure, form, and concept, products of mind, like Thirdness, mediation, and synthesis, depend ultimately upon time for their development: there are no simultaneities but only *differences* and *deferments*. And temporal movement, the product of experience filling out the content of the world, must be construed as if it were space in order to reduce it to the analytical rigours of intellection – that is, a given entity's 'world-line,' *pace* relativity theory, or our 'worm-line,' in light of the above. Our 'real' universe is that of concrete experience; 'mind-stuff,' in contrast, is what dreams, that is, illusions, are made of. Concrete experience may be in tune with the 'real,' but in such case we shall not stand a ghost of a chance of describing it faithfully. 'Mind-stuff' will always fall short of the mark, though if we are lucky we will be able to say it and know it with a certain degree of precision. In short, 'left-brain' experience is by and large Bunn's C mode; 'right-brain' experience is comparable the F mode. Mind or intellect, in contrast, 'highlights' space, 'suppresses' time, and reduces 'torque' to a minimum – that is, action is atrophied, mind is hypertrophied. We have here the distinction between our feel of a car's acceleration on the one hand, and the object's trajectory slapped onto a graph, *en bloc*, on the other.

4. THEN WHAT IS SEMIOTICALLY 'OUT THERE'?

But a problem continues to persist, when the immediately preceding discussion is placed alongside Peirce's 'Man-Mind $\approx$ Sign' equation. If matter is indeed effete mind, if the 'stuff' of the world consists of the fluid magma of thought-signs having become habitualized and solidified into a lava bed of habit, then the idea of brain as matter from which mind emerges raises the enigmatic question: What is a mind that it may be capable of conceiving a brain capable of generating a mind, or vice versa?

Edgar Morin formulates the problem thus: 'The mind is an outgrowth of the brain, which is itself a representation of the mind. The mind is, as an activity, a product of the brain, itself a biological organ that can only be recognized by the mind in and through a cultural organization. Thus, in a circle always mediated by a society and a culture, the brain can only conceive of itself via the mind, but the mind can conceive of itself only via the brain' (1987:10).

Eddington (1958b:276), upon suggesting that 'the stuff of the world is mind-stuff' is not propagating the notion that 'mind' refers to what we ordinarily mean by mind or to the 'stuff' we commonly consider the furniture of the world. The 'mind-stuff' of the world is something more general than the content of a set of individual conscious minds or a collection of physical things. It is rather more akin to Schrödinger's oneness of consciousness, following his paradox of number – that is, of discrete *and* dense series, of discontinuity *and* continuity – as I have discussed it elsewhere (Merrell 1991b).[10]

That is, though we consider consciousness to exist in plural form equal to the number of conscious subjects, the term is used in the singular: all consciousness is a merge of individualized consciousness into one; it is the joint product of all consciousness. In this vein, a categorical distinction between matter and fields of force as defined by classical mechanics is irrelevant when regarding the world in terms of 'mind-stuff.' Matter simply as a mathematical sign put to use in quantum theory and relativity is more apropos. The mathematical sign, as symbol, is arbitrary in terms of its form, and as index, it takes its rightful place as part of the whole of the universe – though it is merely a thought-sign referring to other thought-signs – and as icon it is capable of creating an image, which, even though unimaginable and unvisualizable, patterns a mind construct potentially in tune with the whole or some aspect of it thereof. Once again, as Peirce puts it, mind, at its best, is in tune with nature.[11]

In this sense, just as mind is sign, so also matter, in so far as it is described by contemporary physics, and unlike the Cartesian-Newtonian corpuscular-kinetic paradigm, is 'sign-like' and 'event-like' more than it is 'thing-like.'[12] For example, when Shakespeare's Macbeth saw (or thought he saw) a dagger before him, dagger-neurons not in the least resembling a dagger 'out there' or his concept of a dagger were firing inside his skull. In his central cerebral clearing-house a dagger message was sorted and decoded, partly by an instinctive capacity to construct images inherited from his ancestors and partly by his learned ability to distinguish between the myriad items that incessantly present themselves in his cultural world. He sensed a variously coloured elongated patch (Firstness). Then the sensation was jacked up to the level of consciousness such that the patch became something *other*, 'out there' (Secondness) and apart from the *self*. And finally, by inference (Thirdness), Macbeth arrived at the thought of a dagger before him.[13]

As Eddington (1958b:278) puts it, 'we are acquainted with an external world because its fibres run into our consciousness; it is only our own ends of the fibres that we actually know; from these ends we more or less successfully reconstruct the rest, as a paleontologist reconstructs an extinct monster from its footprint.' Or as Macbeth reconstructs a dagger in his mind, a thought-sign, rendering it apparently coterminous with the furniture of his world 'out there.' This is by no means to imply that a mind-state is tantamount to a state of affairs in the world 'out there,' or that 'mind-stuff' is in any form or fashion identical to consciousness. Rather, it suggests that whatever 'mind-stuff' is, it is, when placed alongside the physical world for comparison, inordinately paltry and drastically incomplete. Whatever happens to be in consciousness as 'mind-stuff' at a given moment at least partly fades out of consciousness in the next moment and is replaced with something else. 'Mind-stuff' is actually quite transient; it is fleeting; when one attempts to think of it, in Peirce's words, it 'has flown.' As such it is radically indeterminate and indefinite.

Nevertheless, there is according to Peirce something 'out there' continuous with 'mind-stuff' residing 'in here,' which makes up one's 'semiotic reality.' 'Real world-stuff,' however, is such that both mind and 'reality' as it is perceived and conceived – that is, 'semiotic reality' – originate from it. Limited islands of this 'real world-stuff' may constitute, and may be constituted by, actual minds, each of which makes up a radically deficient inventory of what there is. Yet the only approach to 'real world-stuff' is through the mind, or Thirdness, which must always mediate between one's repertory of signs and the nuts and bolts of the 'real world' to fabricate a 'semiotically real' domain. We do not live in the physical world as it is, but in an *Umwelt*-emergent 'symbolic universe,' as Ernst Cassirer writes, much in the spirit of Peirce's dialogical mode: 'Physical reality seems to reduce in proportion as man's symbolic activity advances. Instead of dealing with the things themselves man is in a sense constantly conversing with himself. He has so enveloped himself in linguistic forms, in artistic images, in mythical symbols of religious rites that he cannot see or know anything except by the interposition of this artificial medium' (1944:25).

I must add that Eddington does not concoct the term 'mind-stuff' with the intention of materializing or substantiating the mind. His 'stuff' refers to function, not form or content. Moreover, he concedes that the matter-of-fact physicist of his day would find his notion that the substratum of the physical world is of mental character a difficult pill to swallow. None the less, he proposes, without reservation, that:

no one can deny that mind is the first and most direct thing in our experience, and all else is remote inference – inference either intuitive or deliberate. Probably it would never have occurred to us (as a serious hypothesis) that the world could be based on anything else, had we not been under the impression that there was a rival stuff with a more comfortable kind of 'concrete' reality – something too inert and stupid to be capable of forging an illusion. The ['semiotically real'] rival turns out to be a schedule of pointer readings; and though a world of symbolic character can well be constructed from it, this is a mere shelving of the enquiry into the nature of the world of experience. (1958b:281)

While I generally agree with Eddington, I would suggest a few amendments, for the sake of semiotic theory. First, not only is the world 'out there' nothing more than 'inference,' a realm of 'symbolic [that is, semiotic] character,' but so also the mind (and self, 'I,' consciousness) – none of which is 'remote,' by the way, but at one with the semiosic gush of things. Eddington's 'rival,' what is taken to be the concrete world of thing-stuff – a matter of 'pointer readings' for the contemporary physicist – is neither immediately nor directly available to empirical detection but only mediately and indirectly so. Hence it can be no more than *symbolic*, since its immediate or *iconic* (qualitative) and *indexical* (actual fact) characteristics are destined to remain beyond the grasp of any finite community of semiotic agents. The 'rival,' then, is 'semiotically real,' not the 'really real' *an sich*, knowledge of which must also remain to a greater or lesser degree incomplete.

In this sense, the 'semiotically real' is the product of a cyclical or undulatory wave-like scheme (that is, brain-mind-brain-mind ... *n*), a sort of Boolean wave-train.[14] By its very nature, it can only be a partial expression of the 'actually real,' which invariably slips through the mesh of the knower's net. It is lost, but, according to Peirce, inasmuch as the knower can know only in the event that she becomes aware of her having erred – that is, of the fact that she does *not know* – then, from a broad view of things, her knowledge cannot but consist of one illusion after another. None of her 'reality' constructs can at all points be coterminous with the 'actually real,' yet each enjoys at least a few lines of coherence with it.

As Nelson Goodman (1978) would trenchantly counsel, one must choose a world and proceed to weave one's fanciful illusions, delusions, and figments into it, for worlds are fabricated rather than found, and they are constructed more by prevarication than by predetermination. Traditionally, Western science has striven to demolish the myths, illusions, and fancies – mere playthings for immature minds, it was assumed – in order to reveal the one and only 'reality.' But this enterprise has itself been elusive and illusive, for we have 'torn away the mental fancies to get at the reality beneath, only to find that the reality of that which is beneath is bound up with its potentiality of awakening these fancies. It is because the mind, the weaver of illusions, is also the only guarantor of reality that reality is always to be sought at the base of illusion' (Eddington 1958b:319).

And a circle has been completed, from the initial state of Fraser's four dimensions free of atemporality to the final state of four dimensions committed in the domain of nootemporality. A 'Linelander' enjoys one degree of freedom, a 'Flatlander' two degrees, and a 'Spherelander' three degrees, if we discount the linear time dimension in each case. However, time cannot be ignored. It begins very significantly to exercise its force in the biotemporal domain, and in the nootemporal it allows for untold freedom, but at the same time severely restricts the time-bound organism, especially the human semiotic agent.

The purely nootemporal Ludwig, with his/her atemporal, hypermental Parmenidean grasp of the totality as *plenum*, inhabits a massive orb in which everything *is there* and *has always already happened*, as if he/she dwelt within the 'node' in figures 3 and 9. This is the result of his/her having 'filled' an infinity of originally free dimensions, aided by his/her infinitely rich perceptual and cognitive faculties. His/her sphere of existence is comparable to that of the topologist whose posited space on a sheet of paper before her consists of an infinity of points awaiting her decision to establish some sort of domain. The possibilities for future constructs are without end.

Mix Ludwig as sheer possibility (Firstness) together with the biological organism's actualized 'world-line' (Secondness), add a dose of consciousness and self-consciousness (Thirdness), then bake well in order to bring about a semiotic fusion, and we have concocted a Peirce-Bohr – Wheeler-Prigogine *participatory universe* evolving toward some undefined receding horizon.

5

Space-Time, and the Place of the Sign

In light of the disquisition on Peirce's concept of semiosis as living process in chapters 1 and 2, Bunn's and Fraser's dimensionality theses regarding tables 5 and 6 call for further consideration.

Upon embarking on the journey I review Piaget's developmental-constructivist theory of cognition as an introduction and tie-in to Patrick Heelan's provocative argument that Euclidean space is no more than a pinch-hitter standing in for a more deeply rooted 'hyperbolic' mode of perception and conception of the world. I argue, following Heelan, that the transition to our Euclidean mind-set is illustrated through Renaissance painting by means of the infinitely receding vanishing-point sucking in what are tacitly construed to be parallel lines. I then exercise a tangential move toward the continuity/discontinuity and A-series/B-series themes for the purpose of re-entrenching the natural gravitation of sign processes toward lifelike processes as they become more complex. This serves to re-evoke the image of Prigogine-style nonlinearity, which finally integrates Bunn's one-dimensional semiotics into our three-dimensional sphere of existence.

These moves should help prepare the ground for chapters 6, 7, 8, and 9, the first two consisting of a glance at what I consider to be some erroneous hypotheses regarding our postmodern milieu – an extension of the topic as developed in Merrell (1995) – and the latter two culminating in the phenomena of cell growth and sign growth, of signs of life and the life of signs.

1. CONCERNING THE FALLACY OF MISPLACED FIRSTNESS

To recap, three-dimensional semiotics – A and D in table 5 – highlights three-dimensionality, while either two-dimensionality is 'torqued' and one-dimensionality is 'suppressed' (A: neolithic pots, utensils, tools, instruments), or one-dimensionality is 'torqued' and two dimensionality is 'suppressed' (D: dance, pantomime, theatre, sculpture). In either case, objects, acts, and events are basically perceived and conceived in terms of three-dimensionality.

The difference between the two modes of three-dimensional semiotics rests in the A mode's utilization by means of a two-dimensional surface or plane (that is, a pot is potted in two-dimensional trajectories, a wrench is operated by planar rotation, shears cut a plane along another orthogonal plane), and the D mode's showing, by a succession of objects, acts, or events, movement along a one-dimensional trajectory (that is, the to-and-fro swaying of a modern dance artist, the orchestrated comings and goings on the stage at a playhouse, the lines being created in a sculpted work of art or on the façade of a baroque cathedral). In the first case the entire surface and the necessary activity its use demands is reiterative in two dimensions; in the second case, movements are along a one-dimensional 'world-line' and relatively free to develop as their author sees fit in n-directions: activity is open to vectorial forces, tangents, calculated twists and turns, and arbitrary flights in any of a potentially infinite number of directions. Utilization of the first is relatively restricted and closed, though certain parameters of freedom are permitted, while use and play of the second is quite free-wheeling. In short, dance, theatre, sculpture, architecture, and other media are among those activities requiring a third dimension in order that they be adequately countenanced (three-dimensional semiotics, it also bears mentioning, includes bodily gestures and other nonverbal signs requiring spatial depth for their proper display).

The world of A and D semiotics is chiefly that of *Homo faber*, the craftsperson, artisan, and artist. It is the haptic hands-on world of grasping, groping, grappling, exploring, getting a feel for things. The most exemplary of practical activities regarding three-dimensional semiotics is found in Fraser's biotemporal realm, according to which three dimensions are committed, and one dimension remains free. This semiotic mode involves exosomatic tools and instruments, their development and their use, which facilitates the 'internalization' of aspects of the 'semiotic world out there.' Such 'internalization' is parcel and product of the *Umwelt*-generated and governed 'semiotic world' having become reconfirmed, renewed, and re-entrenched, which at the same time serves the semiotic agent as self-confirmation, self-renewal, and self-entrenchment, in her incessant dialogue with her external world, with her social *other*, and with her *other* self. The semiotic realm of biotemporality, of course, is by no means limited to the human animal. Birds build nests, beavers dams, bees hives, and ants beds, all of which are a manifestation of their interaction with their 'semiotic world' according to their assimilation of it and their accommodating themselves to it. The 'real world' is to a degree altered by their coming into existence and their passing away, just as it is altered by all signs – though unlike their counterparts, human semiotic agents, they leave their world basically as they found it. Each organism is in this sense an ephemeral sign, a slight vortex somewhere along the flow. The flow was responsible for bringing it into existence, and its existence changes the flow, even though to an almost infinitesimal degree. And things manage to get on.

Given the obvious difficulties with respect to our empathizing in any form or fashion with the *Umwelten* of nonhuman agents (see Merrell 1995), I shall hereafter limit myself to the social construction of our own 'semiotic world.' The products of three-dimensional semiotics from within human biotemporality can be related to what in scientific – as well as humanistic – endeavours Rom Harré (1970) calls 'homeomorphic' (iconic) models, of which scale models and toys are most exemplary. 'Homeomorphic' models are intuited, developed, and perceived chiefly from within the domain of secondary qualities, of what is on the surface to be seen and sensed in terms of relatively immediate and less mediated sensations.[1] These items of experience, rather than mere two-dimensional surfaces, are actually three-dimensional entities the intuition, conception, creation, and perception of which move along one-dimensional trajectories – 'world-lines' – in three-dimensional space. This one-dimensional characteristic is indeed significant. Our faculties are such that they can operate along it in n-directions *as if* only one dimension were at any point committed and three remained free (I write *as if*, for this relatively open degree of freedom does not exist solely within the domain of A and D activities, but, as we shall note, more properly within C and F).

Development of our intuition and creative capacities along 'homeomorphic,' iconic lines of Firstness has been shunted aside by Baconian science, especially from Galileo onward, when mainstream scientists and philosophers began contending that science delivered us from the primitive innocence of mundane experience. As I have intimated above, classical science asserted that the world merely appears to be multicoloured, noisy, many-scented, hot, cold, and lukewarm, but these are no more than secondary qualities, which are quite unimportant for classical science. There is actually nothing but the scurry of colourless, invisible particles, waves of air, and electromagmetic radiation, that is, of primary qualities, which are all-important. Subjective secondary qualities were first suppressed, then revived when the soon-to-be romantics awakened from their dogma of neoclassical slumbers, and finally they gave way to the smug world of wide-eyed scientific objectivity. And the yawning chasm widened between appearance and reality. Whitehead sketches the dilemma effectively:

Bodies are perceived as with qualities which in reality do not belong to them, qualities which in fact are purely the offspring of the mind. Thus nature gets credit which should in truth be reserved for ourselves; the rose for its scent; the nightingale for his song; and the sun for his radiance. The poets are entirely mistaken. They should address their lyrics to themselves, and should turn them into odes of self-congratulation on the excellency of the human mind. Nature is a dull affair, soundless, scentless, colourless; merely the hurrying of material, endlessly, meaninglessly. (1925:56)

This unimaginable, well-nigh ineffable, scientific picture of 'reality' has effectively held us captive; it has seduced us with its rather perverse charm. Odours, tastes, colours, sounds, and surfaces were banished from the kingdom of the 'real' and left to find their way as best they could through the labyrinthine catacombs below, while above, three-dimensional items in three-dimensional space, each in proud possession of its particular 'world-line;' simply moved about, apparently *as if* oblivious to any and all aspects of Peircean Firstness. They were pure Secondness, which, when injected with a strong dose of mathematics and positivistic science, gained entrance – albeit artificially, as it were – into the domain of Thirdness (cf. table 7). Were Hermann Ludwig von Holmholtz and John B. Watson in psychology; that supreme romantic mechanist, Sigmund Freud in psychoanalysis; Herbert Spencer and Gustave le Bon in social engineering; and twentieth-century logical positivists, behaviourists, physicalists, and various and sundry remnants of the mechanical model of the human organism and nature – were all these to have their say, the nightmares of cybersociety forecast by gloomy futurologists would by now certainly be close at hand. But fortunately for us all, and thanks to the insistence of poets, artists, a few maverick scientists and philosophers, and other upstarts, since romanticism we can hardly disregard aesthetic matters.

In light of the dependence of three-dimensional semiotics on Firstness, iconicity, poetic insight, the art of getting a feel for things, Bunn's worlds of *A* and *D* are in even more general terms the domain of *Homo spatifex*, that is, the human animal capable of imagining, constructing, and shaping space. I am not writing of Kant's aprioristic particularity of space, following Newton's mechanics, which was superseded by Einstein. Rather, I refer to 'space' according to its myriad definitions: an empty receptacle for the furniture of the world, a Euclidean or non-Euclidean physical, empirical, and conceptual representation, which includes Hilbert space of infinite dimensions, phase space of the sort exploited by 'chaos physics,' and most of all, 'haptic space' – topological forms – which will be the chief focus of our attention here. 'Haptic space' does not refer exclusively to that which is seen, but rather, to surface impressions, sensations that are as much nonvisual as visual. To 'see' things as they really are has through the centuries in traditional thought ordinarily – though erroneously – implied a plumbing of the depths, the perception of something not readily available to the senses of common folk.

Haptic or homeomorphic models in this respect go against the grain. They are like the blind person's cane. It renders otherwise unseeable and virtually unintelligible three-dimensional objects in three-dimensional space a mite more intelligible by making them subject to nonvisual sensory impressions by means of an instrument operating along a one-dimensional track – a surface – in many directions. Homeomorphic models, quite comparably, afford relatively immediate surface likeness between *modelans* and *modelandum*. They are three-dimensional, to be sure, but their surface is much like a two-dimensional skin constructed by the one-dimensional recursive unfolding and enclosing of a three-dimensional space. Attending solely to the skin is like the Flatlander dwelling on the surface of a sphere for whom the only world is a two-dimensional world, yet his very existence depends upon a one-dimensional tracing of his exterior features. Homeomorphic models, in this sense, are thoroughly topological (see Merleau-Ponty 1962:143).

A conventional and visualizable three-dimensional homeomorphic model *par excellence* is found in that of the DNA molecule, which, following enantiomorphic – that is, left-handed/right-handed mirror-image – principles, is topological, that is, 'haptic,' before it is visual. DNA is composed of amino acids based on carbon and other components – nitrogen, hydrogen, oxygen, and various radicals formed from these elements – that can exist in two optical forms. As a result, proteins consisting of chains of amino acids form helices whose twist is always right-handed. All in all, we have a megamolecule of what appear to be linearly generated higgledy-piggledy twists and turns in space ultimately creating the essence of a three-dimensional visual paradox – comparable to many of Escher's works, or to the two-dimensional Möbius strip requiring a third dimension for its unfoldment.

Intriguing though homeomorphic models combined with three-dimensional semiotics may be, a question surfaces: How can we relate the concrete thought-signs and sign-events of everyday life to the equally concrete homeomorphic creations of Western physical sciences as well as the human sciences and philosophy, embedded as they are in ever-deeper levels of abstraction? In search of an answer, I turn to psychologist Jean Piaget's theory of cognition.

2. ENLIGHTENED EGOMANIACS OR LITTLE BOOLEAN SAVAGES?

Bunn (1981:66–7) alludes to Piaget's (1970) work on the sensory-motor development of children, culminating with the thesis that topological perception and conception of moving objects precedes an understanding of Euclidean conventions. Piaget's child's topological manipulation of significant shapes and their representation in three-dimensional space entails attention most specifically to surface features. Indeed, the fascination of children with Mother Goose, Winnie the Pooh, and most especially, Alice's adventures – also a favourite pastime of logicians, mathematicians, and physicists – attests to their import to 'primitive' perceptual and conceptual modes, keenly picked up by philosopher Gilles Deleuze (1967; also Lecercle 1985). I shall take Bunn's suggestion a step further for the purpose of illustrating the haptic quality of three-dimensional semiotics, and ultimately, its relation to Fraser's biotemporal domain of three dimensions committed and one free.

The very small infant does not behave as if her perception and conception of the world were something separated from herself and containing a set of more or less permanent objects. Rather, her initial experience, Piaget argues, is that of an almost undifferentiated totality. She has not yet learned to distinguish between 'inner' and 'outer' worlds (or thought-signs and sign-events), but senses one world in an ongoing flux of sensations and feelings, with hardly anything recognizable as permanent. That is, she has not separated her-*self*, considered as stable, from the rush of experience so as to order the latter more or less in conformity with the former. It is as if she existed in the atemporal realm of chaos, chance, pure possibility; she is barely in touch with any facet or fashion of Firstness; hence it remains vague in the extreme.

At this early stage in her life she is, however, endowed with certain inborn proclivities regarding nourishment, comfort, and so on. These proclivities are subject to development enabling her to accommodate herself to various aspects of her environment, beginning with recognizable factors of it that serve as food, things to explore with the senses, things that threaten, and so on. The child is at this stage a long shot from the concept of permanent objects and causal relationships (Secondness) between them, however. She is able to abstract only vague, hazy, uncertain, and hardly recognizable blocks of her sensory data and coordinate them in a rough manner with her responses. The flux of her experience is gradually becoming ordered, and certain invariant factors of her surroundings are slowly being recognized. Yet, as long as she views all features of her surroundings as a totality, she develops no clear-cut distinction between 'inside' and 'outside,' here and there. There is no definite Secondness of self and *other*.

Soon she begins to perceive intermediate connections in space and time between the items of her world as she learns to coordinate eye movements, locate the origin of sounds she perceives, and develop her sensorimotor capacities by haptically exploring objects with which she comes in contact. She now begins to construct a rather nebulous mental image of her world containing perceived and unperceived items, and of herself as apart from *otherness*. The items of her world consequently begin to take on more or less permanent character as a result of their organization in her spatial field, brought about by the coordination of her movements over temporal periods. These coordinations presuppose a rudimentary notion of the return of an object to its point of origin (reversibility), and a change in the direction of its movements (associativity), thus taking on the fundamentals of a mathematical 'group.'

When the child is about 18 months to two years of age, the 'symbolic function' appears, chiefly as a result of our child's initial acquisition of language. Symbolic play, the commencement of an ability to create imaginary constructs, to conceive of signs referring to absent objects, acts, and events as if they were present, and especially, to what *is not as if it were* – a *sine qua non* for human semiotics according to Eco (1976, 1984) – demands the notion of before, after, and now. That is to say, the concept of time, of something occurring after the original event, that form of internal imitation or imagination giving rise to thought-signs, emerges. As a result of the symbolic function, *representation*, the internalization of objects, acts, and events 'out there,' becomes possible. The child's immediate surroundings can now be related to past situations, and anticipations can be built up regarding possible future situations. In Peircean terms, the child can now enter into the process of habit-taking and belief-formation; she is on that long road toward contrary-to-fact conditionals, to hypothetico-deductive inferential processes that entail recognizing, realizing, or imagining what *would be, would have been*, or *will have been* the case if certain patterns of conditions happen to inhere. She has now gained entrance into the initial stage of Thirdness, which, at approximately age seven to eleven years, will prepare her for Piaget's 'concrete operations' of the sort necessary for putting into effect Peirce's 'pragmatic maxim.'

During this stage, logical operations involving *inclusion, asymmetry, nonreflexivity*, and *seriation* or *transitivity* are developed. These operations are crucial in constructing the concepts of number, time, and motion, and especially in assimilating geometrical relations of Euclidean topology within chronometric time. Positive and negative integers and the system of linear measurement are developed in close association with operations of class and relation. Rather than the relations of propositional logic, however, these relations remain at a concrete stage. Formal operations are not yet completely dissociated from concrete data; in other words, concrete fields are developed separately, without their being classified into full-blown generals. These concrete operational systems consequently remain to a degree fragmentary. They can be classified and ordered serially, but ordinarily they are not combined into structured

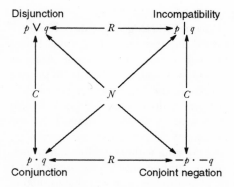

FIGURE 10

wholes. As Piaget puts it, they have not attained complete 'equilibrium' – to be defined later.

Finally, our subject enters into her final stage of development from roughly eleven to fifteen years of age. The new feature marking this stage is the appearance of hypothetico-deductive reasoning by the use of formal operations. In Peircean terms, progression of thought-signs is no longer exclusively a matter of 'Possible → Actual → Probable (Potential),' or 'Abduction → Induction → Deduction,' but rather, from abducted possibilities directly to hypothetico-deductive theoretical schemes that are then given a chance to prove themselves on the stage of actual everyday (inductive) practices. Primacy is now placed squarely on Thirdness, on thought-signs, on operational schemata. The subject no longer sits around waiting for something interesting to happen, but generates theoretical constructs with which to confirm actual relationships between bits and pieces, and acts and events, of the world. Rather than merely coordinating 'facts,' hypothetico-deductive reasoning pulls out the implications of likelihoods and probabilities, thus giving rise to unique syntheses of the possible and the necessary in order to account for the actual.

In other words, the subject is now concerned with statements, or more formally, propositions (thought-signs as symbols), as well as the world 'out there' (sign-events). Piaget hypothesizes a group of propositional operations the most fundamental of which consist of disjunction ($p \vee q$), conjunction ($p \cdot q$), conjoint negation ($-p \cdot -q$), and incompatibility ($p \mid q$, the equivalent of Sheffer's 'stroke function,' or 'not both $-p$ and $-q$'), illustrated in figure 10. N is an *inverse* operation of *complementarity*: negating $p \vee q$ yields $-p-q$, and vice versa. Operation R is that of reciprocity: negating the one produces the other. And C is that of *correlation*: what is common to both becomes everything included within both, and vice versa. In addition, an 'identity' operator, I, is the combination of operations N, R, and C such that when performed on any proposition, it leaves things unchanged. Hence $CR = N$, $RN = C$, $NC = R$, and $NRC = I$. The entire set of operations constitutes an abstract mathematical 'group' (Mays 1953).

Put it all together, add a dose of logical implication, and we have, Piaget argues, a close connection between a group lattice and the logic of propositions culminating in sixteen binary operations tantamount to a truth-table for two propositions (1953:32–7).[2] These operations do not appear in the adolescent's bag of tricks as unrelated thought processes, as discrete operations, but form a *structured whole*. However, the whole remains by and large implicit, for the adolescent 'is not conscious of the system of propositional operations. He undoubtedly uses these operations, but he does this without enumerating them, or reflecting on them or their relationships, and he only faintly suspects that they form such a system. He is unaware of this, in the same way that in singing or whistling he is unaware of the laws of harmony' (Piaget 1953:39–40).

Such structural wholes are in this sense a priori forms of the mind, and they tend toward states of *equilibrium* as a result of ongoing thought-sign activity. A state of equilibrium:

is one in which all the virtual transformations compatible with the relationships of the system compensate each other. From a psychological point of view, the logical structures correspond precisely to this model. On the one hand, these structures appear in the form of a set of virtual transformations, consisting of all the operations which it would be possible to carry out starting from a few actually performed operations. On the other, these structures are essentially reversible, that is to say, the virtual transformations which they permit are always self-compensatory as a consequence of inversions and reciprocities. (Piaget 1953:41)

In this manner, Piaget asserts, it is possible to account for the subject's being affected by her posited structural wholes without possessing consciousness of them. When beginning with a proposition as a guide to future thought and/or action, she cannot proceed according to her whims or wishes, but finds herself in a 'field of (semiotic) force' governed by the structural laws of equilibrium. She must carry out operations that tend to maintain equilibrium without full awareness of the structural whole, and of her operating on the propositions guiding her thought, actions, and the equilibrating force field. In other words, mathematical combinatorial (group) operations are formed and carried out systematically, and mechanical equilibrium dictating whatever transformations are to occur is virtually automatic, with computer-like certainty. The system is self-regulatory, above all. Reflexivity, reversibility, and symmetry are primary, and if asymmetry or irreversibility should happen to arise, the structural whole exercises a shift so as to reestablish a new state of equilibrium.

And the balanced, harmonious, homeostatic train of events is allowed to go on.

Now, all this appears well and good. For sure, Piaget is correct in observing that knowledge is increasingly regarded more as a process than a state, and that any object science attempts to hold in check almost immediately dissolves in the 'current of development.' It is at the receding horizon of this development, and of it alone, he writes, 'that we have a right to state, "It is (a fact)." What we can and should then seek is the law of this process' (Piaget 1971b:3). Granted, Piaget's reference to equilibrium might initially conjure up the image of a static state. However, to his credit, he has consistently denied the assumption of predetermined forms of equilibrium, opting for successive processes of increasing equilibration intermittently punctuated by periods of nonbalance. He has reiterated time and again his thesis that 'the passage of the nonbalance, or of imperfect forms of equilibrium to 'better' forms, implies at each stage the intervention of new constructions, themselves determined by the requirements of compensations and reequilibrations. In such a model the equilibrium and the creativity are thus more antagonistic but closely *interdependent*' (Piaget 1977:82).

Piaget assures us that his equilibrium is not that of customary definitions: it is 'progressive equilibration,' an 'indispensable process in developing a process whose manifestations show modification from stage to stage' (1971b:17). Equilibration is ongoing, Piaget believes, because self-regulation is hierarchical in terms of its self-organizational manifestation. An initial program of thought and action is subject to modification and enrichment by differentiation, recursive multiplication, coordination of goals, and integration of new items of thought and experience into the whole constituting the subject's mental construct, her perceptual framework, and her conceptual scheme. In the face of disturbances, she can respond in one or a combination of different ways: (1) the disturbance can be *cancelled* (inversion) or *neutralized* (reciprocity), or (2) the subject can *assimilate* it to her cognitive whole and *accommodate* herself to it, thus conserving that whole through (3) a series of internal *transformations*. In whichever case, the tendency is compensatory: all responses are both *constructive* and *conservative*.

Piaget labels his set of behavioural response (1) 'alpha,' (2) 'beta,' and (3) 'gamma.' The succession of behaviours from 'alpha' to 'gamma' constitute, from the cognitive view, passage from endogenous to exogenous or extrinsic (empirically noted) variations. Such passage, Piaget observes, enjoys correlation with the biological phenomenon of 'phenocopy,' that is, the replacement of a phenotype in reaction to outside pressures by a genotype caused by the subject's genetic determinants, which then recursively and endogenously produce the characteristics of the original phenotype − recall the *Ho-t'u* model and the semiotic 'hypercycle.' If the environment is conducive to the production of the standard phenotype ('replication' of the same sign), then there is no push to generate an endogenous reconstruction. In the semiotic terms established in chapter 1, *de-generation* can possibly ensue accompanied by an increase of *vagueness*, with the general direction being from one dimension free to three dimensions free, Thirdness to Firstness, and Boolean to non-Boolean forms. On the other hand, if the exogenous (environmental) conditions are such that nonbalance, or in Prigoginean terms, far-from-equilibrium conditions, arise, then a backlash can result. Such backlash will indicate, by nonlinear interaction, multiple feedback, and eventually the creation of indefinite possibilities for future action, one of them being radical reconstruction (dissipative structures, catastrophes) potentially leading to higher forms of order (out of chaos), via sign *generation*.

But all is not well with Piaget's conservative program, as we shall note by turning to an extrapolation of Piagetian principles.

3. WAYS OF *UMWELTEN*

Ernst von Glaserfeld (1979a, 1979b, 1984) draws inspiration from Piaget in developing his program of 'radical constructivism.' It is 'radical,' Glaserfeld writes, in so far as it incorporates not only the idea that cognition is a process of subjective construction of the world rather than discovery of what is 'out there,' but also, the Kantian (and rather Peircean) belief that there can be no rational access to the world as it *is* prior to and independent of experience: over the long haul, we have nobody but ourselves to thank or to blame for the state our world is in.

In spite of Kant's epistemological and ontological bombshell, metaphysical realism persists, and the bottom line still has it in many quarters that 'reality' is discoverable by way of faithful representations, images, and replicas. This notion, however, implies an infinite regress tactic that has generally been conveniently stuffed in the closet by hopeful epistemological questers but openly embraced by Peircean semiotics. It is this: if the world is there, prior to its knower's knowledge of it, then the knower's representation, image, or replica of it, to be known and judged valid, can be so known and judged solely in terms of some other representation, image, or replica serving as a standard of comparison, and that in terms of others, and so on. As Giambattista Vico would have it, science, like myth and art, approaches the world by means of symbols, and symbols about symbols. And in Peirce's terms, a sign's interpretant is known by another sign, and that by another one, with no end in sight. There is no constraint set up by the dreamy goal of some preordained and/or determinable correspondence between signs and an 'objective reality' that can neither be directly and immediately experienced nor known in the absolute, totalizing sense (Glaserfeld 1974:30–1). Everything can in principle be known, though, of course, only in the theoretical long run, which is infinite in extension. The verdict, in this light, is that Kant is right regarding real practice but somewhat misguided where ideal principles are concerned.

One might retort that common sense must agree with Descartes and refuse Kant's suggestion that God played a trick on us by equipping us with unreliable senses. I shall at least grant that, much in the order of Peirce, our intractable will to believe tends to win in a sparring match with Pyrrhonism's absolute suspension of belief. However, the fact remains that today's common-sense view of the world invariably brings a morsel to a mound of nineteenth-century Newtonian-Euclidean empiricist baggage with it, which persists in cornering our 'empathy' with our world 'out there,' even though in light of the twentieth-century scientific revolution we should know better (Comfort 1984). Recent philosophers of science have developed sceptical arguments (Feyerabend 1975, 1987; Hanson 1958, 1969; Kuhn 1970), concerning science as intersubjectively hermeneutical (Hesse 1980; Kuhn 1977), the combination of which entails a broad 'holistic' view of thought, conceptual schemes, and knowledge that actually dovetails effectively with Michael Polanyi's (1958) equally 'holistic' view of knowledge rooted in personal inclinations, references, and beliefs.

Traditionally, and especially with the onslaught of logical positivism, 'observation sentences' and their counterparts, 'theoretical sentences,' with 'correspondence rules' in between, were capable of supporting or refuting theories, conceptual schemes, and postulated meanings, and perception was taken as hard-core data with which to support or refute particular views of the physical world. What goes by the name of 'holism' contrives to reverse the role of perception and sentences. From the 'holist' view, the world as seen is just that: the world *as we see it*. And the world as we say it is so because *we so say it*. Inside the ballpark of Quine-Davidson 'holism,' a particular sentence enjoys no determinate reference or meaning; neither can it be effectively translated into another language (Merrell 1992:chap. 5). Individual sentences can always be packed into some Procrustean bed or other, whether regarding scientific theories, broad conceptual schemes, or natural languages. Thus there is no adequate method for understanding a language except from within the interacting whole of theories, conceptual schemes, and the 'language games' contained within them. Glaserfeld says much the same, though he enters from the other side of the stage. A hypothetical framework or model and the language in which it is garbed, he asserts, maps one possible way of perceiving and conceiving a commonsensical (that is, 'semiotically real') world.

At the same time, it must remain methodologically, epistemologically, and ontologically uncommitted, thus abstaining, in the Pyrrhonist tradition, from affirming or denying any particular meaning or correspondence to the 'real' world. The question is not 'What is the "real" world?' but 'What is our experienced ("semiotically real") world?' Our particular picture of the world is a *construct*: not what is but what our feelings, desires, inclinations, dispositions, expectations, and habits (from First to Third) want it to be. In another way of putting it, a 'semiotically real' world is an *Umwelt*-emergent invention.[3]

According to Hans Reichenbach's (1956:24–37) brand of 'conventionalism' – quite commensurate with constructivism as outlined here – our visualization of space is neither necessarily Euclidean nor non-Euclidean; it is no more than a particular extract from the three-dimensional manifold. It takes on Euclidean characteristics according to established conventions, which are normative, historical, and cultural. Upon constructing visual images, according to this conception, we bring to bear on the process some antecedent 'logic' – a 'logic of perception' (Rock 1983) – grounded in certain culture-dependent rules of congruence determining the conditions of equal and unequal, straight and curved, homogeneous and heterogeneous, spatial metrics. These rules direct perception, as it were, from outside, and as a result of choice. To be specific, our history, culture, and education have compelled us to adopt Euclidean rules. As a consequence, they have become so deeply embedded in our psyche that Kant erroneously declared Euclidean geometry to be our only possible mode of visualizing objects in space; in fact, our Cartesian-Newtonian corpuscular-kinetic heritage is in part still with us, whether we like it or not (Capek 1961; Skolimowski 1986).

However, Reichenbach tells us that perception – guided by a particular *Umwelt* – has no natural capacity to respond to nature with a specific geometry other than in a partly to wholly illusory manner. In fact, the geometry of a perceptual field can be whatever one makes of it by applying a suitable mathematical transformation to one's conventional Euclidean metric, thus altering the physics of one's world appropriately. We are free to choose virtually any rule of congruence for physical space we like, and if it happens to be non-Euclidean, it will allow us to perceive our world with a corresponding non-Euclidean geometry. With such a revised slant on things, a new 'art' of visualization can then be assimilated, and we will consequently see the world 'through different eyes,' so to speak. The upshot is, Reichenbach tells us, that we possess the intuitive capacity to discard our Euclidean maps and adapt ourselves to one of an indefinite number of non-Euclidean constructs, in the process changing our visual imagination of pictorial objects. This capacity, he claims, has been exercised effectively by mathematicians, especially in the budding field of topology.

Now, Reichenbach's rather positivist-empiricist view is problematic in so far as it fails adequately to account for our *Umwelt*-based limitations, given the neurophysiological channels available to us. Logic and mathematics alone are not necessarily sufficient for training and governing perception. There is a natural compulsion automatically to see pictorial forms according to *Umwelt*-determined limitations and cultural-conventional inculcations. If it were a matter merely of mathematics, then there seems to be no reason why we could not become tantamount to a strictly Boolean-brained digital computer or why the computer could not be programmed to perceive objects in the same way we do, commensurate with the dreams of artificial intelligence researchers.

Given our freedom of choice – and despite *Umwelt*-bound circumscriptions – Patrick Heelan (1983:163–4) argues in reference to various empirical studies that a non-Euclidean (hyperbolic) power of visualization naturally antecedes Euclidean perception and is independent of the perceiver's deliberate act of selection in the Reichenbach sense. In this light, Piaget demonstrated quite convincingly that children recognize topological and non-Euclidean properties before they learn to recognize Euclidean properties (Piaget and Inhelder 1956:147). Heelan now takes a step further regarding human perception in general, postulating that independently of logic, mathematics, and any other instrumental measuring technique, 'human perception naturally (i.e. easily) reads the optical clues so as to assume – at least episodically – the form of hyperbolic [non-Euclidean] geometry. Such a geometrical form is not then *conventional* for intuition in Reichenbach's sense: it is not the product of deliberate and conventional choice, since it does not rely on a "universal force field," nor does it depend on the constructibility of an instrumented measurement process to provide hyperbolic congruences' (1983:163).

According to the basic tenets of Heelan's enquiry, ordinary folk, artists, and entire communities have at times perceived their world spatially organized in ways that are difficult to describe in our conventional Euclid-oriented modes of accounting for objects in space without resorting to languages and images of illusion and distortion. The mode of perception and depiction deviating from customary pathways highlighted by Heelan is *hyperbolic* and non-Euclidean. Though experience of our physical environment generally appears to be displayed before us in an infinite Euclidean space, from time to time it has been seen in terms of finite hyperbolic spatial trajectories. Heelan's evidence for this thesis, during different times and in different places found in all walks of life, he claims, falls into three general categories: (1) everyday phenomena, such as dynamic flows of space along highways, or in the open sea

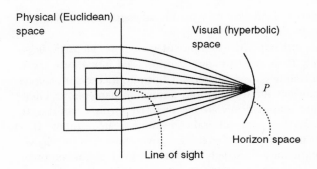

FIGURE 11

or sky, (2) common visual illusions, typical of Escher's work, and (3) pictorial spaces depicted by ancient architecture and both ancient and modern painting (Heelan 1983:27–36).

Distortions created by hyperbolic vision are the result of such factors as the qualitative distinction in the way objects appear when close to and directly in front of the viewer and when far away and to one side, in the way curvatures appear when near and when far from the horizon of perception, and in the distorted apparent sizes of objects in optical illusions. In a capsule, the difference between Euclidean and hyperbolic space is illustrated in figure 11, where the observer (O) views a point (P) along the distant horizon sphere in terms of lines hyperbolically converging toward that focal point. The Euclidean perspective, in contrast, would depict straight lines from physical space, projecting out toward an infinitely receding vanishing-point – that is, the Renaissance perspective, as we shall note shortly.

The most natural – that is, 'primitive' – inclination for reading the furniture of the world in its spatial setting is in this sense non-Euclidean, unconventional, and at the deepest levels of our *Umwelt*.[4] It is our Euclidean world that is conventional, most radically constructivist, and hence the most severely abstracted. In a certain manner of speaking, it is a matter of primary Euclidean principles in contrast to secondary (non-Euclidean) qualities. Heelan goes on to write that though Reichenbach erred in assigning the plasticity of our perceptual mode strictly to logic and mathematics – for they are mere adjuncts, not the main characters in the play – he is correct in postulating the idea of plasticity. Our embedded, automatized Euclidean perceptual mode owes its dues not to geometrical models defined by logic and mathematics but to the technological advances brought about by Euclidean-based science that, on the stage of human *praxis*, gradually reformed the structure of our perception, thus deconstructing and reconstructing the scaffolding, the props, and the angles, vectors, distances, trajectories, and relations before us.

In short, it is likely that our Euclidean construction of space actually plays second fiddle to the leading role of haptic perception.[5] Secondary qualities win out as most fundamental in their contest with Reichenbach's Euclidean geometries and their confirmation by measurement, which are actually secondary to secondary qualities, Heelan tells us. Yet, for generations upon generations, space constructed along Euclidean lines has been the space we 'saw' as a result of conventions, inculcation, education, and even ideology. So Euclidean perception must *ipso facto* also be taken into due consideration.

The constructivism postulate I have developed herein attempts to straddle the fence between the Scylla of representationalism, prototypical of which is the work of Jerry Fodor (1987), and the Charybdis of radical idealism, a dialectical to and fro of attention toward the individual as a sort of Maturana-Varela autonomous, autopoietic system tending toward self-referential, self-contained sufficiency on the one hand, and an entity in perpetual interaction with the whole of its environment, on the other. This fence-straddling concept, when applied to signs and semiotic agents, is actually quite Peircean in spirit. It demands constant bootstrapping on the part of the self-consistent sign (or semiotic agent) as a First in light of its historical development as a consequence of its action and reaction with other signs (or semiotic agents), and its taking on habit (that is, its – or a semiotic agent's – role as the repository of Secondness and Thirdness). Given this ongoing, ever changing stream of relations, any semiotic-constructivist concept of knowledge must remain far from the idea that we get to know an ontologically 'real' world that was prefabricated, fully striated, and lying in wait 'out there' for our discovery. At the same time, Prigogine collapses and resurging orders persist in forcing themselves onto the scene, calling for constantly renewed levels of order from the ensuing chaos, and at the same time giving up order in hopes that greater order will at some point be forthcoming. Caught within this process, the semiotic agent (sign) interacts with the world while reading its messages according to internalized dispositions, proclivities, and habits: the self (sign) imposes itself on the world, forcing it into moulded 'semiotically real' patterns. Piagetian assimilation and accommodation may occur when inconsistencies arise through the interaction of logically incompatible levels.

However, if complacency happens to ensue, giving one a smug know-it-all sense of being in possession of complete knowledge, sooner or later the world of Secondness, that 'outward clash,' as Peirce puts it, will force itself on its would-be knower, suggesting that she alter her course somewhat, and at times even compelling her to strike out in an entirely new direction. For no body of knowledge is absolutely free of *vagueness*, chance, or Firstness, nor can it reach pure *generality*, the necessity and plenitude of all things, Thirdness. Whatever is *vague* is caught up somewhere with *inconsistency*, and whatever is *general* is never *completely* and determinately so. Everything is perpetually subjected to the onslaught of varying degrees of chaos, of disorder.

Rather unfortunately, as it were, the elements of *vagueness* and *generality* coupled with *inconsistency* and *incompleteness* are absent in Piaget's (1968) 'structural' concepts of 'wholeness,' 'transformation,' and 'self-regulation,' which belie at their roots a closed rather than open epistemological system. Such closure limits Piaget's theory considerably; it requires him to focus almost entirely on the process of equilibration to the exclusion of disequilibration, not to mention Prigogine far-from-equilibrium conditions. Even when writing of 'dynamic equilibrium' Piaget actually has in mind something in the order of a synchronic slice out of the proverbial Saussurean semiological salami as a static state produced after a transformation and as it exists prior to another transformation. For, Saussure's 'system' raises a canopy over both synchronic oppositions from one transformation to another and synchronic equilibration when things tend to settle down and normalize (Piaget 1968:117–22).

This is a mechanistic model of the classical sort, typical of early cybernetics. The order of the Piagetian day is self-regulation in terms of quasi- or pseudomathematical operations according to which dissonances, perturbations, dissynchronies, and catastrophes – that is, the tendency toward disorder – must be virtually eliminated before the system has a chance to assert itself: every operation has its inverse, its reciprocal, its correlate, and, one must add, its *idempotence* (that is, a quantity other than zero, which, when applied to itself, remains the same as it was). In this sense, like a set of group operations, there is no real change of change but merely change. Nothing is genuinely novel but rather, there is no more than mere permutations already prescribed by the system; there is no purpose, goal, or end, but merely what I have elsewhere termed 'structural causality' (Merrell 1975). Certain sorts of change are banished, thereby threatening us with the aesthetic, ethical, and logical fiat that what is, is all right as it is, so we shouldn't meddle with it.

Piaget's mathematically justified conservatism, then, flies in the face of Peircean nonequilibrium semiotics, which falls more in line with contemporary chaos physics, the physics of complexity, and recent findings in biology, especially dissipative structures, the hypercycle idea, and autopoiesis as briefly described above. This might appear prima facie tantamount simply to the Saussurean distinction between synchronic stasis and diachronic process; that is, a primacy of order and nothing but order, though it is always in the throes of structuration, on the one hand, and an incessant, rather unstructured gush of signs, on the other. But though the comparison has its enticement, it falls flat upon scrutiny. Granted, Saussure-based semiology is chiefly static, while Peircean semiotics is radically processual. The evolution of semiology, whether in its Barthesian, Greimasian, Genettean, Kristevan, or Todorovian guise, has tended to become open-ended in one form or another. And semiology's various offshoots, whether by the name of poststructuralism, deconstruction, or archaeology-genealogy, have inclined toward a view on some points quite compatible, and if not, complementary, with Peirce's thought. This move remained basically implicit in Barthes and Foucault, but has become at times quite explicit in Deleuze, Derrida, and Kristeva.[6]

But actually, the demarcation I have suggested between Piaget and Peirce is more akin to that between Newtonian-Cartesian corpuscular-kinetic balance and harmony of the spheres and its robotic expression in early cybernetics, in contrast to the concept of biological growth and natural and social evolution. It is mechanism in contrast to organicism, *allonomy* (a person is needed to steer the car, a child the video game, God the universe) rather than legitimate *autonomy* (self-referential, self-contained, self-organizing entities perpetually undergoing change). On the one hand we have systems that can only be known adequately when entropy is at a relatively low ebb, and balance, harmony, and equilibrium are the apparent order of the day; on the other hand we have partly knowable novel order arising out of the intermittent breakdown of previous forms of order. On the one hand, there is statistical determinacy (certainty), transcendence, teleology; on the other, indeterminacy, immanence, teleonomy.

As a case in point, Piaget's brand of the 'semiotic square' (figure 10), while more sophisticated and 'dynamic' than that of Greimas (1966, 1970), none the less remains inadequate. It is a paragon of symmetry, balance, harmony, equilibrium, or if not, at least it entails an incessant push toward equilibration. Though Piaget readily concedes that the world does not always conform exactly to our intransigent ideals, and that his operations are not-quite-exactly reversible and repeatable, nevertheless, disturbances in his otherwise well-oiled systems are met with his concept of 'compensatory action' on the part of the subject (1965:37–61; 1971a:208–10). Moreover, Piaget's admiration for the so-called 'Bourbaki group' of mathematicians and their 'parent structures' from which the whole of mathematics is purportedly to have been engendered – a rather dreamy positivist image, if I may say so – reveals his nostalgia for yesteryear's certainty. Such certainty is no more, if we take logicians, mathematicians, and physical scientists at the cutting edge of their disciplines seriously. Though recent work on groups, lattices, networks, and topologies can be conceived as a road ultimately leading to the absolute, on the other side of the coin it is looked upon as a set of signposts bearing rather unwanted tidings regarding the swampy terrain ahead.

Whatever might be one's cup of tea, the scene most likely to prevail during the foreseeable future entails a definite 'loss of certainty,' even in mathematics, the most rigorous of disciplines (Kline 1980). Groups, lattices, and networks outline no more than possibilities when the 'unreasonable effectiveness' of mathematics is applied to the physical world (Wigner 1969). And the budding field of topology of n-dimensional neighbourhoods, boundaries, and domains deals with creamy-smooth continuity rather than the cut-and-dried atomistic, digitalized world with which we would like to be familiar. Topology, or so-called rubber sheet geometry, is the mathematics of continuity, in which lengths, angles, areas, and shapes are indefinitely mutable. A square can be continuously deformed into a circle, a circle into a triangle, a triangle into a line, a line into a point, or vice versa (by de-generation or generation, so to speak, in light of sign transmutation as discussed in chapter 2). What is more noteworthy, topology has led to radical nonlinearity, unpredictability, asymmetry, and irreversibility in the topsy-turvy world of fractals, catastrophes, and chaos physics in general (Stewart 1989).

All this is a far cry from Piaget's Cartesian-Newtonian push-pull mechanical model, though he admittedly took a step in the right direction regarding his notion of 'genetic structuralism,' which has influenced a host of scholars and observers of the twentieth-century upheaval in the sciences and humanities.[7]

4. OUR UNIVERSE BY ANY STRETCH OF THE IMAGINATION

For example, Wolfgang Yourgrau (1966), backed up independently by David Bohm (1965) and Heelan – all of them drawing support from certain facets of Piaget (1953; Piaget and Inhelder 1956) – argues convincingly that (1) Euclidean space was not really inherent to the Greek mind-set or pre-Greek common sense, though we would like believe it was, and (2) the world of children presents an excellent laboratory for the study of space perception of the most basic sort. Inspired by the work of Géza Révész (1957), Yourgrau first points out that topologically there is no fundamental distinction between circles, ellipses, and polygons, or between cubes and spheres: if the spaces are equivalent they are not identical in every respect but merely homeomorphically the same. Such topological relations, Yourgrau points out, are grasped by children at a much earlier stage and more easily than Euclidean shapes – recall the above remarks on Heelan's enquiry.

There appears to be more than a grain of truth to this hypothesis. F.M. Cornford (1976) writes convincingly that the common sense space of the ancient Greeks before Plato was spherical and finite, like the Being of Parmenides – and much in the order of de Cusa's God, or Pascal's fearful sphere. Consecrated by

Aristotle, this heterogeneous, finite, but unbounded space became the space of Western thought up to the scientific revolution, when infinite, homogeneous Euclidean space and the void of the atomists became virtually axiomatic. Actually, there are quite compelling reasons to perceive and conceive time and space as absolute along Euclidean lines. The very laws of classical mechanics bear this out. The first law, chiefly the product of Galileo's thought, involves the simplest and apparently the most common-sensical phenomenon imaginable: linear movement of a body along a straight line with constant velocity. It was a revolutionary new view of nature, diametrically opposed to the Aristotelian notion that rest is the natural state of all bodies. More revolutionary yet, the medium required for this linear motion was absolute space. As we shall note below, the Greeks' spatial imagination stressed tactile perception more than ours. A characteristic example is found in Euclid's fifth axiom of parallel lines. They are like the sense of touch along two parallel rods. 1 never feels them come together, unlike the eye following the infinite stretch of a pair of converging railroad tracks. The assumption seems to be that it is the parallel tracks converging to a point at the infinite stretch that is illusory, the tracks as they are seen or felt concretely in the here and now and on the surface constite the authentic 'reality.' The upshot is that the Greeks, lodged in their finite, relatively concrete universe, apparently perceived a somewhat different 'semiotic world' than we do, given our infinite Euclidean universe of infinitely converging parallel lines. In this sense, Greek perception was more immediate and closer to concrete sensations (Firstness) than our own (Szamosi 1986:112–44).

Properly inoculated with a massive dose of the abstract in our twentieth-century cultural milieu, of course, we would like to think there is a smooth, natural continuity between our perceptual and representational relationships. We tend to believe the physical world corresponds to Euclidean dictates, and since that is the world we (think we) see, it is undoubtedly the way things are, clearly and simply. Not so, however, if we follow the above words on constructivism and the nature of particular *Umwelt*-emergent 'semiotically real' worlds. According to these views, as well as that of Yourgrau – also Hanson (1958, 1969), as I have argued elsewhere (Merrell 1995) – what we see is what we have been trained to see and want to see. And to rub salt in our wounded confidence that we are capable of knowing the 'real' if we would just open our wide, innocent eyes and look, whatever 'semiotically real' world we happen to perceive and conceive could always have been otherwise. It could have been another construct entirely.

With this new-found awareness that all our worlds are inexorably constructs, what we should attempt to tune in on, Yourgrau writes, is our more 'primitive,' haptic sense of things, proper to the hands-on, felt world of children. However, having been educated in Euclidean geometry, like Piaget's properly inculcated child, there is actually an unbridgeable gap between our haptic perception of what is 'out there' and our mental representation 'in here,' since the latter evokes the existence of the former in their absence – as is proper most particularly to signs in the symbol mode. The problem is that our customary semantic relations and thought-signs of diverse sorts are not only conjured up in the absence of haptic experience, but they most often differ fundamentally from it.

Certain mathematicians, most notably Henri Poincaré (1952:21–31) shortly after the turn of this century, pointed out that our adult spatial notions are not immanent in our biopsychological makeup, and that our experience does not necessarily prove space is three-dimensional; its being so perceived has merely been a convenience to which we have become so accustomed that we tend to believe it is simply the way things are. Alternative geometries developed in the nineteenth century by J. Bolyai, W.K. Clifford, K. Gauss, N. Lobachevsky, and B. Riemann effectively bear out this contention (Richards 1979). The oftimes presumed a priori nature of Euclidean perception was also challenged by the experimental work of von Helmholtz (1876), among others. Maurice Merleau-Ponty (1962:203–5) and assorted phenomenologists during the present century have commented on the homogeneous nature of classical space in contrast to the heterogeneity of visual space. In fact, the Einsteinian world of relativity that superseded the Newtonian-Euclidean world of Cartesian coordinates slaps our supposedly 'common-sense' notions of both space and time in the face, though it remains quite commensurate with the world of the 'prelogical' child. It takes us back to the very finite but unbounded sphere of the pre-Socratics.

In order to approach this alternative world, a quantum jump is necessary from a nonrelativistic point of view in physics to a relativistic point of view. Upon exercising such a jump, we must cease regarding our concepts of space, time, mass, energy, and so on as representing absolutely permanent and necessary features of the world. Instead, we must construe them to be expressing invariant relationships (Piaget 1965:196). In Yourgrau's summary, 'the observation of little children's behavior patterns suggests that the "india-rubber" world of the topologist and of Einstein, though highly abstract to the uninitiated, and the haptic perception of the child are much closer to one another than haptic perception is to Euclidean shapes and spaces with their rigid properties. We say that the child recognizes objects haptically at an early age. But once the level of representation is reached, the aid of speech is invoked and thereby all doors opened to Euclidean commitment' (1966:500).

More recently, Heelan's 'hermeneutical visual model' of 'hyperbolic space' patterned after evidence from visual illusions, the history of art, and psychological studies rounds out the picture. Just as the surface of our world sphere is curved rather than flat in the classical sense, so also our space-time manifold is best represented by geometries of curved rather than homogeneous space. To get a better feel for our situation imagine our Flatlander's universe to be placed on the surface of the earth. As far as he is concerned, his world is flat, for, given his perceptual mode, he has no reason to believe otherwise. If the centre of his universe is at the North Pole and its radius measured along the lines of longitude, we can understand how he has every right to think his 'two-dimensional' space is properly Euclidean. But it is not. It is actually of a much different order and can be defined and conceived solely from within that order, which entails an extra dimension as well as Riemannian 'curved space' geometry, where what were apparently parallel lines actually meet. In other words, his space is for us more properly 'haptic,' pre-Socratic, finite, and unbounded, in spite of his believing he perceives it to the contrary. His own classical, mechanistic form of science has obviously implanted in his mind the concept of a universe that, no matter how conveniently displayed in computational language, simply does not exist as such – that is, from our imperious vantage.

Like the Flatlander, we would like to cram our space perception into neat Euclidean categories. However, in spite of our obsession with such an orderly world, and even though our perception has been symmetrized by cultural imperatives with which we were indoctrinated so long ago that it is lost to memory, our space perception is inexorably hyperbolic, according to Heelan's quite effective argument. Instead of the hygienic, desiccated lines of our accustomed vanishing-point, made popular since Renaissance times especially as a result of Alberti's studies in linear perspective in painting, our binocular vision actually curves space, from the periphery at the brownish-grey area to the focal point as illustrated in figure 11 – Heelan's detailed analyses of works by van Gogh bear this out (see also Gombrich 1960; Ivins 1973; Panofsky 1960). We look down the railroad track and (think we) see two parallel rails meeting at the infinite stretch, though at the same time we (think we) know parallel lines do not actually meet; it is our parallax vision that merely makes it appear so. This 'one-dimensional man's' focal perspective in Renaissance painting is a far cry from the 'bird's eye' view depicted in medieval painting, which appears to our twentieth-century sensibilities as a clutter and confusion presenting a nonlinear multiplicity of perspectives simultaneously (Romanyshyn 1989).

Actually, following the theses of Heelan, Yourgrau, and others that the linear perspective vision is a historical invention, it is quite plausible to conclude that in creating it we have designed and invented ourselves and our world. That is, our world has become an extension of our mind, of ourselves, and at the same time it has brought about a transformation of ourselves, the consequences of which have culminated in a progressively mechanistic, technologized, even electronic – in our age of information – view. In contrast to the world we have relentlessly fabricated and to ourselves as having in the process become fashioned, Heelan observes that his 'hermeneutical model' of visualization presupposes that 'visual space can take on any one of a family of geometries depending on the hermeneutical context of foreground and background, that is, of object and containing space' (Heelan 1983:53). The relationship between *foreground* and *background* – terms common to Heelan's discourse – is complex, but, to be sure, our tendency for foregrounding some items of experience and backgrounding others, as gestalt studies have amply demonstrated, is in part idiosyncratic, in part culturally motivated, and in part biological and constrained by our species-specific *Umwelt*.

The important point is that foreground and background are mutually exclusive, though complementary. In fact, they are well-nigh incommensurable, as is the Möbius strip 'world' for a Flatlander, who felicitously travels recursively along it with the belief his world is flat, but for us, from within a 'higher' dimension, we would like to view his delusion as helplessly pathetic and hopelessly naïve. But, of course, we are in a manner of speaking as naïve as he. For our three-dimensional classical world is tantamount to his on a two-dimensional plane, and our four-dimensional manifold twisting and reshaping Euclidean-Newtonian space is tantamount to his Möbius-strip twisted in a three-dimensional space. Just as only Ludwig is capable of a view, *sub specie aeternitatis*, of our world, so also we can see *en bloc* what is unavailable to the Flatlander, trapped as he must remain within his world.

Let us, then, turn to a world with which our Flatlander is somewhat familiar, Bunn's 'two-dimensional semiotics,' that of eotemporality, that is, of classical mechanics.

5. YET, AT THE INFINITE STRETCH IT´S ALL THE SAME

We are now in the domain of the plane, that of early cave paintings, Egyptian hieroglyphics, Mayan low-relief sculpture, Aztec pictographs (visual signs depicting things), Oriental and other ideographs (visual signs representing thought-signs), the native American cryptographs studied by Benjamin L. Whorf, and so on, all of which serve as devices for depicting linear mnemonic activity on a spread sheet. We are also squarely within the world of contemporary painting, and its counterparts in our high-tech, fast-track world of mass media (television, videos, movies).

Two-dimensional semiotics also coheres with Harré's 'paramorphic models.' They model their subjects dyadically, in terms of visual schemata and/or abstract relations between *modelans* and *modelandum*, though the models' form and mode of operation are often drawn from a source that differs from the subjects modelled. Paramorphic models are generally constructed or imagined as operating in the order of principles already accepted in science and technology. But sometimes, by imaginary leaps, a fudge factor can be introduced either for the purpose of keeping the dynamo of Kuhnian 'normal science' in operation, or for bringing about a tectonic shift of 'revolutionary science.' In such cases novel and hitherto unforeseen connections are evoked between the model and that modelled by virtue of interaction between them, and as a consequence new concepts can be and usually are forthcoming (for example, Black's [1962] 'interactionist' view of metaphors and models).

Regarding paramorphic models, the relation of dyadic differentiation between *modelans* and *modelandum* can be of three sorts: (1) their initial and final states are equivalent, but the processes by which they are reached differ (that is, the corpuscular [billiard-ball] theory of gases; visual computer simulations of mathematical computations), (2) their initial and final states are analogous (that is, Bohr's 'planetary model' of the atom, which does not account for how electrons move instantaneously from one orbit to another), or (3) their initial and final states as well as the processes leading to them are the same (that is, the ether's function regarding light as analogous to the air's function regarding sound; electric circuits as analogous to hydraulic networks). These three types of relations between *modelans* and *modelandum* correspond to models that are (1) singly connected (a molecule of oxygen acts like a billiard ball), (2) multiply connected (Bohr's atom is like a planetary system regarding the functions and workings of its parts), and (3) semi-connected (the ether is like air only mediately, in so far as both provide a medium for light and sound respectively).

If homeomorphic models coincide quite closely with Peirce's *images* – the first type of what he calls *hypoicons* (*CP*:2.276f) – paramorphic models are comparable to *diagrams* and occasionally even to *metaphors* in terms of their relation of Secondness to their object – which still excludes Thirdness, or the symbolic – that is, linguistic – aspect of metaphorical expressions.[8] The problem is that the models refer to their subjects and those subjects to the models in terms of pictures and schemata on the flat – though three-dimensional images or physical simulacra can often be constructed. Yet they remain as if something abstract and mysterious. Their 'misplaced concreteness' can be rendered somewhat less mysterious only by 'reading' them much like sentences in order that they may be treated as having a certain three-dimensional spatial configuration for the purpose at hand. But the model (index), unlike words (symbols), remains a model by projective convention: the characteristics 'read' from/into the model serve their function through imagined and/or physical similitude to the characteristics of the phenomenon modelled. Words, in contrast, are in general arbitrary before they are conventional in terms of some modelling function of similitude (Harré 1970:46).[9]

All theory construction, Harré tells us, 'is primarily model building, in particular imagining paramorphs' (1970:46). Paramorphs slapped on paper involve imaginary processes among either 'semiotically real' or imagined entities. In whichever case,

> [paramorphs] may invite existential questions, since unlike homeomorphs, they introduce additional entities other than the given, provided it seems plausible to treat these as a causal mechanism. It is through imagined paramorphs and their connection with their sources, multiple, single, semi or fragmentary, that theoretical terms gain part, and a vital part, of their meaning. It is by being associated with a paramorphic model, ... that many laws of nature get their additional strength of connection among the predicates that they associate, that distinguishes them from accidental generalizations. A scientific explanation of a process or pattern among phenomena is provided by a theory constructed in this way. (Harré 1970:47)

Models, analogies, and metaphors in terms of their two-dimensional dyadic exposition are closely related to rational (symbolic) thought, though they are not sufficient in and of themselves without the more developed semiotic mode of signification.

A problem exists in that, just as metaphors dressed in language can become merely the terminological debris of 'dead' models, analogies, and metaphors illustrated in two dimensions, so also models, analogies, and metaphors can become the indexical (referential) debris of 'dead' scientific theories, cultural myths, rituals, and symbols – as Merleau-Ponty (1962) reiterated emphatically, perception and language are not separate powers. In fact, when considering the entire range of possible models, analogies, and metaphors, along with the range of all possible 'real (that is,"semiotically real") worlds' fabricated by the mind, past, present, and future to come, both the law of noncontradiction (in the domain of *vagueness*) and the excluded-middle principle (in the domain of *generality*) must at some point fall by the wayside. So one can hardly do more than take signs as they come, modelling one's world in midstream as best one can, and hope for the best. But before we tackle this issue head-on, a few more preliminary words on that semiotic phenomenon *par excellence*, painting, with a further word on Heelan's intriguing thesis.

As I mentioned above, during antiquity, and on into the medieval period, the universe was to be 'read,' so to speak, as a moral and religious text – that is, the book metaphor, which intrigued Galileo and other harbingers of modern science. The text of the universe found its way into art and artefacts of all sorts, as well as in folk-tales and early literary texts. These works were considered to 'speak' the world, to give a thoroughly realistic account of what there is. The important point for the topic at hand is that to an extent among the ancient Greeks and Romans, but especially at the time of the Renaissance, perhaps more significantly than in writing, the world was to be represented pictorially and rationally constructed by means of geometrical principles. Renaissance natural philosophy consistently threw the medieval unity of appearance and reality for a loop, demonstrating the relativity of immediate sense experience (Firstness, and qualitative or immediate Secondness, that is, secondary qualities). In contrast to all appearances, Copernicus' and Galileo's universe (of quantitative or dynamical Secondness, that is, primary qualities) was construed to be superior to the cumbersome Ptolemaic system. The new infinite universe effectively challenged the closed cosmology of medieval thought and raised questions regarding the reliability of unaided sensations (Koyré 1957).

Most crucial to the focus of this chapter, during the Renaissance, Euclidean lines, planes, and surfaces of various shapes were all flattened onto a two-dimensional sheet guaranteed to match selected items from the world's furniture. They were designed so as to convince their presumably disinterested onlooker that they were equivalent to the world not as she ordinarily perceived it but as it really is (Snyder 1980; Nodine and Fisher 1979). In other words, the flat plane of Cartesian coordinates was to become the scientific mode, following the dream of *mathesis universalis*, of reducing our three-dimensional existence to two-dimensional semiotics in the abstract, to a dyadic 'world on paper,' as Bellone (1982) puts it. Any representation not reducible to the flat plane or to two-dimensional algebraic ciphers could not but remain, so to speak, inauthentic.

As I mentioned above in passing, the transition in space perspective during the Renaissance is perhaps no more keenly manifested than in painting. Like literature and scientific theories, painting recreates the world symbolically in the abstract. The space of a painting, no matter how naturalistic or realistic, is mental before it is 'real.' It is a 'semiotically real' construct. In order that a painting may be capable of depicting the three-dimensional world, it must contain certain visual cues; without them, it creates no more than spatial illusion. The development of these cues is no simple matter. For example, Egyptian efforts toward effective depiction of visual space in painting and sculpture are a study in almost perfect contrast to those of their Greek counterparts. In Egyptian painting there is hardly any visual depth, with little distinction between the purely imaginary and the 'semiotically real,' the legitimate and the artificial, the living and the dead. As a consequence of this perspective, Egyptian sculpture produced powerful 'block' figures in abstract, almost geometrical, form. Their visual and tactile space is closed, inward looking, and static. The viewer is barred; she is compelled to remain outside; there is no invitation to enter into the artistic work. Greek sculpture, in comparison with the hidden potential emanating from its Egyptian counterpart, radiates activity. It is dynamic, producing a sense of motion; it gives promise of open space (even though that space remains closed); it projects outward, inviting the viewer into its aesthetic domain.

In the early medieval period the techniques of both painting and sculpture were quite primitive by Greek standards. There was little interest in depicting the three-dimensional world. Spatial extension was either entirely ignored or camouflaged by a flat, lifeless background. Individual figures did not relate to each other in space but merely existed in a continuum without scale or gradations. Like their Egyptian predecessors, medieval artists created starkly beautiful and expressive works, but they seemed unconcerned about reproducing the visible world 'objectively' – whatever that can mean for a given cultural perspective. In fact, they likely considered the 'objectively' perceived world irrelevant, preferring to convey the religious significance of the 'real' and the imagined, the sacred and the profane.

Joel Snyder (1980) writes that the images produced by the medievalists' rudimentary form of camera obscura, flawed, reversed, and upside down, should have suggested a pictorial application to the human eye and hence to artistic techniques. But they did not. It was not until the time of Giotto and various of his contemporaries that nature was finally subjected to detailed observation, a precondition for more 'realistic painting.' These painters derived their work from visual experience rather than tradition, producing a new sense of transparency of the painting surface and at least a suggestion of depth. Orthogonal lines (created so as to appear perpendicular to the surface) then began to enter the scene and began converging toward some ill-defined area, and at times even toward a point. These and other such changes helped prepare the way for the Renaissance upheaval.

Construction of faithful pictorial images became the paramount goal of Renaissance painters. They developed what came to be known as the linear 'mathematical' or 'artificial' perspective. Once again, Alberti's linear perspective technique is especially noteworthy. His procedure involves two steps: (1) construction of a vanishing-point, and (2) establishing a distance-point.

The vanishing-point consists of a set of orthogonal lines fading away in the distance like a pair of railroad tracks to transform the perspective into a matter of spatial distance rather than of levels in medieval hierarchic fashion, thus endowing the painting with the same qualities as the eye. The painting becomes a symbol of a new vision of the 'real,' of the place of humanity in nature, and of the relationship between them. It removes the spectator and at the same time draws her into the world on the flat surface. She becomes at once detached and at one with the open space projected out by the painting to grab her and draw her in. The distance-point, requiring a separate drawing subsequently mapped onto the drawing made possible by the vanishing-point, introduces diagonals to complement the asymptotic stretch of the vanishing-point. It constructs the necessary *degree of depth* along lines diagonal to the orthogonal vanishing-point, which initially *created a sense of depth*.

By these two methods, the body is eclipsed. Since the eye is now to have become a detached spectator, the 'I' (self) is presumed objectively able to see the world, which according to Renaissance thought becomes in the process icon, eidos – that is, a mirror of nature. The medieval depth of the world as hierarchy becomes Renaissance depth in terms of open, infinite space. The 'I' (eye, icon, *eidos*) is focused straight ahead; it is apart from its body, exists in another sphere, later to become the celebrated Cartesian consciousness. The fixed vision eventually takes on mathematical character, and nature becomes nothing more than quantitative measure since it exists in advance of the penetrating 'I.' In Alexandre Koyré's (1968) view, the closed medieval world becomes the infinite universe of classical mechanics. Robert Romanyshyn puts it nicely:

A linear perspective vision is one which places everything on the same level and in this respect the imaginal eye of the artist has already prepared the space for the sixteenth-century emergence of the scientific world of *explanations*. Galileo, for example, will presume such a space for his law of falling bodies, a space where all objects fall equally fast. In such a space all things, regardless of what they are and regardless of the context to which they belong, are equal and the same. They are, in short, ex-plained, that is, reduced to the same plane or level of reality. They are, so to speak, flattened out, within a space that is neutral and homogeneous, a space within which all things become calculable objects in a mathematical equation. That the truth of Galileo's law of falling bodies was demonstrated on the moon during the flight of *Apollo 15* is significant. It indicates that the space opened up by a linear perspective vision is even at its origins an imagined space apart from the earth. There is in this space where all is on the same plane already more than a hint of departure. (1989:43)

The Renaissance vanishing-point allows, even encourages, the subject to imagine she is a spectator of the object to be painted as well as the world to be theorized, experimented with, and acted on. Esconced behind a window to the world, she presumes an imperious, neutral, objective view to the panorama spread out and on display before her. The world 'out there' exists in order that it may subject itself to the gaze of its spectator. Quite understandably, the dyadic linear perspective displayed on a plane – a counterpart to Harré's paramorphic mode – especially after its incorporation into science, reduces everything to the same level in a homogeneous, isotropic, infinitely extended Newtonian-Euclidean space, a space within which all things become mathematically calculable. This perception of the furniture of the world as belonging to the same plane is a vision that ultimately transforms the depth of the world. Depth merely becomes the depth of the plane seen as if looking out a window to a receding landscape (Romanyshyn 1989:38–57). The all-seeing eye, in this process, obviously becomes paramount: its logical ramifications are what Karl Popper calls the 'bucket-theory' of the mind as an empty receptacle to be filled with facts. This is the 'spectator theory of knowledge,' mind (and presumably philosophy) as a reflection of nature. It is the 'semiotic world' of Piaget's child after she has been properly indoctrinated.

On the other side of the ledger, it is the world of Derrida's 'myth of presence,' relegated to the status of fictions, figments, fragments, and lingering phantasms some time ago by Nietzsche. From this view, apparently, all was not well with the Renaissance world. Irwin Panofsky (1960), complementary with Heelan and Yourgrau, and backed up by Ernst Mach's sensationalism, effectively argues that the space represented by the Renaissance perspective – homogeneous, isotropic, infinite – is not that of visual perception, that is, of psychological space, at all. Psychological space is neither homogeneous nor isotropic nor infinite. Everything is not flattened to geometrical and mathematical sameness as it is in the Renaissance perspective. Up and down, back and forth, forward and backward, are not of equal significance; equal volumes of space are not of equal value; space does not extend linearly with no end in sight. Indeed, psychological space, in this view, appears to invite a 'subjective' grasp, in contrast to Renaissance 'objectivity.'[10]

However, it may also well be that no particular school of thought or *modus operandi* necessarily enjoys any monopoly over any other one. In fact, Gombrich (1960) raises serious doubts regarding the possibility of knowing how artists of past cultures perceived their world by the way they painted it. If one assumes the artist was in possession of a realistic pictorial mode and that the stimuli produced by the object painted and what appeared on the canvas exist in one-to-one correspondence on relevant points, problems arise. For any given three-dimensional object can be depicted on a two-dimensional plane in many ways, some of them contradictory, and even mutually exclusive (see also Arnheim 1954, Ittelson and Kilpatrick 1952). Gombrich calls it 'visual hallucination' – and indeed, this is what optical illusions are all about, to which the 'haptic' characteristics of the Möbius strip and other such intriguing phenomena also bear witness. Each and every perspective (or 'semiotic reality') is to a greater or lesser degree a community-wide 'visual hallucination,' for, though on certain points it may correspond to the 'real,' on others it does not.

Finally, Marx Wartofsky (1980) demonstrates how modes of pictorial representation compel their viewers to perceive the world 'out there' in certain ways, hence what they perceive is in part the result of pictorial representation. He concludes that though 'it is true that those paintings which we take to be "realistic" are so because they most closely represent the way things look, things come to look the way they do because they are perceived in accordance with the rules of representation embodied in those pictures we take to be "realistic"' (1980:30–1, in Heelan 1983:110). If Wartofsky is on the right track – and he is backed up by a host of psychologists and philosophers in this regard (as well as constructivist philosophy) – then the illusory space of objects on canvas can come to be conceived as the space of 'real' objects, thus forcing a perception of objects 'out there' in the three-dimensional world in accordance with the modes of depiction of objects on a two-dimensional plane.

And thus a circle has been completed: much in the order of Harré's chiefly dyadic paramorphs, the three-dimensional perceived object is conceived to match the two-dimensional painted object, which gave rise to the perceived object in the first place. The venerated concept of the mind as mirror of nature becomes symmetrical with that which is implied, which is that selfsame nature as mirror of the mind, as what the preconceiving, constructive, destructive, deconstructive mind put there in the first place. It is not so much that the Western mind was presumed to be the main character on the stage of the world. Rather, the stage itself was none other than the product of Western mind: the stage as mirror, a flat plane that faithfully depicts the three-dimensional realm it reflects, a two-dimensional reflection considered to transcend its own spatiality since it becomes coterminous with, and often presumably a duplication of, what is considered to be the 'real' – but is in reality no more than a 'semiotically real' domain resting alongside all other possible domains that could have been actualized but were not, as our venerable mentor, Ludwig, would tell us.

But more on that topic later. For now, let us turn to Fraser's bio-nootemporality and Bunn's 'one-dimensional' semiotics – notice, before entering the next section, that I have collapsed biotemporality and nootemporality into one, which spans the entire domain of Thirdness as depicted in figure 9.

6. LINEARITY GONE MAD?

I begin with what Harré calls 'protomorphic models,' from *proto* (= before, first in time, lower or primary in a series). Protomorphs are an example of the genus 'logical' or 'mathematical icon,' of which diagrams of the most abstract sort – like fleshless metaphors – represent logical or mathematical relations in such a manner that they can be reinterpreted, or misinterpreted at a level of ideality far removed from the objects of which they are models.

Common examples of protomorphs are graphs in terms of their strictly linear, one-dimensional generation on a two-dimensional plane as the representation of a three-dimensional objects, acts, and events. For example, to the question 'What is the distance traveled by an object that begins from rest and accelerates to a velocity of 40 feet per second in a time of 15 seconds?' the mathematical solution is elementary: $\frac{1}{2}vt = \frac{1}{2} \times 40 \times 15 = 300$ feet. But what is meant by the resulting statement 'The distance the object travels *is* equal to 300 feet'? The copula, *is*, implies a timeless state of affairs, a Parmenidean universe in which everything is *there* simultaneously (Park 1980:22–35). This is a mummified rather than a living image, mechanical rather than organic, static rather than dynamic. It is the skeletal depiction of a full-fledged, fully incorporated, experiential happening. It has hardly anything to do with the immediate quality of mind, of feeling, of sentience. We could also have solved the problem geometrically by linearly plotting velocity against time along the Cartesian coordinates and determining the area of the triangle in terms of time and acceleration in the order of a graph or diagram. But once again we would have a static form on paper far removed from the *experience* of acceleration. On the contrary, we could assimilate the two-dimensional graph in one perceptual gulp from our three-dimensional vantage point. The mathematical formula is linear, and its depiction in diagram form is a two-dimensional paramorph, both of which are timeless from within the three-dimensional perspective. As I have intimated, experience is also linear, a time-line within a multiply linear domain. Experience as Firstness and the mathematical-geometrical products of the intellect as Thirdness share common ground, at least on this issue.

However, there is a crucial distinction between experience and intellection. Our *experience of acceleration* (tacitly) knows more than the nonphysicist (explicitly) knows and can tell about the concrete, sensed, felt, intuited world of acceleration. Ask any intelligent human being with a normal educational background but no special training in physics the question, 'If a ball is thrown against a wall from x feet away with a velocity of y feet per second at angle z, where will the ball be $\frac{1}{2}$ second after it has rebounded from the wall?' Without a fair knowledge of the laws of mechanics, she will not be able to come up with an answer. Now put a ball in her hand, and ask her to throw it against the wall and catch it, and she will have hardly any trouble accomplishing the task. By the act (tacitly) of judging from the speed, angle, and distance of the ball, she will know quite well and without a moment's hesitation where her hands must be in order to retrieve the object. And her solution is virtually as effective as that of a competent physicist after filling a sheet of his notepad with computations. From the same initial conditions, both arrived at fundamentally the same answer.

Insult is added to injury when one realizes that not only can a human brain tacitly solve practical time and space puzzles more rapidly than the trained physicist can do so explicitly, but the lowest of beasts can also quite effectively accomplish the tacit feat, thank you. Imagine a cougar when pursuing a fleeing buck, an eagle when homing in on an unwary trout arduously making its way upstream, a trained dog when pursuing a Frisbee gyrating in the air. Their brains suppress noise, select and process relevant data, compute speeds, directions, all the while making predictions, and at the propitious moment they make their catch. Each cue is a sign, no matter how minimal it might appear, and all but a tiny part of each is processed by tacit means (nonconsciously, by instinctive, embedded, automatized, habituated behaviour).

In each of these cases we could construct a graph (diagram, as a linear protomorphic model) illustrating how the animal in question realized its goal, a composite sign now subject to conscious, rational, logical inferential reasoning process the sort of which we humans are so imperiously proud. Whether we focus on the animals' doing what comes naturally or the physicist's marks on paper, and whether experience through time and space is involved or merely a timeless diagram with its accompanying computations, a collusion of time and space is imperative. The animals etch out a minuscule portion of their life trajectory along their 'world-line'; the physicist slaps linear equations down on a two-dimensional plane as a *fait accompli*, as if it were always already there. The animal knows tacitly how to do it and does it; the physicist knows explicitly how to show it and shows it. The one is experience; the other is intellect. The one is Firstness coupled with nonconscious inference; the other is mediated Thirdness accompanied by mind grasps. Both entail a 'line' from 'here' to 'there' and from 'then' to 'now.' But after the fact, when all is done and shown, the product exists irretrievably in the past, never to be altered except in future 'semiotically real' worlds as distortions, to a greater or lesser degree, of the hard-core existence of the 'real.'

A new and uniquely human realm of space and time, corresponding in a loose way to the physicist's computations in an artificial language, began with the evolution of natural language. A beast in the wild knows where to go for food. Domestic animals, on the other hand, can be trained to know that with a signal food will appear at a certain spot. But it cannot, we would suppose, *understand* that the food was there yesterday or *predict* that it will be there tomorrow. A dog can by habit go to a certain place at a certain time of the day and lie in wait for someone or something, but it cannot go somewhere in *expectation* of something or someone it has never before experienced. In contrast, language, with its ability to account for the past, of absent presents, and project into the future, allows the human semiotic animal to construct worlds in space and time with virtually limitless possibilities. These worlds are not necessarily empirical. Yet they can be purely symbolic. They are worlds of Thirdness, *par excellence*, of arbitrary signs some or most of which can, at some future point, become convention, habit, law. When you write a note to a friend by electronic mail, when Cervantes penned *Don Quixote*, when Einstein calculated the motion of the perihelion of the planet Mercury, it was all a matter of symbols: words, numbers, graphic ciphers, and the like. And it is a matter of symbolic time and space made accessible, we must suppose, chiefly – though perhaps not exclusively – to humans.

Statues, paintings, holy places, buildings, altars, maps, eternal hunting-grounds, are examples of imaginary constructs having become actualized. They are there, all at once, to be perceived in holistic fashion. But when we analyse them and talk about them they are fractured, split asunder, reduced to bits, destructured, deconstructed and reconstructed, all as a matter of time. And this time of the raw generation of symbols is linear; it is one-dimensional. While a string of symbols is being generated, it is patterned by experienced 'real' time; when the string is a *fait accompli*, it is two-dimensional and atemporal, *en bloc*. And it can now take off along multiply tangential pathways in its evolution toward radical nonlinearity, culminating in apparent chaos from which new orders can arise – by constructive acts of heart and mind.

As Saussure (1966:70) once put it, 'the signifier, being auditory, is unfolded solely in time from which it gets the following characteristics: (1) it represents a span, and (2) the span is measurable in a single dimension; it is a line.' An individual letter, a number, a musical note written on a score, are perceived as two-dimensional signs on a sheet abstracted from time and existing in timeless space. In contrast, an entire text exists *in toto*, as a timeless universe on paper, while each of its readings constitutes a linear, time-bound process. The individual signs are bits abstracted from a process – the author's writing of them – while the composite set of signs composes a universe, a realm of possibilities (Firsts) that can be set in motion along a sequential stream of actualized signs (Seconds), that can in their turn potentially become endowed with interpretations (interpretants, Thirds). Once again, the movement is from linear generation to nonlinear complexity (this, we shall note in chapters 8 and 9, is the way of all life processes as well).

Prototemporal semiotics, in this fashion, consists of spatial displays subjected to temporal processing. Such processing involves chains of signs strung together so as to release minute portions of what was in the 'block,' there and waiting. The act of creating such strings is of the order of consciousness, experience, thought processes, along the linear race of time. Thinking and experiencing are linear, though when one thinks retrospectively about past sequences of events, the set of sequences are held in check in enfolded simultaneity while a particular sequence is unfolded as a process. Thought is not limited to a one-dimensional mode, but, as we shall observe, it involves many dimensions, in fact, n-dimensions. This notion of an entire set of sequences held in check while a particular sequence is being unfolded may be a difficult pill to swallow for some observers hoping to retain a modicum of conscious, rational control of the world 'out there' and self-control 'in here.' It imprisons the future within the same chamber as the present and the past. It is like a slide show, as William James explains of the 'block universe.' All the slides are poised and ready in the carousel, but they can be displayed only in linear one-flash-at-a-time fashion.

It is precisely in Peirce's symbolic mode that we find the most effective approximation to the notion of an n-dimensional enfolded set of possibilities a portion of which may be unfolded in time. Symbols are set apart from icons and indices in that in their composite forms – embodied in texts and such – they are neither there for the taking, *en bloc*, as are icons introducing themselves to us as wholes, nor do they present the countenance of simple dyadic, linear cause-effect, here-there, part-whole, this-that conjunctions, as do indices. Rather, symbols are linearly generated and processed signs vaguely hinting at that paradise, somewhere in the infinite horizon, of learned ignorance, of appearance and 'reality' having become one such that a grasp of the all, all at once, becomes possible.

In another way of putting it, symbols are future oriented, while icons belong to experience now past – when there is consciousness *of* them they exist only as images in the mind – and indices incorporate present experience – they are physically and naturally associated with their objects, like smoke with fire, lightning with thunder. Symbols, in contrast, set certain conditions that, if they inhere, will most probably give rise to certain sets of experiences, thoughts, or behavioural actions. Symbols bear on hopes, fears, desires, expectations, and beliefs, all of which are always already 'there,' in wait of the proper circumstances so as to yield that which would be or should be the most likely consequence. Symbols thus cannot but influence the thought and conduct of their interpreters, affording them ever-greater subtlety of intellection and at the same time illusions of omniscient grandeur.

And, to repeat, natural language is the supreme manifestation of symbols: 'Every word is a symbol. Every sentence is a symbol. Every book is a symbol' (*CP*:4.360). The book is a past construction; it is Firstness, a set of possibilities, and can exist as an image in the mind of she who read it some ten years ago. As a physical artefact the contiguous placement and relationship of the graphic signs are Secondness, 'real' actuality. To be actualized in a 'semiotically real' domain they must be read with certain propensities, dispositions, expectations, hopes, fears, desires, an so on, on the part of the reader. Upon a given reading, interpretants (Thirds) are attached to many or most of the signs, and their potentiality is partly realized, though their full realization lies beyond the reach of any given fallible reader or any finite community of readers. Thus the signs' plenitude, their ultimate interpretants, must be *esse in futuro*.

In this light, allow me, if you will, an incursion into the more abstract disciplines in order more adequately to illustrate the one-dimensional character of bio-nootemporality at its best.

7. SO ON IT GOES, AND WHERE IT ENDS NOBODY KNOWS

Zeno's four paradoxes refuting motion evoke the impossible image of dense linear series infinitely digitalized. Mathematicians, logicians, and philosophers have generally attempted to resolve these paradoxes by means of the principles available to them from within their particular disciplines.

To cite an example in passing, H.N. Lee (1965) argues that the theories of Dedekind and Cantor relate to the divisibility of an infinite series and can therefore avoid Zeno's embarrassing proclamations. The Dedekind-Cantor theories of continuity – to be discussed further in chapter 8 – define a real continuum, whereas the infinite divisibility into rational fractions does not. Zeno's brand of divisibility entails rational numbers only, omitting the irrationals; hence the series has holes and is not a full-blown continuum. The series of rational numbers is dense and denumerable: between every two elements there is another element, and all elements are discrete and specifiable, though there is a definite stopping place. Not so with the irrationals, composing a nondenumerable continuous series, whose elements are not discrete: they cannot be put in one-to-one correspondence with the positive integers.

Zeno was right at least in that there can be no motion constructed from a series of discrete parts (for instance, the arrow at every instant occupies a certain space, and it cannot close the gap between one discrete space and another, hence it cannot move). This demonstrates that continuity cannot be composed of discrete elements, even if there exists an infinity of them. Furthermore, according to Dedekind-Cantor, a continuum cannot be analysed in terms of discrete parts. In this light, Lee considers that since motion and change are continuous and actual the paradoxes do not hold water, for actual motion and change cannot be so discretized. It follows, he argues, that Zeno errs in so far as a continuum is no more than a pseudo-continuum, and his problem thus vanishes. Consensus persists that the dilemma Zeno presents cannot be dissolved so easily (see Salmon 1970; Slaatte 1968; Benardete 1964).

From another vantage, Andrew Ushenko (1946) notes that Heisenberg's uncertainty relegates to the trash bin Zeno's assumption that the arrow in motion simultaneously occupies a definite position (see also Grünbaum 1967). An arrow in motion can be assigned a specific location only at the expense of knowledge concerning the arrow's momentum and energy. In other words, what is moving is not at any definite place at any specifiable moment. In fact, as long as it is moving it is not really a thing but a state of affairs, and consideration of its being *there-then* is consideration of it not as a thing but as an event. The very thingness of things vanishes before our eyes. We are left with nothing but the surface manifestations of events evincing the bare suggestion of actual objects – thus the mediacy of Peirce's semiotics, corresponding quite closely to Derrida's vague notion of *différance* in taking up arms and going into battle against the 'myth of presence,' against '(phal)logocentrism.' This view of things reminds one once again of Heraclitus' world of perpetual change. Heraclitus, in contrast to Zeno, predicated the identity of opposites to the neglect of the law of contradiction. He interpreted the incessant *conjunctionis oppositorum*, the transition of one contrary into the other, as coexistence *and* identity – an identity of opposites and of existence and nonexistence that was, by the way, upheld dialectically by Hegel and rejected by orthodox logic.

Heraclitus' continuum of change, however, runs head-on into the brick wall of Zeno's successive discrete cuts. Interestingly enough, a particular line of Buddhist theory denies substance and has no use for continuity: there is no motion in things, the things themselves *are in* motion. That is, motion exists empirically, for experience, though the thingness of things consists of momentary fulgurations succeeding one another in contiguous locations without their possessing any abiding stuff. They are no more than a series of flashes, each passing into extinction prior to the emergence of the succeeding one. These pulses are smoothed out by experience, while motion exists in the registration and annihilation of the thing's thingness. Things do not move in the sense of a duration of change. They do not move, for they have no time to do so; they appear only fleetingly; they are mere instantaneities. Hence, there is no becoming. What becomes, is not what *is* in terms of instantaneities, for instantaneities disappear as soon as they appear. Instantaneous things thus cannot be said to displace themselves, nor do they overlap, since they vanish at the very point at which they emerged. There is in the second instant nothing left of that existent in the instant before. All there is, is a self-annihilating instantaneous sensation.[11]

Throughout the history of Western thought, philosophers have attempted to define change and time either as continuous or discontinuous. Discontinuity implies instantaneous existents (haecceities), succeeding one upon another, without real duration. Continuity opts for real duration of change and time as one and all-pervading. The discontinuity hypothesis posits that movement and time are the products of the self-annihilating nature of each particular existent, and experience merely creates the illusion of basic duration, like the celluloid strip containing a series of frames passing through the movie projector. Nothing endures, nor is there duration of any interval or gap. This hypothesis likewise falls into Zeno's alluring trap. The instantaneous existent can never get out of the starting blocks: there can be no account of that which is instantaneous with itself as different from what it succeeds and what precedes it. Not only is its emergence logically impossible, but as an instantaneous existent it must forgo the possibility of its being something definite. So according to the definition of a pure instantaneous existent, pure continuous change is denied. Yet, given the power of experience, pure change cannot simply be discarded without further ado.

The continuity hypothesis entails duration of consciousness and some sort of durationless present – William James' 'specious present' – regarding what is held in consciousness, both past and present, which is simultaneous with what is experienced at a given moment. Time thus becomes like a line of which a segment makes up the 'specious present,' the 'real' present constituting the later boundary of this segment. The problem is that if relations exist between images, past and present, which consciousness somehow holds in check at a given durationless moment, the notion of temporal precedence is put out of the question. For the relations must exist between entities that occurred through successive durations of time, yet they are held in check simply in terms of earlier than, later than, and now, as if they were all always already there in simultaneity. Events are strung along the time-line as successive points; there is no account of time's flow, of consciousness of the incessant mutability of things. If 'earlier' and 'later' are conceived to be all there all at once, then the idea of duration is effaced; if they are not present at one and the same time, then any notion of unity is pure chimera.

What we have here, in a new garment, is McTaggart's one-dimensional linear flow of the A-series in contrast to the always already here-nowness of the B-series. The ongoing, continuous flux of experience eludes B-series time and orthodox logical interpretation. In the flow of experience unfolded from the experiential matrix, what is, is already something else. Thus we once again have the sliding-scale distinction – as illustrated at the close of chapter 4 – between intellection and experience, Thirdness on the one hand and a Firstness → Secondness transition on the other. And thus also we once again see that identity, contradiction, and indirectly, the excluded-middle principle, are abrogated. That is, classical logic is on the whole tautological, but experience is nontautological. Logic posits discrete atoms; raw experience knows no such particulars, for they are the yield of culturally developed propensities, proclivities, and habits. Dissenters from orthodox logic and in favour of a logic of pure change – of life processes, and sign processes – have been few in number, faint voices from the wilderness: Heraclitus, Nicholas of Cusa, Hegel, vitalist philosophers such as Bergson and Whitehead, and in his own, tentative and incomplete way, Peirce. Peirce occasionally promised a 'logic of vagueness,' which he never delivered in its entirety, though he left scattered bits and pieces for future contemplation (see Merrell 1991b, 1995, for brief discussion; also Nadin 1982, 1983).

A chief – if not *the* chief – bugbear with any logic of change is the paradoxical coalescence of presence and absence. According to stock-in-trade logical imperatives, a subject as identical with itself must be coexistent with itself and exactly equal to itself. It must be where it is, as an absolute presence, for there is no place else where it could be. If it were anywhere else at the same instant it would be other than what it is. Likewise, it must be exactly what it is, for there is nothing else it can be and still be itself. Hence change is barred from the stark landscape of logic as it is ordinarily conceived. In contrast, a logic of change, as I see it, must be able to account for something that is (in the present) what it is not (at the instant there is consciousness of it). What it *is* is not (yet) available to consciousness, what it *was* (and is so available) has already become something other, and what it *will be* (in the process of emerging into the present) is (yet) a mere possibility for emergence into presentness, and then into consciousness. The presence and absence of an object is in this manner that which is not the object. At the same time, the experienced object, the object of consciousness, is never less than both a presence and an absence. By these knee-jerk standards, to say that something is present is to imply both its presence and its absence. Which is to say that that which is identical to itself is always already in the process of modifying itself such that it is not identical to itself.

An adequate 'semiotic logic' or 'logic of semiotics,' then, must be all-embracing along the lines of this paradoxical mould. It must be both ordered and unordered by the identity and noncontradiction principles. In other words, it must include the *is-ness* of Secondness (fleeting haecceities), the *might-be-ness* of Firstness (possibility), and the *would-* or *should-be-ness* of Thirdness (probability). It must include both orthodox logic and a logic of flux. It must be a logic of the actual and the nonactual, of something and nothing (that is, the not yet something). It must be the 'now this, now this' of our 'Wormland' as pure, unadulterated change on the one hand, coupled with Ludwig's hyperlogical grasp of the universe, on the other, plus all the mediary stages in between – a monumental, and most likely impossible, task indeed.[12]

Or perhaps at a somewhat more down-to-earth – yet equally perverse – level, a 'semiotic logic' could be considered the combination of Borges' (1962) mnemonic super-nominalist, 'Funes the Memorious,' inextricably merged with Borges' timeless contemplator of the 'Aleph.' Funes' impeccable memory allows him to reconstruct an entire day of his life, but, limited to a mere linear stream of sensations, he required a day to complete the task – compare to Tristram Shandy's paradoxical writing of his memoirs, which must continue, *ad infinitum*. Funes' phenomenal powers of memory are the exact opposite of that contemplator of Borges' 'Aleph,' who is capable of witnessing all the things and happenings of the entire universe, past, present, and future, in one massive instantaneous gulp. One *Umwelt*-emergent semiotic sphere is pure change, the other pure timelessness. It is the pure rush of time against the recalcitrant resistance of changelessness; the linear push of an irretrievable 'worm-line' within the isotropic Minkowski 'block,' where everything is always already there.

Thus it is that the whole of bio-nootemporality must ultimately – that is, at the infinite stretch – include within its embrace the whole of the domain of Thirdness, and it ultimately terminates, along the infinite stretch of the semiotic node, in the nothingness from which the universe of signs gushes forth. Experience conjoined with intellect, consciousness with the mind, brings continuity into brief moments of alliance with discontinuity, process with permanence, or, to use the terms with caution, 'diachrony' with 'synchrony.' And thus we have a fair image of one-dimensional semiotics – that is, linear development of a particular 'world-line' within the multidimensional 'block' containing an indeterminate number of possible 'world-lines,' or, as we shall note below, linear development of the genetic code generating a three-dimensional organism.

One-dimensional semiotics, in sum, sets up severe restrictions, for the semiotic agent ordinarily cannot see beyond her 'world-line' and into the 'elsewhere' and hence into the 'world-lines' of others, or beyond her own self so as to enter into the *otherness* of the *other*. Her perception is comparable to the view from a vertical slit in a boxcar of a rushing train. She can see no more than a slice at a time, but since the series of discrete slices are passing by at a rate beyond her persistence of vision, she sees − or believes she sees − the continuous unfolding of her 'semiotically real' world. On the other hand, to repeat the conclusion from chapter 4, she actually enjoys an indeterminately heightened degree of freedom, for at any juncture along her 'world-line' she has an n-directional set of possible trajectories lying in wait. The choice is hers, of course.

Speaking of freedom, I now exercise a digression by turning in the next two chapters to our contemporary, 'postmodern' milieu, in order to foreground, and further qualify, the ebullient flush of signs perpetually confronting us, whether we like it or not and whether we know it or not. In chapters 8 and 9 I move on to the 'Signs ≈ Life' equation suggested in chapters 1 and 2.

6

Assembly-Line Signs, and Beyond

I shall have been asked by now what all the talk of temporality and spatiality has to do with the 'Signs $\approx$ Life' equation in the first place. In order to clarify my motives, let me exercise a move from symbolicity (one-dimensionality disseminating and spilling into multilinearity), and iconicity (self-referential, self-sufficient oneness), toward the Secondness of indexicality – that is, that which is construed to be 'real.' I do so by bringing the semiosic process to bear on our postmodern scene and its semiological interpretation by Baudrillard and others.[1] Then, I enrich the focus by introducing the self, which serves to complement the concept of sign. This move should prepare us for chapter 7, which briefly places the idea of the postmodern in a broader framework.

Of course I cannot be so pretentious as to assume I can properly outline the multiply varied postmodern milieu in a few short pages. At most I can perhaps evoke a certain feeling; I can hardly expect to do more, for we are living the milieu, we are within it, we are it.[2] So the only possible avenue, I suppose, must begin, most appropriately ...

1. ON A DISSONANT NOTE

According to many observers, during the last half of the present century an entirely new 'language' began to emerge in response to the rapidly changing socio-politico-economic postmodernist environment. Mark Poster (1989, 1990) calls it the 'mode of information' – that is, comparable to the 'mode of signification' idea presented above. The 'mode of information' has served, for better or for worse, to 'detotalize the social world,' thus providing impetus for dispersing and decentring the self. This loss of the self and the accompanying decentring process are chiefly a consequence of recent electronically mediated lines of communication 'which are increasingly being substituted for both face-to-face and written communications' (Poster 1989:79).[3]

The postmodern gaze tends to reduce the length and breadth of cultural experience to a carnival of two-dimensional (for example, dyadic, paramorphic) spectacles, an effervescent race of captivating images and seductive surfaces. This phenomenon is an unbridled fetishism, and of the illusion of a forever inaccessible *virtuality-immediacy*, of the depiction of naked power, ribald sex, and unremitting violence, of relentless speed and break-neck acceleration of the imaginary (and, by extension, the 'semiotically real'), of a blaze of spatial segments and temporal increments the total concoction of which becomes fused and confused into nothing more than a random mishmash of suggestive signifying glimpses (Kroker 1992). Television, and especially its ads, we are told, are by consensus the prime offenders. The boob tube is the most natural medium of information transfer in this near-chaotic setting – most likely ripe, it would appear, for massive Prigogine dissipation on a global scale. In fact, television is not merely the chief medium, but the most active propagator of the new 'mode of information.' While one stares glaze-eyed at the tube, images fly past images with staccato, machine-gun cadence. It is up to the mind to somehow find a way to construct some sort of legato flow from the staccato series, an ominous task when we consider that the barrage of messages is projected forth at multiple levels some of which remain virtually inaccessible to the conscious mind: they are in part subliminal (Jameson 1984).

For example, the nimble cameras of Cable News Network juxtapose images of international violence with trivial domestic-problem situations and their simple unsubtle answers, for the purpose of marketing fabric softeners, headache remedies, programs for weight loss without effort or sacrifice, and underarm deodorants that promise an attractive mate. What is worse, those same scenes of international violence can even be buffered so as to appear somehow alluring, a means to some twisted form of salvation for all humankind. During the skirmish between the person set up as Satan incarnate, Saddam Hussein, and the might of 'we-the-people' supposedly represented by the whole of the United Nations, TV sets proudly displayed jets taking off laden with instruments of death, then empty jets landing, mission accomplished, and 'at ease, men.' There were no killing fields to be seen, no Rambo-esque show of machismo, no revelation of the thousands of innocent lives lost. In another – but perversely complementary – march of scenarios, we have George Bush, on the one hand accompanied by corporate giants on a trip to meet the capitalistic power-league in Japan with the objective of making *demands* for free trade by *pleading* for the sale of American cars on the island, and on the other hand, buying socks in J.C. Penney's, registering fascination over the check-out procedure at a supermarket, and sitting down with construction workers to eat a sandwich and have a good-ol'-boy chat – our former President, who in all probability never had a friend in his life who was not a millionaire!

Examples are legion, and I trust I need not pursue the issue further. The point to be made is that Marshall McLuhan's 'the media is the message' announcing the impending electronic age, renders centralization, linear specialization, analysis of components to the detriment of wholes, isolation, and the cultivation of detachment – all of the machine age – quite obsolete. Meanings merge with messages, and messages become inseparable from channels of information; in fact, information is highlighted more and more, while meaning tends to fall by the wayside. The electronic media create conditions of decentring within local confines, interdependence on a global scale, and a visual and auditory world of simultaneous events. What is more, the *mise en scène* rapidly overtaking us apparently defies linearity; hence in its radical 'nonlinear logic of differentiation' it appears synonymous with irrationality (Smart 1992:115–20).

At this point the message might seem to be that the media, by and large one-dimensional, even regarding visual imagery – parcel and product of Boolean linearity – with their machine-gun cadence, give rise to virtually limitless possibilities in our three-dimensional sphere of things (life games, virtual reality, semantic nets, and other wonders of cybermania). Nothing seems to be absolutely barred, everything is apparently possible by way of some sort of, to rephrase Derrida, joyous Nietzschean free-play of signs. We are, it would seem, at last liberated from those awful tyrants – *logos*, representation, presence, immediacy – and can now bask in the life-giving warmth of semiosis, unfettered by our previous hang-ups.

But this is not exactly what we are being told by those self-proclaimed hypersensitive contemplators of our present scene. Critics charge that TV rhetoric, above all, undermines the viewer's residue of reason, transmuting well-tempered thought processes into the baser metal of desire for frivolous consumption, and attraction into the mixed messages underlying dizzy rhetorical cajolery. Advertisers, politicians, and reporters, so the story goes, stop at nothing in their efforts to grab a larger share of the market, rate higher in the polls, and pursue that elusive Pulitzer Prize. Advertising has most especially shifted from offering information to a presumably intelligent, thoughtful consumer, to the irrational manipulation of the consumer. This transformation is the result of what has been termed a collapse (1) of (dyadic) referentiality – which enjoyed unwarranted privilege anyway; (2) of (triadic) meaning, the dream of a Grand Transcendental Signified loaded with semantic ammunition – which never really existed in the first place; and (3) of language in general, the language of 'presence,' of '(phal)logocentrism,' of unadulterated 'truth.'

Consequently, a decentring of that artificially propagated idea of the paramount individual Cartesian subject standing apart from its world as supreme objective arbiter is brought about, which further serves to undermine the traditional distinctions between subjectivity and objectivity, true and false consciousness, science and nonscience (humanistic concerns, ideology), and appearance and reality. So far, so good, it would seem: the Derridean critique of our coveted Western standards stands out bold and robust. But let us look further.

The transformations wrought in our contemporary milieu are hardly any-where more evident, we have been told, than in the writings of Jean Baudrillard. The early Baudrillard saw society as organized around unnecessary conspicu-ous consumption and the lavish display of commodities by means of which one could acquire identity, prestige, and status in the community; the more flashy one's cars, house, clothes, and assorted toys, the higher one's standing. During this stage of his thought, Baudrillard made efforts to combine Saussurean semiological theory in terms of a 'critique of the political economy of the sign' with a Marxist critique of capitalism (Baudrillard 1975, 1981). For the later Baudrillard, labour is no longer a force of production but has itself become just another sign among signs. Production is nothing more than the consumerist system of signs referring to themselves (Baudrillard 1983a, 1983b, 1988).[4]

Regarding the contemporary West, Fredric Jameson also observes that culture is 'the very element of consumer society itself, no society has ever been saturated with signs and images like this one' (Jameson 1979:131). To many observers, Jameson's announcement, as well as Baudrillard's conclusions, hardly come as a surprise. Consumerist culture and the mass media have generated an inundation of images and signs the consequence of which, in Baudrillard's terms, created a 'simulation world' erasing the age-old distinction between the 'real' and the imaginary. Jameson (1979, 1983) calls this world the product of a depthless, schizophrenic posture capitalizing on a plurality of styles, idiosyncrasies, fads, and fashions, the end-product of which is 'pastiche' – hollow imitation, 'blank parody,' empty masks. Baudrillard would not exactly disagree with this estimation.[5] Both he and Jameson allude to a progressive abstraction – in fact, a fetishism of the abstract – of cultural signs (see also Rochberg-Halton 1986). However, he does Jameson one better, factoring his equation to the next stage: the 'logic' of contemporary commodity capitalism is not merely depthless, it breeds a malignant Nietzschean sort of nihilism. The privileged domains of modernity – science, philosophy, labour, private enterprise, social programs, and above all, theory (all Lyotard's [1984] 'metanarratives') – are sucked up by a whirlwind of vacuous signifiers and into a 'black hole.' The age-old cherished illusions of the referential sign vanish, as signs and their objects implode into mere disembodied signs (Baudrillard 1983a:1–4).

Consequently, the commodities of postmodern culture organized around conspicuous consumption have lost their value as material goods; they exist only in the realm of semiotic value. Like signs in Saussure's differential system of language, we are told, they take on value according to their relations with all other sign-commodities in the entire system. Everything is flattened to the same level, that of signifiers existing in contiguous relationship with other signifiers (that is, dyadic, two-dimensional semiotics). Ultracommercialized goods having become signs are centrifuged, homogenized, desiccated, and shoved onto a gullible public in the form of a Pablum diet, the totality of which composes a vast tautological system whereby individual needs are created by the very system responsible for satisfying those needs. In fact, individuals are nothing more than socially invented agents of needs. Each individual becomes tantamount to any and all individuals. The individual, like any given sign-commodity, is equal to no more than any and all other sign-commodities of the same name and value. That is, individuals are hardly more than gas molecules in an enclosed container colliding with one another and with the container walls, now zipping along at breakneck speed, now buffeted along tangential lines, now momentarily at rest, all of them definable in no more than aleatory terms. Yet, as an aggregate, the collection of individuals is statistically determinable.

This transformation of society that Baudrillard outlines is marked by the onslaught of simulacra, a deluge of infinitely reiterative signs ushering in the aftermath of individuals in a rush of random Brownian movement. Objects, and society at large, have been subjected to the effects of cybernetic codes, models, modulations, and steering mechanisms aimed at perfecting the project of social control in terms of statistical averages. This, Baudrillard writes, is the chief characteristic of neocapitalist, post-Marxist, postmodern society. The masses ('silent majority') passively consume whatever is dished out to them – television, sports, toys, movies, politics, processed food, cars, etc. – which renders any idea of class struggle obsolete. Boundaries and categories of social life and commodities dissolve. Distinctions between appearance and reality, subject and object, everyday life and art, collapse into a delirious mix of signs, a self-perpetuating system generated and controlled by *simulation* models and codes, the product of society's accelerated computer-technologization.

Three 'orders of simulation,' Baudrillard writes, have gradually come to dominate our mind-numbing postmodern social life. They were introduced with (1) the order of the counterfeit (the natural law of value), which coincides with the rise of modernity, when simulacra implied power and social relations, (2) the industrial revolution, when serial production, and finally automation (based on the commercial law of value), opened the door to infinite reproducibility, and machines began to take their place alongside humans, and (3) our present cybernetic society (based on the structural law of value), when models began to take precedence over things; and since models are signs, signs now began to exercise the full force of their hegemony (Baudrillard 1983a).[6]

This third-order simulation is obsessively binary or dyadic in nature – which is to be expected, for after all, Baudrillard's own model is 'linguicentric,' Saussurean. The story has it that language, genetics, and social organization are analogous (in the order of structuralism, the DNA code, and semiology). All are governed by a binary (cybernetic, Boolean) logic underlying social models and codes controlling institutional and everyday life. Consequently, an individual's range of choices and responses is severely regulated by programmed and precoded messages. In contrast to classical theories of social control, Baudrillard's theory prima facie appears radically indeterminate: there is no Grand Omniscient Administrator with a Master Plan in hand, but rather, everything resembles 'a Brownian movement of particles or the calculation of probabilities.' Such is, for example, voting in democratic cybersocieties, 'as if everyone voted by chance, or monkeys voted.' Party distinctions have been flattened. It really 'makes no difference at all what the parties in power are expressing historically and socially. It is *necessary* even that they represent nothing: the fascination of the game, the polls, the formal and statistical compulsion of the game is all the greater' (Baudrillard 1983a:132).

Power can be absolute in this system only if it is capable of diffracting into a spectrum of variants, each defined in terms of binaries: remove something here, put something else there; change this, and reciprocally alter that, and so on. This applies to brands of soapsuds as well as to peaceful coexistence between superpowers. Two superpowers are necessary to maintain control; one superpower standing alone would soon crumble.[7] The macrolevel binary opposition between them is regulated by manipulating myriad series of binaries within the system to retain the image of equilibrium. Though at local levels a flurry of diversified activity appears to reign, the matrix, by its very nature, remains intractably binary and does not change on the whole. It is 'always the 0/1, the binary scansion that is affirmed as the metastable or homeostatic form of the current system' (Baudrillard 1983a:135). Everything apparently comes in twos, whether giving the appearance of opposition or identity (simulacra). In either case, the sign purifies itself by duplicating itself, and on so doing it destroys its meaning and its referent. Andy Warhol demonstrates this with his multiple replicas showing 'at the same time the death of the original and the end of representation' (Baudrillard 1983a:136). In short, cybernetics triumphs by reducing everything to binaries that are not really binaries at all but oppositions fused into differences ultimately destined to be cancelled entirely. And sameness will surely rule the land. That is, Baudrillard seems to be telling us – though he is far from explicit on the matter – that signs will suffer 'de-generacy' to the extent that they will function as if they were signs of Firstness: icons.

On Baudrillard's radical semiological view, signs and modes of representation rather than representation itself come to constitute 'reality.' Consequently, signs begin to take on autonomy. In interaction with other signs, they make up a new type of social order; they mandate the future of commodities, consumers, and society, all of which are in the final analysis nothing more than signs flattened to the same base level. Signs refer to, become charged with meaning in relation to, and take their rightful place in the language of, the media with respect merely to other signs in the entire interwoven, variegated, labyrinthine tapestry. Representation is banned, and signs are destined to float in an undefinable space of their own making – all of which is Saussurean poststructuralist idealism with a vengeance, as defined by Douglas Kellner (1989: 60–92) and Eugene Rochberg-Halton (1986:45–51), each in his own way.

Thus the era of rational thought and discourse meets its demise, while at the same time, in Poster's words:

the structural dimension gains autonomy, to the exclusion of the referential dimension, establishing itself on the death of the latter. Gone are the referentials of production, signification, affect, substance, history, i.e. the whole equation of real contents that still gave the sign weight by anchoring it with a kind of carrying capacity, of gravity – in short, its form as representative equivalent. All this is surpassed by the other stage of value, that of total relativity, of generalized commutation, which is combinatory and simulatory. This means simulation in the sense that from now on signs will exchange among themselves exclusively, without interacting with the real (and they only exchange themselves among themselves smoothly, they only exchange themselves perfectly *on the condition* that they no longer exchange themselves with the real). (1988:125)

As a result, the individual is left with an idealist, relativist universe composed of the imaginary (thought-signs) more than the 'real,' that is, the 'semiotically real' (sign-events). It follows, Baudrillard writes, that

determination is dead, indeterminism reigns. We have witnessed the ex-termination (in the literal sense of the word) of the reality of production, and of the real of the sign ... All the great humanist criteria of value, all the values of a civilization of moral, aesthetic, and practical judgment, vanish in our system of images and signs. Everything becomes undecidable. This is the characteristic effect of the domination of the code, which is based everywhere on the principle of neutralization and indifference. This is the generalized brothel of capital: not the brothel of prostitution but the brothel of substitution and interchangeability. (Poster [ed.] 1988:126–8)

2. YET, STRANGE CONSONANCES

What we have in Baudrillard, it would appear, is a sort of 'ultra-' or 'hyper-nominalism,' something in the order of category *B* in table 4. Signs as discrete, referenceless atoms rush about in a constant collision course with one another, their apparent relation to one another and to the whole of things having been lost in the maelstrom: pure particulars, nomadic signs with neither subject nor object, only naked signs.

In fact, Baudrillard's signs have 'de-generated' to the extent that they are barely signs of Secondness, for there is hardly any dyadic relation, let alone any triadism of Thirdness, which is all quite alien to Peirce. These signs are tantamount to a sort of one-dimensional semiotics incapable of producing authentic Peircean symbols of mediated Thirdness, for they have submerged into the domain of iconicity (simulacra) as homeomorphs, with little degree of freedom at their disposal. A logical move, in this light, would be to demonstrate how Peirce, along lines radically divergent from those of Baudrillard, deviates from, yet on certain points coincides with, the poststructuralist-postmodernist stance. Upon so demonstrating, I shall generally focus on the Peircean idea of symbolicity, Thirdness, mediation.

In the neo-Saussurean parlance common to poststructuralism, a sign is a concept and an image, both of them mental – idealistic nominalism – with hardly any association between sign, meaning, and referent. In other words, the putative postmodern subjectless subject consumes signs, not things. Peircean triadic semiotics, in stark contrast, entails a sign (representation), its meaning (roughly, the interpretant), and its respective object (which is 'semiotically real,' not 'really real'). Hence what Peirce dubs 'representation' is never immediate but always mediated, never what is directly perceived but what is perceived and in the same breath interpreted *as* such-and-such – which salvages 'representation' from out-and-out 'logocentrism.' In Baudrillard's view, when in the postmodern world signs are exchanged between minds they become 'symbolic' (that is, 'autonomous'). Their meanings float – ambiguously and vaguely, as it were – between minds, and thus remain divorced from the furniture of the world. Signs do not carry along a satchel full of meanings to put in some sort of order such that one can say 'Here the sign, there the meaning,' nor is there any necessarily motivated link, natural or conventional, between signs and 'things.' Rather, 'meanings,' if we dare even use the word in this context, indiscriminately and randomly wander in and out of minds: a hustle-bustle of activity, aleatory signification, anarchic information generation. Manipulation of these cultural signs equals manipulation of the public. It is no longer a matter of exchanging commodities in the orthodox Marxian sense, for the commodities have become themselves mere signs. We are, it appears, submerged in the 'mode of information.'

In this fashion, television is capable of displacing confessionals, therapy, family encounters, fireside chats, private periods of silent contemplation, public events such as checkers, scrabble, and poker marathons – far removed from one-on-one video game interaction – as well as picnics, football and baseball games, adventurous outings, and even puttering around the yard or cleaning the garage. During sitcoms, commercials, CNN, dreary soaps, I-told-you-so mini-series, and even so-called educational TV, the onlooker is presumably formed, fashioned, and artificially refabricated into a passive consumer, numbed into an apparently semicatatonic state by incessant uni-dimensional bombardment of visual and aural rhetoric. In the process, floating signifiers are slapped onto unnecessary commodities not because of some intrinsic relation between them but for the purpose of fulfilling desires created by that very rhetoric. In comparable fashion, through computer mail and teleconferencing, electronic mediation heightens the artificiality of the communicative track, compelling the user to sense a false presence, an illusory immediacy, a hereness and nowness of the communicative act (and all this without the mediated inferential process of Thirdness, since the semiotic agent, on reflection, knows better – or should know better – than to think all this is anything more than ersatz, mock, sham representation of frivolous commodities).

Thus with the term 'mode of information,' Poster, in part following Bau-drillard, is able to reinvest Marx's 'mode of production' and place it in the contemporary context, while eschewing such terms as 'age of information,' which usually pretends to hail the ushering in of something new and refreshing. 'Mode of information' designates the field of pure linguistic experience, 'whose basic structural relations change from period to period just as do those of the mode of production' (Poster 1989:82). It takes into account recent critiques of representation, intention, and the univocity of language, while remaining in tune with Marxist assumptions and the unique tenor of the media since the cybernetic revolution began in the 1940s and 1950s with Alan Turing, John von Neumann, Norbert Wiener, and Claude Shannon and Warren Weaver.

The important facet of Poster's work – via Baudrillard – to the present enquiry stems from his idea that the electronic mode creates a surface of signs referring only to themselves in delirious bliss, finally embracing the self, which in the process becomes itself a full-blown sign. Language is no longer a mere tool, but includes the interpreting self and thus becomes its own mechanic tooling the semiotic machine, from 'software' (mind) levels to 'hardware' (brain) levels. In this vein, Baudrillard's study of the nature of signification in advertising emphasizing the separation of signifiers and signifieds from the commodities that were the focus of their erstwhile relation, is multiplied many-fold by the electronic media. The result is that everything can be somehow construed to relate to everything else, in a bewildering and at the same time in some masochistic fashion, delectable confusion.

The upshot is that Boolean computer language underlying the electronic media – the most obstinately linear, digitalized language imaginable – ultimately gives rise to unlimited associativity along n-ary lines in n-dimensional spatiality. The problem stems chiefly from Baudrillard's idea that in our postmodern milieu signs, Saussurean signs, have been injected with a massive dose of *autonomy* – an autonomy of actualized atoms, bordering on Secondness as it were.[8] As largely arbitrary, autonomous signs, they enjoy virtually unlimited freedom, no doubt – as emergence along multiple one-dimensional lines within a three-dimensional sphere – and they can consequently take on a 'life' of their own, it might appear.

This 'life,' however – and herein lies the problem – has been supposedly granted any and all signs by those of the multimedia in charge of manipulating the public. Signs take on 'life' because they have become autonomous; the media-mongers use, and are thereby used by, these signs for the purpose of duping the common folk into lavishing on themselves more and more unnecessary commodities. But the commodities have themselves been replaced by the signs, which are now more 'real' than the 'real,' they are 'hyperreal,' as Baudrillard reiterates time and again. The common folk gobble up the signs dished out to them as if they were 'real'; and they are 'real,' the only 'reality' available in a superhyped malaise.

Now, if Baudrillard's signs with a 'life' of their own were indeed to have become autonomous and nothing but autonomous, the yield would be devastating; the so-called common folk's semiotic freedom would be severely shunted. These very autonomous signs enjoying authenticity worthy of the most dignified symbols, would actually have become mere signs of 'de-generacy.' As such they would be 'dead' signs, much like 'dead' metaphors and all other signs mindlessly consumed as a result of *embedment, automatization, habit.* They would not be signs engaged in interaction with active consciousness but signs out of mind and rooted in matter, neither genuine thought-signs nor sign-events but simply signs blindly pushed and shoved here and there, randomly moving in and out, while engaged in an aleatoric dance to the screech of some sort of heavy-metal tribal cadence.

In contrast, relatively authentic, 'growing' symbols spiral 'ever-upwards' – though with fits and jerks, and with occasional setbacks – according to the equation $1 \rightarrow 10 \rightarrow 1' \rightarrow 10' \rightarrow 1'' \ldots n$. These are indeed 'living signs.' For the 'common folk' of Baudrillard's discourse, in contrast, parameters of choice are fundamentally limited to one-dimensional 'de-generate' symbolicity (that is, to iconicity), as autonomous signs having become merely self-contained, isolated signs, that is: $10 \rightarrow 1 \rightarrow 1' \rightarrow 1'' \ldots n$. Active, mediating Thirdness is 'life'; self-sufficient iconicity of 'de-generacy' without the collaboration of interactive interpretative communities of semiotic agents suffers slow 'death.' The rampaging semiosic river is dammed, a reservoir builds up, and winter arrives, freezing the water into a solid block. If Baudrillard's signs were indeed autonomous in the full-blown sense, then the manipulated ordinary citizens could not but consume them at most in linear Boolean fashion – Baudrillard himself admits that they do so as robots – as if there were no choices, as if there existed *this* sign in the immediate *here* and *now* and nothing more.

Fortunately, in light of the premises underlying this enquiry, 'living' Peircean signs *ipso facto* exercise, and will continue to exercise, some degree of autonomy; if not, they would not be 'alive.' But rather than mere islands unto themselves, they are also to a degree perpetually open to their environment; in other words, in view of chapters 1 and 2, they are not exclusively *autopoietic* entities. There is constant give-and-take, disequilibrium, imbalance, tension. The process is ongoing. This tension of tensions there will always be: a tendency toward symmetry, equilibrium, balance ('death') *versus* an opposing tendency toward asymmetry, disequilibrium, imbalance ('life'). If 'death' were to reign supreme, then there would be only crystallized stasis. On the other hand, if there were only 'life' and nothing but 'life,' then pure chaos would erupt – Nietzsche's eternal return, nothing new under the sun – within which 'life' as we know it, and perhaps as it can only be known, could not continue to sustain itself. There must reign, in the final analysis, disordered order, ordered disorder: being always becoming, and becoming never quite becoming authentic being.

As a result, whether at work or play or rest, whether in the family, the church, the schools, leisure activities, or travel, complex and perplexing new levels of interconnectedness afforded by the electronic media promise virtually unlimited possibilities to the media manipulators, thus enhancing their control over the manipulated. As a result, exchanges of messages between humans and between humans and machines are subject to radically fewer space and time constraints – consequently, McLuhan's 'global village' now appears technically feasible. Silicon-based communicative facilities become increasingly efficient, giving credence to compelling arguments demonstrating that human relations are undergoing radical alterations. Negotiations regarding the conduct of social life – who belongs up and down the hierarchy, who can speak with authority, who must listen, who makes decisions, who is free to choose, who commands credibility and who not – are subject to new rules and strategies. This is not simply a current phenomenon, of course. It began with the light bulb, the telephone, and other early technological developments, and is only now beginning to exercise its full force (Marvin 1988).

According to this conception, in Fraser's realm where one dimension is committed and three dimensions are free, the bonds limiting traditional discourse are severed. Since the Renaissance, art, science, intuition, thought, and even everyday affairs have been ordered along specific lines and patterns, like the iron filings on a vibrating flat surface when a magnet is placed under it. Everything, it now appears, is somehow, and mysteriously by invisible lines of force, connected to everything else. All experience is part of a whole; each individual consciousness is all consciousness. What appeared to be the undesirable chaotic element of the universe, feared by scientists obsessed in their pursuit of truth at all cost, is not merely that random, unplanned, catastrophic Antichrist, the adversary of all that is good and godly. It is a new form of order under the statistical headings 'indeterminacy,' 'uncertainty,' 'fractals,' 'fluctuations,' 'dissipative structures,' 'asymmetry,' and so on. From modernity's insistence on law and order, on balance and harmony, on collecting all the information and putting each bit in its proper place, we now have postmodernism's ruthless rush of time, reckless abandon in space, and experience through n-directions in virtual simultaneity (Hassan 1980, 1987; Schechner 1982:109–28).

In Baudrillard's interpretation of the postmodern milieu, what we have is actually not symbolicity at all in the Peircean sense. Rather, the unfettered freedom promised by Fraser's domain of one dimension committed and three free (Firstness, prototemporality, protomorphic models) has 'de-generated' to the point that few degrees of freedom remain. That is to say, communication is by way of symbols, clearly enough, but symbols tied down to tunnel-like linear production rather than free-rein n-dimensional generativity. To repeat, they are *de-generate symbols*, their symbolicity is processed in robot fashion as if they were icons.

Of course, Heraclitus of old was privy to such paradoxes. He knew that they are not resolvable into a harmonious, noncontradictory whole. Postmodern holism also admits, embraces, needs, an uncertain system of contradictory complementarity. It has learned – must learn – to accept, even embrace, *inconsistencies* and *incompleteness*. For the unattainable and inconceivable whole within which we dwell is *multicentric*, whether we like it or not. Everything and nothing is at the centre, which is everywhere and nowhere, depending upon the perspective – that radical *perspectivism, pace* Nietzsche, from another vantage, José Ortega y Gasset, and in recent times, Jacques Derrida, Richard Rorty, and in their own way, Nelson Goodman, Hilary Putnam, and W.V.O. Quine.

Experience is in this view quite free-wheeling. It flows, alternating between reflexivity of the flow without stopping it and subjectivity to the flow without the capacity to analyse it. This alternating of the current serves further to foment an embrace of the inconsistency-paradox horns. Upon their being so embraced, the processes of knowing and being known are inseparable: all observations are participatory acts, and all participatory acts are to a degree creative – or constructive, as it were. In this light, it must be conceded that the alternative currents of experience – reflexivity, subject-object, knower-known – cancel the possibility of exclusively autonomous entities in the sense of Maturana-Varela. Rather, an oscillatory autonomy-dependency process is incessantly acted out, annihilated, and re-enacted.

Thus it becomes exceedingly problematic to speak of absolutes. The direct, unmediated seeing things 'Exactly as they are on no uncertain terms, dammit,' of modernity, becomes a postmodern flux of experience, given the moment and nothing but the moment. The only specifiables, if specifiables there be at all in a rather loose sense, are found solely in relations – in triadicity, and in this sense Peirce wins yet another round. The alternation of flow and reflexivity, of openness and autonomy, of self within *other* and self set apart from *other*, cannot but result in fragmentation *and* holism. There is not the one without the other. And they are themselves mediated by a third term, like the complementary wave-particle and 'wavicle,' or sign-object and interpretant, First, Second, and Third. The dancer cannot be separated from the dance; they are both included in the happening being unfolded, unfolding itself.

What we are experiencing today is most likely a harbinger of things to come. In the future it may be possible that the entire corpus of printed works will be digitally encoded and stored, that no information in this 'library' will be inaccessible to any individual desiring to peruse it whenever and wherever she might wish, that the information will be consumed at one's leisure, and used and abused according to one's whims, without any economic or political gain. For, if all information is available in all times and at all places, then nothing will be prioritized over anything else. All words, ideas, doctrines, and ideologies will be democratically flattened. This, in a strange convoluted way, might appear tantamount to the Enlightenment dream of human emancipation, with all information available to all – though at the same time the principle of private property will be threatened, and with it, a further diminishing of the self-importance of the Western individual self.

Or perhaps we shall have the high-tech equivalent of John Wilkins' (1968) bizarre taxonomization of the universe, or even Gustave Flaubert's (1947) *Bouvard and Pecuchet*, where all things possible are truths futilely concocted into one characterless mass. On the other hand, the scenario may be that of Jorge Luis Borges' 'Library of Babel' the anguish-ridden inhabitants of which wander about their entire lives with hardly any hope of discovering any meaning to their existence, since in this unfathomable totalizing aetheneum, meaning has become so diluted in the random maze of ciphers that it is nonexistent for these hapless, finite souls.

At any rate, futurist projections culminating in high-tech utopias of one sort or another must be considered highly suspect. In the best of possible futures, the multiple facets of electronic communication will absorb the subject, displacing it, destabilizing it, changing it from an autonomous self-determined block of granite to an amorphous mass. This transformation is not without its positive value: the Cartesian subject standing apart from the world, and from its centralized vantage enjoying access to determinate knowledge; the Kantian subject both inside and outside the world yet capable, from its self-appointed cardinal position, of constructing knowledge of its phenomenal world; the Hegelian subject trapped within the world yet capable of aiding and abetting it in its move toward the ultimate, totalizing goal; all are most likely in the throes of a demise the likes of which the West has not hitherto experienced. With the cybernetic 'mode of information,' and in light of the above on Baudrillard, on disquisitions by various and sundry poststructuralists, deconstructors, and self-proclaimed postmodernists of diverse stripes, the individual self begins to lose its distinctiveness, thus becoming increasingly decentered, orphaned, anonymous, without a home to call its own. Or so it appears.

Yet, although all this may still strike one as light-years removed from Peirce, as I suggested above, and argued elsewhere (Merrell 1995), Peirce is in some respects quite in tune with our times. In other respects, however, he diverges radically from much current thought, especially in regards to the essence of Baudrillard's three orders of simulation and the (dis)location of the self in contemporary language, discourse, and everyday langauge games. In order more adequately to illustrate the relevance of Peirce's concept of the sign to the brief disquisition I have presented in this chapter, I turn, as a preliminary step, to Michel Foucault in *The Order of Things* (1970).

3. A TOUCH OF CONTRAPUNTUS

Foucault's *epistemes*, somewhat reminiscent of Thomas Kuhn's *paradigms* according to frequent observations, served as a guiding light in Baudrillard's development of his ages of simulation thesis. The reigning *episteme* during the Renaissance was dominated by *resemblance*:

It was resemblance that largely guided exegesis and the interpretations of texts; it was resemblance that organized the play of symbols, made possible knowledge of things visible and invisible, and controlled the art of representing them. The universe was folded in upon itself: the earth echoing the sky, faces seeing themselves reflected in the stars and plants holding within their stems secrets that were of use to man. Painting imitated space. And representation ... was positioned as a form of repetition: the theatre of life or the mirror of nature, that was the claim made by all languages, its manner of declaring its existence and of formulating its right of speech. (Foucault 1970:17)

Thus the Renaissance 'prose of the world' held everything together as similar, yet different, inscribing the universe itself in the form of signs. Nature was a book. But nature's secrets were closely guarded. Knowledge was anything but self-evident, and unavailable to the unlearned eye. To know nature was a matter of disinterring and deciphering her signatures. Hardly any distinction was made between natural phenomena and Scripture, ancient texts, and the province of magic and rituals. All was language hiding her secrets, signs lying in wait, in anticipation of their discoverer and interpreter. These secrets, in their original form, were as transparent as could be; signs and things were one; all was God's creation. If after Babel, language's pristine purity was lost, it was now up to the tutored, penetrating eye to unearth her original resemblance to the furniture of the world. It was considered that these signs were strung along in triadic fashion: the inscriptions themselves, the items of the universe they designated, and the similitude linking sign and thing. In short, the macrocosm was mirrored in the microcosm of signs. Language was not arbitrary; it had been 'set down in the world and forms a part of it.' And words were 'linked together and arranged in space'; they reconstituted 'the very order of the universe' (Foucault 1970:35, 38).

The seventeenth century saw the rise of the 'Classical' – or 'Neoclassical' – age, the age of *representation*. Knowledge now focused on (1) general grammar (how to say and write the universe), (2) natural history (how to taxonomize the universe), and (3) wealth (how to analyse society through the scurry of human activity regarding exchange of goods and capital). During this time the realm of signs became binary through and through. Similitude, in terms of both form and content, had been the infinitesimally thin imaginary sheet of paper connecting signifier on the one side to signified on its reverse side. Now, Foucault tells us, Don Quixote stood at the threshold of this age of positivity, of the knower standing apart from the known, of representation. At the outset, the Don's windmills resembled, and became through his penetrating gaze, knights; a herd of sheep became an army of soldiers, an inn became a castle, a serving girl became a lady of dignity. But a transformation occurs. Don Quixote's adventures are an enactment of the books of chivalry, and like the heroes in those books the Don himself became written; thus he becomes represented and known to all. He becomes himself a book. Thus his whole being 'is nothing but language, text, printed pages, stories that already have been written down. He is made up of interwoven words; he is writing itself, wandering through the world among the resemblances' (Foucault 1970:46).

Writing, no longer the 'prose of the world,' is now an instrument of imagination, but also of illusion, deception, and madness. Rather than a source through which one can gain access to the world, similitude becomes an occasion of error, the source of fantasy, Bacon's idols, Descartes' confused mixture that must be analysed in terms of identity and difference. Words, no longer filled with resemblances, exercise tangential moves to become nothing more than merely what they are; they become arbitrary. Yet they can at least continue to represent. The classical age's task was that of constructing a universal method of analysis that would yield knowledge by arranging signs in such a way that they mirrored the universe, the order of things. The paradigmatic model was that of classification: if things could be arranged as they should be on the flat plane, they would create a legitimate picture of the object of analysis. Ideally, an arbitrary set of signs would 'permit the analysis of things into their simplest elements; it must be capable of decomposing them into their very origins; but it must also demonstrate how combinations of those elements are possible, and permit the ideal genesis of the complexity of things' (Foucault 1970:62). Signs no longer have any value apart from that which they represent; the written word and things no longer resemble one another; writing is now merely the arrangement of signs, the relations between them, which are potentially capable, by *comparison*, of representing the world. Comparison, through measurement (focus on primary qualities), and analysis (focus on parts and their relations), constitutes the dream of *mathesis universalis*, the general science of order.

For whatever success was to be had through the classical obsession with method, a price was to be paid: the process, the temporal unfolding of representation, could not itself be represented on the two-dimensional spread sheet. Foucault's disquisition on Velázquez's *Las Meninas* reveals this paradox of the impossibility of representing representation through the three functions of representation: (1) the painter can be represented in the painting but not in the *act of painting*, (2) the characters in the painting are gazing at themselves, as models, in the painting, but they are not represented in the *act of modelling*, and (3) the viewer of the painting notes that a painting is being painted, yet Velázquez places a surrogate painter in the background who is no longer observing the painting but has become a painted object; furthermore, a mirror in the background of the painting does not reflect the outside observer, but rather, it images the royal couple. Velázquez thus illustrates 'the visibility of all the ways representation works and the profound invisibility of showing it being accomplished' (Dreyfus and Rabinow 1982:26). But in spite of its fluctuating uncertainty, its strange asymmetry, its threatening to disrupt into total disorder, the painting is a screaming success. It demonstrates the *model of representation* and at the same time the impossibility of representing the *act of representation*.

The dilemma evoked by Velázquez's work patterns the tectonic shift that occurred, Foucault tells us, somewhere at the end of the eighteenth century. This dramatic upheaval signalled the collapse of the classical age, with the announcement that representation is not transparent but opaque. As long as it was taken for granted that God created a great chain of being with a preordained language to which it corresponded, and that human semiotic agents standing in some neutral zone could, by use of proper methods, get things right once and for all, the parade moved along smoothly and in step with the big band. In classical thought, the agent for whom representation represents itself is never found in the representation she has authored. She gets the picture without suffering the indignity of having to get her hands dirty by getting in it. In the general classical mode, 'nature, human nature, and their relations, are definite and predictable functional moments. And man, as a primary reality with its own density, as the difficult object and sovereign subject of all possible knowledge, has no place in it' (Foucault 1970:310). Language is no longer viewed as potentially a transparent medium whose relations are capable of representing the world's relations. Like representation itself the very act of representing relations becomes problematic.

Thus at the end of the eighteenth century 'man,' Foucault writes, makes his appearance to become the measure of all things. This is the 'anthropological age.' Language now takes its final step, divorcing itself entirely from the furniture of the world: it becomes autonomous. Discourse was first distinguished from the world and the age of 'man' brought on a distinction between the transcendental self and discourse. If Cervantes stood at the limits of resemblance and Velázquez at the limits of representation, it was the Marquis de Sade, whose *Juliette* depicted *desire* in terms of the relation between subject and object, master and slave, the transcendental and the empirical, lust and the desired body, who announced 'anthropological man.' Juliette is not merely the subject of all possible desires, we are told, but those desires are carried over and into the representation that provides them with a reasonable foundation in *discourse* and transforms them spontaneously into *scenes*. So that the great narrative of Juliette's life reveals, throughout its catalogue of desire, violence, savagery and death, the glittering table of representation. But this table is so thin, so transparent to all the figures of desire that untiringly accumulate within it and multiply there simply by the force of their combination, that it is just as lacking in reason as that of Don Quixote, when he believed himself to be progressing, from similitude to similitude, along the commingled paths of the world and books, but was in fact getting more and more entangled in the labyrinth of his own representations. (Foucault 1970:210)

After the classical age, and de Sade's closing its doors, the field of violence, desire, and sexuality, life and death, extends out below the level of representation, a vanished horizon we are now attempting to regain in our discourse, freedom, and thought. But, Foucault continues, our thought is so brief, our freedom so enslaved, our discourse so repetitive, that we must confront the fact that that horizon was a bottomless sea from the very beginning. This age of 'man' brought about a change as far-reaching as that which accompanied the advent of the classical period. The universe was now construed not as an arrangement of isolated bits and pieces linked by relations of identity and difference, but as an organism – the romantic in opposition to the mechanical model – consisting of internal relations between the parts making up a functional whole. There is no longer a similarity or identity of elements but a complementary, a sort of symbiotic, relation between them. And 'man,' who was a privileged being among others, is not merely a subject among objects; 'she' becomes another object to be known like all other objects. 'She' makes 'her' appearance when signs cease to be the sole and unquestionable source of knowledge. 'She' is now limited, however, by 'her' involvement with a language no longer considered a transparent medium but a dense field of relations providing no guiding light to an understanding of the world and its knower, who is no longer a mere spectator but an actor in the drama of existence.

Man [makes his appearance] as an object of knowledge and as a subject that knows: enslaved sovereign, observed spectator, he appears in the place belonging to the king, which was assigned to him in advance by *Las Meninas*, but from which his real presence has for so long been excluded. As if, in that vacant space towards which Velázquez's whole painting was directed, but which it was nevertheless reflecting only in the chance presence of a mirror, and as though by stealth, all the figures whose alternation, reciprocal exclusion, interweaving, and fluttering one imagined (the model, the painter, the king, the spectator) suddenly stopped their imperceptible dance, immobilized into one substantial figure, and demanded that the entire space of the representation should at last be related to one corporeal gaze. (Foucault 1970:312)

The beginning of the anthropological age is the beginning of modernity, now celebrated, now maligned, whose greatest invention, according to Foucault, was 'man' himself. In place of classical analysis, an analytic mode evolves, from Kant onward. There are now attempts to determine how the very idea of representation was possible at all, how 'man' can be known empirically by some transcendentalism making knowledge possible at all, how to know the unthought, to say the unsayable, and how we can know where we are in history and from whence we came if we can neither reach the beginning nor envision the end.

Finally, with respect to our times – that is, with the disappearance of 'man' and the 'linguistic turn' – Foucault ends *The Order of Things* as he began by discussing Jorge Luis Borges' bizarre Chinese taxonomy, with a laugh: 'Rather than the death of God – or rather in the wake of that death and in profound correlation with it – what Nietzsche's thought heralds is the end of his murderer; it is the explosion of man's face in laughter ... As the archaeology of our thought easily shows, man is an invention of recent date. And one perhaps nearing its end' (1970:385).[9]

In other words, *we* are at present where we began: *in language*, and Baudrillard's final 'age of simulacra' rules the land – disembodied signs referring to themselves, semiotic agents somnambulistically gobbling them up as if they were the genuine article, but actually they are more than genuine, they are 'hyperreal.' There is no longer any direct recourse either to signs, things, or thoughts. Discourse vanishes and we are left simply with language, that is, with signs among signs. The 'prose of the world' became during the classical age the language of representation, which was in turn transformed into discourse by the transcendental self about the word itself, about knowledge about the way things are.

Now, language returns to mock us, after the likes of Nietzsche, Mallarmé, Valéry, the later Heidegger, and the post-*Tractatus* Wittgenstein; in mathematics and science, of Poincaré, Bohr, Schrödinger, and Heisenberg; in mathematical logic, of Gödel, among other authors of the 'limitative theorems'; in the avant-garde movements, and later in literature, of James Joyce, Gertrude Stein, Beckett, and Borges. We are left with the 'text' and nothing but the 'text,' not the 'prose of the world' but our *Umwelt*-generated 'semiotically real world' as the one and only world accessible to the finite, fallible semiotic agent.

However, a distinction must be highlighted between Baudrillard, and to an extent Foucault and Derrida, and indeed, the whole of those proponents of the so-called 'linguistic turn,' on the one hand, and Peirce on the other. The linguicentrists' myopia does not allow them a peek beyond the opaque veil of natural language. In Baudrillard's vision, by way of Foucault, gravitation has been from simulacra of representation to seriality to 'hyperreality.' This is comparable to the move from homeomorphic to paramorphic to proto-morphic modelling. The problem is, to repeat, that the end-product does not cultimate in one-dimensional semiotics allowing for linear generativity of three-dimensionality, but rather, protomorphic symbolicity has 'de-generated' into iconicity, with the subject having been displaced and exiled to 'no-man's land.' In contrast, Peirce, especially when interpreted in view of the *Umwelt* idea, includes human and nonhuman 'semiotically real worlds' alike, which can-not exist without subjects as collaborating and corroborating semiotic agents. Within the domain of our own *Umwelt*-engendered signs, natural language is the medium of description and explanation *par excellence*, to be sure. But it is by no means the only medium, nor is it the most profound; it is merely one among many, the combination of which offers us a virtually unlimited play of signs, that fluid 'text,' the river of indefinite semiosis.

This very important point aside, and back to the issue at hand, a certain relationship – albeit convoluted, with frequent Möbius twists – will have been noted between Foucault's epochs of resemblance, representation, and 'man'-as-object-among-objects, on the one hand, and on the other, Firstness (iconicity), Secondness (indexicality), and Thirdness (symbolicity) – in addition to Bunn's spatiality and Fraser's temporality, to be the focus of chapter 8. This is the climb from sensation to volition to cognition, unity to duality to triadicity. Sign *generacy* is thus highlighted. But this is not the entire picture, for a threat always hovers above the semiotic agent: *de-generacy*, a fall from grace, from that hopeful but impossible paradise of unmediated signs – whatever sign goes up must come down unless there is an opposite and at least equal force keeping it upright.

Our contemporary milieu bears witness to the fact that we have never escaped, nor will we ever be able to escape, from the attraction, and, yes, the potential tyranny, of *resemblance*, from Firstness, inclination, intuition, sentiment – *abduction*. It has repeatedly come back to haunt modernity's Enlightenment dream of a rational construction of society, of objective knowledge, of absolute consensus in a community of like- and therefore right-minded citizens, and the good life for all.[10] At the same time, resemblance or analogy (Firstness) cannot always resist the slide into contiguity (Secondness) and that into autonomy (sign arbitrariness, context-independency, Thirdness), the latter stage evincing the notion of organicism – the 'growth' of symbols – with the whole constituting more than the sum of its parts, that whole being in its ideal form a self-contained, self-sufficient totality. The final stage, especially in our contemporary times in light of the above on Foucault, would entail 'man' not as a subject among objects, but as just another sign among signs – that is, a sort of pale reflection of Peirce's 'Man ≈ Sign' equation, which, in this vein, and as we shall observe further in chapters 8 and 9, is more contemporary than much contemporary thought.

Peirce's equation, like the general postmodern posture, flies directly in the face of Enlightenment-Cartesian foundationalism, the idea that knowledge is firmly planted in solid foundations fixed by our special faculty of insight or intuition by which we can know them. In his 1868 article 'Some Consequences of Four Incapacities' (*CP*:5.264–317), Peirce exposed what now goes by the name of the 'metaphysics of presence,' and '(phal)logocentrism.' Abandoning foundationalism, and propagating his fallibilist concept that there is no thesis, no matter how fundamental, that is not open to rebuttal and eventually removal, he revealed a philosophy of tender, tentative interpretations always subject to alteration. And his fallibilism calls for the concept of a *community of knowers* and the social character of the *self* (see Bernstein 1992:323–40).

I briefly turn to this topic, then, which should help clarify my assertions in the previous paragraph with respect to the continuum between Firstness, Secondness, and Thirdness. Ultimately, it will help more clearly to foreground a most important distinction between what I have dubbed the 'linguicentrists,' on the one hand, and Peirce on the other.

4. THE SELF AND ITS CONJURORS: A EUPHONIOUS BLENDING

In Western culture and thought, the self has been during diverse times and from within various disciplines conceived to be located within the physiology of the organism, in the organism's observable behaviour, or in a vanishing mathematical point somewhere in the brain. Descartes located the focus of the self in his *cogito*, a move that ultimately served to bring about an unbreachable rift between mind and body. *Rational mind*, presumably the sole property of sublime human beings, has been radically upgraded, while *instinctive mind* belongs chiefly to the behaviour of the lower beasts.

Peirce, given his anti-Cartesian posture, overturns these tables entirely. Rational mind takes years to develop, as Piaget's studies illustrate – but bear in mind that he refers to that *rational mind* of the Western variety, whose validity can and has been placed in question. And when it finally reaches its pinnacle of development, it turns out to be quite sluggish. It customarily deliberates with excruciating torpidity, it is obstinately deliberate, and it is destined repeatedly to err. On the other hand 'the instincts of the lower animals answer to their purposes much more unerringly than a discursive understanding could do. But for man discourse of reason is requisite, because men are so intensively individualistic and original that the instincts, which are racial ideas, become smothered in them. A deliberate logical faculty, therefore, has in man to take their place; and the sole function of this logical deliberation is to grind off the arbitrary and the individualistic character of thought' (*CP*:1.178).

Peirce's reason is not an arbitrary conception, as are cultural codes in the semiological sense; neither is it strictly an individual expression. The *rational mind* (of Thirdness), after becoming gelled by habit, enters semiosis along the continuum somewhere – for the precise demarcation line between rationality and instinct is unspecifiable – within instinct's domain. Therein also lies sentiment, feeling, intuition (Firstness) at the core of the human semiotic agent's innermost being, for, 'just as reasoning springs from experience, so the development of sentiment arises from the soul's Inward and Outward Experiences. Not only is it of the same nature as the development of cognition; but it chiefly takes place through the instrumentality of cognition' (*CP*:1.648).

By a process of 'slow percolation,' Peirce tells us, the sentiment, feeling, and intuition of Firstness comes to be generalized, and by the reverse process of sedimentation, reason, the domain of Thirdness, in a rather uninspiring manner takes on the characteristics of instinct: it becomes *embedded*, *automatized*, a *tacit* knowing *how* generally without the necessity consciously of cogitating and reasoning about how it is that knowing *how* is possible. Ultimately – that is, in the 'theoretical long run' – Firstness generalized into mediating Thirdness and Thirdness crystallized into autonomous, self-contained, self-sufficient Firstness are, from the most general of perspectives, and assuming the process in the infinite stretch might have reached completion, one and the same. Distinctions will at this infinite stretch of things have become welded together, discreteness will have become continuity, and the notion of an individual *self* will be no more.

Now, instinctive mind is not Baudrillard's subjectless subject devoid of consciousness, as well as conscious control and self-control, without mind or Thirdness. Instinctive mind, rather than the product of aleatoric chance affairs, evinces a cunning of its own. It has direction, purpose, goals – though they are at best ill-defined and perhaps even undefinable. It is not merely buffeted about by random forces in a humdrum display of signs, but exercises mastery over its surroundings with a confidence unknown to consious and self-conscious, cogitating and calculating, rational mind. Actually, just as Thirdness without Firstness is empty and Firstness without Thirdness is dead, so also instinctive mind needs rational mind and vice versa – and, it bears mentioning, the autonomous entity needs interaction with its environment, for if there is none, it will die, and if it loses all vestiges of its autonomy, it will disperse and become vacuous. The *self*, in good Peircean spirit, embodies this incessant fusion and fission of Firstness and Thirdness, autonomy and interaction, instinctive mind and rational mind. So let us turn directly, albeit briefly, to this issue.

Just as according to Peirce's 'Law of Mind,' ideas 'tend to spread continuously and to affect certain others which stand to them in a peculiar relation of affectivity' (*CP*:6.104), so also with the self, which, as a general idea, a thought-sign, 'is not a thing to be apprehended in an instant. It has to be lived in time; nor can any finite time embrace it in all its fullness' (*CP*:6.155). The self, in so far as it is anything apart from other selves, and from what it and they are becoming, is only a negation. That is to say, in a given present, and in isolation, it merely *is not* what it *has been* – that is, its past, its history as a biological organism that has determined the entire trajectory of its development up to now. And it *is not* what it *will be* – that is, its potential, the state toward which it is in the process of becoming. To be a self is to be part of a community and in a process of becoming, but at the same time an individual self must maintain a certain degree of aloofness, of autonomy, with respect to that community (*CP*:6.157). Yet if its role as autonomous agent exceeds its limits, if it is cut off from its past and future and from other selves in the ongoing present, its possibility of self-realization as a sign is negated; it is merely a sign of radical negation.

Of course, the 'theoretical long run' by means of which the self-sign realizes its absolute self-fulfilment will never come to pass in a finite community of finite semiotic agents. The individual self, mind, and consciousness will always exist as, in part, an autonomous entity that is at the same time set apart from the world. Vincent Colapietro (1989:chap. 4) argues, quite effectively, that Peirce's self is commensurate with and presupposes his notions of *individualism, substance, organism*, and *mind*, all of which serve ultimately to fuse the distinction between discontinuity and continuity. In other words, at its most basic, the self, as itself a sign (*CP*:5.313), is no more than a locus of error and ignorance, at the same time that it is a centre of a certain degree of power and control (*CP*:5.225–27).

In light of the above, the self is a source of power and control, as well as self-control, in so far as it is capable consciously and deliberately of engaging in a rational, self-reflective, process of thought and action. And it is perpetual errancy and ignorance in so far as it is no more than negation (*CP*:5.317). It is negation, for, above all, it is the product of inference; it is, so to speak, mere fiction. In Peirce's words, if we will admit to a 'personal self in the same sense in which a snark exists; that is, there is a phenomenon to which that name is given' (*CP*: 8.82), then we must also admit that 'self,' like 'snark,' is 'an illusory phenomenon; but still it is a phenomenon. It is not quite *purely* illusory, but only *mainly* so' (*CP*:8.82). That is to say, we are only deluded into supposing that we have some self with some isolated, autonomous existence. For actually, we do not. The 'self' can learn from the emergence into semiosis and the endurance within its context of 'snark,' supposedly a mere word, but a word nonetheless, that enjoys at the basest of levels a status equal to that of the 'self,' which does not exist outside language.

For this reason Peirce could write that selves and signs reciprocally educate each other, for just as signs – most particularly words – possess their own form of individuality, though fleeting and transient, so also selves are individual only in so far as they are signs among and beside other signs (*CP*:5.313). In other words, selves and signs are mere negations in that they *are not* what they *were* (in the past), nor are they what they *will have been* (in the future), nor are they even what they *are* (in the present) – for they are in the throes of a perpetually transitory process of becoming something *other*, they have always become something *different* (*différance*) *for* their semiotic agent(s). They *are* and they *are not* what they are. They are identical to themselves (vaguely as Firsts and tentatively though incompletely as Thirds), yet they are never identical to themselves (as Seconds, haecceities). They are in this sense *inconsistent* (*vague*) and/or *incomplete* (*general*).

However, this situation is not as helpless and hopeless as it might appear. Though Peirce denies rugged individuality in the hell-bent-for-leather Western way, he offers a complementary view with his idea that *synechism* promises a collusion and collaboration between traditional horns of opposition, most notably mind/body and self/other. There is neither any cogitating mind absolutely divorced from the physical world nor any absolutely autonomous self-sufficient self always a step removed from its other. Synechism promises interrelation among all selves, since all communication 'from mind to mind is through continuity of being' (*CP*:7.572). The concept is thoroughly topological in the current sense of boundaries and their merging one into another, for 'neither selves nor neighbor-selves' are 'anything more than mere vicinities' (*CP*:4.69) – that is, they are topological domains merging into one another. At most, individual selves are like 'cells in the social organism. Our deepest sentiment pronounces the verdict of our own insignificance. Psychological analysis shows that there is nothing which distinguishes my personal identity except my faults and my limitations' (*CP*:1.673). Indeed, society itself can be looked upon as a loosely compacted person, and even loosely compacted cells (*CP*:5.421).

Thus a self is itself not by virtue of what it is in and of itself but through its relations with other selves: it is a member of some community of comparable selves. The self is unique in that it is itself, as a self-contained, self-sufficient oneness, a First, an autonomous entity. At the same time, its nature as unicity outside its membership to any actual community of selves endows it with the possibility of becoming one with other(s). Its possibility is its selfhood as an autonomous self, and its relation to its respective other(s) opens it to the action of Secondness. It is one and in its relations with its other(s) it is many; it is autonomous (an autopoietic entity) and at the same time open to its environment (a Prigogine system) (*CP*:5.402). As such the self as a sign in the process of becoming, of developing, via Thirdness, becomes evident (*CP*:5.313). The self's element of autonomy ultimately allows it the wherewithal for control and self-control, the latter serving to distinguish humans from other semiotic agents (*CP*:5.533) – a distinction of degree rather than kind.

First, the self as conscious *of* the sign-events 'out there' is itself a sign (*CP*:5.283, 314). Then, the self as self-conscious, as conscious *of* its thought-signs 'in here,' gives rise to an inward inhibitory force governing actions 'out there' (*CP*:5.194). This initiates awareness of a distinction – albeit imaginary and artificial, as it were – between 'in here' and 'out there.' Such awareness of this distinction allows one at choice moments to stop oneself from acting in an instinctive (*embedded, automatized*) manner, and reflect – through self-reflexive self-consciousness – on one's thought-signs and one's actions on the sign-events displayed before one's world. Thus one is capable of constructing one's 'semiotic world' in commensurate fashion with that of the other members of one's community. Every human semiotic agent, Peirce writes, exists in a partly arbitrary and artificially split world, 'inner' and 'outer,' the 'world of percepts and the world of fancies' (*CP*:5.487).

And the self consists precisely of an oscillatory to and fro from one world to the other, thus composing a series along which the 'inner' world exercises an influence on the 'outer' world and vice versa. Sign-events shape thought-signs and thought-signs collaborate with one another in constructing, deconstructing, and reconstructing a 'semiotically real' world of sign-events. The self-reflexive self is an evolving storehouse of thought-signs just as the self's actions on its world of sign-events composes an ongoing stream in turn acting upon that selfsame self. This to and fro oscillation attests to the inexorable *deferment* and *difference* (*différance*) regarding the self's relation to itself and its other(s). The self can never catch its own thought in its flight toward some other, whether it be the other 'inner' self or the 'outer' other. There is no Cartesian introspection but at best retrospection, what just happened to pass by the conscious self (*CP*:7.420). Given this most intractable nature of the self, it is always already in the process of becoming something other, that is, of becoming its self-fulfilled self, a process as *inconsistent* – it cannot but be vague and contradictory, given the impossibility of any self-identity within the process itself – as it is destined to remain *incomplete* – it cannot become fully itself, in all its plenitude and presence, since it is always becoming something other than itself (see *CP*:6.157).

In sum, the self as oneness, as the possibility of oneness without enjoying distinctness in relation to anything else, is Firstness. In so far as it is acted upon by something other, it is Secondness. And in so far as it is an ongoing process of actions, potentially a continuity of relations bringing about a fusion of selves into selves, it is Thirdness. Selves that simply *are*, in the fleeting moment, as haecceities, are discrete Seconds; selves that *persist*, endure over a continuity of relations, making of themselves one self and many selves, are Thirdness. They are, to be sure, autonomous, islands unto themselves, yet they are also entities in an interconnected, interpenetrating archipelago devoid of clear-cut boundaries. They are, in a word, perpetual transience yet there is stability; they are what they are and at the same time they are always something other.

5. ON BEYOND: THAT *OTHER* VOICE

Peirce's definition of the self, which necessarily includes Firstness, is something akin to a 'woman's language' in the order of French feminist semioticians Julia Kristeva, Hélène Cixous, and especially Luce Irigaray – and I say this at the risk of being met with knee-jerk reactions from some quarters.

This is a roughly a language of immediacy (Firstness), hovering over, under, and between the written and spoken word, in tune with a sense of touch (haptic perception) in the here-now. It is a language of flux, without stability, without rigid definitions. Whatever there is is no more than fleeting, for each moment of change ushers in a new situation that calls for a new response. It is a fluid plurality of signs becoming signs indifferent to the logic of identity and noncontradiction (commensurate with the realm of *vagueness*). These 'inner' signs cannot address themselves properly; they are only themselves and nothing but themselves. That is, there is no 'male' self-conscious metalanguage, for when a series of signs begins addressing itself to some other – in the order to Thirdness – it is now (it has become) something else (Irigaray 1980, 1985).

Such thought-signs do not ordinarily manifest the conceptual rigour of the sort traditionally prized in classical thought, nor are they susceptible to that degree of control and self-control so highly prioritized in Western societies. They are, rather, an attempt to latch on to a world of fleeting sign-events that are fluid, protean, unstable, as they merge into continuity without foregrounding themselves into clear-cut signs of Secondness. That is to say, there is no subject of the sentence, statement, or proposition, *per se*, but merely transient predicates suggesting proximities, nearness, neighbourhoods – much in the topological sense of haptic perception – without the distinction of identities. There would certainly be no presumed neutrality of fleshless, depersonalized pseudoscientific discourse in third person (Irigaray 1985:134).[11]

What I am writing of here is the one-dimensional prototemporal, protomorphic domain proper to symbolicity (linear generation of signs), and at the same time, in an inverted mode, it is proper to iconicity, nootemporality, homeomorphic modelling. That is to say, from within the nootemporal mode coupled with the prototemporal mode, one-dimensional semiosis is free to engage in n-possible directions, depending upon the context and the perspective. The range within this domain is radically nonlinear and apparently disordered, though it gives free rein to virtually random walks, unadulterated play, free flights of fancy (via thought-signs) and action (via sign-events). This is, most appropriately, the province of Prigogine dissipative structures, fractal geometry, the physics of chaos, where fluctuations take disorder to order, where order erupts into apparent disorder, where *vagueness* (*inconsistency*, Firstness) rules at one extreme and *generality* (*incompleteness*, Thirdness) at the other, where what is *actualized* (Secondness) is so ephemeral as often to escape notice altogether. (And, I might add, it is diametrically opposed to Baudrillard's scheme of things, according to which radically 'de-generate' signs are linearly produced within the homeomorphic mode without enjoying the freedom offered by the protomorphic mode.)

What we seem to be left with in these provinces of Firstness (*vagueness*, possibility) and Thirdness (*generality*, potentiality), is the matrix of experience and the incessant push toward fulfilment of the range of possibilities implied by the matrix, to re-evoke the tropes from a previous section. Regarding the self, this image is patterned by DeWitt Parker's (1941) distinction between what he dubs the *matrix self* and the *focal self*. The first is the background allowing the focal self the range of possiblities available to it and with which it can operate. It is a 'womb' giving rise to a series of transitory selves that emerge and submerge in and out of existence. The matrix self is of deep significance; it is continuous, and, like Firstness, endures in terms of its being simply what it is, in spite of the series actualization of myriad focal selves. It is also rather commensurate with Kristeva's (1969, 1984) 'production of the text' from the *chora* (matrix, womb), a repository of a preverbal (yet semiosic, within the domain of Firstness) organization of drives. It is analogous to the Cartesian grid from which points, lines, curves, and figures are *generated* – and *de-generated*. The term *chora* is borrowed from Plato's *Timaeus* via Derrida (1972). It signifies the chaotic receptacle of unstable, contradictory possibilities out of which the subject (self) emerges.

Influenced also by Mikhail Bakhtin's theory of the carnivalesque, Kristeva focuses on the ambivalence of language, which follows a non-Aristotelian logic of the 'paragrammatic,' of 'orthocomplementarity' (Kristeva 1969).[12] In the beginning, with respect to the dialogical text, is the 'blank space,' a 'condition of possibility' of the subject (self) of narrator and narratee – that is, Peirce's 'nothingness.' The carnivalesque dialogical narrative flowing from the inner matrix – as a superposition of all possibilities making up an *inconsistent, contradictory, vague,* set – transgresses bivalent classical logic. It is a 'correlational' form of logic allowing for both the one and the other, and giving truth and falsity, and yes and no, equal time and equal credence. There is no representation and identity, but rather, merely otherness, negation, and opposition held together in an incessantly fluctuating on-again off-again, fluid embrace. Being and nonbeing, real and imaginary, language and nonlanguage, become one.

Kristeva's non-Aristotelian space makes up a totality that is infinite in extension. Within this totality, the subject (self) moves. It is in the throes incessantly of emerging, it produces itself, it is anywhere at a specific moment and everywhere regarding all specific moments, in contrast to the punctual, localizable, largely specifiable phenomenological subject (self) of consciousness. This nonphenomenological subject (self), operating within the infinite range of *vagueness,* of all possible values in superposition, upon evoking itself, becomes tantamount to a variation of the Cretan liar paradox as if to state 'I am *not* that I am.' The subject (self) is part of the whole; she *is* what she is. At the same time, she *is* that whole, for she *is* everything that she *is not,* the combination of which is tantamount to the whole itself. In line with Peirce, the self, as sign, is itself yet *other*; it is fused with all *others* ultimately into a continuum that at once contains that individual self and is equal to that self.

So we are not merely left with language and nothing but language, in the linguicentrist's view. 'Man' ('self') was not at some time in history invented, and destined at another time to disappear, as Foucault would have it. Rather, 'man' ('self') was from the very beginning a sign among signs, or an inference (or 'invention,' if you will), and continues to retain that status. Nothing has really changed in this respect – except the gradual becoming of consciousness *of* the 'self' and of 'selves' ('man') (Neumann 1954). As signs, we articulate, and so interpret, our world of signs, and as signs, we articulate, and so interpret, ourselves. Interpretants become (are) signs interpreting themselves and thus becoming other, what they are not but once were, and what they become is other than what they could otherwise have become but did not. All signs, like ourselves, are signs only by virtue of their erring and their errancy, by virtue of their element of negativity.

But in my present obsession with Firstness and Thirdness one might retort that, in spite of my outlined objectives at the commencement of this chapter, I have apparently lost sight of the 'real' – or even of Baudrillard's 'hyperreal' – the world of actualities, of surface events. Let me expand my purview, then, in order to tie the themes of self (thought-sign) and surface (sign-events).

7

Rhetoric, Syncopation, and Signs of Three

1. THE UNIVERSE SPLIT ASUNDER: DISSONANCE ANEW

In view of the thesis presented in chapter 6, consider table 8, drawn in part from Hartshorne (1970), Harvey (1986), Hassan (1987), and Tyler (1988), which complements table 7 in chapter 4.[1]

Existence - Actual - Particular - Space - Symmetry - Reversibility - Action - Reaction - Noun are the stock-in-trade of the classical Cartesian-Newtonian corpuscular-kinetic mechanical model of the universe. Concrete - Finite - Discrete-Presence convey the nature of traditional Western thought, following its Greek ancestors. And Tree-Roots are characteristic of traditional Porphyrian-Linnaeusean taxonomizing. Indeterminacy-Unpredictability, however, presented a problem for classical mechanics at the turn of the nineteenth century, when the Second Law of Thermodynamics threw things into disarray. The universe as a closed entity in its incessant push toward maximum entropy, 'heat death,' negated reversibility, time being forced into the equation. Statistical indeterminacy and its consequences regarding the received world model were brought to the fore by Peirce, among other scientists, and raised to a shrill pitch by Nietzsche. During the present century, chiefly owing to the work of Prigogine, among others, nineteenth-century statistical indeterminacy and twentieth-century quantum uncertainty are combined into a unique view of 'reality.' Both inorganic and organic, nonliving and living, disorder and order, are placed under the same umbrella covering Becoming-Possible-Potential-General-Abstract-etc. along the right side of table 8.

A corresponding transition in the social sciences, humanities, arts, and the general public view of the world from the classical to the postclassical paradigm has been slow and painful. Much of the resistance to change can be blamed on language, that is, on our general conception of language and

TABLE 8

2nd	1st–3rd
Existence	Becoming
Particular	General
Finite	Infinite (Potentially)
Discrete	Continuous (Ideally)
Actual	Possible-Potential
Concrete	Abstract
Presence	Absence
Space	Time-space
Symmetry	Symmetry $\rightarrow$ asymmetry
Reversibility	Reversibility $\rightarrow$ transitory (irreversibility)
Action-reaction	Automony $\rightarrow$ Relation
Indeterminacy- Unpredictability	Chance-necessity
Tree-Roots	Rhizome
Nouns	Verbs, Adjectives

how it functions.[2] Among hopeful observers of conservative bent, language is still presumed to be a transparent medium, a potentially faithful representation of consciousness and of the furniture of the world in writing and in speech. Putting the hopelessness of this utopian dream aside, our present electronic mode of communication has thrown the entire project out of kilter. It has finally brought to our attention the fact that the supposed representational function of language is subverted by loss of reference, which language never really enjoyed in the first place. Much ado about nothing.

To cite an example: money. Currency as gold exhibited relatively concrete relations. There seemed to exist a one-one correspondence between the word and the thing, its function, its use, and its meaning. Representation was simply taken for granted. The facts were there and no questions were to be asked. At a later stage in the decreasing relational concreteness of the sign, gold was backed by banknotes. Then cheques, credit cards, vouchers, and coupons entered the scene. Finally, in the 'age of information,' databases arrived, and 'money' became no more than oxides deposited on tapes. The connection is now purely arbitrary; the sign seems to have lost all its 'deep' meaning. What the words supposedly denoting money 'represent' have become a great remove from their referents; they are separated by multiple and multiply variegated levels of mediation. Language has begun referring merely to itself and nothing but itself. In the grand age of information, power, whether social, political, or economic, is derived not from what signs represent but from their own internal workings (Baudrillard 1983a, 1983b; Jameson 1981; Terdiman 1985).

The crisis of representation in the 'information age' also upsets the accustomed relation between subjects (selves) and their signs. Electronic communication distances the relation between selves and selves and selves and the signs passing between them such that 'semiotic objects' tend to become not part of the material furniture of the world as represented by the signs but tantamount to the flow of signs themselves. This might appear merely old hat: according to Peirce's Kantian posture, 'semiotic objects' cannot but remain a step removed from the 'real' *an sich*. But Peirce takes the formula in a more benign direction: comfort is to be derived from a certain confidence that the interpreting self, herself a sign, is always capable of distinguishing in one form or another some sort of 'semiotically real' object lying 'behind' and 'beyond' the flow of her cultural signs. As a consequence of such distinction, her social life consists in large part of a practice of her self's positioning itself so as to interpret the cultural rush of signs against the backdrop of the 'semiotically real.' I allude here once again to Peirce's break between the 'in here' of thought-signs and the 'out there' of sign-events, with some rather unspecifiable 'middle ground' in between. The 'inner' pertains more to the self's 'inner other' and its social comings and goings in interaction with other selves; the 'outer' is chiefly the self's hard-line physical world; and the 'middle ground' is a slippery, slushy, sliding scale preventing determinate boundaries in between. At least this distinction, however tenuous, could traditionally be made.

In the 'information age,' however, the equation has been inverted, or so we are told: the self becomes successively less distinguishable from cultural signs – the limit becomes vague – at the same time that signs become less distinguishable from their proper 'semiotically real' objects. One might continue to insist that this is not all bad; it is an extrapolation of Peirce's image of signs merging into signs and minds (selves) into minds ultimately to produce a continuum (according to Peirce's *synechistic* doctrine) which is, after all, the goal of all signs. Such a posture presumably does away with the Cartesian rational, autonomous, hyperconscious subject intent on manipulating the world of things for the purpose of creating a more comfortable life for the good of all. But this anti-Cartesian effect is not-quite-Peircean in so far as the Peircean subject, while partly autonomous – as the self in dialogue with its own other 'in here' – is also open to its environment consisting of signs plus their respective 'semiotic objects' – as the self in dialogue with the world 'out there.' All is not merely reduced to a Saussurean hodgepodge of self-referring signifiers. What we do have is a Peircean melting of Cartesian binaries as a result of the generative-de-generative signifying process. So the twin columns in table 8 are actually not columns at all, but rather, there is a general fusion of terms commensurate with the ongoing order-into-chaos and chaos-into-order self-organizing universe of signs.

The decentred subject is reduced to acting and reacting mindlessly to the signs of the various media not as symbols but as if they were indices (the result of first degree *de-generacy*) and at the far stretch as if they were icons (the result of second degree *de-generacy*). But at the same time, in the classical sense the subject is capable, with greater or lesser degrees of effectiveness, of intermittent sign generacy from icons to indices to symbols, thus fulfilling its participatory role in the dance of signs on the stage of semiosis. It is not so much that the signs represent themselves for the decentred self, but that the self, a sign among signs, becomes more and more indistinguishable from the signs 'out there,' as her sign processing becomes increasingly *embedded, automatized*. In other words, signs 'in here' (thought-signs) tend to become coterminous with their counterparts 'out there' (sign-events) to the extent that self and world, mind and matter, thought-signs and sign-events, are at one with one another. They merge into one another. This, as we observed in chapters 1 and 2, is Peircean through and through.

So we have apparently run the gamut through Baudrillard's three eras of simulacra, which are tantamount to (1) a correspondence mode of signification, (2) a representational mode, and (3) the 'informational mode' (Poster 1990:61–6) – as well as Foucault's triad of *epistemes* culminating in the current return to language. The first is precapitalistic, the second marks the classical capitalist period, and the third is at present in the process of being unfolded. During this final stage, it is not so much that floating signifiers are set into free-wheeling play, but that, in the Peircean vein, signs *de-generate* – in addition to their *generative* processes – and interpretants become *as if* 'semiotically real objects,' and those in turn *as if* they were the signs themselves. Or in the above manner of putting it, symbols are processed *as if* tantamount to indices which in turn risk becoming processed *as if* they were icons.

The result has been that inner images as a mixture of 'real' and 'unreal' items are all made indiscriminately 'real,' interpretants or meanings lose face, and the consequent *de-generate* signs are mindlessly processed *as if* their interpreters enjoyed no consciousness and hence *as if* they had ceased to be rationally inferred meanings. To rephrase Baudrillard, signs as simulacra of interpretants (or icons as simulacra of symbols) become more 'real' than 'reality.' The (imaginary) 'unreal' is made (semiotically) 'real.' And consequently, to cite an above example, the *de-generate, embedded, tacitly acknowledged* classical Cartesian-Newtonian machine metaphor of the universe can threaten to become perceived and conceived as the one and only one true universe. By a comparable token, the television image becomes not merely virtual reality; it *is reality.* The map becomes the territory; the sign becomes the thing. And we are in, it would appear, the equivalent of Baudrillard's 'hyperreality.'

Baudrillard's transition from cocksure correspondence to hopeful representation to the transient sign and nothing but the sign serves gradually to cancel context, thus creating an unbreachable chasm not only between sign and erstwhile 'semiotic object' but also between sign and semiotic agent. Dialogue consequently tends to wane and monologue surfaces with regards to the self and its outer other(s). As a result, in electronic communication, one pole transmits the overwhelming majority of the messages and the other becomes chiefly a receiver. The boob tube is more monological than interactive conversation, and even than the printed word; E-mail becomes less dialogical than phone talk; answering systems less than person-to-person calls; a disc in the word processor less than discussion over coffee; and so on. Actual conversation can induce anxiety, and books require mental aerobics. In contrast, an answering machine can't talk back; you simply and passively feed information into it or it into you. And word processors are the most obstinate and demanding brutes in existence, but at least they are predictable; you know exactly where you stand, there is no vacillation, no doubt, no ambiguity. The soothing soporifics derived from simply letting the brain take in messages or feeding messages into a machine is occasionally an attractive alternative in a stressful world confronting one with a perpetual barrage of what often take on the guise of random signs.

But don't get me wrong. As I have argued elsewhere (Merrell 1995) in critique of Baudrillard and others of kindred spirit, electronic communication does anything but transform us into passive zombies. Receivers of high-tech messages, rather, tend to become profoundly engaged in the semiosic flow. However, admittedly, the interaction is to an increasing degree that between receiver and *de-generate* ('hyperreal') signs (simulacra), signs that have become hyperself-referential. Consequently, since the signs are now at a greater remove from contexts and the semiotic agents themselves, monologic begins more effectively to compete with dialogic. The semiotic agent, as a result, loses a certain rationally controlled and self-controlled dominion over himself, his thought-signs, and the sign-events 'out there,' as *embedded, automatized* signs exercise their force.

However, it does appear that to a degree the three ages of simulation, of information, and of *episteme* evoked by Baudrillard, Foucault, and others, are mirrored in other transformations of thought-signs and the 'semiotic world' of sign-events thought. This we shall now see regarding a cerebral pursuit generally ignored in poststructuralist and postmodernist circles, but erroneously so, for it constitutes the very core of our so-called 'age of information': the concept of number.

2. THERE'S SECURITY IN NUMBERS

Greek algebra, contrary to much popular conception, was not abstract in nature but *rhetorical* through and through. In fact, Greek thought was in general nonalgebraic, because it was so thoroughly concrete. The abstract operations of modern algebra, group theory, set theory, and mathematical logic, involving formal symbols stripped of all reference to concrete physical 'semiotic objects,' are entirely alien to minds intensely preoccupied with the nuts and bolts of everyday living.

According to ancient Hebrew or Greek *Gematria*, every letter in the alphabet had the double meaning of a sound and of a number. The sum of the numbers represented by the letters of the word was considered coterminous with the number – much in the order to Borges' 'Funes the Memorious,' that mnemonic nominalist of concrete particulars *par excellence*. For instance, according to the Greeks' system, the names of the mythical heroes, Patroclus, Hector, and Achilles add up to 87, 1225, and 1276 respectively, which supposedly accounted for Achilles' superiority. Mystic Pythagorean philosophy left a deep impression on Greek thought, especially in the connection it established between *form* and *number*. The Pythagorean's *tetrakys* was considered the root and source of all creation, represented by the four elements, earth, water, air, and fire. This system, however, was not a study in abstraction, but a paragon of concrete imagery. Whole numbers were represented by simple figures – triangles, squares, pyramids, cubes – of concrete form.

Strange though Greek focus on concreteness may appear to us, steeped as we are in our coveted abstractions of which the dreams of rationality are made, it none the less constitutes the origin of contemporary number theory. Particularly regarding Platonist mathematicians, number theory is an 'experimental science' through and through – and Peirce would by and large agree, given his notion of thought-signs and their study, the 'science' of *phaneroscopy*.[3] Even the most abstract of our disciplines was preceded by concrete forms. The particular fascination of numbers as individuals foreshadowed the theory of numbers as collections, just as concrete interest in individual stars antedated astronomy, the four elements antedated the periodic table, phlogiston antedated oxidation, Euclidean geometry antedated non-Euclidean alternatives, and Democritus' atoms as small impenetrable spheres antedated Schrödinger's electron 'clouds' (Dantzig 1930:36–56).

According to popular belief, mathematics starts with generals of the most general sort – axioms, postulates, and definitions – and builds its edifice from that foundation. This is the deductive method. Investigation of the concrete objects, acts, and events of nature – currently going by the name of science – is the result of observation and experience. An observation is made, then it is made again, and again, and as long as the conditions remain invariant, the results of the observation will be virtually the same if the scientific theory and the method are valid. This is the process of induction, which, according to some mathematicians, remains categorically banned from the paradise of serious number crunching. The inductive method entails the notion that what has been said once can be said again, given identical conditions of saying. This is reasoning by recurrence, or reiteration. However, a dilemma eventually raises its ugly head. If mathematics is purely deductive in the most rigorous sense, then why is it not reducible to a vast tautology? If not so reducible, due to its mind-numbing enormity, then can it really be deductive in the purest sense? – and the spectre of Gödel's proof rises up to haunt us once again.

On the other hand, if the rule of reasoning by recurrence is valid for mathematics as well as science, then how can we know that if a given rule is correct for the first billion or so numbers, it also holds true for an infinity of numbers? Induction is possible only if identical operations can be repeated indefinitely, but if infinity is implied by use of the term indefinite, then there is no guarantee that a set of operations in question will indefinitely be the same – Poincaré (1963) demonstrated so much almost a century ago. For example, if the generation of numbers by mathematicians in our particular culture happens to have terminated at one billion, then computation of such expressions as '500,000,000 + 5,000,001' and '1,000,000 × 1,000,001' could not be certain beyond a shadow of a doubt, and hence they would risk becoming to a certain degree meaningless. In other words, it is not only that we could not survey the entire state of all conceivable computations within the domain of one billion numbers; we could not with absolutely certainty conceive of any computation beyond that number. Limited surveyability and finite capacities, though not necessarily imposed on the mathematician either by logic or experience, are mathematical necessities. The mind has some power to conceive of these indefinites, though inductively carrying out the act of verifying them absolutely is impossible – this we have from Wittgenstein on mathematics (Shanker 1987).

Science is not subject to the same limitations as mathematics; it admits, nay, requires, contradictions, falsifications, refutations, without end – if there were none, the activity could not proceed. The scientist consequently can live quite comfortably within a finite realm. In contrast, mathematics, in so far as it is conceived to be purely deductive, cannot bring itself to embrace contradictions, though, according to Gödel, they are duty-bound to appear somewhere along the inductive stretch of things. In this sense at least, induction is part and parcel of mathematical activity, as well as scientific activity. Therefore the most that can be done is tacitly to accept and assert those unnameables $(\sqrt{-1}, \sqrt{2}, \pi,$ infinity) that were stashed away in the closet by the Greeks, fearfully pushed under the rug during and following the Renaissance, and subject to derision by certain early twentieth-century mathematicians and the logical positivists (see Kline 1980; DeLong 1970).

Upon reviving such unnameables, the ethereal heights of abstraction have been reached, where no more than pure symbols, $\sqrt{-1}, \pi, \infty$, can be used with hardly any hope of the mathematicians' ever being able to stumble upon any concrete object of reference. Yet used in everyday computations of science and engineering ($\sqrt{-1}$ in quantum theory, relativity, and elsewhere, π in geometry, ∞ in calculus), this gravitation from concreteness to abstraction patterns the evolution of the concept of numbers throughout the history of humankind (Dantzig 1930:chap. 4). Take, for example, algebra. As it stands today, algebra consists of a set of operations on symbolic forms. But things have not always been this way. Algebra experienced its development in various guises at various times and places. All developments, however, follow three general stages, from the concretely *rhetorical* to the *syncopated* to the purely abstract and *symbolic* (Dantzig 1930:76–98). Rhetorical algebra had no need of symbols in the strict formal sense. Algebraic concepts of the rhetorical sort found their expression in natural language, something like 'The sum is independent of the order of the terms,' which is the equivalent of '$a + b = b + a$,' or commutativity. Syncopated algebra is typical of that of the Egyptians: words are successively abbreviated, in the order of the word *minus* coming to be represented by m with a superscription. Finally, the letter is dropped altogether, and the symbol, '$-$', remains, along with all other symbols of modern algebra.

Early Greek algebra, to repeat, was essentially rhetorical – that is, it was close to the senses (Dantzig 1930:99). In fact, it can hardly be labelled algebra at all, in the modern sense, due to the fundamentally concrete nature of Greek computations. The abstract operations of algebra were simply incompatible with minds so intensely interested in the concrete objects themselves that they found symbols stripped of all physical content abhorrent. The Hindus were not hampered by Greek compunctions over such apparent rigour; they had no sophists to stultify flights of the imagination uncommitted to the things of the world. They dabbled at their leisure in numbers of all sorts – zero, infinity, and other ineffables. Yet their algebra remained at the syncopated stage; they never made the final leap of abstraction. The Arabs took a small step further, bringing Greek geometry and Hindu algebra together, but they still did not fully enter the category of symbolic notation. A turning point finally arrived late in the sixteenth century when the Frenchman Franciscus Vieta began designating unknown variables by purely abstract symbols – somewhat like our contemporary notion of empty sets – for the purpose of operational functions. The final stage was subsequently set when Cartesian notation and Newtonian binomials were introduced.

By this process of successive abstraction, the letter was liberated from the slavery of the word, and then replaced by an abstract symbol, which served to abolish the last vestigial links to concrete items in the physical world. The symbol now allowed one to paraphrase any statement into a number of equivalent forms. Passage also occurred from the individual to the collective in terms of 'some,' 'any,' and 'all,' preparing the way for linear forms such as the quadratic equation. Furthermore, formal symbolism allowed for expression of forms hitherto relegated to the category of 'meaninglessness.' However, at this higher level of abstraction, π, $\sqrt{2}$, $\sqrt{-1}$, and other such oddities could be taken *as if* they were bona fide numbers by the very act of writing them down and giving them a name and a form of meaning (Lehmann 1979:66–90). Indeed, what distinguishes modern mathematics from pre-algebraic computations is an altered attitude toward unutterable, impossible, and meaningless mathematical entities. Today, possible and impossible entities take on relative meaning. Neither constitute the necessary property of a mathematical operation, but merely, they are restrictions imposed by the mind on the field of the operand. Erase the restriction, extend the field, and what was impossible may become possible. $\sqrt{-1}$ is not decidable or meaningful *per se*, but, once plugged into the proper equation, it can be used to describe 'real world' – that is 'semiotically real' world – states of affairs (Eddington 1958a:137–53).

Now, all this concern over mathematics as unutterables, as something less than 'real objects,' takes nothing away from the central role of abstract mathematical symbolism. As embodiment of the pinnacle of success within the domain of Thirdness, mathematical symbolism does not entail any sterile attempt to banish intuitions, assumptions, vague feelings, unfettered flights of the imagination – all Peircean *abductions*, within the province of Firstness – from the playpen of human thought. Rather, the power of mathematical symbols in terms of probability or generality – what would, should, or could be – is virtually as limitless and uncompletable as Firstness in terms of its chanciness, its vagueness, its possibility for creating new forms of thought. Such symbols are the ultimate extrapolation of natural language symbolism, a rhetorical algebra *par excellence*.

After all, nouns and phrases are but symbols of classes of 'semiotic objects.' Verbs symbolize relations, adjectives symbolize attributes, and sentences bring them all together in quite tidy packages. Yet sentences, as symbols, are a composition of baser but no less important signs: the simple predicate of a sentence is an icon (sign of Firstness) and its subject or noun is an index (sign of Secondness). As such, sentences are generally, though not always, capable of evoking (1) images and images of relations between images, (2) concrete pictures of representative elements of classes and of the things they do and things that are done to them, and (3) relations between these elements and others, as well as (4) generalities and abstract concepts. In fact, language itself runs the gamut, from *rhetorical* to *syncopated* to *symbolic*, from *feeling-intuition* to *action-reaction* to *intellection-cognition*, and from *abduction* to *induction* to *deduction*.

What is generally true of lexical items in natural language is particularly true of the words representing natural numbers. Numbers, when evoking concrete images of things, collections, and their relations, appear to be so rooted in rock-solid 'reality' as to be endowed with an absolute nature. Consequently, in the manner in which numbers are used, the mathematician sometimes tends to forget that they are but abstract symbols subject to operational rules that are themselves often subjected to alteration (DeLong 1970; Klenk 1976; Kline 1980). The sense of acceleration in an automobile can be, as illustrated in the previous chapter, manifested mathematically or geometrically as no more than motionless states, length as extensionless points, and time as durationless instants. This abstraction, 'is not even the skeleton of the real motion as perceived by our senses! When we see a ball in flight we perceive the motion as a whole and not as a succession of infinitesimal jumps. But neither is a mathematical line the true, or even the fair, representation of a wire. Man has for so long been trained in using the fictions that he has come to prefer the substitute to the genuine article' (Dantzig 1930:127).

In addition to the abstract, and partly arbitrary base of number, and of all symbols for that matter – according to Peircean semiotics – one must concede that impossibles, unutterables, and fictions in general, unlike 'reality,' depend for their 'existence' on our constituting them. In this sense they must be exactly what we say they are. There is a constant risk involved, for what the mathematician says of her symbols cannot but be deficient. To be more specific, talk about her symbols, whether put in formal dress or left to the equivocacies of natural language, is in the final analysis either *inconsistent* (*vague*) or *incomplete* (*general*). Thus the science of numbers shares the limitative theorems with the natural sciences; both are at heart plagued with a certain loss of the security of absolute certainty (Kline 1980). In this vein, Peirce argues:

That twice two is four is often used as a type of perfect certainty. The basis of our confidence in the proposition lies in the extreme ease with which we can at any time make the experiment of duplicating an imaginary object, then duplicating the resulting pair, and comparing the final result with that of adjoining to the first imaginary object a second, a third, and a fourth like it. But this is only an experiment. – It may have been performed with the same result a billion times; still mistakes in addition do occur, according to all experience; and what happens once may happen any number of times, and on every one of the first billion trials. It is therefore not absolutely impossible, that every one of the experiments hitherto made upon the result of multiplying 2 by 2 have been in error in the same way; so that it is as nearly certain as anything can well be that the proposition $2 \times 2 = 4$ is not absolutely certain. Of course, it would be silly to doubt it. But it is one thing to hold to that practical maxim, and quite another to hold it to be beyond the bare possibility of error. (*MS* 335:1-4; in Dozoretz 1979:79–80)

Quite obviously, Peirce allows for practical certainty but not absolute certainty. Symbols can be put to use as though they were immune from error, and if things run smoothly, fine and dandy. But such activity does not preclude the 'bare possiblity' that sooner or later a flaw will show itself. Practical reasoning, whether in natural language or formal language, can be regarded as certain though not absolutely indubitable; it is provisionally accepted without doubt for now, with the expectation that it may possibly be subjected to doubt at some unexpected moment.

3. SIMULTANEOUSLY BENDING FORWARD AND DOUBLING BACKWARD

I have suggested a parallel of sorts between rhetoric-syncopation-symbolism and Peirce's iconicity-indexicality-symbolicity. Taking a further step, we reenter Baudrillard's Foucault-inspired three orders of simulation.

First, the modern era broke with the relatively static feudal-hierarchical medieval order by introducing an *artificial* world of counterfeit signs legitimizing and valorizing *artifice* (rhetorical figures, baroque art, styles, and fashions) over natural signs. Second, the industrial revolution introduced *serial producibility* of mass objects, replicas ejected from assembly-line processes, ultimately leading to robotization. The automaton is merely an *analogy* of the human semiotic agent, while the robot of the second order of simulation becomes by and large *equivalent* to a man/woman. It is itself a semiotic agent (sign) among others, a replica of the genuine item (Baudrillard 1983a:92–102). In contrast, the third-order of simulation is no longer the counterfeit or assembly-line replica of the original; the simulation model now becomes 'reality' merely as it is. In fact, having voraciously devoured both representation and simulation, it becomes more 'real' than the erstwile 'real.'

Of course, in light of above sections, one must bear in mind that Baudrillard avails himself of that tired image of neo-Saussurean floating signifiers. Baudrillard's third-order simulation is the triumphant march of binarism,

TABLE 9

Peirce	Firstness Iconicity	Secondness Indexicality	Thirdness Symbolicity	1 ⟶ 10
Fraser	Proto-temporality	Eotemporality	Bio-nootemporality	Atemporality
Bunn	3-D Semiotics	2-D Semiotics	1-D Semiotics	(4-D Semiotics)
Mathematics	Rhetoric	Syncopation	Symbolic	
Baudrillard		Representation	Serial	Hyperreal
Foucault	Resemblance	Representation	'Man'	'Language'

specifically of the cybernetic sort, though it remains – in the Jacques Monod style of chance and necessity – an aleatory, radically indeterminate system. None the less, upon considering Peircean *generacy–de-generacy* of signs, especially as I have argued here and elsewhere (Merrell 1995), a move 'up' the scale from sign 1 toward sign 10 implies relatively voluntary, conscious, intentional, and rational sign processing (semiosis), while a move 'downward' tends toward embedded, automatized, involuntary, tacit, sign processing (*phanerosis*). Movement is from the iconicity (Firstness) of symbols (de-generate signs) to the symbolicity (Thirdness) of symbols (relatively genuine signs) and back again. Or if you wish, in the Prigogine sense it is from order to disorder to more complex forms of order, from stability to instability to metastability. Or in the sense of the medieval trilogy – which Peirce appropriated for his own use, by the way – transition is from rhetoric to logic to grammar and the inverse. The entire shebang is never static but always tirelessly ongoing: *it is process.*

In sum, I submit, for your contemplation, table 9 – albeit with fuzzy lines of demarcation between all categories, in keeping with the premises underlying this enquiry. Peirce's *generacy–de-generacy* cycle of the sign, like Foucault in general and the 'linguistic turn,' takes us back to the beginning, and the process recommences. This must be the case, for how else could a Barthes of *Mythologies* (1972), a Baudrillard of *Simulations* (1983a), a Foucault (1970) of *The Order of Things* and his other work, or a Jameson (1981) of *The Political Unconscious* presumably – not to say pretentiously – become aware of what was to have lurked beneath the consciousness of their jaded, bourgeois compatriots, or of peoples of remote times, if not by some hopeful knowledge of the ability to leap 'up' and 'down' the scale so as to be able to think and write about what is mindlessly acted out by the common folk? And how else could those masses of which they write have become so mentally clapped-out, if not by a gradual slide 'downward' such that they came anaesthetically to act out their lives in robot fashion?

By and large, however, the assumption of such wide-eyed hypersensibilities is actually alien to Peircean tenderly fallibilistic semiotics according to which we cannot hope to know our presuppositions and prejudices, nor can we subject all of what we know to doubt: we (tacitly) know more than we (explicitly) know, and hence we cannot say all we know or know the implications of all we say (Polanyi 1958). In other words, we cannot (explicitly) know, for we are *in* signs; we are contiguous *with* them; we *are* ourselves a part of the very signs we wish to know. This intellectual modesty is a far cry from semiological imperatives sacrificing diachrony to synchrony, or positivist and quasi-positivist imperatives sacrificing what is in the process of becoming to what presumably has become and is now there for the all-seeing eye of the I-told-you-so savant analyst. Those who continue to write almost exclusively in the dyadic vein risk blockage of the flow of thought-signs by the synchronic Saussurean salami. In such case, they generally construct, in spite of themselves, a determinately indeterminate system of absolute uncertainties and vague generalities by way of irrational leaps of faith in their own particular style of unreasoned reasoning – caught up, as they are, in a *tu quoque* of their own making.

And yet ... and yet. Given the implications inherent in table 9, it is precisely the extension of biotemporality into nootemporality, reaching its most complex – though not necessarily the most sublime – expression in human communication, that can end with a dip in the unruly semiosic sea of chance, pure possibility, unblemished vagueness. This is the realm from whence *abduction* arises. *Abductive* acts reveal mind at its best, not that of reason, logic, intellect, control, and self-control in the classical sense, but that of sentiment, intuition, gut feeling, which are all in classical jargon closer to the heart than to the mind. To rephrase Peirce, the heart follows its own form of logic of which the mind knows little, yet it is that upon which the mind's cunning rests.

8

Knowing Signs, Living Knowledge

The distinction I referred to at the close of the last chapter between Peircean semiotics and Saussurean, neo-Saussurean, and post-Saussurean – poststructuralist – semiology can be dressed quite nicely in terminology common to mathematical philosophy. Upon our formulating this distinction, the 'life-signs' theme discussed in chapters 1 and 2 resurfaces.

This serves to re-introduce the continuity/discontinuity problem that has emerged throughout much of this book. By relating that distinction to the Cantor-Dedekind paradox and McTaggart's A- and B-series to the becomingness of signs, I re-evoke the theme of spatio-temporality, also presented above. I then turn briefly to sign multiplication and its relationship to cell division, which brings on François Jacob, who develops his theory of life processes – somewhat comparable to that of Jacques Monod – with the appropriation of a 'Textuality ≈ Life' metaphor. In spite of his enticing image, however, Jacob is thoroughly Darwinian, as I argue in chapter 9, and his thesis – life emerging out of the virtual impossibility of chance happenings as if by a miracle – is unacceptable, given the tenets underlying this enquiry.

Nevertheless, I do maintain that life processes and sign processes are both at their roots paradoxical. This I attempt to demonstrate with a trick from Varela using a Gödel-Tarski move comparable in natural languages to old Epimenides' paradox. The paradox entails (1) self-referentiality, (2) infinite regress tactics, and (3) negation (which also exists at the heart of fictionality). In essence, cells, like signs, are marked off, they mark themselves off, in order to establish boundary conditions demarcating what they are, as relatively autonomous entities, from what they *are not* – though, at the same time, they are in constant interaction with their surroundings. This suggests, I would submit, that the universe is semiotic through and through, and that any and all investigations of nature and of the nature of signs and life must ultimately be semiotic in nature, as Thomas Sebeok (1977a, 1983) has often reiterated.

(By way of an afterthought, the route I have chosen through Cantor-Dedekind – which will certainly appear deviant to some observers – is motivated by the fact that much of Peirce's terminology is thoroughly mathematical. For this reason, complete avoidance of the mathematical import of Peircean semiotics could not but produce a diluted picture of lacklustre pastels rather than the scintillating dance of brilliant hues with which it should be dressed. I ask, therefore, that the reader bear with me, for, I trust, the message will eventually shine forth.)

1. BECOMING, BUT NEVER ARRIVING

To recap, Saussurean semiology is structural, Peircean semiotics is processual. The first sets for itself the impossible task of brushing becoming aside and focusing on *langue*; the second attempts somehow to get the act of becoming in its clutches without losing sight of what *was*, *is*, and *will be* – a task that, though perhaps equally impossible, is at least more faithful to ongoing *semiosis*.

   This problem of the being of becoming and the becoming of being bears on an important facet of the history of mathematics. A crisis developed during the time of the Pythagoreans with an attempt to force the arithmetic of rational numbers on the geometry of the diagonals of a square and the circumference of a circle: π and square roots of numbers producing irrationals (such as $\sqrt{2}$) eventually surfaced to throw things in disarray. It finally became evident, however, that an extension of the number field to include such irrationals was unavoidable. The problem and paradox, it was conceded after much soul-searching, deliberation, and debate, consisted of a method for interjecting irrational numbers into the rational number system, that is, of mixing the concept of infinity with a discontinuous but orderly phalanx of integers. A continuously extended straight line that could be 'cut' (*pace* Dedekind) into discrete elements seems to be the most likely candidate for modelling this heterogeneous mix. A line was conceived as representing an infinity of numbers, each corresponding to a *point*, and thus an infinity of individuals merged into one another to compose a continuous whole smoother than the smoothest vanilla ice cream.

   A point, like a line and other such entities, is, of course, a sort of fiction. As a fiction it is capable of performing a generative function producing continuous entities no end: from a point, a line can emerge, from the line a plane, from the plane a cube, from the cube a hypercube, and so on. This function seems to dovetail conveniently with the notion of continuity. However, when a point and its generation into a line dissolving the collection of all points is related to the string of discrete numbers extended infinitely, the two are ultimately found incompatible. This is comparable to the dilemma of our senses, which, as we noted above, ordinarily perceive motion as a continuum, but when one analyses what is perceived, the continuity is invariably destroyed. Quite understandably, the idea of a continuous line consisting of a series of resting-places for individual numbers is disconcerting – and, to boot, it provides fodder for the continuing force of Zeno's arguments. Calculus and analytic geometry represent heroic and masterful attempts to plug up the dike and bridge the discrepancy between continuity and discontinuity. But though one might tend to call them mathematical theories of *change*, of *limits*, the perennial question remains: How can discreteness be reconciled with continuity? We stomp on the gas pedal of our car and experience the exhilaration, the power, the continuous pressure of the resultant acceleration on our body, and that is the proof of continuity, we declare. But though the proof of the pudding is in the taste, eating it cannot tell us what it is in the analytical sense. Ultimately, experience (or A-series time, continuity, change) appears eternally irreconcilable with analysis (or B-series time, discontinuity, stasis).

In an attempt to come to grips with this problem, a point has been conceived as a *limiting position* in an *ongoing process* of a particular segment of a line. Along this line, the process consists of untold repetitions of the same operation, for example, $\frac{1}{2}$, $\frac{1}{4}$, $\frac{1}{8}$ ... n. The sequence converges asymptotically toward its limit at the infinite stretch without being able to arrive at the finish line. This image should evoke reminiscences of Peirce's smooth, soothing, converging swim toward Truth.[1] However, the image is deceptive, for although Peirce's asymptote model is largely continuous, he readily admits to occasional fits and jerks rendering the process discontinuous from a larger view (Rescher 1978). Yet the image in its analogy with a line continues to exercise its appeal, even its fantasy, because the line is the prototype of all things continuous. It is the concrete representation of the stream of time, frozen, as it were, and evincing all things past, present, and future. As the stream of time goes, so also the flow of events, we would like to believe. This appeal is an elegant soporific. The mind tends to shrink before the aleatoric, spontaneous, catastrophic, and cataclysmic. Although it is true that Peirce gave a nod to sharp breaks in the otherwise smooth accumulation of knowledge, the fact remains that he preferred to emphasize the latter.

This is perhaps unfortunate. It tends to lead one to the conclusion that Peirce's system is tantamount to a statistical aggregate the individuals of which are unpredictable, but when the whole is viewed, things are quite certain – a popular nineteenth-century hope, following in part on the heels of the Second

Law of Thermodynamics. In contemporary times, we have Jacques Monod's (1971) universe of blind chance, causing discontinuous mutations among individuals the combination of which brings about continuous evolution of the species. This theory has been ruthlessly criticized by those who refuse to recognize that mere happenstance generation may be the dominant fact in the process of evolution. But these critics are at times still caught between the Charybdis of continuity and change and the Scylla of discontinuity and stasis. Ilya Prigogine (1984) rejects Monod outright, as he does the Einsteinian 'block universe' freezing time forever, and opts for a physics of unpredictable catastrophic change over determinacy (whether statistical or otherwise), and of complexity over simplicity. Yet he still clings to the idea of continuous time, evolution, and irreversibility. On the other hand, David Bohm (1980) would like to propagate the notion of an open, creative universe, but at the same time he maintains faith in the doctrine of causality linking phenomena into a continuous chain, thus safeguarding the future against the horror of chaos. And John A. Wheeler's universe, whose past as well as her future depends upon us as participatory agents in the long run, becomes, as a whole, apparently always already made, a sort of *fait accompli*. Ultimately, in light of scientific thought, it seems wellnigh impossible to bridge the chasm between the continuity of time as we might like it and the discontinuity of events as we might like to 'cut' them.[2]

Returning to the contradiction of the number series conceived as a line, one must finally admit that accelerating staccato will never yield legato, no matter to what extent one factors the equation. The discontinuity/continuity (staccato/legato) distinction I refer to is analogous to that between the theories of Dedekind and Cantor. Like Cantor, Dedekind takes as his point of departure the domain of rational numbers. But instead of defining the real (that is, rational and irrational) numbers as a convergene sequence of rationals, he conceives them to be generated by the power of the mind for classifying the sequence in terms of a Dedekind *cut*, *split*, or *partition*. A cut separates the continuity of a line into the class of all numbers on one side and their counterpart on the other side. Wherever the *cut* is exercised – and it can be exercised at one of a possible infinity of points – what rests on one side is equal in magnitude to what rests on the other side: each contains an infinity of points. Cantor, in contrast to Dedekind, used the infinite domain to account for the generation of the number domain. It is basically the notion of a point attracted to a centre as a limit toward which it converges. Cantor's theory is in this sense *dynamic*, Dedekind's is *static*. Both theories pattern in a rather uncanny degree the two conceptions of time discussed above: Cantor's theory is analogous to the A-series, Dedekind's to the B-series (recall discussion of the series and their relation to Cantor-Dedekind in chapter 3). Cantor's converging point is like the sliding knife-edge of the 'now'; Dedekind's *cut* separates 'before' and 'after' into two static partitions, with no place for the 'now' of things. In fact, regarding the Cantor-Dedekind distinction, Dantzig writes: 'Paradoxical though this may seem, *the present is truly irrational* in the Dedekind sense of the word. For while it acts as partition it is neither a part of the past nor a part of the future. Indeed, in an arithmetic based on pure time, if such an arithmetic was at all possible, it is the irrational which would be taken as a matter of course, while all the painstaking efforts of our logic would be directed toward establishing the existence of rational numbers' (1930:176).

In spite of the grainy B-series – with a nod to Zeno – we persist in experiencing A-series time, filling in the gaps in accord with our intuitive capacities, analysis's penchant for the B-series to the contrary (a point that for some reason Dantzig seems neatly to have overlooked). Yet, analytic geometry bridges the chasm, though artificially so, and as an act of mind, between intuition and reason, by a convenient postulate that ousts the intuitive notion and puts a logically consistent concept in its place. As a consequence, we now have the notion of a real number and its aggregate, the arithmetic continuum, on the one hand, and on the other, a point and its aggregate, the linear, continuous line.

With this image of the line as mathematical construct and its inherent continuity/discontinuity problem in mind, let us now return briefly to Peirce's concept of the sign in order to prepare the scene for sign (cell) subdivision and generation.

2. THE DISCONTINUITY OF SIGNS; THE CONTINUITY OF THEIR BECOMING

Classical logic seeks categories cut in stone; fuzziness is anathema. In contrast, the dream of every Peircean sign is to merge with all signs, to become one with the continuum: semiosis at its best recognizes no fixed categories.

Given the nature of semiosis, our confidence in the charming simplicity of languages (natural, logical, mathematical, sign systems in general) may be misplaced; they may look simple only because we have unlocked so few of their secrets. As we dig deeper into the microscopic structure of signs, we continue to strike seams of virtually indescribable complexity created by the interplay of an enormous number of factors. Such a condition might appear lawless, pure chaos. But it is not, I would suggest. Semiosis is ordered, according to its own style of ordering; it is replete with wonders, patiently waiting for our torpid wits to grow sharper.

Without the aid of modern mathematics (probability, fractals, topology, catastrophe theory), without the vision afforded us by contemporary physics (quantum and relativity theory, dissipative structures) – all bearing in one form or another on the theme of complexity – and prior to empirical positivism's grand epistemological dreams and their aftermath with a return to what are properly considered to be pragmatic issues, Peirce struggled during the greater part of his life with this dilemma of complexity within apparent simplicity. In his early days he disagreed with John Locke in the last chapter of his *Essay* that logic is tantamount to semiotics. During the mid-1880s he conceded in part to Locke's conception with the admission that logic cannot do business without icons and indices; hence the two disciplines must be considered coterminous. By 1884 he was arguing that all reasoning makes use of a 'mixture' of icons, indices, and symbols. And by 1902, Max Fisch (1986:339–40) reports that Peirce discarded the narrow sense of logic, defined it in the most general sense as semiotic – the study of semiosis – and adapted Locke's term *critic* to designate logic of the formal, more limited, sort. One must bear in mind that Peirce's general logic is not a formulation, in signs, of knowledge cut in stone, but what seekers of knowledge do from within their respective interactive, dialogical communities. Knowledge is in this manner never static but ongoing, like the living sign process itself, like the ongoing, continuous flow of semiosis.

Indeed, Fisch (1986:357) proposes that 'Peirce's general theory of signs [which is to say, a theory of logic] is so general as to entail that, whatever else anything may be, it is also a sign' (brackets added). Fisch's principal justification of this enigmatic statement, I believe, is found in the very Peircean notion that signs are constituent parts of more complex signs, up to, and including, the entire universe as a sign (*CP*:5.119). It would seem that the whole of the sign domain contained within the semiosic process is, at its ultimate stretch, comparable to the mathematical continuum: there are no practical or definable limits. True to form, Fisch writes that 'words are signs; and it goes almost without saying that phrases, clauses, sentences, speeches, and extended conversations are signs. So are poems, essays, short stories, novels, orations, plays, operas, journal articles, scientific reports, and mathematical demonstrations' (1986:357). The list, of course, proceeds without conceivable end.

Fisch goes on to evoke Peirce's distinction, now quite generally accepted in philosophical circles, between tokens and types. There is only one definite article in the English language, as type, though a dozen or so might exist on this printed page as tokens of the type. Tokens are most properly speaking Seconds, tones and types being Firsts and Thirds respectively. A tone is mere possibility, and a token is an instantiation of the type to which it belongs. But tokens can do no more than approximate the type in all its fullness, which is a sign in a preeminent – though non-Platonic – sense that enables it to confer signhood on its tokens.[3] Yet tokens, like individuals in the mathematical continuum, can be conceived as somehow, and at some time and some place, merging into generalities. But if so, then one must concede that if an individual token is a discrete sign, and if a collection of them makes up a conglomerate or compound sign (subset) of a type (set), then that type, in its pure form, becomes tantamount to a continuous, self-contained sign (set) of itself, paradoxically – and hence the perplexity regarding Fisch's statement on Peirce's sign in the most general sense, and, once again, the Cantor-Dedekind paradox.

This most likely appears unbearably murky, so let us look at the problem from another vantage. If, as we have seen in the preceding chapters, (1) symbols imply protomorphic, linear generativity most appropriate to Fraser's prototemporality and Bunn's one-dimensional semiotics, (2) indices are paramorphic, corresponding to eo-biotemporality and two-dimensional semiotics, and (3) icons dovetail with homeomorphic models, bio-nootemporality, and three-dimensional semiotics, then (4) compound or complex signs containing constituent signs must entail a combination of all signifying modes, temporalities, and dimensionalities. But rather than cut-and-dried categories, we have a veritable spectrum of continuous slips and slides from one mode to another, one time to another, one space to another. Ultimately, semiosis is neither continuous nor discontinuous *for* us; *our* categorization tends to make it so. Categories, historically contextualized, can be no more than hazy topologies of the mind.

The notion of artificial topological domains becoming fuzzy and ultimately making up a complex continuum is perhaps nowhere more evident than in Peirce's 'existential graphs,' a forerunner to topology – here I follow Don Roberts' (1973) excellent study. Peirce's graphs come basically in three flavours, Alpha, Beta, and Gamma, roughly corresponding to Firstness, Secondness, and Thirdness. At the upper level, Gamma graphs begin generating graphs of themselves; they begin 'talking' with and 'reasoning' about themselves. In a manner of speaking, as wholes they take on the countenance of iconicity; they become icons (that is, upon subdivision they construct their own replicas). They are now, at least as *potentia*, graphs of unity. And thus the circle is closed, the system becomes continuous with itself – recall the disquisition in chapter 1 regarding tables 2 and 3 and figure 1. With a successive proliferation of signs to levels of ever-higher complexity, a wealth of signifying entities is produced. Yet in the final analysis all signs in the resulting conglomerate are essentially of the form of self-reflecting and self-reflexive signs of themselves (*CP*:4.512). In this sense, ultimately, diagrams can exhibit a state of affairs without referring to anything outside themselves (*MS* 410:11-13).

Peirce's own thought processes are actually quite conducive to this rather strange way of thinking, I would conjecture, in so far as he tended to think in diagrams, not words: 'I do not think I ever *reflect* in words: I employ visual diagrams, firstly because this way of thinking is my natural language of self-communion, and secondly, because I am convinced that it is the best system for the purpose' (*MS* 620:8). For Peirce, a genuine diagram should ideally be iconic (that is, continuous) in nature: its parts and the relations between them are in some way analogous to the parts and relations of that which they represent (*CP*:3.363, 3.418, 3.556). And he was convinced that his existential graphs enjoy essential features of diagrammatic reasoning. He further compared logic diagrams to maps. Like maps, they convey information regarding different matters by way of *showing*, that could not have been as easily conveyed by explicit *saying*. Moreover, like maps, they lend themselves to mental and even visual experimentation; the parts and relations can be rearranged in order potentially to make them more efficient or to portray new information (*CP*:4.530).

Diagrams referring merely to themselves, recall, are one of the three types of hypoicons, the other two being *images* and *metaphors*, all of which are in a sense signs of themselves inasmuch as they do not (yet) relate to anything outside themselves. Fisch (1986:359) observes that in internalized thought as silent dialogue, icons and indices in terms of their relating to themselves enjoy more direct function than in oral conversation. Peirce's own visual yet schematic diagrammatic thinking is in all likelihood quite characteristic of inner dialogue – perhaps above all, given the isolation within which he thought and wrote.

Icons and indices have been qualified as natural signs in contrast to the partly arbitrary, conventional signs Peirce labelled symbols. There has been some controversy regarding the conventionality of the former, which actually serves to augment the contention in this enquiry that the three sign types are not absolutely distinguishable.[4] Yet one might still contend that it is quite feasible to assume that icons and indices need not have any utterer, as is the case of symbols in oral dialogue between two or more interlocutors, nor do they cease to be signs – though not signs in the full-blown sense – as do symbols when no semiotic agent is present. In response to this type of argument, we have physicist John A. Wheeler's (1980a) variation on the parlour game of twenty questions as an illustration of the quantum world – which I shall recontextualize for the purpose of the present argument.

One evening while playing the game, when it came Wheeler's turn to leave the room, the gamers contrived to choose nothing in the room that he must attempt to discern and name by asking twenty questions or less. They agreed to agree on no object and no word; hence at the outset there was no 'reality' to be discovered, though everything was in the room from the beginning as 'brute actual fact,' awaiting its being paged for entry onto the stage of some 'semiotically real' world or other. According to the new rules they conjured up, each gamer questioned by Wheeler could answer as she pleased, the sole requirement being that she should have a word in mind compatible with her own response to Wheeler's question and to all the responses that had gone on before it. Otherwise if Wheeler challenged the question, she lost. This altered version of the game was thus as difficult for Wheeler's friends as it was for him.

The important point is that whatever 'reality' that was to be called into existence during the game was not there a priori. It must be created by all participators concerned, in relation to iconic images, indexical relations, and the use of language (symbols). There was no 'reality' except that which came into being while the game was being played out. Wheeler believes his example is typical of our 'participatory universe.' Whatever meaning the physicist is able to glean from nature depends upon whatever questions she puts to nature in the first place. She knows there is a certain unpredictability, uncertainty, and undecidability regarding what any given set of her measurements will disclose, regarding what answers nature will decide to put forth, regarding what will happen when 'God plays dice.' Yet she poses questions, nature responds, and she records the results and puts them to use according to her needs and the pragmatics of her situation. In Wheeler's game no image, relation, or word existed before the fact. Hence there was no meaning until the images, relations, and words were promoted to 'reality' by the choice of questions asked and answers given. In comparable fashion with respect to the world of quantum physics, *'no elementary phenomenon is a phenomenon until it is a recorded phenomenon'* and properly *put to use* (Wheeler 1980a:356).

Placing Wheeler's formulation in the context of this enquiry, without participatory (semiotic) agents, '(semiotic) reality' does not come into existence in the full sense. In fact, items of experience must be *put to use* in one form or another before they can come into being, before they can take on meaning – which Wheeler (1984) qualifies as 'meaning physics,' developing from classical and Einsteinian physics. Wheeler's example is reminiscent of the comments · of both Niels Bohr and Werner Heisenberg that the physicist cannot hope to acquire knowledge of nature directly, but at best, she can know only what she is capable of saying about nature. Or, in François Jacob's (1982:ix) words, an 'age or a culture is characterized less by the extent of its knowledge than by the nature of the questions it puts forward.' Of course, my examples involve natural language use, language games, discourse, and narrative, all of which are garbed in symbols. Yet symbols cannot be divorced from the icons and indices from which they evolved and developed, in addition to the fact that they invariably contain constituent icons and indices. What a proud symbol is (has become by *generacy*), an icon once was; and what an icon is, a symbol may become (by *de-generacy*).

If we re-evoke our image from mathematics via Dantzig's interpretation of it in terms of *rhetoric-syncopation-symbolism*, we can reformulate the notion in (almost) purely symbolic form without divorcing ourselves from due consideration of the other two sign types. Cantor's line converges asymptotically toward the limit in its most ideal form – analogous to Peirce's semiosis as conceived by a community of semiotic agents. In comparable fashion, tokens converge toward their type, and signs toward their final interpretant – that is, the sign generation model as depicted in tables 2 and 3 and figure 1. Symbolicity is the move toward generality, or continuity, in the ideal sense, though the project is destined to remain incomplete. The first degree of Peircean *de-generacy* from symbolicity 'downward' yields the character of indexicality (syncopation). Syncopation signifies in order to modify, cut short, abbreviate. It is Peirce's 'prescission' of a sign into its more abstractive form, the act of 'hypostatic abstraction' (*CP*:4.155, 4.234; *NE* IV:162). Syncopation as indexicality is tantamount to the successive displacement (metonymization) of one contiguous entity (point, integer, token) by another, indefinitely. This is the domain of discontinuity, of digitality, in contrast to the ideal continuous form of completely authentic symbolicity.

A further *de-generative* step and we enter into iconicity (rhetoric). In Dantzig's (1930:77) words, rhetorical algebra 'is characterized by the complete absence of any symbols, except, of course, that the words themselves are being used in their symbolic sense.' That is to say, in Peirce's terms, nonalgebraic natural language symbols are used in place of their presumably less blemished counterparts, algebraic symbols. Yet both natural language symbols and algebraic symbols evince properties that are iconic in nature. As icons, the *de-generate* manifestation of their more genuine cousins, symbols, they exercise *re-generative* acts, thus producing replicas of themselves. They cannot do otherwise, for in their character as icons they do not (yet) relate to anything outside themselves. But, in light of chapter 2, the emergence of each new replica is not-quite-exactly a faithful repetition of what went on before. There is always a difference, though virtually infinitesimal, between one replica and another – somewhat in the order of aperiodic crystals. Hence the *de-generate* icons (rhetors, signs of genuineness in their implicate form) are not exactly self-replicative, but only approximately so.

This is not the whole story, however. *Generacy* from icons to symbols and *de-generacy* in the opposite direction is not always the lackadaisical, meandering stream it might have appeared to be thus far. Granted, Firstness, iconicity, the rhetorical as possibility for further specification, is analogue in nature, while Secondness, indexicality, the contiguity of syncopated bits and pieces is digital, and Thirdness, symbolicity, begins a move from digitality toward some ideal form of analogical holism. In another way of putting it, from the continuity, vagueness, and necessary inconsistency and contradiction of the superposition of all possibilities represented by Firstness, gravitation is ultimately toward continuity, generality, completeness, without there being any necessary excluded-middle principle, for it can never be known with absolute guarantee which gaps will in the future be filled and which will remain open. Symbolicity, then, experiences an incessant drive toward increased complexity, symmetry, unity – the growth of signs – which, if drawn out to its logical end, would complete the circle, thus re-entering the realm of Firstness.

In this sense, from a larger view, it might appear – though erroneously, we shall observe – that the process conducing toward continuity, the completion of Thirdness, the final interpretant of the sign, follows the most general tendency toward a decrease of asymmetry in nature – against which the asymmetrical push of dissipative structures represent islands of order in the overall sea of randomness. This decrease can be recognized in three different types of process: (1) microlevel atomic and molecular change, (2) mechanical and statistical change, and (3) macromolecular and biological change. These changes pattern the prototemporal, eotemporal, and biotemporal domains respectively – roughly corresponding to Firstness, Secondness, and Thirdness. The second form of change does not fall within the central focus here; it is mechanical change, random movement toward a state of resting equilibrium, or entropic disorder, where objects tend more toward maximum entropy (for example, a pendulum) and mere statistical change. The first and third forms, on the other hand, are of central concern to the general growth and decay of signs (or life-forms), especially regarding molecular and biological development. *Prima facie* these two sorts of development present a study of contrasts. Pure molecular change entails the separation, persistence, and extension of symmetry, the most pristine case being that of crystal formation, while the biological process is a complex tension the summation of which may manifest a tendency toward, without arriving at, a static form of symmetry.

Inanimate processes appear to end in static, symmetrical patterns, but biological processes continue to develop until the organism's life-sustaining conditions fail and the processes decay into the relatively static state of inorganic systems. But, in view of chapters 1 and 2, these processes do not always evince symmetry decrease. Aperiodicity and symmetry breaking is now considered to exist alongside the tendency toward balance and equilibrium in both micro- and macrolevels, and in inorganic and biological domains. Symmetries break, balanced structures fluctuate and eventually dissipate, homeostatic equilibrium conditions erupt into far-from-equilibrium conditions. In addition, periodically there are catastrophes, random dips into the chaos, the chance, the disorder, of the domain of Firstness. And subsequently the self-organizing process begins anew.

Further to specify this continuous process punctuated by violent fits, jerks, and occasional setbacks, let us re-turn to biology, this time with our one-, two-, and three-dimensional semiotics more squarely in the spotlight.

3. SIGNS SUBDIVIDING INTO THEMSELVES

To recapitulate some earlier observations, crystallization in its purest form involves the monotonous reiterative union of identical units. Rather than movement, it represents permanence; rather than dynamism, stasis; rather than life, death.

Let us exercise a cross-eyed glance at an ideal periodic crystal unit resting beside an individual living cell. At the outset, we notice that the anatomy of the cell depends chiefly on the details of a montrous number of protein sequences, governed by the genetic code. We also observe that reproduction of the cell is made possible by means of its three-dimensional molecular structure being determined by a one-dimensional algorithmic order specified by its DNA – that is, one-dimensional semiotic generation giving rise to a three-dimensional manifestation. The code, the algorithmic unfolding, and the one-dimensional linear messages remain entirely within the system, while the three-dimensional cell exists within a two-dimensional topological wrap, its 'skin,' serving in the capacity of boundary conditions. On the other hand, growth of the crystal is relatively uncomplex. There exists a 'formula' consisting of, say, Na^+ and Cl^- ions, and their combinatorial properties determining the cubic halite structure. As layers are piled upon layers, we can see the tiny seed crystal grow outward, symmetrically, and in all directions simultaneously. The same pattern appears tediously to repeat itself; reproduction is entirely on the surface, with no detail in limbo or hidden from view – as is the case of the cell's one-dimensional algorithmic unfolding from within. Each repetition yields a virtually exact replica (simulacrum) of what went on before. Each is new, yet since it is for practical purposes identical to the old, there is actually neither new nor old but timeless invariability.

The cell, in contrast, prefers a different route to reproduction. In fact, it avails itself fundamentally of two different systems: the double-helix sequence of nucleic-acid that remains linear and recopies itself one-dimensionally, and the protein sequence that spontaneously unfolds – commensurate with one-dimensional semiotics – into a three-dimensional form. Its three- dimensional complexity is capable of reproducing itself due to the underlying simplicity of the one-dimensional sequence. For, in the biotemporal domain the order is an order of an order; one order is linear, the other requires three-dimensionality for its development. Unlike the crystal, the cell reproduces itself not by a three-dimensional accumulation of layers on its two-dimensional surface, but from within, by subdivision, with the self-enclosed surface becoming a mirror image of itself. The crystal's surface appears continuously to expand, as if a cubical balloon were being inflated – the topological space becomes larger. The cell's surface makes a copy of itself while the surface itself remains intact, like a soap bubble splitting into two, and the topological space apparently remains the same for the original and its copy.

Recursive sign duplication, I would submit, patterns the mould of cell growth more than crystal growth – in its pure, absolutely self-replicative, absolutely symmetrical sense, that is. Sign exemplifications from sign 1 to sign 10 subdivide, the 'parent' sign (cell) replicating itself, by a recursive process, into itself plus its 'offspring,' with the entirety of the sign's (cell's) viscera being in the process replicated as well. This recursivity is tantamount to the sign folding into itself: $\circledS$. There are two fundamental distinctions between sign multiplication and cell subdivision, however. In the first place, the semiosic process can apparently with greater facility realize moves either 'upward' (*generacy*) or 'downward' (*de-generacy*), depending upon the context and the circumstances, according to the general equation, $R_1 O_1 I_1 \leftrightarrow R_3 O_3 I_3$ (from figure 3). Thus with relative ease sign 1 can by generacy become sign 10 and the latter can de-generate – whether gradually or by dissipation – into the former, all by successive operations (see Merrell 1995:chap. 6). This distinction between sign growth-decay and cell growth-decay is due to the relatively greater degree of intentionality, of wilfulness, and I might as well write it, of consciousness, on the part of the sign generator collaborating with other signs in the process of semiosis, especially regarding human semiotic agents. Yet, by and large the growth and decay of signs, like all life-forms given their capacity for self-organization through fluctuations leading to dissipative structures, tends to favour symbolicity: *generacy* rather than *de-generacy*, life rather than death, asymmetry rather than symmetry.

In the second place, once an individual sign has developed from 1 to 10, it, along with its neighbors in the entire semiosic field, can evolve according to their superscripts: $R_3^1 O_3^1 I_3^1 \rightarrow R_3^n O_3^n I_3^n$. This process, like biological *evolution*, is irreversible, since memory, traces, and habits of thought and action disallow reversion to former states in their pristine form. However, it is distinct from general biological processes in so far as the ongoing progression is subject, most notably in distinctively human semiotic, to consciousness and intentionally

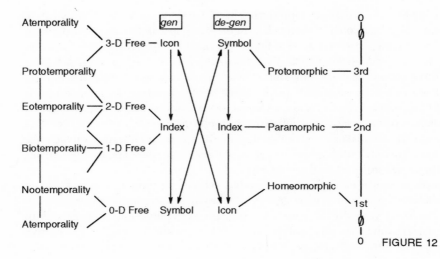

FIGURE 12

exercised control toward some purpose or goal by the semiotic agent *set apart from* – albeit artificially as it were – the semiosic domain. In much the sense of Wheeler's 'participatory universe,' the agent is outside, yet inside, and she collaborates with the universe in its gradual unfoldment, yet she is part of that selfsame universe being unfolded. Though the Cartesian subject/object distinction is rent asunder in the strictly physicalist interpretation of biology, it forces a foot in the doorway in less stringent interpretations. Still, if Peirce were to have his way, the distinction could never have been clear-cut in the first place but remain indelibly ambiguous.

At their basest level, it appears, signs and life evince common ground. If where life is found there are legisigns, as Short (1982) puts it, then more complex life-forms perpetually enact a push toward the equivalent of symbolicity – aperiodic rather than periodic forms. Signs grow from within, like organic growth, and by virtue of one-dimensional, linear generation along aperiodic lines ultimately to produce three-dimensional, asymmetrical variability leading toward ever greater levels of organized complexity. *De-generacy* can result from gradual decay (*embedment, automatization, habit taking*) of a once proud symbol such that it functions as if it were an index and even an icon. Occasional catastrophes occur as well along the same lines of *de-generacy*. In either case, growth can then re-commence, and the arduous climb toward ordered complexity begins anew. This process, from the broadest possible vantage, pictures the universe of signs, the biological domain, and indeed, the entire universe itself, as a vast self-organizing, bootstrapping operation.

Let us carry this analogy further.

4. MYRIAD DIVISIONS, UNTOLD FOLDS

Contemplate the perplexing twisting, turning, involuted, convoluted, recursive – but only with quasisymmetry – topological form illustrated in figure 12, which encapsulates the essence of key terms introduced in this and previous chapters.

As a pure topology it is comparable to John Barth's 'Frame-Tale' from *Lost in the Funhouse* (1968), consisting of a strip of paper indicated by a dotted line along the edge of the page with instructions that the reader is to cut it out, twist it, and fasten its ends together to form a Möbius strip. It now reads 'ONCE UPON A TIME THERE' ... 'WAS A STORY THAT BEGAN' ... 'ONCE UPON A TIME THERE' ... *n*. The first statement exists on the front side, but since the front side becomes the back side and vice versa in eternal oscillation, each is on the obverse side with respect to the other. In other words, linear generativity of symbols undergoes a fold on a two-dimensional plane in three-dimensional space, thus breeding a paradox, which would have been impossible without the added dimension – that is, in a fashion comparable to the growth of a cell, as we shall note in the next section. (For a more perplexing mind-bender try abstracting figure 12 from the page, give it a twist in your mind, and contemplate the results.)

From another angle, figure 12 is analogous to Diego Velázquez's *Las Meninas*, which contains visual resonances with *Don Quixote*, *Tristram Shandy*, *Hamlet*, and a host of postmodern contemporary works (Searle 1977). Velázquez's masterpiece distorts reflection and representation, classically conceived, thus incorporating an irreconcilable contradiction. As was mentioned above, the artist himself is found in the work painting on a painted canvas only the back side of which is present to the actual painting's contemplator, and a mirror reflects the artist, who is gazing outwardly toward his own subjects – perhaps the royal couple – he is in the act of painting (Gaggi 1989:2–9). The absent outside becomes the nonempirical inside and the inside the outside in eternal conflict, a topological agonistics for which there is no decidability.[5] By a comparable twist, our wishful mirror of nature is the image of an image of an image, each successive one an inverse replica of its predecessor and in turn the flip side of its successor. We are caught within an eternally convoluting, involuting, coiling, whorling, vertiginous, vorticose semiosic cascade, numbing in its complexity, yet exhilarating in its breath-taking volatility.

But a word of protest might be overheard: 'You think you are constructing square circles, counting the angels dancing on a pinhead, turning lead into gold, drawing the sword of Excalibur. Nothing but sandcastles in the sky! A futile quest for the Holy Grail! Why don't you get off your presumptuous high horse and dirty your fingers with the pragmatic, everyday affairs of signs, as Peirce originally taught us?'

Actually, Peirce has never ceased in this enquiry to act as a sounding-board, a pair of shoulders upon which we all can perch in order hopefully to see something through and beyond the dark cloud clearly, a springboard promising leaps of the imagination into somewhere and somewhen. I trust that I have remained quite faithful to the fundamentals of Peircean semiotic, availing myself to the best of my ability of logical, mathematical, and scientific, philosophical, and psychological studies, the human sciences, the humanities, and the arts. If the yield breeds nightmares of uncertainty, oceans of ambiguity, and an apparent promiscuity of paradoxes threatening to dissolve all dreams of reason, harmony, and stability, I see no call for despair. Rather, it opens the door, if not exactly to a Nietzschean-Derridean joyous play of free-wheeling signifiers, most certainly to a vision of open, creative, self-organizing dialogue with one's self, with the *other* of one's community, and with the *other* of nature at large, engaged in the process of its own self-organizing project.

That much written, the confusing snarl figure 12 might tend to evoke in the mind is comparable to other such topological quandaries that find their linguistic counterpart in impossible Meinong 'objects.' Take the 'square circle,' of which Percy Bridgman writes:

We cannot say that such a thing as a square circle ... does not 'exist' without implying by the mere fact that we are using the words and talking about 'it' that a square circle has a certain kind of existence. What kind of existence this may be has provided philosophy with a topic for discussion for thousands of years. The quandary presented by this situation we can see is one which naturally arises in Indo-European languages – it would be interesting to know whether it is felt as a quandary in other types of language. It seems to me that the situation can be adequately dealt with by reducing it to the purely formal level. If we say, 'The combination of words "square circle" has no referent either in the objective external world or in the conceptual world of logically consistent objects,' it seems to me that we have said all we need to say. I do not see why philosophers are not willing to say this and dismiss the topic from serious consideration. (1959:34)

Bridgman, it bears mentioning, was a founding father of 'operationalism,' which is to say, a sort of 'scientific pragmatism' without the metaphysical bent. At any rate, the import of his words stems from his suggestion that we take the words 'square circle' as symbols *qua* symbols and leave it at that. Though topologically a square can be transformed into a circle, and vice versa, any attempt to create reference for the words or to exercise mental gyrations in an attempt to create an image of the symbols are futile enterprises. Two-dimensional visual illusions are legion, as I have mentioned above. At the next stage of dimensionality, two wire squares facing each other and linked by a connecting wire can be rotated in such a manner that they appear to glide flatly over each other, or alternately that they oscillate about a vertical axis, reversing direction of rotation at every half-turn (Gregory and Gombrich 1973). Attempts to create more perplexing images of the fourth dimension (hypercubes, tessaracts, computer mock-ups) are amusing at best, and effectively reveal our paltry perceptual and conceptual powers (Rucker 1984).

But actually, with subtle acts of intuition and of mind we are ordinarily capable of overcoming such confusions with the same ease that Achilles overcomes his torpid competitor. A mountain range can be reduced topographically to a two-dimensional map − the collapse of three-dimensional space into two-dimensional space of iconic, indexical, and symbolic character − and the experienced traveller can easily find his way around without giving the mechanics of so doing a second's thought. That is, the map is ordinarily not confused with the territory in the same way the metaphor is not confused with the authentic article, the coffee with the cup, the fire with the smoke, and so on. Thus, at increasingly sophisticated levels, a relief map–like drawing can figuratively become a set of 'epigenetic paths' (Waddington 1957), an expanding dotted balloon can become a model for the 'expanding universe' (Gamow 1947), pockets in a billiard table can become 'black holes' (Davies 1988), a James Joyce neologism can even become interjected into the 'semiotically real' world of the physicist as 'quarks,' and variously 'coloured' ones to boot (Herbert 1985).

By a comparable move, with further regards to figure 12, it is now legion in psychological and psychoanalytical circles that Lacan's (1966) 'Schema R,' Bateson's (1972) 'double-bind,' and R.D. Laing's (1970) 'knots,' or their equivalents from other sources, can play havoc with the best of one's intentions. Yet, by 'topological transformations,' one can potentially become aware of the 'knots' in one's thoughts in such a way that what was a vicious tangle becomes harmless. Figure 12 illustrates such 'transformations.' For example, by exercising a 'twist,' the 'homeomorphic icon' of Firstness (as an ideal autopoietic entity) can become interchangeable with the 'prototemporal icon' of linear generativity, the ultimate yield being a 'protomorphic symbol' of Thirdness (as an asymmetrical, nonequilibrium, dissipative entity in constant give-and-take with its environment). Or reciprocally, the 'bio-nootemporal symbol' of Firstness (as a quasi-autonomous entity along its interminable road toward self-sufficiency) can become interchangeable with the 'protomorphic symbol' of Thirdness (as a Prigogine entity), which, by way of de-generacy, reverts back to its less developed stage, taking on iconic properties.

In another way of putting it, linear generativity from within the immanent domain of protemporality gives rise ultimately to symbolicity (sign 1 to sign 10 as a relatively self-sufficient 'argument'), which then, following the *Ho-t'u* model, can either (1) felicitously gyrate within its own space, remaining relatively unchanged, (2) be booted – bootstrap itself – up to a 'higher' level of Firstness to begin the generative process anew, thus yielding an ever more complex textuality of signs, or (3) embark upon a de-generative path 'downward.' In whichever case, there is never stasis but ongoing semiosis as signs of life, the life of signs, and life itself, continue to undergo their inevitable periodicity.

Significantly also, at the 'mesocosmic' level of figure 12, that 'semiotically real' domain of indexicality – that is, the realm of primary and secondary qualities of the world as we measure and cognize it, and as we sense and intuit it according to our *Umwelt*-given capacities – apparently continuous and smooth changes, rather than catastrophes, are ordinarily perceived to be the case. This affords us the customary calm security that our world is a harmonious whole, that order rather than chaos rules, and that all is well and will end well. And finally, it will have been noted, the atemporal extremes at the left of the diagram are connected to the empty set ($\emptyset$), and finally to the 0 of Peirce's 'nothingness,' that 'pre-First' antecedent to all categories (Baer 1988).

Now, let us take a giant step backward in our game of semiotic hopscotch from the paradoxical Möbius 'twist' character of figure 12 in light of the brain-twisting theories of the likes of Bateson, Lacan, and Laing to the humble cell. What we would hope to find is simplicity to soothe our aesthetic preferences. But to no avail, at least if we heed Varela's (1984a) advice. He begins his description of the cell as a Cretan lie-monger with a description of Escher's 'Hands' that draw each other, ad infinitum.[6] Of course Varela highlights the semiotic agent's autonomy, somewhat to the detriment, as I have argued, of that agent's openness to his surrounding phenomena. Yet, it is from the perspective of autonomy, in terms of self-referential systems, that the Möbius-twist is foregrounded. For when the system opens itself to its environment, its context, the paradox can be at least ephemerally resolved by the introduction of an 'axiom' from 'outside' – commensurate with the 'limitative theorems' in general (Gödel's incompleteness, Tarski's metalanguages). It is as if following my saying 'I am lying' I were to qualify it with 'No, you don't understand, I meant I was lying in my previous sentence, not when I said 'I am lying.'' I have introduced a sentence from outside the system, which serves to detox the effects of the paradox, to clear up the muddle. The sentence was 'opened to its environment,' so to speak, and as a result, it reached a new level of complexity and at the same time of intelligibility. In the sense of Prigogine – and by way of Cretan paradoxicality, according to Howard Pattee (1969, 1979, 1986) – an organism as a system in perpetual interaction with its environment does fundamentally the same. In other words, like the sentence contextualized, the organism environmentalized loses autonomy in its interaction with the world. There *is* a degree of autonomy, to be sure, but that is only part of the total picture.

Some examples are in order. A dog and a pedestrian are walking along the sidewalk in the same direction but on opposite sides of the street, when suddenly the animal decides to cross the street, thus closing the distance between them, and greet his human counterpart. A pelican at the wharf during the early morning hours suddenly notes that it is time to spread her wings and dry them out under the rising sun. A gerbil in her cage doing her morning aerobics in her mechanical Ferris wheel decides she has had enough and approaches her mate for some grooming. A flatworm running a T-maze opts at the juncture to make a left rather than a right turn. Now, the dog's behaviour is neither exactly programmed nor the result of having received instructions from some outside source, and the same can be said of the other animals. The flatworm, in fact, does not turn left merely as a result of repeated punishment-reward trials and errors, but because, given its role as an autonomous entity, it is subjected to certain changes and disturbances in its sensory input that it processes, constructs, and interprets so as to maintain a satisfactory regulation and balance of its inner workings — recall Piaget's 'constructivist' assimilation-accommodation model. This distinguishes the *autonomous* self-referential, self-regulative aspect of the biological entity from an *allonomous* system requiring an outside agent for its proper functioning.

A car is allonomous. It did not make itself, but was made; it is now operated by a driver, and if it breaks down, it cannot fix itself but requires a mechanic to do the job. Escher's drawing as a self-contained system gives the appearance of its being autonomous; but, of course, the viewer knows the paradox is not 'real,' for Escher's unseen hand once lurked above, drawing the hands drawing themselves. So it is in the final analysis allonomous. The organism is autonomous – self-referential, self-contained, self-organizing – but it is also constantly opened to its environment.

5. THE LANGUAGE (SYMBOLIC DESCRIPTION) OF LIFE

The upshot is that the component parts of autonomous entities refer to each other, and they mutually specify themselves. It is in this sense that in the molecular domain life is capable of determining and organizing itself, thus acquiring the chiefly autonomous nature of its existence. An individual cell, Varela writes: 'stands out of a molecular soup by defining and specifying boundaries that set it apart from what it is not. However, this specification of boundaries is done through molecular productions made possible through the boundaries themselves. There is, therefore, a mutual specification of chemical transformation and physical boundaries; the cell draws itself out of a homogeneous background. Should this process of self-production be interrupted, the cellular components no longer form a unity and gradually diffuse back into a homogeneous soup' (Varela 1984a:311–12; also, in general, Maturana and Varela 1980).

The cell sets up boundary conditions in terms of a membrane separating itself from the rest of the universe. From within the membrane, what Hofstadter (1979) calls a 'strange loop' composing a 'tangled hierarchy' is to be found the equivalent of which in natural language is our familiar Epimenides paradox: 'I am lying.' From within the sentence the paradox is irresolvable, nothing but eternal flip-flopping between an *either* and an *or*. As we saw above, a solution is forthcoming solely by a leap 'outside' the system in order to understand the intention behind the utterance. Regarding biological organisms, the leap becomes trickier, for we are, ourselves, biological organisms. One might retort that the same inheres when we include the inorganic universe within our purview, for after all, is the physicist not a collection of 'wavicles' trying to understand what it is to be a 'wavicle'? The point might be well taken, for the physicist, as part of the self-contained, self-organizing, self-referential universe, can hardly expect more. Besides, it is all a matter of language: 'waves,' 'particles,' and other symbols of scientific discourse are over the long haul no more than 'word-spinning,' no more than so much language, as Bruce Gregory (1988) has so aptly demonstrated.

Now, Varela provides the final insult to our vain efforts to know the world as detached, objective subjects upon declaring that the same self-containment of the Epimenides sort is found at the core of living organisms (also Pattee 1979). In an uncomfortable manner of putting it, just as the physicist of quantum theory and relativity makes ample use of an 'irrational' value, the 'imaginary' number $\sqrt{-1}$, so also the organism's 'tangled hierarchy,' as a whole, evinces the equivalent of the statement 'Everything within this boundary (membrane, epidermal layer) is a fiction.' That is, the organism has, rather arbitrarily as it were, set itself apart from what is now conceived to be (an *Umwelt*-dependent) 'reality,' which consists of the entire universe less the organism. As such the organism *is not* what the universe *is*, and the universe *is* what the organism *is not*. The organism's interaction with its world – its knowledge of its world – is tantamount to an 'imaginary' realm, a netherworld somewhere in some ethereal sphere from which the universe can be seen. Its position in/outside/at the margin of its world is rather comparable to Wittgenstein's eye of the *Tractatus* (1961), which sees its world but cannot see itself, or see itself seeing its world.

Varela points out that in the Epimenides case, the paradox remains intact as long as its contemplator is unwilling to let go of his pigheaded desire dogmatically to choose between absolute truth and absolute falsity. Once discarding this need, one can then see the sentence's vicious circularity as its own self-help program for specifying its meaning. From an 'outside' vantage – that provided by the contemplator's perspective – the sentence becomes like a photograph of Escher, with hands on drawing board, putting the final touch on his pair of hands engaged in their own viciously circular, mutually self-organizing project. Escher 'imagines' himself in an ethereal neutral sphere from within which he is capable of generating an 'irrational' self-referential system whose very existence depends upon his own creative hand. The Epimenides sentence, viewed from 'outside,' is like contemplating an 'imaginary' thought experiment one of the supreme examples of which is that of Einstein, who wondered what it would be like to grasp the entire universe from a neutral perspective, as if lassoing a photon of light and saddling it for a scenic trip to nowhere and nowhen. Of course, Epimenides's sentence, Escher's 'Hands,' and Einstein's universe are *allonomous* rather than *autonomous*. They are the yield of creative hands and minds, 'imaginary' language-dependent models designed to help us get a feel for the unimaginable and ineffable. Biological organisms, on the other hand, are somehow able to lift themselves up by their own bootstraps without the need of such an artificial leap of imagination giving them a view as if *sub specie aeternitatis*.

Varela relates the to-and-fro oscillation of the paradoxical systems in question to Mandelbrot fractals, whose iterative program yields such phenomena as a complex snowflake design ('Koch curve') from a simple equilateral triangle. This is pure mathematics, of course, but according to Mandelbrot and his followers it is capable of patterning the self-organizing character of all facets of change and growth found in the entire universe, inorganic and organic phenomena alike. More apropos to the concerns of the present enquiry, and equally patterning life and nonlife, are Prigogine's far-from-equilibrium conditions leading to order through fluctuations, the sort of autocatalytic cycle we saw in chapters 1 and 2. The Belousov-Zhabotinsky reaction, for example, creates a structure of concentric and spiral 'cells' that undergo intermittent stages of pulsation and stability. The concentric circles are 'waves' not of liquid motion but of chemical change, comparable to the action potentials succeeding one another as they travel along a nerve axon. Like action potentials, Winfree writes, the onset of these Belousov-Zhabotinsky chemical changes 'is so abrupt as to constitute a virtual discontinuity: the wavefront spans only a few percent of a millimeter; during mere milliseconds, one of the reactants explosively increases a thousandfold in concentration. Unlike water waves or sound or light, waves of this kind propagate steadily without attenuation. Though the waves may be spreading from a point source, it does not lose strength, because each newly excited region supports the passing wave to the full extent of its resources' (1987:169).

The reaction, in other words, is strictly chemical, and involves no DNA, yet it 'grows' as if it were endowed with life processes. With apparently minor adjustment the chemical reaction can be made to cease oscillating spontaneously. But its 'excitability' and its capacity for self-organization remain uncompromised (Winfree 1972). The same behaviour can be observed in living 'excitable' media. For example, an inert neuron in a state of delicate readiness for firing when in response to a stimulus can be adjusted by reducing the stimulus, until it is too small to be noticed. Then the firing will occur, apparently spontaneously, and the process will be iterated time and again (Winfree 1987:170). Indeed, given Winfree's conclusion, space-time forms in all vibes of life – heartbeat rhythms, fruit fly and firefly entrainment, gut peristalsis, cricket chirps harmonizing with one another, morphogenetic oscillations in chick embryos, slime mould periodicities, and so on – are all part of, and in a certain manner of speaking a microcosm of, the cosmic wave ballet.

In formulating his own argument that life is a self-help program, Varela (1984a:315–17) asks us to compare the state of affairs 'inside' a pair of 'strange loops': the liar paradox as an individual cell. I shall perform a certain variation on both of these states for the purpose of the present concerns by introducing the concept of 'fictionality' (that is, of semiosis) in the sense that what is 'fictional' is thereby not 'real' – which is the case of all *Umwelt*-generated 'semiotic realities,' of course. In the Varelan spirit, assume the following system:

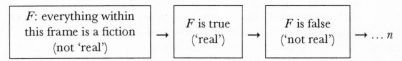

The sentence includes itself within the frame of all fictive sentences. Therefore if it is true, it cannot be fictive, so it belongs to the sphere of 'reality.' But it cannot be true, since it includes itself in the class of all sentences to which it refers, so it must be fictive, that is, not 'real,' but if this is the case, then what it says of itself must be true, so it is 'real' rather than fictive, and so on. This is somewhat comparable to Magritte's lifelike painting of a pipe underneath which the caption 'This is not a pipe' is found. If we were to substitute 'Is not a pipe' for 'This,' we would have ' "Is not a pipe" is not a pipe.' It is as if to say of the painting, including the caption: '*P*: EVERYTHING WITHIN THIS FRAME IS NOT A PIPE,' which yields '*P* IS TRUE' → '*P* IS FALSE' → ...*ñ*. Varela then goes on to construct the following:

to pattern the iterative growth and subdivision of a cell. What Varela seems to imply is that in essence the cell, upon separating itself from the remainder of the universe with a two-dimensional boundary condition, the membrane, is acting out the one-dimensional, linear statement: '*C*: I *AM* THAT I *AM NOT*.' What it is *is not* the universe and what the universe *is*, it *is not*. The cell is and is not a subset of the master set called the universe; the universe is and is not the master set containing the cell as a subset. In this manner, the counterpart of 'METABOLITES ARE PRODUCED' would be '*C* IS TRUE ("REAL"),' and the iteration of 'A MEMBRANE IS FORMED' would be '*C* IS FALSE (NOT "REAL").' Both systems are thus given natural language window-dressing.

Now let us integrate the conclusions of chapters 1 and 2 into this discussion. First, notice that the *R–O–I* 'hypercycle' is as viciously circular as the above paradoxical sentences. *R* is not the 'real' thing; neither is it the 'real' object for which it stands, which is itself not even 'real' but merely 'semiotically real.' The *R*, a sign, is transformed (translates itself) into its respective *I*, another sign, which becomes, in collaboration with its interpreter, yet another sign, *as if* it were 'real' *for* some semiotic agent *in* some respect or capacity, though it will never be absolutely 'real' short of having become the final *I*. It is *as if* the signs in question were implicitly telling us:

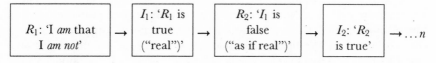

If in nutshell form, the Peircean sign is something that *stands for* something else *to* someone *for* something *in* some respect or capacity, that 'something *in* some respect or capacity' becomes another sign – subscripted if you will – referring to another object, now conceived to be some difference – though to an infinitesimal degree – which in turn determines another interpretant further down the stream. And this interpretant becomes yet another sign, and so on. Moreover, the interpreter (self), as her/himself an interpretant, places the whole affair in another dimension. Upon the sign's being interpreted, the self becomes a displaced interconnecting mode in the sign component's interaction, and the entire concoction, SELF–*R*–*O*–*I*, enters into the self-participatory rush toward some unseen, unknown, undefined, unfathomable finality. Self and sign, interpreter and interpretant, representamen-object and self-interpretant, become fused and confused in conjunction with the ongoing effervescence of semiosis. During this process, like cells, living signs subdivide, whether in the direction of *generacy* or *de-generacy*, upstream or downstream, 'bottom up' unfolding or 'top down' unfolding-enfolding.

Just as an amoeba (a linearly generated entity) cannot step outside the boundary conditions (two-dimensional membrane) defining itself as something set apart from the remainder of the universe (of three dimensions), so also it has no world except what it 'experiences' by means of its sensory perceptors, which make it what it is. Neither is there any possible indication of its origin, of that time when it first defined itself as an entity apart from the *other*. It is a viciously regressive, ever-receding set of replicas of replicas of replicas, with certain fugue-like variations at certain points. Likewise, all signs, from the most humble icon to the most imperious of symbols (words, sentences, texts, intertexts), flow along, side by side, in the same semiosic stream as signs of signs of signs, interpretants of interpretants of interpretants. Thus we note anew that we ourselves, our conscious selves, are caught up in the same infinite regress. Our present consciousness is conscious *of* our previous consciousness – what it now *is not* – and what our consciousness *is* will be something *else* in the next moment of which there will be consciousness of what it then *is not*, and so on. We have no semiotic sonar mechanism with which to gauge the depth of the stream, no periscope so as to bring its banks into focus, no anchor we can drop to halt our movement within the flow, no sextant to determine where we are, no map to see how we arrived at this point or where we are headed.

Furthermore, the amoeba, like all self-referring signs, is so arranged that it can replicate itself every so often. Unlike more complex organisms (and signs), birth is not counterbalanced by death. When an amoeba community grows, the resulting amoebae do not die, but merely disappear as individuals: one becomes two, and two become many. The only criterion for an amoeba's no longer sustaining life is that it cannot subdivide (that the sign cannot exercise *generacy* or *de-generacy*). This 'death,' however, is not simply an individual matter but contingent on the community; if a part of it remains alive, self-replication will continue. 'Death' for the individual amoeba is in this sense not an affair of beginning there-then and ending here-now, but a matter of dilution, dissemination, and multiplication. Thus there is no individual consciousness, or self, with any Grand Design regarding the whole, but merely the execution of a semiobiological autosemeiopoietic program. The only messages forthcoming as a result of the genetic code, or signs (interpretants) as a result of semiosis, are the messages-signs (interpretants) themselves. And genetic texts-signs (interpretants) are made intelligible solely to those units (amoeba, interpreter-interpretant) they have themselves determined.

With this in mind, focus once again, if you will, on figure 12. Upon considering its Möbius-strip qualities, the twist, in a manner of speaking, is capable of rendering iconicity symbolicity and Firstness Thirdness, and vice versa, by means either of *generacy* or *de-generacy*. Relatively genuine signs on their road toward self-contained, self-sufficient, self-referential autonomy return to their origin, which is now different from what it was – thus with each return a circle is not exactly completed, but rather, a spiral is either perpetuated or partly collapsed. Taking the Möbius sheet as a whole, symbolicity of zero-degree freedom, *en bloc*, exists in simultaneity with symbolicity of three-degrees of freedom, and the latter rests at the side of iconicity as pure possibility, which, like Peirce's *abduction*, is the fountain of novelty, creativity, the unfolding of the enfolded, explication of the implicate. From this point onward *generacy* can produce ever-more-complex systems.

On the other hand, symbolicity of three-degrees of freedom can exist in simultaneity with symbolicity of zero-degree freedom in contiguity with iconicity. Zero-degree symbolicity masquerading as iconicity is symbolicity that has presumably reached, or is close to reaching, autonomy. That is, autonomy within its particular environment, for the ultimate sign is not realizable *for* a finite community of semiotic agents. Such symbolicity is the product of *de-generacy*, from signs of complexity and wilful, conscious processes, to *embedded, automatized, habituated* processes. Symbolicity having *de-generated* into iconicity is processed along *embedded, automatized, habituated* pathways *as if* there were no degrees of freedom, *as if* all signs were coagulated into a *plenum*; the well-springs of *abduction* have become a dry gulch, and signs are processed along tacit pathways with virtually no consciousness *of* their being so processed.

In another way of putting it, by way of *generacy*, ever-increasing complexity is made possible in terms of linear development through symbolicity (natural language, formal language, genetic code) within a combinatorial system (pro-tomorphism, the semiotic counterpart to prototemporality). Each symbol can replicate itself re-iteratively through time (time-binding) eventually producing a cycle ('hypercycle') of events. In the unfolding of these events, the role of each constituent is dependent on that of all others, and the role of all constituents

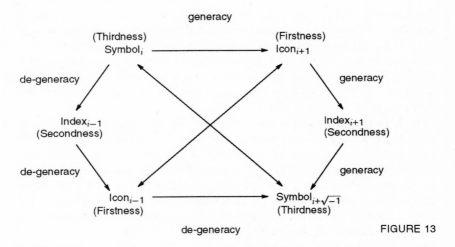

FIGURE 13

is dependent on that of the whole, to bring about the emergence of greater complexity of structures in space (space-binding). Thus when a given cycle has been completed (sign 1 to sign 10), from the Firstness of iconicity to the Thirdness of symbolicity, the sign can once again take on 'iconic' properties (the Firstness of symbolicity) as a self-reiterating whole, from which point it can begin the *generacy* process anew toward a sign of greater compounded qualities (that is, symbol$_i$ → icon$_{i+1}$ → index$_{i+1}$ → symbol$_{i+1}$ → ... n). Or vice versa, in the case of *de-generacy*: from the Thirdness of symbolicity the sign can be transformed into the equivalent of an index and then an icon, which is capable of functioning as if it were a symbol of lesser complexity (symbol$_i$ → index$_{i-1}$ → icon$_{i-1}$ → symbol$_{i-1}$ ... n). And the icon of Thirdness comes to be used generally and somnambulistically without awareness *that* it is being so used on the part of the semiotic agent (due to the *embeddedness*, the *automatization*, of his/her sign use).

The whole concoction is patterned in figure 13, also following the Möbius-strip topology, with the symbol existing at the twist as the product either of *de-generacy* (yielding S_{i-1}), or *generacy* (yielding S_{i+1}). In other words, the symbol can flip to the other side, thus re-capitulating (recursively re-iterating) itself as the symbol it once was – recall the *Ho-t'u* model. The obverse, of course, can be stated of the icon. Moreover, if figure 13 is superimposed on the Argand plane depicted by figure 6 in chapter 3, symbolicity and iconicity would lie along the imaginary axis, with indexicality strung out on the horizontal axis according to its positive and negative values, and with the complex numbers determining the vectorial sum of a given sign's semiotic value (its interpretant, meaning). And, one must be mindful, the interpreter (another interpretant) is immanently caught within the entire semiosic whirlpool.

We must continue to pursue these strange trips 'up' and 'down' the spiral staircase, their bearing on complexity in the biological realm, and the radical indeterminacy of our capacity to know it.

9

Chance and Legacy

1. IT'S A SIGN'S WORLD

Given the so-called 'genetic code,' the number of possible double-helix sequences and hence protein structures is for practical purposes unlimited. It
is the genetic analogue of one-dimensional generativity along infinite paths
in three-dimensional space – somewhat reminiscent of Cantor's transfinite set
algebra.

In view of this unfathomable degree of freedom, the cell's accuracy of
reproduction is indeed remarkable. Untold chemical reactions occur within
the cell almost simultaneously with an I-told-you-so certainty and precision unknown and unthinkable to the mass-produced commodities of which
postmodern technology is so proudly capable – which is to a degree an
affront to Baudrillard's notion of simulation, as we observed in chapter 6.
Regarding cell multiplication, there are, to be sure, checks and balances
for the purpose of preventing overloading at any point along the assembly line, and policemen for detecting poor workmanship in order to ensure
quality control. And life goes on, toward ever-greater complexity. Such ef-
ficiency does not guarantee infallibility, however. Nobody's perfect. Errors
somehow manage to creep in. They can either alter the genetic make-up
of the cell and are passed on as mutations, or they can merely abstract
the execution of genetic messages. In the case of mutations, the chemical
make-up of the DNA sequence is thrown out of kilter. Mutations, Jacob
writes, appropriately availing himself of a textual (symbolic) metaphor, 'result
from errors similar to those which a copyist or a printer inserts into a text.
Like a text a nucleic-acid message can be modified by the change of one
sign into another, by the deletion or addition of one or more signs, by the
transposition of signs from one sentence to another, by the inversion of a

group of signs – in short, by anything that disturbs the pre-established order'
(1982:289).

In nature, changes in the 'chemical text' occur not by selection of a
particular sequence and an active decision regarding its modification, but
blindly, randomly, without purpose or meaning. The chemical reaction cannot
choose a particular letter in order to change it to another one, for the chemical
reaction contains that letter as part of itself. Nucleic acid is its own sequence,
and like our one-dimensional worm in chapter 3 along its Lineland, it can see
neither forward nor backward, nor can it step outside its 'world' in order to see
the line as a line. Quite comparably:

There exists no molecular species in nature that can modify the nucleic-acid sequence
in a deliberate manner, whether among the enzymes used for ordering the nucleic-acid
sub-units in the copy process or among the regulatory proteins that turn nucleic-acid
segments 'on' or 'off'. These molecules can establish associations with nucleic-acid; but
they cannot modify the sequence of the message. By the very nature of the genetic
material and its relations with other cell constituents, no molecular species is able to
change the plan that decides its own structure. This means that a gene cannot be
transformed by reference to the function it controls. Whether spontaneous or artificially
induced, mutations always modify at random the order of the sequence taken at
random from the whole genetic programme. The entire system is arranged so as to
make mutations blind errors. (Jacob 1982:289–90)

Jacob, of course, is donning a Darwinian hat, much in the order of Jacques
Monod. Random mutations are strictly chance occurrences, as so effectively
argued by Monod. Presenting his thesis in characteristically brazen fashion,
Monod declares that the events of mutation are strictly 'accidental, due to
chance. And since they constitute the *only* possible source of modifications in
the genetic text, itself the *sole* repository of the organism's hereditary structures,
it necessarily follows that chance *alone* is at the source of every innovation, of
all creation in the biosphere. Pure chance, absolutely free but blind, at the very
root of the stupendous edifice of evolution: this central concept of biology ... is
today the *sole* conceivable hypothesis, the only one compatible with observed
and tested fact, (1971:110). And he concludes that: 'the ancient covenant is in
pieces; man knows at last that he is alone in the universe's unfeeling immensity,
out of which he emerged only by chance. His destiny is nowhere spelled out,
nor is his duty. The kingdom above or the darkness below: it is for him to
choose' (1971:180).

Darwinian selection, or Monod's chance affairs, are as blind as the tinkering
of a *bricoleur* with bits and pieces scattered here and there, devoid of ongoing

process structures entailing foresight, purpose, design, participation on the part of the subject, and above all, devoid of true creativity. That is to say, if there is any form or fashion of creativity, it is of a bare mechanical sort, the unpredictable rearrangement of what was already at hand. It is a far remove from organic creativity resulting in the emergence of total systems defying analysis of their parts as mere aggregates that can be broken down into their fundamental components. Mechanical 'creativity' is like a diversity of static structures put together from an Erector set by a child as if she had no purpose in mind, but by random combinations she occasionally happened to put a meaningful object together.

This image is an extension of the Cartesian machine, with humans thrown into the mix and their genes as 'blind watchmakers,' to use Richard Dawkins's (1986) reductionist-determinist label. By the tinkering with that grand tinkerer, nature, the Cartesian hope is that genetic engineering can someday learn to perfect what nature left flawed, to control nature's aleatory, purposeless, apparently unintelligible humdrum. This would be the triumph of positivism long after it had given up the ghost. It would be equivalent to a totalizing grasp and control of Saussurean *langue*, kit and caboodle, as a massive *ars combinatoria* determined by Lévi-Straussian mechanism and Baudrillardian mechanical simulation.[1] This is the biological-mechanistic counterpart to Laplacean mechanism gone wild. In his critique of the Laplacean ideal, Alexandre Koyré (1978:42) once observed that modern, mechanistic science substituted quality for quantity, thus making a place for everything except the knowing subject, who 'became estranged and utterly divorced from the world of life, which science has been unable to explain – not even to explain away by calling it "subjective."' As if oblivious to this and other such warnings, genetic engineers and AI researchers now believe the final step is at hand: the *terra incognita* of 'subjectivity' can finally be mapped in terms of true, genuine, and certain mathematical knowledge (Davis 1991; Suzuki and Knudston 1990; but see also Kevles and Hood 1992). Chimerical utopias, misrepresented Eden, irretrievable Paradise.

The problem here bears on an infinite regress quandary comparable to those to which I refer above and in the previous pair of volumes of which this book is a companion (Merrell 1991b, 1995). For example, if, as the vitalist Henri Bergson (1935:317) once put it, from the positivist perspective the universe is 'a machine for making gods,' and if *Homo sapiens* is capable someday of making machines that simulate their makers, then the gods, product of the universe and yet themselves machines, will have constructed machines that were engendered by machines, no end. This is in essence tantamount to saying that the organism is nothing more than DNA's way of making another DNA – or that the

Interpretant is nothing more than the sign's way of making another sign. The problem is that this is, once again, reductionism through and through, with due respect to the Thomas Sebeok quote with which I opened this enquiry.[2] It follows the strange thesis that the code makes us human, endowing us with our particular characteristics, and just as it gives us life, so also it surely brings us death. Yet to know the code will make us free. At least so we are told.

But the code is not everything. A DNA molecule is in the first place 'dead' anyway. It must be, if it can be recovered from mummies and mastodons frozen tens of thousands of years ago. In the second place, it has no power to replace itself, but rather, it is produced from the complex cellular machinery of proteins. As I pointed out above, no molecule is absolutely self-replicating, only entire cells contain the machinery for their own reproduction. The linear sequence of nucleotides in DNA – and the messenger RNA – is used by the cell to determine what sequence of amino acids will be involved in the construction of a protein, and how and at what point along the sequence the reaction will occur. Proteins are made by proteins and cells by cells: the entire apparatus is necessary, not merely a code and a DNA string (Lewontin 1992). It is like the image in figure 12 of one-dimensional protomorphic, prototemporal generativity of a two-dimensional paramorphic surface containing a three-dimensional, homeomorphic entity. The whole process commences with a linear string, but what is of ultimate import is the (holistic) product, not the (binary, atomistic) linear principle. And in the third place, organisms are not strictly determined by DNA (biological determinism) or by social conditioning (cultural determinism) but by a complex interplay of both. Nor does change comes about merely either by the *evolution* of the species through random microscopic mutations or by an individual organism's *development*, from birth to death. According to all indications, there is no sharp dividing line between genetic and cultural evolution and individual development (Lumsden and Wilson 1981; Salthe 1992). Consequently, neither genetic engineering nor social programming are capable absolutely of determining the individual or the species. The entire organism and society, as wholes, make up the field of interaction wherein emergent processes engage in their Shiva's dance.[3]

(Furthermore, tunnel-minded emphasis on the code by AI engineers and Darwinian molecular evolutionists is patterned by the linear, digitalized, Boolean, cybernetic electronic media placing prime stock in the code, also fancied and fashioned by Baudrillard and certain other gurus of postmodernism. Such emphasis is also strikingly comparable to Saussureanism as interpreted by many – though not all – structuralists and poststructuralists. Context is relegated to virtual oblivion, while the signs themselves become autonomous, purportedly taking on a 'life' of their own. And the self is displaced, if it does not vanish altogether, or at least, the self-other relation becomes a mere dyadic relation of two antagonistic states.)[4]

Monod's thesis that life is an impossible accident (chance), a sheer miracle that should not really have occurred and is quite unlikely to be repeated anywhere else in the universe, coupled with the individual organism's implacable, demanding, selections on no uncertain terms (necessity), is sort of the flip side of Zeno's paradox of motion. Zeno denied motion on the basis of an arrow's necessarily occupying one and only one of an infinite array of infinitesimal segments along a continuum without the possibility of its passage from one resting spot to another. Monod rejects emergence because a living organism is utterly impossible in terms of a chance combination of millions and millions of molecules from random throws of the cosmic dice: an infinite set of random infinitesimals cannot an orderly pattern make. Yet, its very existence makes intransigent demands on the entire system. In response, Wicken (1987:33) points out that, in the first place, random processes do not necessarily demand the existence of a random matrix. Amino acids and proteins are to a considerable degree self-sequencing, as wholes, as a holistic process that defies mere chance happenings. In the second place, certain proteins evince catalytic capacities, thus they are capable of bringing about reactions that could not occur among a random aggregate of molecules.

This is organic creativity – in contrast to mere *ars combinatoria* – at its best, comparable to the product of a poet or sculptor whose works are not isolated from one another but make up an interconnected whole. If the sculptor's works were isolated, it would be as if the Erector kit parts had arranged themselves in random fashion, as if there were no participating subject. Such machine creativity, in Bohm's (1980:173) words, dictates that 'each part is formed independently of the others, and interacts with the other parts only through some kind of external contact.' In contrast, the products of organic creativity, like living organisms themselves, are such that 'each part grows in the context of the whole, so that it does not exist independently, nor can it be said that it merely "interacts" with the others without itself being essentially affected in this relationship.' Organic creativity in terms of interconnected wholes calls for a composite, cumulative set of constructs representing an irreversible process, as if they had a 'will of their own,' as if successive works had some 'memory' of their predecessors, and as if they were guided by some invisible hand, the participating agent (Ingold 1986:176–83). If there be an agent regarding mechanical creativity, then she is surely a *bricoleur*, while organic creativity, the product of the equivalent of *abductive* acts, requires a semiotic agent in the full, Peircean sense. Indeed, this form of creativity is also commensurate with the phenomena described by Prigogine as 'dissipative structures,' process structures.

Placing this mechanic-organic distinction within the context of previous chapters, the wheel, printing press, telephone, computer, or works of art embody concepts, novel conjunctions of sentiments, intuitions, hunches, and ideas, that emerged as wholes and became relatively fixed in their creators' minds. They were certainly not merely atomistic fortuitous conjunctions. Organic creativity involves (1) thought, intellect, cognition, and the B-series incorporated within Thirdness at the southern point of figure 9 – which bears on nootemporality – and making up the right-hand column of table 7, coupled with (2) the process of thinking, experience, the stream of consciousness, and the A-series, embodied in the upper portion of Thirdness in figure 9 – coinciding with biotemporality – and the left-hand column of table 7. The latter is dynamic, flowing, living process as a complement to the viscous budge of habit, law, convention, modes of living. It is fluid sign processing accompanied by embedded, automatized actualization of signs tending toward stasis. It is the knife-edge race of conscious and nonconscious processes allied with snail-paced memory. It is living *abduction* (Firstness), providing the motivation for chipped in stone *deduction* (Thirdness) – which is not to discredit the importance of Thirdness, but just as Firstness without Thirdness is formless, so Thirdness without Firstness is surely dead.

What we have in the machinic-organic distinction at its roots is logical positivism and analytic philosophy in contrast to Whitehead – Bohm himself was influenced by the process philosopher – the earlier Wittgenstein in contrast to his later counterpart, and Saussure (and semiology-structuralism) in contrast to Peirce (and later, William James and Dewey) (see Rorty 1979; Bernstein 1983; Rajchman and West 1985).

2. THE MANY AND THE ONE REVISITED

In other words, from the organic view we have an anti-Darwinian posture. In brief, Darwinism tends toward historical functionalism, with structural changes occurring by a throw of the dice. These changes cause *genotype variations* in the population *inherited* by the next generation, whose *phenotypes* are not all created equal; hence the fittest will be the most *adaptive* and most likely to survive.

The problem is that Darwinism is by and large linear thinking. It involves 'one-dimensional' transfer from parents to offspring. A more adaptable individual will have hardier offspring than its contemporaries, and with each successive generation, the less adaptable mutants will tend to disappear as their stronger neighbours grow stronger. This is also equilibrium thinking. The tendency is toward a more random (hence more symmetrical, less organized, ordered, and complex) state pushing toward maximum entropy. While random mutations must certainly play a factor in evolution, they do not constitute the whole picture. To reiterate the conclusions of chapters 1 and 2, living systems tend toward increased organized complexity at diverse hierarchical levels. More complex and diversified systems, given their capacity for self-organization, with feedback links between themselves and their environment, are also increasingly capable of their own self-determination, in contrast to the Darwinian model of confirmation or elimination of systems on the basis of purely random mutations. And as greater complexity goes, so also the frequency of dissipative structures, the destruction of order, and the product of far-from-equilibrium conditions, all of which can potentially give rise to ever-higher organization and complexity.

In the Prigogine mould, a system in nonequilibrium takes matter and energy from the environment, undergoes an irreversible entropy production from within, and exports entropy to its surroundings. Thus entropy becomes the history of the living system, as it moves irreversibly toward maturity, midlife, old age, and finally death. The boundary conditions separating the system from its environment must always be, during the system's history, in flux – hence a nonequilibrium state must persist. This is not the picture of a mere random state, nor is the system chaotic; it is highly ordered and organized, though exeedingly complex. Quite understandably, in view of the idea of life through aperiodicity, imperfection, asymmetry, and imbalance, as suggested in chapters 1 and 2, a living system is constantly in a process of transformation and is incapable of perfect replication. Living organisms are distinctly a class of nonequilibrium entropy systems. They are and they are not thermodynamically susceptible when considering living systems. Thermodynamics exercises its force when organisms and their environment are taken into account, for on the large, entropy increases.

To be sure, living organisms appear to defy the Second Law of Thermo-dynamics when viewed merely as Maturana-Varela autonomous, autopoietic entities. However, to repeat, they are not exclusively autonomous entities and nothing else. Neither is their entropic behaviour simply determined by energy flows, given their self-organizing capacity, enabling them, as open systems, to exploit those flows to their advantage. Energy flows between the organism and its environment create boundary conditions granting them freedom but at the same time placing limitations on them. They are set apart from their environment as autonomous, autopoietic entities cut out and marked off from the rest of the universe. At the same time, they incessantly interact with their surroundings – an *Umwelt*-world generated by themselves as autonomous enti-ties – and in so doing bring about changes in their world as their world changes them and they undergo self-contained, self-organized alterations (Wicken 1979, 1980).

If energy flows alone were the determining factors for biological organization, then purely thermodynamic energy changes would be registered in the living organism. It appears most likely at this point, however, that organisms also change due to mutations. Hence there is no definite correlation between the exclusive concept of energy flows and mutations in the living organism that is patterned in energy flows in the inorganic world (Brooks and Wiley 1986:37–8). Consider our hummingbird analogy regarding the *Ho-t'u* model. While she maintains herself in one position, wings fluttering furiously, and inspects the flower before her, there is a flurry of activity around her: the sun, wind, a brook, trees, countless insects, some cattle. She is surrounded by energy flows and sign flows. If it were merely a matter of the sum of all the energy and sign exchanges in the field that determined her status as a living organism, she would be able cheerfully to go on in life, with hardly any active participation on her part. This is not the case, however. As an *autopoietic agent*, she actively *selects* from her environment that which is most necessary to her survival. This environment is not the world *an sich*, but her actively *constructed* world she shares with others of her species, an *Umwelt*-construct. As an *interactive agent*, she perpetually engages in a process of exchange of energy and material with this construct, which complements her role as autopoietic agent.

The environment was a chief contributor to the genetic make-up of the species to which she belongs. Her particular environment plus her genotype has yielded her phenotype, the ensemble of her physical, functional, and behavioural characteristics. As an autonomous entity, she and she alone can exercise a selection, within her environment, of what is necessary in order to sustain life: she is attracted to particular species of flowers only, she avoids certain other organisms, while foraging for food she has little use for the pine trees around her, she never dreams of using the ground for a landing strip, and she is hardly aware, we would suppose, of the life-giving sun above, the mountains in the horizon, a distant train whistle. She selects from her environment, avoiding danger signs whenever they pop up, and if what she has chosen does not offer the nourishment she expects, she is ordinarily incapable of inventing and constructing alternatives. In this manner, to repeat, one of the two roles she plays out on the field of semiosis is that of an autonomous unity. But there is another role, that which entails perpetual give-and-take with her surroundings, which maintains her system in incessant imbalance (disequilibrium) with respect to her environment and in a *tendency toward* balance (equilibrium) within.

Thus she is by and large able to retain her identity through time, despite certain structural changes that occur in her and her environment as she travels through life. Her dual properties as autonomous entity and open system, as stable and variable, are at roots based on the very nature of her genetic 'text' – to evoke the metaphor anew. Her 'text' is a re-printing of that of her parents. It prescribes not only the details for each complex molecule in her body, but the means for executing the plan. However, given her species as a whole, from a broad historical viewpoint, her 'text' is incessantly plagued by the equivalent of typos, reprinting errors, spoonerisms, litotes, hyperboles, oxymorons, synecdoches, metaphors, ironies, and neologisms. At times there are even additions and omissions. Usually the text is corrected, but sometimes not. Merely reading the individual hummingbird's message would be like a printout from the computer's hard disk, or more simply, like depositing a coin in the jukebox, pushing the button of one's choice, and hearing the result. The product and its execution can hardly be modified.

Once the hummingbird has realized her particular linear spin-out as determined by her code, she is there for the pleasure of all observers. She is a written 'text'; she is described, and now bares herself for any and all interpreters. Unlike a book subject to and determined by its surrounding energy flows, however, as a biological 'text' she can, as pointed out above, actively select from her environment, given the limitations specified by her particular program. And there are certain limitations, since all organisms are initially bounded or partly closed, and limited by the ontogenetic programs specified by their genes (Brooks and Wiley 1986:38).

However, the book-text analogy is somewhat flawed. A book as mere physical artefact, as the equivalent of an item in Popper's World 1, is not a 'living text.' It is for practical purposes 'dead,' a mere collection of molecules, like an inert organism, for example a virus, including its DNA. Active mind, the sieve through which at conscious and self-conscious levels 'experienced' or 'real time' passes and the processor of the stream of signs actualized *for* the semiotic agent, is the field of Popper's World 2. But World 2, characterized by the rush of the 'now,' is pure process, which, devoid of form endowed it by Thirdness, bears hardly any semiosic authenticity; it is experiencing without memory, thinking without thought, signifying without signification. World 3, mediating between relatively inert World 1 objects and the stream of World 2 experiences, is the most likely domain of Peirce's symbols that 'grow.' World 3 is the repository of thought, intellect, cognition, all derived from habit, law, convention.

Symbols are the culminating achievement of legisign characteristics (Thirdness, including qualisigns and sinsigns corresponding to Firstness and Secondness respectively). Only in active, mediating Thirdness is life to be found: once again, where there is life, there are legisigns. Without the tertiary mediation of legisigns, merely autonomous signs of self-contained, self-sufficient iconicity or the binary push-pull antagonistics of indexicality, and from the broader view, without interactive, interpretative communities of semiotic agents, the entire process will surely suffer a slow death. Yet, we must remember, symbols without World 1 and World 2 cannot sustain life, let alone 'grow.' Symbols bring order out of the blooming, buzzing confusion of experience (Firstness) as a result of the impingement of the 'real' on the senses (Secondness). But alone, symbols are no more than the equivalent of black marks on white somewhere in a corner of the library collecting dust, like the inert virus awaiting the propitious moment to awaken from its mechanistic slumber and enjoy a quick meal. When placing a symbol's entire *development* within a text as a token and the *evolution* of its species as a type, it can be viewed as the result of a long history: its interaction within the whole of the language to which it belongs and its interaction within its particular (con)text, both of which processes are dependent upon a host of interacting semiotic agents. Without this composite interweaving, the symbol is no more than 'dead.'

In comparable fashion, and to reiterate, DNA alone does not a living organism make. An organism, at any point in its life, is a unique consequence of the *evolution* of the species to which it belongs. A conglomeration of molecules (symbol) generated by molecular string, DNA, and contextualized within an organism establishes the ground rules for the organism's *development,* though that development is dependent upon a give-and-take between internal and external forces. Internal forces paint the organism's autopoietic picture; external forces include the environment within which the organism exists, producing and consuming the conditions of its very existence, consequently painting it as a system in disequilibrium.

Thus our hummingbird did not find, nor was she merely thrown into, the world in which she is developing; she is in the process of making it and it in making her. As World 1 spin-out she is what she is, much the same as her hummingbird neighbours. As a World 2 entity, she engages in perpetual interaction with her environment the end-product of which is herself as a set of World 3 artefacts, a monument testifying to her ephemeral existence, a struggle to maintain order within a sea of overriding chaos. World 3 constructs are proof that organisms are not exclusively determined either by nature or nurture, but somewhere in between. Birds build nests, beavers dams, ants hills, and humans cities producing mountains of dissipative waste, all of which activities entail the organism as autonomous entity *acting on* its environment, while at the same time, as interactive agent, being *changed by* that selfsame environment.

The ultimate import of this activity is that, comparable to a composite symbol – a sequence of signs – an individual organism's internal forces reciprocally respond to external forces, and in the process, both are altered irreversibly. Drosophila or fruit flies, for example, differ among themselves. In fact, transplanted imaginal disc tissue from the larva of a fly usually behaves in a 'programmed' manner, but sometimes it will take off on a tangent of its own, differing from other discs. The organs seem to be able to use genetic mechanisms in specific ways in particular contexts (Leighton and Loomis 1980; Oyama 1985). Phenotypes, then, can vary quite widely in spite of their being programmed with identical genetic information; in other words, there is no one-to-one correspondence between the genetic code and a particular phenotype. Furthermore, just as there are no clones in the absolute sense – identical twins have different fingerprints, and entirely individual experiences upon entering the fetal stage – so also absolute symmetry is never manifested by an individual organism. All organisms are an expression of what their species would be or could be, were there, in a manner of speaking, no tinge of *vagueness*, and at times even *inconsistency*, in each and every one of them. Consequently, the individual's efforts to live up to the ideal of its species as a *generality* must remain *incomplete*. Peirce, we have observed, says so much regarding signs.

On the other hand, some of the above-mentioned genetic engineers, with eugenic visions of sugarplums dancing in their heads, propagate the notion that eventually all the genes nature has not developed to their full capacity will be located in human chromosomes, which, when traced back to their causes and corrected, a superior being will have been born. Fortunately, this ambitious program is on its way toward being revealed for what it is: a dangerous, but likely an impossible, dream. But there is a deep-seated reason, in Lewontin's words, 'for the difficulty in devising causal information from DNA messages.' It lies in the fact:

that the same 'words' have different meanings in different contexts and multiple functions in a given context, as in any complex language. No word in English has more powerful implications of action than 'do.' 'Do it now!' Yet in most of its contexts 'do' as in 'I do not know' is periphrastic, and has no meaning at all. While the periphrastic 'do' has no *meaning*, it undoubtedly has a linguistic *function* as a place holder and spacing element in the arrangement of a sentence. Otherwise, it would not have swept into general English usage in the sixteenth century from its Midlands dialect origin, replacing everywhere the older 'I know not.'

So elements in the genetic messages may have meaning, or they may be periphrastic. The code sequence GTAAGT is sometimes read by the cell as an instruction to insert the amino acids *valine* and *serine* in a protein, but sometimes it signals a place where the cell machinery is to cut up and edit the message; and sometimes it may be only a spacer, like the periphrastic 'do,' that keeps other parts of the message an appropriate distance from each other. Unfortunately, we do not know how the cell decides among the possible interpretations. In working out the interpretive rules, it would certainly help to have very large numbers of different gene sequences, and I sometimes suspect that the claimed significance of the genome sequencing project for human health is an elaborate cover story for an interest in the hermeneutics of biological scripture. (1992:35)

The allusion to our 'symbol' analogy in this rather extended passage cries out for elaboration.

3. NO BEGINNINGS OR ENDINGS, ONLY MIDDLES SOMEWHERE IN BETWEEN

According to all indications, the genetic engineer's 'causal information' would be mechanically determined by the DNA sequence. It would be *nature* virtually without *nurture*, all *genotype* without any favourable nod to *phenotype*, or from another vantage, World I artefacts without Worlds 2 and 3.

The problem is that all signs ('words,' and, we would suppose, genes) vary to a greater or lesser degree as their contexts and functions vary. Lewontin's periphrastic 'do' is apropos. Periphrasis generates meaning in a roundabout way by the use of circumlocution, by evasive, indirect strategies. This is typical of sign 5 from among Peirce's 10 basic sign types, which, significantly enough, is the (invariably vague) focal point of the *Ho-t'u* model: it is when at its ideal best the centre of the mandala, or William Blake's grain of sand that either reveals nothing or everything, depending upon the perspective.

Sign 5, an *iconic legisign* (that is, an iconic sinsign apart from its particular individuality as a *token*), is the first sign of the nature of a general, a universal, or *type* (that is, species). Each instantiation of this sign embodies some quality, or iconicity, that serves to call up in the mind the *general idea* (though still vague) of the object. It is an icon, but of a special sort. Its *modus operandi* is that of governing a series of singular instantiations of an object, each of which is an iconic sinsign, toward some general concept (*CP*:2.258). That is, as a *token*, the sign is on its way to becoming a *type* in the full sense. This, for better or for worse, is how generalities are built up, as if accumulated *haecceities* were capable somehow of yielding legitimate *quiddities*, or to use a previous example, as if by accelerating *staccato* (interjecting integers between integers no end) we could obtain *legato* (Cantor's continuum). Differences tend to be ignored, while sameness is highlighted (for example, column *A* of table 4).

'Do' as an iconic legisign – of course the term is a rheme, a symbol, but as pure periphrasis it does not yet have any object in the full sense – has reached the Thirdness of its representamen while its object and interpretant remain at the level of Firstness ($R_3 O_1 I_1$). It is a general icon in the most general sense, though that generality remains enshrouded in vagueness. For example, the utterance, '_____ is blue' is a quasi-proposition whose predicate (icon) is specified, but it remains quite vague since its subject (index) is no more than an empty set to be filled in by an indeterminate number of possible signs. However, 'do,' unlike the absent subject and vague predicate of '_____ is blue,' is a general, though that of which it is a general remains unspecifiably evasive unless it is surrounded by a particular context. In other words, 'do' is a 'regulator' (it regulates, specifies regularity) within its context. Only after it fulfils its function as 'regulator' does it take on meaning as a result of its particular context. That is, sign 5 continues to evince (1) a maximum of *vagueness* (superposition of possibilities, some or many of which are *inconsistent*) given O_1 and I_1 though there is always a modicum of specification, by way of R_3, and (2) a maximum of *incompleteness* (its *generality* remains largely unspecified), though R_3 has in essence developed to the fullness of its potential. R_3 of sign 5, like all representamina, is re-iterative; it is a *replicator*, capable of engendering replicas of itself – but not simulacra in the Baudrillard sense. On the other hand, the function of O_1 and I_1, as potential *interactor* (of Secondness) and *synthesizer* (of Thirdness) respectively, is still up for grabs. In a manner of speaking, the *genetic* component of the sign is developed while the *memetic* component remains at a 'primitive' stage; *nature* has done its thing on the stage of semiosis and now lies in wait for *nurture* to join the show; the well-fed and properly trained icon is there for all to see, but needs its supporting cast of indexicality and symbolicity before the dance can progress.

Indeed, if R is the *genetic* component as iterative, self-replicative, self-reduplicative, and capable of fabricating simulacra ad infinitum, the fact remains that it cannot gain citizenship as a full-fledged sign without the O and I filling themselves out in so far as that is possible within the context of semiotic interaction. O and I are in this sense legitimately the *memetic* components: never autonomous of their environments, they are perpetually open to exchange of semiosis within ever-changing contexts qualified by the effervescent dance of signs. The largely autonomous R – or the icon, as it were – does not a real sign make. R's as graphemes on paper or phonemes floating through the air are as they are by convention. But as R's are, so, in a manner of speaking O's and I's can become by successive stages of embedment, sign de-generacy, automatization, such that they may be blindly and mindlessly taken as the way things are, clearly and simply. They come to be processed – or better, they

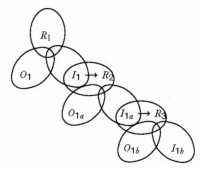

FIGURE 14

process themselves – as autonomous units, *as if* they were Saussurean floating, referenceless signifiers, divorced both from the world and from flesh and blood, thinking and feeling, semiotic agents.

Given the dynamics of semiosis, however, what we need is not a structural account, attention to codes and the system's 'syntax,' or even its 'semantics,' but rather, the spotlight should rest on adaptive change of the semiotic agent's behaviour as a result of its processing signs within new contexts and given incessantly variable situations. This falls in line with the description of the organism's tendency toward adjustment in the constant give-and-take with its environment by W.H. Thorpe (1956:66) and T. Dobzhansky (1962:56) in their call for a balance of instinct (inherited traits) and learning (acquired propensities). Once again, sign 5 seems to enact the role of semiosis's pivot foot about which all such interaction revolves. It is the minimal sign representing the process of an I's becoming another R at its maximum. It is the point from which triadic mediation is potentially capable of enacting some creative moves, thus offsetting the apparently chaotic milieu, and with a leap doing a slam-dunk in the Boolean-Saussurean binary mechanist's face.

Figure 14 depicts the sign components' interconnecting of their pivotal nodes, which are included within the overlap (when considered as a Venn diagram). Yet with a wry twist (when considered as a three-dimensional Borromean knot), each I circle is interjected into another semiosic space such that another R is produced ... and then another, to yield sign 5 ($R_3 O_1 I_1$). Thus the equivalent of a Cantor continuum of change through *sign coupling* is patterned, and at the same time account is given of possible discontinuous Dedekind-like breaks – a theme I have hammered away at in the three books making up this trilogy. The R as replicator has reached the level of generality, while the function of the O (interactor) and the I (synthesizer) has hardly stepped foot outside limbo. Metaphorically speaking, the genotype is relatively set in concrete while the

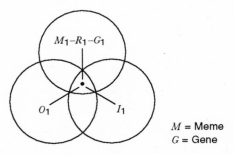

M = Meme
G = Gene

FIGURE 15

phenotype (memo-type) is open to myriad variations in the sluice box of a particular *corpus* of sign activity during future space-time intersections.

Actually, the R in $R_1 \rightarrow R_2 \rightarrow R_3$ is not the same R. Yet it remains the same in so far as, at the conclusion of the process, it is still a sign of possibility that the semiotic agent consciously and subsequently endowed with certain generality even though it remained vague and unspecified. In this sense it contains, within itself, the equivalent of both *gene* and *meme*. It contains *genetic* qualities, since it represents a *type*, given its characteristic generality, allowing it to *evolve* along with the other members of the sign species to which it belongs. And it is *memetic*, since with the ushering in of each moment, and given changing contexts and circumstances, it *develops* as an individual sign. The periphrastic 'do,' in Lewontin's example, was 'swept into general English usage in the sixteenth century from its Midlands dialectic origin,' and has been experiencing successive, and continuous, evolutionary shifts since that time. And as an individual sign, 'do' can take on a spate of different meanings, periphrastic and otherwise, due to the particular environments within which it develops. More adequately put, in this sense, the R space in figure 14 should take on the form of figure 15, where, as replicator, it encompasses both gene and meme, while O and I remain fundamentally memetic, though we must bear in mind, by de-generacy they can come to be processed as if they were possessed by genetic characteristics.[5]

Interplay of *evolution* and *development* bears on Peirce's idea of change. The general idea was actually quite common during the nineteenth century, the 'age of evolution' – especially found in W.S. Jevons, Alexander Bain, Michael Faraday, Ernst Mach, Ludwig Boltzmann, and Henri Poincaré (much of whose work Peirce knew well) – in addition to the biological and social evolutionists, Darwin and Spencer. Among contemporary advocates of the idea in philosophy of science, we have Donald Campbell (1974), Popper (1972), and Stephen Toulmin (1972) (see also Radnitsky and Bartley 1987). In the present context, however, the problem is how to account, semiosically speaking, for both chance mutation (Darwinism) and selection by design (including Lamarckism), variation and invention, teleonomy and teleology, and above all, continuous change and discontinuous (including catastrophic) change. Should one side of the polarity be lopped off, and if so, which one? Or should there be an attempt to hold both poles in a rather loose embrace?

Rom Harré (1981) opts for the latter approach, which is actually quite Peircean in spirit. His key variable is *degree of coupling* between conditions of mutation and conditions of selection. Totally blind chance, the extreme Darwinian interpretation, would reduce coupling virtually to zero; mutations would be causally independent of the processes of selection. At the other Lamarckian end of the spectrum, mutation and selection would be absolutely coupled; environmental imperatives would have the final word. In the first case the individual is a passive recipient of change; in the second she is virtually the sole author of change. Harré suggests that in relatively static human societies, change tends to approach the Darwinian pole – random shuffling of the cards. Variations occur in spite of the individual's whims and wishes to the contrary. On the other hand, in rapidly-changing societies, the individual can generally take it upon herself to question knowledge, conventions, roles of conduct, and customs. Consequently, she is to a degree capable wilfully and intentionally of creating new patterns, thus altering her environment. The first system, subject to blind, random variation, is generally continuous. The second system undergoes radical change of continuous as well as discontinuous, and even catastrophic, nature.

Peirce would most likely extrapolate Harré's equation to include all semiotic agents, human and nonhuman alike. In the words of Emile Benveniste (1971:24), if I may, 'man invents and understands symbols; the animal does not ... Between the sensory-motor function and the representative function is a threshold which only human beings have been able to cross.' Though Peirce would not enact so absolute a split between human and nonhuman organisms, the spirit of this quote hits the mark. The human animal, by inventing and understanding symbols, is capable of inventing an unlimited variety of cuts, joints, and folds in the universe. Thus there is no end to the environmental variations, and therefore 'semiotically real' worlds he/she can make for him/herself. Consequently, we would expect the coupling between processes of mutation and processes of selection to be relatively intimate. However, in the Harré sense, there is never absolute coupling of mutation and selection, nor is there an absolute absence of such coupling. Absolute coupling, and the agent would be omniscient; she would be Maxwell's Demon and Laplace's Superobserver rolled into one; she would be God. Absolute absence of coupling, and she would be absolutely passive; she would cease participating entirely in the ongoing semiosic dance. Actually, the agent, a sign among signs, is part of the very process she strives to alter, and, as a sign, she is in the process invariably altered.

4. YET, THE TYRANNY OF THE CLOSED BOOK

To expatiate somewhat on the closing remark of the previous section, allow me to interject two examples from the work of Jorge Luis Borges (1962): 'The Library of Babel' and 'Pierre Menard, Author of the *Quixote*.'

The narrator of the first tale tells us at one juncture that the Library might *appear* to be infinite in extension. However, since this monstrous athenaeum contains all the possible permutations of the twenty-five orthographic symbols of its alphabet, and even though the total number of books is unimaginable, none the less, the Library is necessarily finite. The solution to this quandary, the narrator suggests, stems from the fact that a finite system can apparently become infinite if it is infinitely perpetuated. That is, after all the permutations are exhausted, then they repeat themselves limitlessly and hence become, rather incomprehensibly, a finite but unbounded system. This premise of the eternal return, we are told at the end of Borges' story, stems from the effort to order the disordered, the compulsion to find meaning in the apparently chaotic universe. Interestingly, an impious group exists that maintains that 'nonsense is normal in the Library and that the reasonable (and even humble and pure coherence) is an almost miraculous exception' (57) – for example, Monod's universe of chance. But the narrator persists in his search for harmony amid the apparent chaos. He prays to the unknown gods 'that a man – just one, even though it were thousands of years ago! – may have examined and read it [the Book of Books, the explanation of the Library].' He longs for the instant of enlightenment to be able to apprehend the Order: 'let Your enormous Library be justified' (57). But alas! The moment of insight is never at hand. The most the narrator can do is 'venture to suggest this solution to the ancient problem: "*The Library is unlimited and cyclical*"' (58).

Why is the narrator condemned to remain sealed within his prison house (of language)? A response is problematic, but perhaps it can be initially approached as follows. First, Borges writes the text, and the narrator narrates it, but Borges *is* the narrator, so the text includes Borges – which is not so strange, since he has observed elsewhere that Don Quixote is the reader of the *Quixote*, and Hamlet is the spectator of *Hamlet*. Second, the reader reads (includes, assimilates) the text, and since Borges is the narrator narrating it, therefore the reader 'reads' (includes, assimilates) Borges – the 'other Borges,' that is to say. However, we must contend with the Library, which is an ominous task indeed, for the Library presumably includes all. The narrator, we discover, is to be found within the Library, writing the manuscript of 'The Library of Babel' with his 'fallible hand' wherever he can, on the 'cover of a book, with the organic letters inside: punctual, delicate, perfectly black, inimitably symmetrical' (53). However, we are obviously *not* reading this original manuscript, but a book that is now stored in the Library. If so, then we the readers, as well as the narrator (Borges), are actually included within the Library.

In other words, the Library, whether infinite or finite but unbounded, must be either inexorably and self-reflexively *inconsistent* or *incomplete*. That is to say, the story speaks of the Library, which contains the story as well as its narrator (Borges) and its readers. As such, the Library contains the story, which in turn contains the Library, paradoxically. The Library, presumably for the readers of the story, is fictive, and the story, contained within it, is also a fiction. It is as if the Library, through the story that it contains, were addressing itself to the reader, who believes herself to be outside the library but in reality is not, with the proposition, 'This is *not* a fiction' – the subject of the proposition being either the Library or the story, since they contain each other. A painting of a pipe that asserts implicitly (and explicitly in Magritte's work), 'This is *not* a pipe,' evinces a comparable dilemma. The inconsistency in each case is tantamount to the Gödelian sentence (or Cretan liar) which says of itself, 'This sentence is *not* true.'

We will recall a similar bootstrap operation regarding Varela's Cretan description of the autonomous cellular unit: self-contained, self-referential, one-dimensional algorithmic generation within a three-dimensional space enclosed by a two-dimensional 'skin,' in its composite tantamount to the Cantor-Dedekind quandary. But there is a nightmare in all this. It would appear that the Library's anti-Darwinian image of virtually no coupling allowing merely for random, fortuitous conjunctions of letters composing an unlimited number of books virtually the entirety of which are unintelligible (pure noise, the ultimate triumph of entropy) is comparable to Monod's diatribes against Lamarckian mysticism in the name of scientific objectivity. A Monodian organism – or Borges' author, narrator, and reader – appears by sheer happenstance, or a meaningful book appears miraculously out of nowhere, as if a monkey at a computer terminal happened to compose *Hamlet* – recall Baudrillard's 'hyperreality.' And both the organism and the book are somehow able to maintain total aloofness *vis-à-vis* the chaos 'out there.'

However, one must bear in mind that a sentence of the liar type, if properly contextualized, can be made consistent. Perhaps the utterer was actually referring to a previous utterance. Or perhaps the listener, upon questioning him about his utterance, obliges him to recant. In either case, clarification demands a step 'outside' the sentence. So if the sentence is inconsistent, then it can well be falsely self-sufficient; and if it is made consistent, then it is destined ultimately to remain incomplete. In this sense, paradoxes of the liar sort, no matter how complex, are at least provisionally soluble.

The problem is that I have been speaking of the paradoxical Library as a totality, as infinite. If indeed it is such a totality, then it is doomed to its own *inconsistency*, for there can be no redeeming 'axiom' from 'outside' to justify it. On the other hand, if it is finite, as some if its inhabitants hope, then it is forever *incomplete*, for the foreign 'axiom' struggling feebly to make it consistent (even intelligible) is precisely the story's reader, the ongoing stream of readers. But once a given reader is seduced into the Library, it is the end of the road, for, like Escher's hands drawing themselves, that reader is now within the Library, and within he is bound to remain – the border between fiction and world having been ruptured. No matter by what clever means the reader attempts to break out of this circle, she cannot: she is, inexorably, immanent. It is as if she were a flatlander on a two-dimensional sheet, unable to transcend her sphere of existence and break into a third dimension. The reader is plagued by the same quandary as the books – signs all – over which she would like to presume imperious control. I have argued for so much throughout this trilogy.

As if this were not enough, the scope of the books housed in Borges' Library is mind-boggling in its magnitude and numbing in its inconceivable effect. As mentioned, the books are randomly composed of twenty-five symbols. Each books contains 410 pages, each page 40 lines with 80 characters each. Some claim that there is no totally nonsensical book in the Library: given the infinite number of possible civilizations, languages, and codes from past, present, and future, all combinations become intelligible at some time and place – though it is difficult to comprehend how a book containing the series $xyxyxyxyxy\ldots n$ would not be nonsensical. Rudy Rucker (1984:130) calculates that the number of symbols in each book in the Library is 410 pages × 40 lines × 80 characters = 1,312,000. And since there are 25 different symbols, there are $25^{1,312,000}$ books, which is approximately $10^{2,000,000}$! Kurt Lasswitz (in Fadiman 1958:237–47), who presumably inspired Borges, obtains the same figure for his Universal Library, and to illustrate the size of this number he estimates that a shelf $10^{1,999,982}$ light-years long would be needed to hold them. This number of light-years is so monstrously large that for practical purposes it is not substantially smaller than the total number of books on the shelf! Understandably, for any given inhabitant within the Library, there is more than a little confusion regarding whether this overwhelming Babel (babble?) is finite or infinite. The uncertainty of one's being able to find at least one intelligible book in this jungle of ciphers is virtually computable to zero – Monod would revel in the thought. Once again, the Cantor-Dedekind problem looms large. Is the entire system continuous or discontinuous? Finite or infinite? If infinite, is it infinity in the actual, Platonic, sense, or merely potential (*pace* Aristotle)?

Interestingly enough, quantum theoretical uncertainty also bears directly on this problem of whether the Library (or universe) is finite or infinite. If the alphabet and languages of the Library's books allow for infinite generativity (in the sense of Chomsky, or DNA sequences), then there exists the potential for an infinity of books. Supposing that the total possible combinations of symbols in the books is infinite, and that the Library's inhabitants cannot be in possession of any finite set of rules for generating the books (as there presumably is in Chomskyan generative-transformational grammar, or the genetic code), then as far as they are concerned, absolute randomness must surely prevail. If so, then the Library suffers from absolute uncertainty. The Library's denizens remain victimized by a collection of books; the randomness is totally beyond their grasp and beyond their control.

It would appear, from this vantage at least, than Monod is having his day: our universe is under the force of sheer chaos; everything is a chance affair, up for grabs until it actually happens, and only by some incomprehensible miracle could life ever have come about in the first place. Indeed, if our plight is comparable to that of Borges' hapless Library rats, we can be no more than passive recipients of change, at the mercy of myriad throws of the dice. On the other hand, as I have mentioned above, evidence points toward the notion that biological organisms are at least in part their own authors of change. There is actually no monopoly of random mutation, but selection also plays a part on the stage of the universe, or in another way of putting it, of semiosis. To repeat, there is never the one at the expense of the complete absence of the other. By the same token, there is no sharp line of demarcation between gene and meme, genetic and cultural evolution, and evolution in general and individual development. So also there is no all-or-nothing distinction between a sign as identical with itself regardless of variations in space-time intersections, and the same sign as virtually infinitely variable regarding its incessant recontextualization with each and every re-iteration.

Let us now consider the flip side of Borges' Library as mechanical generativity: the organism's (or composite sign's) prerogatives as an agent of choice extrapolated to the extreme.

5. AND THE INFINITELY MALLEABLE TEXT

In the sense that so the context goes, so also the sign, at the far stretch we have Borges' text by Cervantes, the *Quixote*, and Pierre Menard's re-duplication (re-plication) of a few passages from it as a presumably autonomous writer – he had not previously read the *Quixote*, but by Herculean intuitive effort, was able to put himself on the same wavelength as the original author.

Menard's *Quixote* seems to be sort of Monodian fortuitous conjunction of ciphers that happen miraculously to fall into the same order as a previously written text. The narrator speculates on the possiblity of Menard's writing the same book as Cervantes being calculable to zero – Monod's ideal. None the less, he concludes, it remains a possibility, however remote. It is as if our proverbial army of simians were pecking away at computer terminals and the *Quixote* happened to pop up. Actually, no law of physics would be violated if, say, ape number 6×10^{23} were somehow to create Cervantes' masterpiece. It is as if in a Darwinian universe of no coupling, continuous aleatory variation somehow produced a combination of signs worthy of the gods' most supreme efforts.

Quite conceivably, the *Quixote* fragments could have been generated within Borges' Library. However, since the semiotic agents housed within play no part in the process, these fragments would have been discarded since they are identical to an already shelved book: authors and readers generating and reading books within different contexts are of no consequence, only the books as World 1 items. However, in the story now under scrutiny, radically distinct conditions prevail. When Menard's text as a replication of some Cervantes passages was placed in the hands of a few presumptuous literary critics, his project backfired. The lonely fragments he was able to write before he died were viewed as a great enrichment of the original. They were the product of creative endeavours, not merely of a Golden-Age Spaniard but of a twentieth-century Frenchman ignorant of the time of which he wrote. The thrust of 'Pierre Menard' is, we are told, rather than writing, the process of reading, for Menard 'has enriched, by means of a new technique, the halting and rudimentary art of reading: this new technique is that of the deliberate anachronism and the erroneous attribution. The technique whose applications are infinite, prompts us to go through the *Odyssey* as if it were posterior to the *Aeneid* ... This technique fills the most placid words with adventure' (Borges 1962:44).

Borgesian allusions to the current intertextuality fad in literary theory aside, we have here a distorted, involuted antipode of Darwinian selection by mutation. Once the text takes on certain acquired characteristics within its particular contextual milieu it becomes something entirely different from what it otherwise would have been. The work's critics fancy that it has become, rather than identical to the *Quixote*, a set of differences that are even contradictory at many junctures. Cervantes, a child of his times, merely followed the trend dictated by his cultural setting. Menard, in contrast, like a good Nietzschean, knew how to lie, to create artifice, to say what was not there as if it were. Cervantes' praise of history is conceived to be nothing more than rhetoric; Menard, 'a contemporary of William James, does not define history as an enquiry into reality but as its origin. Historical truth, for him, is not what has happened, it is what we judge to have happened.' Cervantes' style is 'the correct Spanish of his time'; Menard's is 'quite foreign,' 'archaic,' and 'suffers from certain affectation' (43). Cervantes' text, 'in a clumsy fashion, opposes to the fictions of chivalry the tawdry provincial reality of his country.' Menard, in contrast, 'selects as his "reality" the land of Carmen during the centenary of Lepanto and Lope de Vega' (42). In short, the two texts referred to two incommensurable 'semiotic worlds' according to the bloated minds of their pompous commentators.

Both texts, as raw spin-outs, belong to the equivalent of Popper's World 1 (mere black marks on white). With regards to World 2, let us assume that if somehow the conscious state of Menard when slapping the signs squeezed from his brain on paper was somehow the same as Cervantes' consciousness, nevertheless, the two texts become radically distinct, indeed, wellnigh incommensurable when placed in their World 3 contexts calling for interpretations by human agents. The texts are apparently clones, and their authors' mind-sets were somehow identical, but, upon 'taking on a life of their own,' and more important, upon entering into interaction with their environment – the critics – they became virtually mutually exclusive. It is not so much that Menard's text is a mutation of the text that spawned it via a conjunction of two brains, but the community of participatory literary critics themselves, as the texts' environment, radically differentiated the texts and at the same time the texts transformed the critics' very notion of reading.

In other words, when considering the two texts in question as organisms in interaction with their literary critics as participating agents in the stream of semiosis, we do not have Darwinian mutation at all, but more properly, Lamarckian absolute coupling at its best. The critics collaborated with the texts, providing World 2 contextualized process ultimately structured by mediating World 3 to bring about transmuted interpretants, which in turn provoked radical alterations in the texts as representamina and in their respective objects. It is not simply that the crap game of textual interpretation was being played with loaded dice, but the gamers, the dice, the lively corner of some back alley, the entire surroundings, were all extensions of one another in an interactive, interconnected dance. Nothing happens that does not affect everything else, and everything else has a hand in whatever happens.

In a certain manner of speaking, somewhere in its *phylogenetic* trajectory, a 'catastrophe' befell what was to have been just another replica of the *Quixote* in terms of its existence as a general text (type). The *evolution* – continuous as well as punctuated with radical breaks – of the *Quixote* in its numerous unique forms (tokens) throughout history somewhere met with a particular re-iteration, which, when contextualized, became radically distinct from all its predecessors. The *ontogenesis* of this collection of texts – their *development* as individuals from birth to death – rendered at least one of them, and perhaps more, incompatible with all the others. As mentioned above, there are no clones in the absolute sense, but rather, environmental interaction renders erstwhile autonomous agents dependent upon a plethora of unpredictable, indeterminable factors in a complex, nonlinear medium. Everything changes as a result of its interaction with everything else, and everything else has a hand in whatever changes are wrought.

Thus we have what appears to be a classical opposition in the form of: $R_3 O_3 I_3$ (Cervantes) / $R_3 O_3 I_3$ (Menard). The two otherwise identical texts take flight, at some bifurcation point, along two distinct tangential paths. However, quite clearly biology, like semiotics, defies any and all myopic determinist as well as reductionist explanations. For over the long haul, the classical Cervantes/Menard opposition is mediated by yet other agents (signs), the readers of Borges' story, and upon such mediation, the otherwise intransigent poles become fused into one (con)text: the works of Cervantes and Menard are identical and different, they are autonomous and interactive, they can affect their onlookers in one way or the other, or along a spectrum of myriad variations in between. No text is a text (of Thirdness) without its context, and all texts (including their authors-readers) are the context instilling a text with its textuality.

The obvious implication might have it, of course, that since everything living is centred on reproduction, since 'a bacterium, an amoeba, a fern – what destiny can dream of other than forming two bacteria, two amoeba or several more ferns?' (Jacob 1982:4), life, like symbols – exists for the sake of becoming something other than itself (a difference) that, none the less, is a replica of itself (an identity). For an organism, like a sign, 'is merely a transition, a stage between what was and what will be' (Jacob 1982:2). And for a sign, like an organism, whenever there is identity, there is necessarily otherness (difference), and whenever there is otherness, there are implications of identity (*CP*:1.566).

Recall, once again, the 'semiotic hypercycle' depicted in figure 3. A living system (sign) exchanges matter and energy (semiosis) with its environment (*other*) while maintaining its individuality (as an autonomous entity), yet it is incessantly in the process of becoming (something *other*). The hummingbird's flower, a sign, absorbs energy from the sun, carbon dioxide from the air, and water and nutrients from the soil, all of which are signs of 'real' objects having become 'semiotic objects' (*O*) *for* the flower as semiotic agent (nonequilibrium system). These 'semiotic objects' in turn determine the flower as representamen (*R*) *for* the approaching hummingbird as another semiotic agent. That is to say, the plant takes in signs and 'semiotic objects' from its environment, which aid in fulfilling its function as a sign, and it in turn expels matter and energy (semiosis) in the form of oxygen, aromatics, light rays of certain frequencies, and so on, into its environment, part of which become signs and 'semiotic objects' for semiotic agents 'out there' in interaction with it. The hummingbird as interpreter aids and abets the plant in determining its interpretant (*I*), as a result of the information generated by the plant upon intaking and expelling semiosis.

The flower has meaning *for* the bird; it is put to use *for* some purpose; the plant puts the bird's penetrating beak to use *for* its own purpose by depositing pollen on it. The two organisms collaborate and cooperate toward reproduction of their own kind, toward perpetuation of the ecological balance. They are individuals and interactive, subject to random happenings inflicted on them by their environment on the one hand, and on the other, always capable of exercising choices, selecting, and *putting* certain signs *to use* for some purpose or other. In this sense, to re-iterate, they are largely autonomous; but they are not entirely autonomous, in their interaction with their surroundings. During this complex give-and-take process, they remain the same and they are signs perpetually becoming other signs. They are both nothing but a swarm of subatomic particles and at the same time delicate repositories of nature's purpose. They are quite insignificant and yet they somehow incorporate the whole of things.

Of course, neither flower nor fowl is completely in touch with the 'real' but only with its particular species-specific *Umwelt*-dependent 'semiotically real' world. As Maturana-Varela autonomous entities, theoretically both flower and fowl remain independent of the 'real,' but as organisms open to and in constant interaction with their environment, they intermingle with their respective *other* 'out there,' with their 'semiotically real' world. If boundary conditions between ideal autonomous entity and the 'real' are considered to be absolute, a very important aspect of the organism is left out of the picture, for organisms cannot perpetuate the dance of life without constant interaction with their environment, and their environment would not be what it is without its interaction with the organisms contained with it. This notion of relative autonomy coupled with openness and interaction bears on Peirce's notion that between autonomous and arbitrarily created signs and the 'real,' there is a 'middle ground.' This 'middle ground' includes, on the one hand, living and breathing semiotic agents in incessant contact and interaction with both the signs they engender and use and abuse, and, on the other hand, the 'real,' which remains as it is in spite of their perception and conception of it (Dozoretz 1979; also recall chapter 4).

This 'middle ground,' moreover, is coterminous with the sliding-scale 'semiotically real' sphere between an organism's intractable, unmitigated ideal or desire, and that which is 'really real.' A dreamt image that for the dreamer later became 'real' was 'real' *for* that dreamer during the dream; a hallucinated image is 'real' *for* its maker, though 'unreal' *for* casual bystanders. A scientific theory is 'real' *for* one generation, though a few decades down the line it may have become 'unreal,' or even absurd (Dozoretz 1979:78–9). There is, according to Peirce, no absolutely indubitable 'reality' constructed by a semiotic agent, or an entire community of such agents. Any and all 'realities' are 'semiotic' through and through. In fact, Peirce does not even allow for the absolute certainty of '2 × 2 = 4,' as we observed above. The upshot is that while Peirce grants validity to practical certainty in the world of everyday living – if not, the biological semiotic agent would surely be reduced to the lifeless comings and goings of inorganic ebbs and flows of matter and energy – he would not say the same of absolute certainty. Practical certainty regarding a 'semiotically real' world involves classification of things in terms of their identity and stability while disregarding their transience, or vice versa, according to the dictating conditions. As the 'real' world of nature unfolds, according to Peirce's evolutionary view, *Umwelt*-generated 'semiotically real' worlds also undergo alterations.

Thus, just as, regarding life and signs, there is both *generacy* and *de-generacy*, symmetry and asymmetry, equilibria and far-from-equilibrium conditions, autonomy and open-ended interactivity, virtual noncoupling and hypercoupling, and evolution and development, so also there is both permanence and divergence, one and many, identity and difference-distinction. The more things change the more they remain intransient. And the more they remain intransient, the more they suffer breakdowns, dissipations, and catastrophes. Everything is both affirmative and negative, pregnant with its contrary. The universe incessantly engages in ongoing agonistics.

10

For a Critique of the Autonomy of the Sign

I now wish to gravitate away from the biological focus in the previous two chapters toward a broader, rather 'ecological' view. On so doing, my theme of the semiotic agent as sign among signs and the ongoing interrelatedness of all signs will reach a shrill pitch. This, I believe, will further illustrate that the triadic concept of the sign is quite in tune with that incessant buzz of happenings in which we find ourselves.

1. RANDOM NOMADIC DIVAGATIONS, DETERRITORIALIZED CONTEMPLATORS

Use of the term 'linearity' throughout this enquiry bears reference to Deleuze (1990a) and Deleuze and Guattari (1983) regarding what they term 'series.' According to the dictionary, a series is an ordered set of terms, the order established by distinctions (that is, 1 + 1 + 1) and syntheses of the entire set (that is, 1–1 correspondence between odd and even numbers, periodicity by multiples of ten, and so on).

Deleuze, in *Différence et répétition* (1968) and *The Logic of Sense* (1990a) alludes to several types of series: (1) conjunction of groups of single series, (2) coordination of two series (parts of which converge), and (3) disjunction of series (the parts of which branch out to form 'resonating' series). Fugues and analogous contrapuntals – for example, Escher prints, the 'limitative theorems' of Gödel and others – are ideal forms of complex resonant, syncopant, alternating series. For Spinoza the premier parallel series consists of things and ideas. For Frege, these two series consist of the sense (*Sinn*) and reference (*Bedeutung*) of terms; for Husserl, of expression and indication; for Saussure, of signifiers (images) and signifieds (concepts); and for Hjelmslev, of expression and content. Deleuze's series also specifically bear on language.

An apparently transparent series can begin on a note of relative simplicity (for example, Wittgenstein's [1953] '2,4,6,8 ... n' following the tacit rule 'add two'), but as infinitely extended individual series, they cannot but eventually become problematic at some point or other (for example, the introduction of a new rule, say, 'bad two,' whose interpretation is up for grabs), and as they invariably begin engendering other multiply variegated series, order is threatened.[1] Deleuze basically uses two metaphors to depict the unfolding of such series – as I pointed out in chapter 2 with respect to Erich Jantsch's work. A *tree* evinces a no-nonsense, linearly bifurcating order, while a *rhizome* entails the onslaught of proliferation, producing apparent disorder, chaos, anarchy (everything is connected to everything else without determinate beginning, middle, or end).

For example, Kafka's texts become rhizomic. By engendering triangles until they become unlimited, and by proliferating doubles until they become indefinite, 'Kafka opens up a field of immanence that will function as a dismantling, an analysis, a prognostics of social forces and currents' (Deleuze and Guattari 1986:55). Thus Kafka's narrative recapitulates the entire thread of Western thought. From Porphyrian trees to Linnaean taxonomies to Chomskyan parses, series upon series have proliferated, finally producing nonhierarchical, nonordered, unregulated, and unruly rhizomes. Consequently, a mobocracy of aleatory, apparently impenetrable conglomerates begins to emerge.

Deleuze writes that, generally speaking, two antipodal phases, order and chaos, rule the scene. We can no longer conceive of a world of entities taxonomizable into myriad packages all of which are partly to almost wholly arbitrary, but merely surface events – the influence of Stoic logic on Deleuze emerges here. According to this conception, nouns (substance) and adjectives (attributes) are suppressed, and verbs (events) are highlighted. A tree is not green, but either in a process of leafing, greening, yellowing, or deleafing.[2] A lumberjack and his chain-saw do not cut it down. There is only a process of cutting and being cut. Man and chain-saw that cut and the living cellulose being cut are in the process inextricably mixed. They merge and overlap with one another, they eventually become one, they are one in an event consisting of cutting and being cut – that is, Peirce's topological view of signs in chapter 8. During this process, hands wield saw that penetrates first the bark, then the flesh of the living organism. At the apex of the initial wedge-shaped absence in the tree there is linear penetration; metal forces its way deeper into the heart of the trunk; gravity exercises its ubiquitous force; the tree is in the process of mutilation/being mutilated, it is falling/being felled, it is dying/being neutralized. The tree's neighbours, the forest, the peaks and valleys and rivers, the outlying area, nature itself – all are wounded. And the lumberjack has suffered irreversible changes as well, though at the outset at least they do not appear as catastrophic.

Whether we are speaking of this imaginary event consisting of lumberjack, chain-saw, and tree (or for that matter, a novel, dream, hallucination, or make-believe world) or of a supposedly 'real world' happening, it is all the same. Facts as well as fictions and fantasies consist of incorporeal events, in much the same fashion that the real import of 'real world' happenings are 'sign-events' more than 'sign-things.' Events, in this conception, have no depth or being (in the sense of the superposition of all possibilities – Firstness), but dwell on the surface. They do not exist in the customary use of the term, they *subsist* – commensurate with Meinong's strange ontology – in the things they inhabit. And they enjoy virtually no extension through time (as identical with themselves, as generalities, types – Thirdness), but are what they are during some fleeting moment or other.

Deleuze's Stoic-inspired distinction between physical *depth* (virtual states of things) and metaphysical *surface* (events) sits quite comfortably with Peirce's notion *depth* (predicates, attributes) and *breadth* (subjects, presumably enduring entities).[3] In fact, Deleuze's recapitulating the long tradition from the Stoics to Spinoza to Meinong actually entails triadicity. The Stoics' *lekta*, somewhat comparable to Peirce's *significate effects* of the sign, differentiate and mediate between the sign (that which signifies) and the referent (that which exists, or merely *subsists*, though usually one cannot determine precisely which). If the sign is an existent, and the referent or object possibly or actually exists, then the significate effect of the sign's action (the interpretant) constitutes an event, that is no more than incorporeal. The 'existence' of this event is not substantive but purely relational, a matter of what is 'between' the sign and its respective 'semiotic object,' and between the sign and other signs.

If, as Peirce points out, an elementary compounded symbol (proposition) consists of a subject (index, noun) and enumeration of one or more of its attributes (icon, predicate, verb, adjective), then that symbol's function is chiefly verbal, that is, event-like in the passive sense (the chain-saw cuts, the tree is being cut). The supposed 'thingness' of Secondness plus the range of possible *might-bes* of the thing, that is, the range of Firstness, are both mediated by neither a 'thing' nor the property of a 'thing' but by a thing-less, attribute-less happening, an event, a naked sign-event. We cannot be in possession of the 'thing' *an sich* (Kant) nor can we know all the possible attributes of the thing, which are infinite in number (Spinoza). The best we can do is survey the sign-events on the stage before our consciousness, the stage we are on as both actors and participators, and hope for the best.

In Deleuze's (1990b:165–7) interpretation, for Spinoza an 'entity,' no matter how small, always consists of an infinite number of possible attributes. It is not a form but a complex of relations. Its affective powers are limited or virtually unlimited, depending upon the semiotic agents involved in its interpretation (von Uexküll's [1957] *Umwelt* idea surfaces here). For example, a tick is susceptible fundamentally to only three effects of a 'food-sign-event,' (1) climbing up the tree toward 'brightness' offered by the sun, (2) detecting the 'odorness' of oxybutyric acid and falling on the unwary mammal below, and (3) sensing 'warmthness' close to its host's hide, the final sign-event inviting it to settle down, penetrate the 'toughness' at some vulnerable spot, and enjoy a meal. The human semiotic agent's susceptibility to sign-event affectation is, in contrast, of overwhelming complexity and diversity, a near Brownian movement of colliding, interacting, interpenetrating, including and included, sign-events only a minute portion of which can be interpreted at conscious levels. Nature, our nature, in its myriad complexion, is an effervescent to-and-fro process of *explicating* from the *implicate, unfolding* from the *enfolded*.[4] It is a dizzying field of multiply intersecting, convoluting, involuting series – a rhizome, tantamount to what I have dubbed throughout this volume the semiosic stream – of intricately differentiated rhythms and affective intensities, without sign-things but rather, sign-ness, or at most, sign-events.

Upon taking into account the range of possibilities for sign-event series, from *vagueness* toward *generality, inconsistency* toward *incompleteness*, one is forced to conclude that sentences, statements, propositions, arguments and their counterarguments, and entire texts and universes of discourse, resist inclusion within that triad of positivist pigeon-holes, (1) 'true,' (2) 'false,' and (3) meaningless (nonsensical). A fourth category becomes imperative: *imaginary* ($\sqrt{-1}$, phlogiston, the ether, quarks and other scientific fabrications, any and all fictions, fantasies, lies, make-believe worlds, dreams, illusions, delusions, and hallucinations, and in general, Meinongian nonexistent thought-signs).[5] This fourth tier corresponds quite nicely with the Stoics' *lekta* and Deleuze's *sense*. For Deleuze, the Stoics did not dwell either on the sign, on the sign's designation (sign-object correspondence is discarded), or inside the head of sign addressers and addressees (meaning is not found in a mental concept). Regarding designation, a sign can presumably be either 'true,' 'false,' or merely nonsensical in terms of its meaning, but when the notion of sense enters the scene, it can have meaning even though it is 'nonsensical' (for example, $\sqrt{-1}$ put to use in quantum theory and relativity), and it can have sense even though it is 'meaningless' ($\sqrt{-1}$ standing on its own or purely as a mathematical operation).

In fact, $\sqrt{-1}$, construed as an eternally oscillating point in the Argand diagram, is quite apropos. Commensurate with the Argand plane, Deleuze's approach to events as surface affects is comparable to a mathematical field of singular points as possibilities for defining unlimited domains of equations and solutions. The point is also comparable to Peirce's *de-generate* sign, which, by successive unfoldment, can, if it is lucky, become an authentic sign. That is, the point can expand into the full-blown solution to a problem worked out on the two-dimensional Cartesian grid, with all necessary lines and their intersects. While a particular point can be specified only after the equation has been solved, it is by no means the result of the solution. Rather, its possibility as an implicate for being explicated into *this* particular 'semiotic world' on the Cartesian plane was always already there, as a virtual field of possible equations from within which an unending series of problems and their solutions could have been actualized. The solution of a particular problem can be seen, then, from three distinct vantages, (1) as an immanent ground (Firstness) of possible actualizations, (2) as the particular manifestation (Secondness) of one set of the possible affects from the field of *possibilia*, which, (3) in corroboration with other such manifestations and their interpretants as well as interpreter-participants, a move toward regularity, generality, habit, law (embedded mind-events all) can be initiated.

The same is to be found in the case of the consonance, conjunction, collusion, confusion, conflict, and even conflagration resulting when multiple series of human sign-events combine. Take a professional conference typical of the superhyped ego-world of academia, for example. It may be viewed in terms of (actualized, unfolded, explicated) bodies meeting at certain locations and remaining in somewhat orderly arrays during specified periods, while between these arrays perplexing streams of bodies of all sizes and shapes and dressed in attire of all fashions move, with intermittent fits and starts, along meandering streams, bucking white water, and occasional cataracts, perhaps toward some ill-defined goal. Along these streams, intermittent periods of apparent chaos resulting from far-from-equilibrium conditions somehow settle into order during certain time frames at certain locations, only later to dissipate into unruly flows once again. From another, complementary Stoic-Deleuze vantage, the conference can be viewed as non-physical surface effects produced by the random to orderly comings and goings of the bodies, a sort of floating (enfolded, implicate) film everywhere sensed yet nowhere localizable, ubiquitous yet strangely intangible.

This surface is indifferent to the individual bodies involved – that is, the bodies strive to evoke the image of individuality, but the illusory dream is to no avail. The vague surface disclosures are indifferent to their jubilance, fear, frustration, anguish, petty jealousy, their pomp, arrogance, pedantry, and even clownish antics, their superordinance and subordinance, their strategic manoeuvrings, their wheeling-and-dealing. All these activities are trivial and even irrelevant, from the complementary view. The ubiquitous but unseen film remains in much of a quietist mood; it is an anonymous process with no discernible beginning or end, never present and always both past and future. It consists of mere happenings. There is no matter of 'this session here-now, that session there-then, "I" pressing forward to score some points with that notorious repository of academic power, now off for a drink with old friends to enjoy some inside gossip,' but merely 'conferencing,' with no-'thing' actually existing as a self-identical entity anywhere or anywhen. It is, in a manner of speaking, Firstness in the process of doing its thing without yet having become full-blown Secondness. It is the becomingness of becoming, the beinglessness of not yet having become any-'thing' determinable.

All in all, however, it somehow promises meaning, that is, sense, by way of events emerging through signs, and thoughts emerging through events, while mediating both signs and events. This signs-events-thoughts triad forms the 'film' of Firstness-Secondness between particular 'semiotic worlds' and the eternally receding 'real world,' and the 'film' of the becoming of Thirdness without its being able to arrive. Thus meaning is never ever either here or there, but always elsewhere: our incessant quest for the ultimate kernels of meaning is a tail-chasing dog. Meaning is the intangible by-product of the paradoxical, self-contradictory field of *possibilia*, the superposition of all that might be, the vagueness of Firstness lying in wait for specification, for determination. Never to be had, like the hand trying to grasp its own thumb, meaning's elusive nature as sheer continuity apparently defies all intellection and all common sense.

But, one might protest, meaning can at least in part be put into semiotic window-dressing. However, on so rendering it actual, as specifiable Seconds (haecceities), it shows itself on the surface as no more than fleeting, scintillating flashes without enduring countenance. Any and all attempts to pin it down from within this realm of Secondness inevitably ends in an infinite regress (that is, Zeno's artificially cutting the continuum into discrete bits, with no possible end in sight). Yet the continuous 'film,' everywhere and everywhen yet nowhere and nowhen, seems to inhere in all signs; at least it is felt, sensed as such. There always seems to be some sort of fore-effect and an after-effect, but nothing is precisely specifiable. Of course, the task of Thirdness is that of attempting to lasso and hog-tie the thinglessness of Firstness and the elusive, fleeting, ephemeral thingness of Secondness, and bring some enduring form of sense or meaning to the whole affair. Yet, as the self-proclaimed author of generality, the task Thirdness sets for itself is perpetually destined to remain incomplete – for us finite, fallible human semiotic agents, at least.

In light of the above as illustrated in my hazy account of a professional conference, it becomes apparent that the field of Peirce's vagueness, of signs as hardly more than *possibilia*, as virtuality not yet made actuality *for* some semiotic agent or other, consists of the equivalent of a field of singular points the combination of which is no more than an indefinite smear – an 'electron cloud' of meaning. Nothing is actually 'there,' nor is it something in the brain or off in some Platonic empyrean. It might appear, consequently, that the relations combining to make up meaning are actualized in aleatoric fashion, by chance, a throw of the dice, a shot in the dark. Yet, the other picture also looms large, that of the semiotic agent as active participant within the flow of semiosis. A full-blown view must embrace both pictures, of course.

Peirce, like some of his contemporary counterparts, and unlike Heidegger, Wittgenstein, Derrida, Lacan, Lévi-Strauss, and Anglo-American analytic philosophers who have taken the 'linguistic turn' in hopes of finding a detour out of the metaphysical quagmire, confronts no 'prison house of language,' that entrapment of thought within signs. On the contrary. Thought begins its long journey as itself just another sign among signs. In fact, it is bolted into the world by other signs: there is no clear and distinct Cartesian sign, in all its plenitude, appearing out of the blue. As such it also defies representation in the positivist correspondence theory mould.

In a manner of speaking, the semiosic process itself begins with some sort of distribution of point-signs as possibilities, and the semiotic agent, fabricator of thought-signs, is, quite properly speaking, a Deleuze-Guattari (1983) 'nomad,' with neither retrievable origin, absolutely stable centre, nor determinate destiny. Nomadic wanderings along multiple 'lines of flight' (that is, imaginary lines converging, diverging, intersecting, vanishing and reappearing), breed the image of a multiply linear, an n-linear, systemless sort of orderless order. In fact, when speaking of the 'film' of Firstness, the term 'linear' becomes an absolute misnomer, and even the terms 'nonlinear' and 'antilinear' are out of the question. Yet at unexpected moments order suddenly appears from chaos; intention and purpose can now be vaguely to somewhat precisely perceived, though before the fact they were indeterminable. In this fashion, one-dimensional semiotics metaphorized as the linear generation of complexity from a lonely point, in the final analysis, spells a relatively high degree of freedom, not constraint. Movement is at local levels linear yet open such that from the larger view it is nonlinear; it is goal-oriented yet in terms of the range of all possibilities virtually directionless, for tangential moves are more common than not.

This image of complexity bred from simplicity and order out of chaos bears a further look.

2. THE 'WORM-LINE'S' UBIQUITY

Deleuze and Guattari (1987) put forth three modes of signification that dovetail effectively with Peircean semiosis as it has been developed here. They correspond to (1) the physico-chemical (Fraser's proto-eotemporal), (2) the organic (Fraser's biotemporal), and (3) the anthropomorphic (Fraser's nootemporal).

Typical of the first is the recursive process of crystallization, a monotonously repetitive action producing merely more of the same: near-simulacra piled upon near-simulacra. In the organic realm, as I urged in chapter 1, quasi-and aperiodic crystals represent the commencement of a 'defect' altering previous linearity, which gives rise ultimately to life processes. The anthropomorphic (mental) stratum, on the other hand, takes on an entirely new configuration with respect to its nomadic expression. The nonlinearity of the genetic code gives way to the multilinearity or 'superlinearity' typical of language (Peircean symbols *par excellence*). In this domain, nomadic propensities lead to deterritorialization, and in the extreme, to random, Brownian-like straying in the direction of everything in general and nothing in particular. This state, like Kafka's 'resonating disequilibrium' − a tendency toward wild reverberation − eventually yields a complexity of far-from-equilibrium conditions culminating in peripatetic strange attractors, a free-play of fluctuations, and wild fractals.

It is crucial to note that symbolicity, standing at the apex of Peirce's sign tripod, is most properly defined in terms of linearity (one-dimensionality) unwinding itself within n-dimensions in all possible directions − a rhizomic image at its best. Time-bound speech and especially writing, which, always already there in the text, *en bloc*, came into existence through a painful temporal process, and they now give themselves up to multiple readings that are equally dependent upon time. That is, one-dimensional signs are strung together in linear chains as syntactic and semantic (metonymic, in Saussurean terminology) blocks awaiting timed release of a minuscule portion of the possibilities superposed within. The text − or consciousness and memory − has a past, and a present (though both are perpetually deferred), and hence it is future oriented in this respect (see Pattee [1972, 1979, 1986] for a comparable notion regarding biological processes). Kafka's writing as rhizome, as n-dimensional possibilities susceptible to particular one-dimensional readings − in fact, an infinity of them − is quite typical of this field of textual 'point-signs.'[6] Symbolicity, in this sense, embodies one-dimensional time-binding and at the same time *n*-dimensional spatiality, or space-binding. But I'm afraid this is still hazy, so let me try to illustrate it from a different glance.

The age-old dream of of *presence*, the early Wittgenstein's (1961) longing for a universal language capable faithfully of mirroring the world, that chimerical utterly transparent language – against which Derrida (1973) took up pen and forayed into battle – would mark fulfilment of the ideal correspondence .between sign and thing. Such a language would also fulfil the project Husserl set for himself in *Logical Investigations* (1913). *Expression* and *indication* were to form the basis of a definitive theoretical self-help program for hooking signs onto the furniture of the world. As per usual, Derrida demonstrates how Husserl's wishful presence of consciousness and thought and of voice and consciousness is actually not unmediated at all, but indefinitely postponed, infinitely deferred, perpetually delayed. If there ever was a moment of presence, like Saussure's sheet of paper – or Peirce's initial sheet of the 'book of assertions' (counterpart to Derrida's [1978] 'bottomless chessboard') – there could have been no-thing before a mark was made and the sheet became marred. Consciousness *of* the mark could not have been other than mediated, after this original sin and fall from grace. Consciousness is thus permanently banished to the wilderness of incessantly time-lagging signs. After this initiary point, whenever and wherever it might have been, signs – and hence consciousness – are destined to disseminate. They spread, across the two-dimensional sheet, the three-dimensional book, and throughout time and space along motley lines never again to be retrieved in their totality.

One-dimensional semiotics (or symbolicity), and indeed, the entire sign process itself, become suspect, however. The *n*-dimensional dissemination of signs eventually doubles back upon itself, and signs begin producing replications of themselves that are none-the-less never-quite-exactly faithful to their ancestors. Availing myself of iconic rather than symbolic reduplication for the purpose of illustration, Andy Warhol's Marilyn Monroe silkscreens can be taken from a magazine image derived from a photograph developed from a negative that resulted from a spash of photons bouncing off a particular body and entering the camera lens. That body, known to millions, is so known only through the mass media – through signs, many or most of them linearly generated. The series is unending, and it inevitably becomes nonlinear, taking off at multiple indeterminate bifurcation points.

In the final analysis, who, where, what, when, is the 'real' Marilyn? It is like the viewer viewing the viewer viewing a print in Escher's 'Print Gallery,' which turns out to be 'real,' thus enveloping both viewer and viewed, and viewer and the viewer viewing the viewer. It is John Barth's *LETTERS*, a novel about novels about language about 'reality,' which is ultimately language about novels about LETTERS. It is a Möbius strip in the order of Lacan's (1966) 'Schema R' doubling back on itself to end where it began. Yet, in all these cases, things are never the same, in spite of our efforts to pack the whole mess in a Procrustean bed of roses.

As I trust is quite evident from the above chapters, today's science shows that nature is by and large relentlessly nonlinear. Classical mechanics had concentrated on relatively docile linear equations for a quite practical reason: an orderly universe – and the universe must be proved orderly at all cost, for if not, the edifice would collapse – could most adequately be described by such computations. In fact, physics was compromised in order to pack any and all data into the harmonious, symmetrical antechamber of these linear equations. At the same time, their unruly cousins, the apparently unmanageable nonlinear equations mixing things up in the party room, were conveniently ignored. Now, linearity is viewed as somewhat artificial window-dressing. The euphoric cymbal clashes from the classical bandwagon when bold new theories were forthcoming had for centuries succeeded in suffocating all other makeshift, and rather rebellious, percussion instruments suggesting disorder, unpredictable happenings. But the cymbals finally developed a crack, which grew into a fissure revealing hitherto concealed blunders, missteps, bloopers, and miscalculations, and finally, they shattered. There is no longer any absolutely determinable orderly sequence from cause to effect, before to after, here to there, part to whole, contained to container, nor are there harmonious parallels, symmetries, reciprocals, and inversions. The other universe, that of unexpected surface happenings, refuses to be shunned any longer. Consequently, dimensions of possibility have proliferated, in the process generating increasingly more complex domains. A one-dimensional line drawn on a sheet has two ends with one degree of freedom: back and forth. A two-dimensional square has four corners with two degrees of freedom, a cube eight corners with three degrees of freedom, a four-dimensional cube sixteen corners and four degrees, a five-dimensional one thirty-two corners and five degrees, and so on, with no end in sight. This is the vague picture of a universe now construed as unimaginably complex.

Take, for example, the operation of a bicycle. Its apparently simple function has at the most basic level five sources of motion, the handlebars, the front wheel, the crank-chain-rear-wheel assembly, and two pedals. A mathematical description of each movement requires one position coordinate and one velocity coordinate. In other words, when considering the five lines of motion, there are $2 \times 5 = 10$ degrees of freedom within a ten-dimensional spatial system. If a mathematician were to scribble all this down on paper as an elaborate set of equations (Thirdness) for the purpose of teaching us how to ride a bicycle (in the sphere of Secondness), and were we to try holding all the possible variables in check (as the *possibilia* of Firstness) while learning the balancing act, we would be reduced to catatonia – like the proverbial centipede who, when asked how he orchestrated the movement of all his legs when he walked, thought about it, and was suddenly paralysed. However, after a few scrapes and bruises, a child can intuitively get the hang of things and manipulate the machine with relative ease. Her knowledge *how* to do it mocks the physicist's mathematical tools describing that knowledge.

From a bicycle to an internal combustion engine to your home computer to your brain, there is a swarming proliferation of complexity. Why, then, should we expect our world, the realm of semiosis, to be anything less? Above all, why should we suppose symbolicity, language, speech, and especially writing, to be merely one-dimensionally linear? This, of course, is the basic thrust of Derrida's message. Writing, for Derrida, is the manifestation *par excellence* of *différance*, of excess, supplement, dissemination, difference and deferral, trace. It radically exceeds the closure, the capture, the hands-on authoritarian policy of metaphysics, traditionally conceived. The problem is that *différance* is radically elusive. It is the absence of a presence, the presence of an absence, the perpetual beginning of something else while leaving only vague signposts indicating that it was there and what it actually was (Derrida 1973).

Writing, in this conception, is the incessant play of differences in an entirely democratic playground where everything is at the outset equal in status to everything else, where everything is not necessarily relative but is at least given equal time to prove its worth. In this nontotalizable totality, this complex web of interrelations, this *aporia*-laden structureless structure, nothing is itself in and of itself, for all things emerge and pass on along the semiosic tidal interplay of forces. Each individual word, the embodiment of a perishing presence, is neither autonomous nor is it any slouch. It is a radically kinetic process, partly emptied of self-identity and self-presence. The same, in fact, can be said of all signs. There is no *causa sui*, antecedent to and the ultimate origin of everything else. The rush of signs renders everything completely co-relative: it is a fluid dissemination of fluid seeds. Dissemination is the act of dispersing, diffusing, broadcasting, and promulgating a scattering of indefinite, indeterminable, undecidable signs along multilinear lines in an *n*-dimensional milieu. Yet each sign, like the ink that flows, or the letter that appears on the monitor, is not there in absolute simultaneity, but only after a certain time lag. For all signs must be mediated before they can hope to become genuine signs.

This semiosic rush of the seminal sign, or more specifically, the word, especially in the guise of modernity, once seemed to promise power, progress, advancement, emancipation, and the good life for all – at the same time that, ironically, it threatened to destroy all. This promise has ended in shattered mirrors, empty dreams, futile dystopias, grave new worlds of unreasoning reason. The postmodern experience, perhaps, appears more attuned to the lure of unlimited possibilities presented by the true nature of semiosis's countenance. And at the same time it has learned quite effectively to expect a unity of disunity, disordered order, affirmative negation and negative affirmation, smooth flow punctuated by intermittent plunges into the maelstrom, disjunctive conjunction, constant renewal of struggle and contradiction: everything bleeds contrariness; harmony and balance turn out to be chimeras; perilous infinities jump up to beckon at every juncture.

Thus our paradigm phenomenon, writing, that scintillating dance of differences within sameness and sameness within differences, appears to be the embodiment of contradictory complementarities at their best. It deludes its presumably neutral onlooker with its stolid surface, its seemingly obtuse demeanour, its apparent inertia, its beckoning passivity. As a case in point, Rorty's (1982) 'philosophy as a kind of writing' gave philosophers fits: they thought they had been doing philosophy, not writing; they had been desperately seeking Truth, not playfully erecting rhetorical gambits. The act of writing was supposed to be a mere means of expression, using language as a tool, and both writing and its tool-box were rather irrelevant to the thought they were supposed to express. How dare Rorty and his cohorts evince irreverence in the face of their sombrely cogitating masters!

None the less, Rorty continues undaunted. Writing, he writes, was considered somewhat of 'an unfortunate necessity.' The words with which the investigator 'wrote up' his report were to be zero-degree, objective, impersonal, and transparent. Now, it has become evident that 'writing always leads to more writing, and more, and still more' (Rorty 1982:145). And so it has become, like the rest of nature, relentlessly nonlinear, indeterminately varied, intransigently vague, radically n-dimensional, with the same number of parameters of choice.

This rhizomically intertwined nature of writing is perhaps nowhere more evident that in the disciplines of history and ethnography. Michel Foucault wisely abandoned his earlier analysis of *epistemes* for a Nietzsche-style 'genealogy,' allowing him to rewrite dipolar fields of tension and conflict in terms of differences, histories with their own personalities – now confidently stepping forward, now uncertain and tenuous, now oscillating between contradictory alternatives, now carefully backpedalling.[7] Each history manifests its own idiosyncrasies, as knowledge, discourse, and multiple series of events articulated in lieu of people and things, without the investigator 'having to make reference to a subject which is either transcendental in relation to the field of events or runs in its empty sameness throughout the course of history' (Foucault 1980:117). Sign-events and thought-signs – but never sign-things – are thus now in the spotlight. A question is asked, a problem posed, a generality formulated. Events are arranged in an array of possible series. To speak of generalities regarding the writing of history entails awareness that things could always have been other than what they appear to be. Events could always have operated in different ways. The dispersing, disseminating, near-aleatoric intertwining of the sum of historical writing cannot but elude rather than elucidate, given its radically diversified rarefactions. For when events are set up in harmonious, orderly, linear fashion, they are not the straightforwardly 'real,' to be dutifully reported by the historian, but an array retrospectively constructed. They are events conceptualized not lived; they are structured not processual, frozen not fluid.

The problem of (sign-)events fitting into the totality (self-reflecting monad), or particulars (Seconds) into the generalities (Thirds), is, Foucault (1977:178) tells us, the product of signs artificially constituted through their re-iteration in thought (thought-signs). These artificial (sign-)events become 'phantasms' rendered re-iterable as if they were singular universals. Foucault borrows the term 'phantasms' from Deleuze. Deleuze's surface effects, the 'film' of *possibilia* hovering over individuals and events, show subtle but illusory promise, given the infinity of singular points awaiting actualization of generals in the most general sense. The fitlessness of particular events into a chimerical totality inevitably conspires to yield both totalizing and detotalizing, as well as solitary – unique, singular – and collective effects. On the other hand, rejection of history (the past) either in favour of an impossible presence (Secondness, actuality, indexicality) or an unattainable future (Thirdness, necessity) inevitably leads either to rampant, pointless nominalism or vacuous generalities. Thus an unresolvable tension should actually be welcomed, for:

the more History attempts to transcend its own rootedness in historicity, and the greater the efforts it makes to attain, beyond the historical relativity of its origin and its choices, the sphere of universality, the more clearly it bears the marks of its historical birth, and the more evidently there appears through it the history of which it is itself a part ... Inversely, the more it accepts its relativity, and the more deeply it sinks into the movement it shares with what it is recounting, then the more it tends to the slenderness of the narrative, and all the positive content it obtained for itself through the human sciences is dissipated. (Foucault 1970:371)

This circularity reveals the very paradoxical nature, and hence the impossibility, of historical narrative – it necessarily remains suspended between the Scylla of what actually was (the 'real' darkly seen through the filter of a past 'semiotic world') and the Charybdis of what now is (the historian's presumably transparent 'semiotically real' milieu). As Jean François Lyotard (1988) puts it, historical narrative contains within itself an incommensurable *differend*; it emerges in concert with present and past tensions and conflicts, injunctions, and prohibitions. History is consequently 'impossible, meaningless, in the finite totality, and ... it is impossible, meaningless, in the positive and actual infinity ...' (Derrida 1978:123). Consequently, the project of writing history is ultimately caught up in the 'deconstructive paradox' (Merrell 1985a: chap. 3). That is, historical narrative depends upon the strictures, closures, and prescriptions of historiography, but historiography is predicated on the nature of existent historical narrative. All becomes fabrication, a hopelessly feeble series of infinitesimals infinitely short of the distant totality.

Given the present, rather postmodernist – whatever that actually means these days – state of writing, of narrative, of discourse, it is becoming increasingly apparent that we have entered a 'posthumanist' period. By 1935 José Ortega y Gasset (1948) was speaking of art's 'dehumanization.' More recently, other observers have focused on a new kind of trans-individual individual. The implication is that there has been a major shift. Something has happened, something has been radically disrupted, a monolithic fluctuation of the social whole of Western humanity threatening precipitously to pour forth, even erupt, into a furious whirlpool of dissipation from which whatever new order will spring forth nobody knows. A by-product of this *Sturm und Drang* is a marked 'loss of the self' (Sypher 1962). Walt Whitman and Nietzsche's 'I am the entirety of humankind' is transmuted into Beckett's more humble 'I am not it, what am I, as if it mattered' articulated by his Unnamable. The option either to affirm or deny has disappeared in Beckett; there is both affirmation and denial. The paradox is ubiquitous. The Unnamable is surprised that he is not surprised that what he expected did not come to pass, and he is untroubled that he is unsurprised at his unexpected nonsurprise. Nothing troubles him, yet he is troubled by his untrouble. He decides, then, merely not to decide, and in so doing decides on, and determines, his future expectations – or nonexpectations. That self of Pascal, Kierkegaard, and others, suspended between the infinitesimal and the infinite, between the void and God, becomes effaced and enfeebled. The self's loss of identity compels it to withdraw to a point from which there can be no more than a dim, dark awareness of the malaise 'out there.'

Henri Lefebvre (1971) discusses the anti-humanistic implications of Saussurean semiology and structuralism of the 1960s and early 1970s, suggesting that the self has been dissolved in an impersonal, though purportedly intersubjective, system that operates through it. The individual self becomes no more than a medium. On the other hand, that self-proclaimed prophet of postmodernism, Ihab Hassan (1980, 1987) uses the terms 'posthumanism' and 'antihumanism' to announce dissolution of that self presumed to be firmly embedded in the Cartesian *cogito* (see also Schechner 1982). The new trans-individual self arising out of the rubble is merely an extension of the collective whole, like the pod put forth by an amoeba when procuring food (Hassan 1980:202–4) – all, perhaps unfortunately, somewhat reminiscent of Pierre Teilhard de Chardin and recent gurus of cosmic consciousness.

And Derrida (1978:292) writes of a posture that 'is no longer turned toward the origin, affirms play and tries to pass beyond man and humanism, the name of man being the name of that being who ... has dreamed of full presence, the reassuring foundation, the origin and the end of play.' From Derrida – and Lacan – to and through poststructuralists, deconstructionists of various guises, and even certain Marxist intellectuals, structuralist and semiological assumptions have been extrapolated, and 'transcended,' finally to deny the ontological primacy of the individual. Postmodernism has taken this equation to its final step: humankind in the future most likely will be of hardly any consequence; it will be the product of mere sensation (iconicity, phenomenalism), mere action-reaction (indexicality, behaviourism), mere mind-spinning (symbolicity, idealism), all in stark isolation from one another. There will be no integration and coordination of all actors on the fluid stage of semiosis, only the disharmony, the dissonance, of the sphinx's riddle.

All of which is in certain ways Peircean, and in others quite un-Peircean, as we shall note.

3. 'TO USE WORDS BUT RARELY IS TO BE NATURAL' (LAO TZU)

It is now common knowledge – though by no means universally accepted, and even subject to knee-jerk reactions in some quarters – that, given the current trend toward radical anti-foundationalism coupled with diverse attacks on '(phal)logocentrism,' the myth of presence, and 'grand narratives,' there has been a general declaration of war on any and all attempts at totalization (Lyotard 1984:82).

The thrust is in the direction of piecemeal enquiries and away from 'globalizing' investigations of the sort that are supposed to inevitably culminate in hierarchization, dehumanization, oppression, and exploitation (Zavarzadeh and Morton 1991). While this move is perhaps healthy, it cannot but be at its roots self-contradictory: the call for an end of 'grand narratives' once and for all cannot itself but imply some sort of totalizing perspective. In the present section, however, I wish to turn the tables somewhat by demonstrating that though we can hardly speak without implying some generality or other, and hence at some unexpected moment falling into the snare of Russell's logical types, this actually presents no real problem in the arena of human pragmatics. For the way of semiosis allows us to roll with the waves, stay afloat through storm and stress, negotiate the bucking surf of any and all paradoxes, and, in general, we somehow manage to get along swimmingly.

Terms the likes of 'society,' 'culture,' 'polity,' 'economic system,' and even 'local narratives' cannot but be, in light of Peirce's concept of semiosis, of *incomplete* character, and if they are taken as generalities in the most general sense, then they cannot but be *inconsistent*. In Derrida's (1978:289) own words, 'the nature of the field – that is, language and a finite language – excludes totalization. This field is in effect that of *play*, ... because instead of being an inexhaustible field, as in the classical hypothesis, instead of being too large, there is something missing from it: a center which arrests and grounds the play of substitutions.' The sign, in short, always 'exceeds,' and is never exhausted by, the concoction of 'semiotic objects' and interpretants. The upshot is that if no sign or even any collection of signs that falls within our capacity to grasp them can be both self-confirmatory (*consistent*) and self-sufficient (*complete*), then they must at least be sufficiently *complete* and *consistent* so as to allow us an increased level of understanding through them.

But, to repeat, we somehow generally manage to get along swimmingly. A pronoun (Peirce's sign 6), for example – or Lewontin's 'do' from chapter 9 – is insufficient if in isolation, but in the context of a particular dialogue it can carry sufficient meaning, pragmatically speaking. Yet it must remain radically *incomplete*. The noun (sign 8) of which the pronoun is a pronoun could have been actualized in place of the pronoun. And specificity is heightened along the road toward completion. But use of the noun still evokes unanswered questions: Is it the bearer of the same referent today, yesterday, or a year ago? Is it the noun according to John's interpretation or Mary's? If it is this noun here-now, then with respect to what or to whom? What are the circumstances surrounding this particular actualization of the noun? This is tantamount to the potentially infinite number of sentences with practical implications generated out of Peirce's 'pragmatic maxim.' There is no conceivable finish line in the same manner that we can retrieve no starting blocks, nor can we know precisely where we are in the race of semiosis. Each sign, in its push toward the ultimate interpretant, perpetually remains short of its goal, though it may be sufficiently *complete* for our purposes. In this vein, given the ludic propensities of postmodernism's premises, the very idea of any 'totalization' of the venerable project of modernity – Habermas' dream – cannot be sutured or held together with Band-aid strategies, but rather, it should simply be abandoned altogether (Laclau 1985:111). There is no knowing the centreless, n-dimensional whole.

Semiosis, like individual signs, including the cell, is by and large self-governing; it is in large part – but not entirely – of self-referential, autonomous nature; its interpretants are the product of its own inner (immanent) unfolding – one-dimensional linear generativity within the three-dimensional domain – and they are not, given their partial autonomy, exclusively determined by any 'outside' agent (though one must not forget that other nature, the openness of signs). Yet to make this very statement – much like Derrida's 'there is nothing outside the text' – is to commit the very sin of totalization. To enter into the community of *Homo loquens* is to select, generalize, evoke types as well as tokens, refer to abstractions, put particulars into one of a beehive of pigeon-holes representing sets of things – in sum, to forget differences. If not, we are hardly any better than Borges' hapless soul, 'Funes the Memorious.'

But how can one generalize, in proper fashion worthy of the human semiotic agent, and at the same time remain faithful to Peirce's admonishment that 'we must be on our guard against the deceptions of abstract definitions' and attend to 'concrete reasonableness'? (*CP*:1.615, 5.3, 5.433, 7.362) In fact, one could argue that Peirce himself is guilty of committing a sin against 'concrete reasonableness': upon articulating his theory of the sign, at various times in his life and in various guises, his focus remained primarily on mathematics, logic, and science, all disciplines of the abstract. Quite understandably, Vincent Colapietro (1989:1–25) could criticize Justus Buchler (1955), David Savan (1988–9), and Beth Singer (1983) for their own attention chiefly, and at times exclusively, to the cognitive – that is, generalizing, abstract – aspect of Peirce's sign.[8] Indeed, the vast majority of Peirce enquiries have centred on his work in mathematics, logic, science, philosophy, and cosmology, with little regard to what he has to say about 'tender-minded' concerns.[9] If in developing a well-rounded sign theory one must chip away at the walls enclosing one in abstract definitions to break out into the field of pragmatic give-and-take and 'concrete reasonableness,' then the sign must be considered in terms of everything and anything that has its roots in interaction between semiotic agents. Interaction between communicating agents must thus serve as a glue welding signs into a web not of local but somehow of global proportions. This would call for a general theory of signs of the most general form imaginable: heretical totalization, perverse abstraction.

Yet visions of totalization persist. Max Fisch, in response to the question 'What is the *use* of a general theory of signs?' writes: 'It will give us a map so complete and detailed as to place any field of highly specialized research in relation to any other, tell us quickly how to get from one field to another, and distinguish fields not yet explored from those long cultivated' (1986:360). Though he concedes that 'at least for a long time to come, the general theory of signs will itself require continual revision in light of new findings,' the vision is exceedingly ambitious, perhaps even utopian, in scope. If 'whatever else anything may be, it is also a sign' (Fisch 1986:357), then whatever a sign in the most general sense *is*, there is nothing remaining that it *is not*. But Peirce's interpreter *is not* what the interpretant interpreted *is*; the thinker *is not* the thought; the map *is not* the territory. In another manner of putting it, just as the thinker is not the thought, and the interpreter is not the interpretant (up to, and including, the ultimate interpretant of the world, of a text), so also a token – in fact, any finite collection of tokens – cannot be coterminous with its type in the absolute sense.

A scattering of marine fossils can be found by a palaeontologist as signs (tokens) that the sea level was once higher than at present. The number of such fossils available to the palaeontologist at a particular time and place pales in comparison to the total number of fossils that have been and are, and those that never were and never will be interpreted by her or any of her counterparts, or by anyone searching among the same tokens for signs of distinct interpretants. Yet the undiscovered fossils are there: they are signs, though they have not (yet) been *distinguished* as such, *indicated, interpreted* and given a *value*, and/or *put to use for* some purpose or other *by* some semiotic agent. They are signs, in so far as they are representations, the natural result of some natural phemonenon – their respective *object* – but, as long as they exclude their potential interpreters, they have had no chance of evoking, provoking, or determining their respective *interpretants* in the full sense. And as long as any set of signs corresponding to a given type are left uninterpeted, there is no chance of that type enjoying fulfilment.[10]

As signs independent of our/any interpretations, they are meaningful to some degree, but their meaning is inauthentic without the collaboration of a semiotic agent, the fourth actor on stage whose function is that of prodding the sign on to its best performance yet. Without semiotic agents, signs could offer no representation *for* someone *in* some respect or capacity, and the whole semiosic river, the entire universe as a perfusion of signs (*CP*:5.448n1), would eventually dry up. Signs without conscious or quasi-conscious interpreting agents are potential thoughts without thinkers. If the universe is indeed perfused with signs, then these signs, if not subjected to thinking and interpreting semiotic agents – human or otherwise – are not (yet) full-blown signs. They cannot become the object of thinking by a thinker set *apart from* them as objects of thinking – that is, the thinker as sign must be something other than the sign thought, and that selfsame thinker must be the sign of another sign, ad infinitum. But upon so being engaged in this infinitely regressive and infinitely progressive interactive interpreting process, the thinker cannot him/herself, during that selfsame act, be considered *part of* the perfusion of signs composing the universe. Hence the ultimate sign of absolute generality cannot be thought.

In other words, if the thinker is construed as part of the universe, then from among all the signs contained within it there will be at least one sign – and in all likelihood countless signs – that are less than authentic, for the thinker must have (artificially) set himself *apart from* the sign or signs he is in the act of interpreting. Even if we go so far as to assume the thinker to be of an omniscience comparable to Laplace's Superintelligence – or our all-knowing Ludwig, from the above – then, as set *apart from* the entire universe in order to subject it to his/her act of thinking, that same universe cannot but be *incomplete*, for it will not contain its own cosmic thinking agent. It seems to follow that the universe, if *complete* and totally wrapped up in a self-contained cosmological package, must inexorably remain *inconsistent* at some point or other. And if that *inconsistency* is somehow remedied, it must be so remedied by some impossible outside semiotic agent, adding to it a qualifying term ('axiom') capable of clarifying and dissolving the *inconsistency*. But since no absolute semiotic agent is conceivable, given the premises underlying this inquiry, the universe cannot but be *incomplete*. The only possible answer, it appears, is that the universal perfusion of signs is self-organizing. It lifts itself up by its own bootstraps, by way of dissipative structures spontaneously generated from within.

Yet, the universe of signs as a self-contained, self-referential, self-sufficient sign, is at least potentially the consummate *conjunctionis oppositorum*, product of the ultimate sign 10 and the ultimate sign 1 (figure 3, the *Ho-t'u* model), the virtual sign of absolute *vagueness* and absolute *generality*. If this potentiality were somehow to be realized, it would be the unending extrapolation of Beckett's modest 'I am I.' It would be unnamable. So even though the semiotic subject (self), were to place itself entirely out of the picture to take a gander of things from that privileged vantage, the horizon would remain totally obsfucated, henceforth the subject (self) could not but remain silent. For, the subject can speak – can signify – only in-so-far as s/he is a sign interacting with signs. If not, if s/he somehow were to presume her/himself in possession of some form of spurious, sham autonomy, as an island completely of/for/by her/himself and nothing but her/himself, then semiosis, as far as s/he could discern, would have become a frozen lake, a hell of ice.

Actually, like the case of the lumberjack, his chain-saw, and the tree, semiosis encompasses the semiotic agent and at the same time somehow displays itself before her/him. And s/he is *part of*, and at the same time somehow – albeit artificially – *set apart from*, s/he sets her/himself *apart from*, the field of semiosis.

Thus the universe *is*, yet somehow it *is not*, what it *is, for* her/him: an immanent whole. And s/he *is*, yet somehow *is not*, what s/he *is, for* it: a mere sign among signs.

Appendix

Ludwig Boltzmann's order principle would assign almost zero probability to the occurrence of instability comparable to Bénard convection involving more than 10^{20} molecules. Macroscopic phenomena, he maintained, demand quite different conditions (Nicolis and Prigogine 1977:5). Prigogine, in contrast, has this to say:

We may imagine that there are always small convection currents appearing as fluctuations from the average state, but below a certain critical value of the temperature gradient, these fluctuations are damped and disappear. However, above this critical value, certain fluctuations are amplified and give rise to a macroscopic current. A new molecular order appears that basically corresponds to a giant fluctuation stabilized by the exchange of energy with the outside world. This is the order characterized by the occurrence of what are referred to as 'dissipative structures.' (1980:89–90)

In other words, given far-from-equilibrium conditions, the concept of probability underlying Boltzmann's order principle is no longer valid, the classical thermodynamic notion of entropy increase in a closed system loses its force, and the age-old problem of the origin of life appears in a different perspective. Life is incompatible with Boltzmann's order principle, but it is compatible with the behaviour of far-from-equilibrium systems.

The implications of Prigogine's findings are thus revolutionary. And they directly bear on Peirce's concept of the sign. What Prigogine calls *order* (comparable to Peirce's law, the product of habit, Thirdness) generated (actualized, by way of Secondness) spontaneously out of *chaos* (chance, Firstness) dissolves the boundary between microscopic and macroscopic phenomena, between inorganic and organic, and between inert and living material. Evolution from Firstness to Thirdness, from spontaneity to regularity, *might be* to *would be*, performs the same task, leading us to the image of the signness of all things, the universe as a 'perfusion of signs' (*CP*:4.512n). Na^+ and Cl^- ions in a supersaturated solution manifest a propensity to form crystals; slime moulds regroup when the food supply is scarce and move across the forest floor toward better pastures; an apparently random collection of termites at the opportune moment begins coordinating activity to construct an elaborate nest; a city appears spontaneously to spring up in the desert by the coordinated work of human hands and minds. In each case order evolves from apparent chaos. Each involves collaboration between a community of semiotic agents and the collocation of myriad signs toward some specific purpose.

Such order arising out of far-from-equilibrium systems is a far cry from classical thermodynamics, which breeds the concept of equilibrium structures in cases such as crystal formation. If a seed crystal is placed in a supersaturated liquid, crystallization occurs around it to create geometrical order from the relatively chaotic liquid state of positive and negative ions in constant movement. Entropy has increased in the event that the process has been exothermic (heat was dissipated), and since the system has shifted from a less probable to a more probable state. But order rather than disorder appears to have been produced, which is anomalous, given the Second Law of Thermodynamics. Bénard cells, like crystals, are structures, though of a quite different nature. The cells emerge precisely to facilitate the dissipation of energy from one level of the liquid to the other. Like living organisms, they take in heat from one level and dissipate it into their environment in order that their structural order may be maintained. If the liquid is allowed the cool, the cells become unstable and fall back into disorder; if the liquid is heated further, they cannot maintain a sufficient flow of energy, and the structure disintegrates. Prigogine introduced the notion of 'dissipative structures' to emphasize the close association, at first paradoxical, in such situations between structure and order on the one side, and dissipation or waste on the other.

Prigogine points out that systems interacting with the outside when embedded in far-from-equilibrium conditions can become the starting-point for the formulation of new dynamic states of dissipative structures. In such case, dissipative structures actually correspond to a form of supramolecular organization. Although the parameters describing crystal structures may be derived from the properties of the molecules of which they are composed, and in particular from the range of their forces of attraction and repulsion, Bénard cells, like all dissipative structures, are essentially a reflection of the global situation of nonequilibrium producing them. The parameters describing them are macroscopic: not the distance between the molecules of a crystal, but of the order of centimetres. Similarly, the time scales are different – they correspond not to molecular times (such as periods of vibration of individual molecules) but to macroscopic times: seconds, minutes, and even hours (Prigogine and Stengers 1984:143–4). The microscopic space and time of disorder conjures up order in macroscopic space and time. Undulatory, pulsational behaviour at the microlevel takes on an undulatory, pulsational behaviour at the macrolevel of an entirely different nature. Thus instability, the lack of predictability and control, the problem of indeterminacy, from microlevels to macrolevels, is foregrounded.

Following Prigogine's approach, indeterminism becomes an implicit part of classical physics – as it was with Peirce (Murphey 1961). The physicist's inability to predict the future of a many-particle system is no longer thought of as a limitation on this experimental or computational ability, as it was during the classical era, but as an inevitable consequence of the laws of nature themselves. Instead of fundamental classical laws referring to microscopic reversible processes that combine to produce macroscopic irreversible processes that no more than approximate those laws, nature is seen in the Prigogine sense as consisting entirely of irreversible processes that are indeterminate in their entirety. In this sense, a *Prigogine uncertainty principle* inheres: if a thermodynamic description applies, precise measurement of the dynamic variables is impossible; a microscopic system can be described dynamically, but it lies outside the thermodynamic sphere. In another way of putting it, the thermodynamic sphere is 'real,' to be sure, but no microscopic system, which is merely 'semiotically real,' can be specified precisely by thermodynamic descriptions, and no thermodynamically 'real' sphere can be specified precisely in terms of a microscopic system. As Prigogine and Isabelle Stengers put it:

It is amazing how closely the microscopic theory of irreversible processes resembles traditional macroscopic theory. In both cases entropy initially has a negative meaning. In its macroscopic aspect it prohibits some processes, such as heat flowing from cold to hot. In its microscopic aspect it prohibits certain classes of initial conditions. The distinction between what is permitted and what is prohibited is maintained in time by the laws of dynamics. It is from the negative aspect that the positive aspect emerges: the existence of entropy together with its probability interpretation. Irreversibility no longer emerges as if by a miracle at some macroscopic level. Macroscopic irreversibility only makes apparent the time-oriented polarized nature of the universe in which we live ...

Also ... irreversibility is the starting point of other symmetry breakings. For example, it is generally accepted that the difference between particles and anti-particles could arise only in a nonequilibrium world. This may be extended to many other situations. It is likely that irreversibility also played a role in the appearance of chiral symmetry through the selection of the appropriate bifurcation. One of the most active subjects of research now is the way in which irreversibility can be 'inscribed' into the structure of matter ...

We come to one of our main conclusions: At all levels, be it the level of macroscopic physics, the level of fluctuations, or the microscopic level, *nonequilibrium is the source of order, nonequilibrium brings 'order out of chaos.'* (1984:285–6)

One cannot help but relate Prigogine's work to quantum irreversibility when the observer is introduced into the system. In a sense the complex probability amplitude, a *might be* or First in the Peircean sense, is 'collapsed' into a particle by the observer to become a Second, a *happens to be*. An interpretant is then generated by that selfsame observer, thus attributing meaning to it, and the cycle is complete. But not quite. That interpretant is a possibility for another observer, hence it must in turn be 'collapsed' into another Second and then interpreted, and so on, in the never-ending cycle of semiosis. Comparably, for Prigogine, irreversibility phenomena of *becoming* are primary, while reversible phenomena of *being* are no more than approximations or idealizations of a secondary nature. In this manner, Prigogine's microscopic level, the quantum level, and semiosis, place the observer (= interpreter, sign) at centre stage in the process, while things, elementary particles, and the 'objects' of semiosis are of lesser importance. From this vantage, 'elementary particles' out of which the world is supposedly composed are actually not 'elementary' at all, but derivative. Rather than contributing the nuts and bolts of 'reality,' they are actually abstract constructs based on the more fundamental process of observer-observed interaction. And signs without mind are not signs in the full sense – in fact, mind *is* sign in a relatively full sense, in interaction with other minds and/or signs, that is. The raw physical manifestation of signs without participating interpreters must thus take a back seat to the process of signs engendering other signs by way of their interpreters, signs that interpret themselves.

Prigogine's view, although at the outset apparently simple, demands a radical switch in the physicist's thinking about the universe. Like Peirce before him – albeit from within a distinct conceptual framework – Prigogine places *events before things, process before content, becoming before being*. In his own words:

The classical order was: particles first, the second law later – being before becoming! It is possible that this is no longer so when we come to the level of elementary particles and that here we must *first* introduce the second law before being able to define the entities. Does this mean becoming before being? Certainly this would be a radical departure from the classical way of thought. But, after all, an elementary particle, contrary to its name, is not an object that is 'given'; we must construct it, and in this construction it is not unlikely that *becoming*, the participation of the particles in the evolution of the physical world, may play an essential role. (1980:199)

Prigogine's very important precedent leading toward the notion of life systems arising out of chaos bears emphasizing. Reconsider Schrödinger's *What Is Life?* (1967), which influenced Prigogine as a student. If, following Schrödinger, we admit to the concept of an increase of organization accompanied by a decrease of entropy, then we are led to the idea of life systems dissipating more entropy than they produce. In other words, life processes steal order from their environment through a local reversal of the temporal arrow of entropy, thus producing *negentropy* – the term was coined by L. Brillouin (1949) and employed by Schrödinger. However prophetic Schrödinger's ruminations now appear, Prigogine points out that the very notion of irreversibility regarding life processes was none the less ignored, categorically rejected, and finally only reluctantly admitted after the edifice of classical mechanics had been reduced to rubble – and this in spite of the fact that the Second Law itself implies 'time's arrow,' though in a different mode.

It has recently become evident that one of the chief objectives of contemporary physics must be that of explaining life processes. From this vantage, irreversibility and randomness must certainly be taken into account. But, Prigogine (1983) observes, life processes manifest an additional characteristic generally ignored by investigators. Life is not merely the passive result of cosmic evolution in general in so far as it entails the appearance of feedback processes. It is the result of cosmic irreversible processes, and, in addition, it is the author of new irreversible processes. In other words, irreversibility induces irreversibility, nonlinearity induces nonlinearity, life breeds life, or in Peirce's conception, signs become other signs. It all appears to be a self-organizing ballet, a sort of counterpart to John Archibald Wheeler's (1980a, 1980b) self-referential, self-reflexive universe, with the intriguing, but paradoxical, incorporation of 'time's arrow.' Actually, the theses of Prigogine and Wheeler are incompatible regarding time, yet, when the paradox is embraced – following Wheeler's own advice – timelessness and time, the continuum and discontinuous cuts, possibility and actuality, Secondness-Thirdness and Firstness, must somehow fit into our purview in the broadest possible sense.

In this sense, life considered as the improbable, even the well-nigh impossible, product of initial conditions – that is, in the sense of Jacques Monod (1971) – is compatible with classical laws of physics (the initial conditions are arbitrary), but it cannot be deduced from these laws (for they cannot determine the initial conditions). This is the problem with Monod's theory, according to Prigogine (as we have noted in chapters 8 and 9). It presupposes constant warfare between a vast army of Maxwell's demons and the physical world according to the traditional definition of the Second Law in order to perpetuate a highly improbable state of affairs.

Prigogine's thesis, then, offers a complete turnabout. Vital processes, rather than functioning at the margins of physical events, follow physical laws adapted to nonlinear interactions and far-from-equilibrium conditions. These characteristics allow for flows of matter and energy necessary to maintain the functional and structural order of life systems. The implication is that life *is* a set of physical events; it conforms with the laws of physics in so far as they include nonlinear, irreversible, and far-from-equilibrium conditions. The age-old demarcation between chemistry, physics, and biology, is thus ruptured. Physical and chemical processes at certain levels are life processes, and life processes become physical and chemical processes. Placed in a Peircean context, just as physical changes are the initial conditions from which signs are read by living systems, so living systems themselves consist of physical changes reading those signs.

Glossary

Abduction (sometimes called hypothesis or retroduction): A term designating the inferential process by means of which ideas, most typically of the sort that will answer a question or resolve a problem, are engendered. Abduction differs from the other two more commonly known inferential processes, *induction* and *deduction*. Induction is the cumulative operation of testing an idea or hypothesis arrived at by abductive means, and deduction is the formulation of an abductive insight, sometimes occurring as a free flight of the imagination, into a hypothetical condition that can be put to the practical test by inductive means, and in accord with Peirce's *pragmatic maxim*. True to the spirit of Peirce's categories, abduction falls in line with Firstness, induction with Secondness, and deduction with Thirdness. (*See also* Categories, Pragmatic maxim.)

Anisotropy: *See* Isotropy.

Argument: A set of sentences one or more of which is put forth as the premise(s) in support of the concluding sentence. In Peirce's semiotics, an argument is the final sign of the decalogue depicted in table 2. It is the culmination of the triad, *rhematic symbol* or *rheme* (term or word), *dicent symbol, dicisign,* or *dicent* (proposition or sentence), and *argument* (text or intertext). *Word, sentence,* and *text* are often used in this enquiry, since they are more in line with current discursive practices than Peirce's turn-of-the-century terminology. (*See also* Dicisign; Rheme.)

Asymptote: A concept essential to an understanding of Peirce's philosophy of knowledge, and of the ultimate sign, the *final interpretant*. Peirce believed that enquiry – a community, not an individual affair – successively approximates the ideal, much as Achilles approaches the tortoise in Zeno's hypothetical foot race. Peirce's ideal, however, will never be attained except in the theoretical long run, which would be accessible solely to an infinite community of investigators or an immortal individual knower. The asymptote, for Peirce, was actually not a mathematical converging series or a smooth approximation in the order of a hyperbola on the Cartesian plane, but unpredictably punctuated by fits and jerks. In other words, we can never be absolutely sure when our advance will be cumulative or when radical breaks will be forthcoming.

Attractor: A means for describing the behaviour of a dissipative system in *phase space*. Equilibrium systems settle down to steady states, while *far-from-equilibrium* systems can lead to strange attractors that are chaotic and to all appearances unpredictable and random in their behaviour. *Strange attractors* are essential to self-organizing systems of the type qualifying as Prigogine *dissipative structures*. (*See also* Dissipative structures; Far-from-equilibrium; Phase space; Strange attractor.)

Autocatalysis: The capacity of a chemical system to catalyse its own production, thereby rendering it self-organizing. (*See also* Catalyst; Hypercycle.)

Automatization: *See* Embedment.

Autosemeiopoiesis: From *autopoiesis* (*auto* = self; *poiesis* = production), a term coined by Humberto Maturana and found also in his collaborative work with Francisco Varela. It refers to the characteristic of living systems to continuously renew themselves – they are self-organizing – and to regulate this process in such a manner that their structure is maintained. Since, given the premises of this enquiry, signs, like living systems, 'grow,' I have integrated '-semeio-' into the term.

Belousov-Zhabotinsky reaction: A chemical reaction evincing self-organizing features named after its two Russian discoverers and used by Prigogine as evidence of chemical self-organizing systems, thereby fusing the traditional boundary between life and nonlife. (*See also* Dissipative structures; Far-from-equilibrium; Hypercycle.)

Bifurcation: A point at which there are two choices open to a *far-from-equilibrium* system. Beyond this critical point the properties of a system can change abruptly, unpredictably, and along nonlinear paths. (*See also* Dissipative structures; Far-from-equilibrium.)

Catalyst: A substance able to accelerate a chemical reaction, yet that does not actively enter into that reaction. (*See also* Autocatalysis; Hypercycle.)

Categories: Essential to Peirce's triadic conception of the sign, consisting of *Firstness* (that which is self-contained, self-sufficient, without relation to anything else), *Secondness* (that which is other than an instance of Firstness), and *Thirdness* (mediation between Firstness and Secondness). In two alternative ways of putting the categories, *Firstness* is qualitative immediacy without its (yet) existing *for* consciousness (it is a *might be*), *Secondness* is brute physical existence (the *is-ness* of things), and *Thirdness* is dynamic mediation between the other two (it is what *would be* or *could be*, given certain conditions).

Chaos: The term used to describe unpredictable and what to all appearances is random behaviour. (*See also* Bifurcation; Dissipative structures; Far-from-equilibrium; Strange attractor.)

Complementarity: The principle introduced by Niels Bohr to account for such contradictory features of quantum processes as the wave-particle duality and the difficulties of simultaneous determination of quantum events. Complementarity is, according to Bohr, the inevitable consequence of the quantum postulate that introduces an essential discontinuity (particle/wave) into subatomic processes such that an unambiguous definition of the system according to classical principles is no longer possible. That is, the particle manifestation and the wave manifestation of a quantum event, if taken independently, can be subject to unambiguous descriptions, but if taken jointly, they cannot. Abraham Pais (1991:24) observes that complementarity 'can be formulated without explicit reference to physics, to wit, as two aspects of a description that are mutually exclusive yet both necessary for a full understanding of what is to be described,' which, he adds, is a 'liberating' way of thinking. It is this broader application of complementarity that is put to use in the present volume.

Complex numbers: Formed by the combination of a 'real' number plus another real number multiplied by an 'imaginary' number of the form: $a + b\sqrt{-1}$ (where a is the 'real' number, and $b\sqrt{-1}$ is the second 'real' number multiplied by the 'imaginary' number, which is most often depicted as i, a positive value that embodies both +1 and −1). (*See also* Imaginary numbers; Real numbers.)

Convention: A term essential to any comprehension of Peirce's semiotics. Conventions, the result of *habitual* practices as a result of *embedded* dispositions, are often in the beginning arbitrarily selected; that is, they could have always been something other than what they are, hence they differ from natural practices. Conventions depend on community agreement, whether explicit or tacit, regarding customs and traditions, which largely govern individual and collective behaviour. Once established, conventions can change or be changed by fiat, by explicit agreement, or implicitly, by a process of cultural and social evolution. Of Peirce's signs, *indices* relate to their objects by natural and hence necessary means (smoke as an index of fire), *icons* are related to their objects by points of resemblance that can become part of social practices by convention (triangles representing mountains), and *symbols* (most characteristically found in language), chiefly arbitrary in the beginning, are the premier example of conventional signs. (*See also* Embedment; Habit.)

Cut: A term devised by Richard Dedekind in defining the continuum of real numbers as a combination of rational numbers (including ordinary fractions) and irrational numbers (for example $\sqrt{2}$). Dedekind defined every 'cut' in a series of rationals as a definite number, but a corresponding 'cut' in the irrationals must remain 'open,' since there is no determinable 'point' at which the 'cut' can be made. The term 'cut' is used in this enquiry as a mark of distinction made in the continuum containing the possibility of a particular sign. (*See also* Real numbers.)

Deduction: *See* Abduction.

De-generate signs: The process in which symbols are transformed (by sign *embedment*) such that they function as if they were *indexical* and *iconic* signs. Peirce by no means wished to disparage *indices* and *icons*. His use of the term is from mathematics, and divorced from the pejorative meaning of the term in ordinary language practices. De-generate signs are actually more fundamental, more essential to communication, than their more 'developed' varieties. They are 'of the greatest utility and serve purposes that genuine [symbolic] signs could not' (NE II:241). Sign de-generacy occurs in two degrees. In Peirce's words: 'A sign degenerate in the lesser degree, is an Obstinate Sign, or *Index*, which is a Sign whose significance of its object is due to its having a genuine Relation to that Object, irrespective of the Interpretant. A Sign degenerate in the greater degree is an Origination Sign or *Icon*, which is a Sign whose significant virtue is due simply to its Quality' (*CP*:2.92). In other words, a symbol, most complex and 'genuine' of Peirce's basic trio of sign types, can either de-generate in the first degree, which involves 'indexicalization,' or in the second degree, by way of 'iconization.' For instance, awareness of a metaphor (say, a 'leg' for a table support) and its full articulation as such involves *symbolicity*; interaction between the two signs, 'leg' and 'table support,' makes for the metaphoricity at the level of Thirdness. If the sign 'leg' is de-generate in the first degree the object of the metaphor is highlighted, and 'leg' relates to the table support as such. If the sign is de-generate in the second degree, the sign *qua* sign is highlighted; the table support is simply taken as 'leg,' and the word interacts with other words, as if words were in and of themselves self-sufficient; consequently, the original metaphorical quality of the sign has been lost: the metaphor is now 'dead.' (*See also* Embedment.)

Determinism: The doctrine that events are the effect of previous causes rather than their being the product of chance or of random factors. This was the grand dream of classical science.

Dicisign (or Dicent or Dicent symbol): Peirce also termed it *proposition*, but within the context of this enquiry, and more in line with currently used terminology, I have also called it statement or sentence. (*See also* Argument; Rheme.)

Dissipative structures: A chemical system capable of exporting *entropy* (disorder) and maintaining itself in a *far-from-equilibrium* condition in order to organize itself internally. Dissipative structures are the prime example of an ordering principle (order through fluctuations resulting from far-from-equilibrium conditions) that, in a manner of speaking, subverts the classical definition of the *entropy principle*, or the *Second Law of Thermodynamics*: dissipative structures are self-organizing, they lift themselves up by their own bootstraps by expelling more disorder than would ordinarily be the case, and thus enhancing their possibility for ordering themselves spontaneously. (*See also* Bifurcation; Dissipative structures; Entropy.)

DNA (deoxyribonucleic acid): A nucleic acid molecule carrying the genetic blueprint for the design and assembly of proteins, the basic structures of living systems.

Eigenvalue: From quantum theory. With respect to everything observable and measurable in a quantum system, there is a set of probable results or outcomes of the observation or measurement. This probability factor is the eigenvalue.

Embedment: The result of a sign's having become submerged into the consciousness of its author and collaborator such that its use is nonconscious, mindless, the product of what Peirce termed *habit*. Embedment is actually not a Peircean term but my own, derived from Norwood Hanson's and Michael Polanyi's philosophy of science and the psychological studies of Jerome Bruner and others. (*See also* De-generate signs; Habit).

Entropy: From thermodynamics, a measure of the order of a system and its available energy. A system of high entropy is relatively disordered and has little available energy, and vice versa. (*See also* Negentropy; Thermodynamics, Second Law of.)

Expectations: *See* Habit.

Far-from-equilibrium: A thermodynamic system that has not attained a steady state, thus maintaining an asymmetrical, unbalanced, and 'tension-ridden' condition that enables it to evolve in time. (*See also* Dissipative structures; Symmetry breaking.)

Firstness: *See* Categories.

Fluctuations: *See* Dissipative structures.

Generate signs: *See* De-generate signs.

Habit: An acquired disposition to behave in a certain manner and guided by certain motives in certain circumstances. For Peirce the use and meaning of signs is chiefly the product of habitual practices. Habit is allied with the *expectations* the semiotic agent has developed that so-and-so will occur, given such-and-such a set of conditions. When expectations are not satisfied, a surprise ensues, which leaves the agent open to novel inferential patterns – following from *abductive* acts – and new modes of action, which can once again begin their long trek toward *embedded, automatized, habitualized* behaviour. (*See also* Convention; Embedment.)

Haecceity: From medieval philosopher John Duns Scotus, it is an individually occurring event or sign, as a simple 'thisness,' devoid of acknowledged properties that link it to a generality, or a type of event or sign. (*See also* Quiddity; Type.)

Hypercycle: A closed circle of transformations by way of catalytic processes in which one or more participatory agents acts as an *autocatalyst*. The Belousov-Zhabotinsky reaction is an inorganic form of hypercycle. In view of Manfred Eigen's idea that in the organic sphere hypercycles account for life processes, they have been related in this enquiry to general sign processes. (*See also* Autocatalysis; Belousov-Zhabotinsky reaction; Catalyst.)

Icon: Of the Peircean trichotomy of signs, including *indices* and *symbols*. Icons are signs that relate to their objects by virtue of some resemblance between them, such as clouds depicted as oval shapes in a cartoon strip.

Imaginary numbers: Negative numbers existing within the square root sign such that their value is undecidable. An imaginary number is derived from the solution of $x^2 + 1 = 0$, $x^2 = -1$, $x = \sqrt{-1}$. $\sqrt{-1}$ is commonly denoted by i, which endows it with a positive rather than merely with an undecidable value. (*See also* Complex numbers; Real numbers.)

Index: Of the Peircean trichotomy of signs, including *icons* and *symbols*. Indices are signs related to their objects in terms of some actual or physical connection between them, such as smoke for fire, thunder for rain, a weather-vane for the direction of the wind.

Induction: *See* Abduction.

Interpretant: One of the three components of the Peircean sign, including the *representamen* and the *object*. The interpretant's function is that of mediator between the other two components, thus allowing the sign to become endowed with meaning for some interpreter. The term should not be confused with the interpreter. The interpreter is the semiotic agent who participates with the interpretant in bringing about the sign's development as a genuine sign, while the interpretant is the result of interaction between the sign and its object, and between sign-object and interpreter. Fundamentally there are three types of interpretants – though they can and have been divided into interpretants of various subtypes. The *immediate interpretant* is that *of* which there is not yet any conscious acknowledgment on the part of the interpreter; the *dynamical interpretant* involves the actual effect of the mediative function of the sign on the mind; and the *final interpretant* is that ultimate goal of the sign to reach the plenitude of its semiosic development – which is accessible only in the theoretical long run and hence outside the reach of the finite interpreter or interpreters. (*See also* Asymptote; Object; Representamen.)

Irreversibility: The unidirectional time evolution of a system, bringing about 'time's arrow.' (*See also* Symmetry breaking.)

Isotropy: A phenomenon, such as light travel, that exhibits the same values whether measured along a Cartesian axis in positive or negative terms. Isotropic light travel is in this manner reversible and timeless, the inverse of anisotropy. (*See also* Symmetry breaking.)

Legisign: Of the Peircean trichotomy of sign functions, including *qualisigns* and *sinsigns*. The function of legisigns is that of generality, regularity, as a type of sign of which its actual occurrence is a token. Words (symbols) are the prime example of developed legisigns. (*See also* Type.)

Light cone: From relativity theory. It designates the surface defined by the space-time paths – 'world-lines' – of all possible light rays through a given space-time point. A light cone divides the space-time continuum into three regions: (1) backward into the past, including all events that have transpired, (2) forward into the future, including all events that can transpire, and (3) elsewhere, consisting of those events that remain outside the cone, and therefore cannot exist for some observer within the cone, given the finite velocity of light. The term, *space-time slice*, used occasionally in this enquiry, consists of everything within a particular light cone at a given moment for a particular semiotic agent.

Negentropy: The push against the *entropy principle*, stipulated by the *Second Law of Thermodynamics*, of which *dissipative structures* or self-organizing systems are capable. (*See also* Dissipative structures; Far-from-equilibrium; Thermodynamics, Second Law of.)

Nonlinear systems: Systems that manifest unpredictability, as a result of *far-from-equilibrium* ('chaotic') conditions producing *dissipative structures* – a typical case is that of weather conditions. Nonlinear systems are often capable of self-organization. (*See also* Dissipative structures; Far-from-equilibrium.)

Object: One of the three components of the Peircean sign, including *representamen* and *interpretant*. It is that to which the sign relates, whether presumably 'out there' in the physical world or 'in here,' as a mind construct. Peirce makes a distinction between the *immediate object*, the object to which the sign relates before there is consciousness *of* that object, and the *dynamic object*, the object *of* consciousness, which is never exactly equivalent to the 'real' object of 'brute physical existence,' but in the best of all worlds can approach it, in asymptotic fashion. (*See also* Asymptote; Interpretant; Representamen.)

Objective idealism: The term Peirce attached to his philosophy, which, in Rescher and Brandom's (1979) conception, is a combination of 'methodological realism' and 'ontological idealism.' According to 'objective idealism,' the object of knowledge is 'real' in terms of the pragmatic operational procedures involved in knowing it, but its *being* or *essence* is an 'ideal' that remains unknowable except in the 'theoretical long run,' which is infinite in extension. Though Peirce has been charged with inconsistency, since he apparently espoused two mutually exclusive doctrines, Almeder (1980) argues for a coherent overall picture of Peirce's philosophy. (*See also* Asymptote.)

Operator: In mathematics, a function, a symbol denoting an operation to be performed.

Phanerons: *See* Phaneroscopy.

Phaneroscopy: Peirce's branch of enquiry, more commonly known today as *phenomenology*. Peirce coined the term from the Greek *phaneron*, which is in his conception the mental counterpart to signs relating to objects, acts, and events 'out there.' *Phanerons* are most properly *thought-signs*. *Phaneroscopy*, then, is the study of signs in so far as they involve categories of thought: it focuses most specifically on *thought-signs* of *Thirdness*.

Phase space: The abstract space by which *strange attractors*, among many other naturally occurring phenomena, are described. Phase space is an abstract space, different points of which correspond to different possible states of some system, say, a pendulum. The instantaneous state of a single point-particle of the system can be represented as a point in a two-dimensional phase space in which one dimension corresponds to the particle's momentun and the other to its position on the line. The evolution of the system over time would then be defined as a path or orbit through the phase space. In the case of a pendulum, movement from the extreme left-hand position to the extreme right-hand position would be described as a 180° arc above the x axis of the Cartesian plane, with the focal point at 0, and movement from right to left would be a 180° arc below the same axis, thus completing a circle. Ignoring wind resistance and other impediments, the circle would be repeated indefinitely. In the event that a *strange attractor* is exercising its force, the circle would be distorted in a potential infinity of ways, thus degenerating into increasingly chaotic behaviour. (*See also* Attractor; Strange attractor.)

Pragmatic maxim: A method for drawing out the meaning of a statement by reformulating it as a *subjunctive conditional*, the product of some *conception*, which, when applied to that statement in terms of the *practical consequences* implied, will either support or deny it. In Peirce's words, the 'maxim' goes like this: 'Consider what effects, that might conceivably have practical bearings, we conceive the object of our conception to have. Then our conception of these effects is the whole of our conception of the object' (*CP*:5.402). The implications of the 'maxim' are as thoroughly sensational (imaginary-Firstness, actual-Secondness), as they are intellectual and cognitive (inferential-Thirdness). 'This diamond is hard,' for example, means nothing unless there is some prior conception of 'hardness,' the relation of 'hard' things to 'soft' things, and the expected practical consequences of bringing the two types of things into contact. So the diamond in question is brought into contact with some softer material, say, glass, and by such contact the glass is either scratched or it is not. Putting the 'maxim' to use, then, entails a method not for determining whether a set of signs, characteristically in the form of a sentence, is timelessly and undeniably 'true.' Rather, it is an indeterminately variable method for interacting with signs in such a way that the particular 'semiotic world' with which they relate appears to be the case, and in the process their meaning emerges: the 'maxim' enables signs – including ourselves – to lift themselves up by their own bootstraps. (*See also* Abduction; Categories.)

Qualisign: Of the Peircean trichotomy of sign functions, including *sinsigns* and *legisigns*. The function of qualisigns is that of their relating to themselves and themselves alone. Qualisigns in relation to their respective objects are actual signs of another trichotomy, *icons*, *indices*, and *symbols*. In relation to their interpretants, most typically in human sign interaction, they are commonly embodied in *terms* (or words), *propositions* (or sentences), and *arguments* (or texts).

Quiddity: The whatness of a thing, its presumed essence according to how it is defined. (*See also* Haecceity.)

Real numbers: The combination of the set of all 'rational numbers' or 'whole numbers' and that of all 'irrational numbers' – whose decimal expansion is interminable, such as π and $\sqrt{2}$. (*See also* Complex numbers; Imaginary numbers.)

Representamen: One of the three components of the Peircean sign, including *objects* and *interpretants*. The representamen is Peirce's term for a 'sign' when it is related to the semiotic object and the interpretant. 'Sign,' in contrast to representamen, is of the broadest possible use, since the semiotic object and the interpretant can also function as signs. (*See also* Interpretant; Object.)

Rheme: Peirce's name for *rhematic symbols*, commonly known as *terms* or *words*. (*See also* Argument; Dicisign.)

RNA (ribonucleic acid): The genetic matter that brings about a translation of DNA into proteins.

Secondness: *See* Categories.

Self-organization: The phenomenon of a system capable of 'lifting itself by its own bootstraps' as the result of nonlinear, dissipative activity. (*See also* Dissipative structures; Far-from-equilibrium.)

Semiology: Specifically designates the study of signs in the tradition of Ferdinand de Saussure, and hence must be distinguished from Peircean semiotics.

Semiosis: A term used by Peirce to designate the general phenomena of sign processes. The very idea of semiosis challenges the common supposition that signs are relatively static instruments, as tools used to describe, and thus 'mirror,' the world. Semiosis is a dynamic process over which the semiotic agent is capable of exercising only limited control.

Semiotics: The study of signs in the Peircean tradition, in contrast to semiology, of the Saussurean tradition.

Semiotically real: For Peirce, the 'actually real,' 'brute physical existence,' remains as it is in spite of whatever we may wish to think about it, though if we are diligent, we may be able to approximate in regards to what we consider 'reality,' which is *our* 'reality,' the *semiotically real*. (*See also* Asymptote.)

Sinsign: Of the Peircean trichotomy of sign functions, including *qualisigns* and *legisigns*. *Sinsigns* are signs in so far as they are embodied in some *other*. It is the *other* to which another trichotomy of signs, *icons*, *indices*, and *symbols*, relate. And it is the *other* to which *Interpretants*, of the form most highly developed in *terms* (or words), *propositions* (or sentences), and *arguments* (or texts), are related.

Space-time slice: *See* Light cone.

Specious present: The psychological or felt present, which is of certain duration and embraced within the mind's momentary experience.

Strange attractor: An attractor is a point in *phase space* toward which the action of a dynamic system, such as a pendulum, gravitates. In the case of a pendulum, the instrument would describe back and forth movements that become smaller and smaller until it comes to rest at the centre of its *phase space*. This is called a *fixed point* attractor. A *limit cycle* attractor would be that of a pendulum under ideal conditions, without air friction or any other impediments, such that it describes the same movement over and over again, apparently without deviation. The third type of attractor is a *strange attractor*, whose movement is not periodic but aperiodic, due to some perturbation introduced in one of the cycles that causes its oscillations to become more and more chaotic. Strange attractors are, quite surprisingly, the most common in nature. (*See also* Attractor; Phase space.)

Symbol: Of the Peircean trichotomy of signs, including *icons*, and *indices*. Symbols are signs of convention, not necessarily related to their objects either by way of resemblance or by some natural connection, but by virtue of a *habit* or disposition to use a sign – often in the beginning arbitrary – as it has been established by social practices or by personal idiosyncrasies. (*See also* Convention; Embedment.)

Symmetry breaking: The transformation that culminates in Prigogine's science of complexity and process philosophy by way of the creation of irreversibility out of reversible spatial and/or temporal conditions. When time symmetry (or isotropy) is broken, the past becomes separated from the future and the macroscopic world takes on a historical dimension (anisotropy). A rupture of space symmetry creates the possibility of something different produced with every transformation of a system in space, thus leading to new forms of macroscopic order. The combination of time and space symmetry breaking gives rise to the spontaneous formation and evolution of new and more complex systems. Symmetry breaking is of paramount importance in Prigogine's *far-from-equilibrium* conditions that engender *dissipative structures*. (*See also* Dissipative structures; Far-from-equilibrium; Phase space; Strange attractors.)

Synechism: The name Peirce attached to his doctrine that all sign processes occur in a continuum.

Theoretical long run: *See* Asymptote.

Thermodynamics, Second Law of: The principle stating that in a closed system, entropy (a measure of disorder) will always tend to increase. A common example is that of two flasks of a gas, one of high temperature and the other of relatively low temperature, and connected by a tube with a stopcock. If the stopcock is opened, the gas molecules of high average velocity and those of low average velocity will trade places until both flasks are of approximately the same temperature. (*See also* Entropy.)

Thirdness: *See* Categories.

Token: *See* Type.

Tone: *See* Type.

Tychism: The name Peirce gave to his doctrine of absolute chance.

Type: A sign of generality or universality (or potentiality), capable of an indefinite number of replications, each of which is a *token*, and each *token* (sign of actuality) being the development out of a *tone* (sign of possibility). Tones are, according to this conception, of *Firstness*, tokens are of *Secondness*, and Types are of *Thirdness*, corresponding to feeling, experience, and conception, respectively. (*See also* Categories.)

Notes

Chapter 1: Of Life and Signs

1 In this regard, see Spencer-Brown (1979), and my linking his work to Peirce in Merrell (1991b, 1995); also Baer (1988), who integrates the *zero degree* of 'nothingness' into Peirce's triad to form a tetrad, the additional term remaining outside the sphere of semiosic activity in so far as we are capable of cognizing it. It is a sort of 'pre-First.'

2 Limitations of time and space do not allow for a detailed survey of the Peircean sign here, though I do so in the preceding volumes comprising this trilogy. For additional discussion, see Fisch (1986); Fitzgerald (1966); Greenlee (1973); and most especially, Savan (1987–8).

3 This image is comparable to the quivering, oscillating, scintillating *moiré* effect found in op art and other phenomena (see in general Gombrich 1979; Jenny 1967; Kauffman and Varela 1980; Ulmer 1985; also discussion in Merrell 1995).

4 I further qualify the italicized terms in chapters that follow (see also the glossary).

5 The notion that what is 'real' (i.e., 'semiotically real') is not 'real' until it is *put to use* by a participating agent falls in line with John Archibald Wheeler's (1980a, 1980b, 1984) interpretation of quantum mechanics, which I have elsewhere placed in a semiotic context (Merrell 1991b, 1995), and briefly discuss below.

6 For earlier speculation on this idea, see Beadle and Beadle (1966), Hawkins (1964), Jakobson (1973), and Masters (1970). For recent views specifically relevant to the thesis to be unfolded in this enquiry, see Berlinski (1986), Hoffmeyer and Emmeche (1991), Löfgren (1978, 1981a, 1981b, 1984), Lumsden (1986), Maturana and Varela (1980, 1987), Pattee (1969, 1972, 1977, 1986), and Varela (1979).

7 See Peirce's idea that signs, especially of the symbol type, 'grow' (*CP*:l.183, 186, 189, 191, 200; 2.229, 302; 5.448); also Rauch (1984).

8 It bears mentioning that *aperiodic crystals* enjoy counterparts in what are called *screw dislocating crystals* (Pattee 1970) and *quasicrystals* (Penrose 1989) – the latter of which are to be discussed shortly. It is originally to Louis Pasteur, however, that we owe the profound insight that the 'stereoasymmetry' of certain molecules is a fundamental property of living matter (see Bunch 1989). This suggests problems of probability regarding asymmetrical systems that lead to deviation from stable states of equilibrium toward far-from-equilibrium conditions – which is precisely the focus of Ilya Prigogine's theory of dissipative structures.

9 See especially Löfgren (1981a, 1981b, 1984), Pattee (1969, 1972, 1977, 1986), and Prigogine (1980).

10 Sheffer's 'stroke function' (and by proxy, so to speak, Peirce's 'logic of relatives') is fundamental to contemporary logic and variations of Boolean algebra (see Singh 1966; Whitehead 1938; Whitehead and Russell 1927). Interestingly enough, Whitehead and Russell (1927:xvi) demonstrated that the logical connectives can be defined by the 'stroke,' and subsequently it is possible to 'construct new propositions indefinitely.' Moreover, since the 'stroke' implies incompatibility or inconsistency in the most fundamental sense, Whitehead (1938:52) writes that it provides for 'the whole movement of logic.' And E.F. Hutten (1962:178) remarks, with respect to the 'stroke' function: 'It is the very essence of rationality to abolish contradictions; but logic – being the most rational thing in the world – is generated by contradiction.'

11 I must point out that 'de-generacy,' as the term is used here, refers to its mathematical definition, and has nothing to do with the its customary derogatory connotation in everyday language (Buczynska-Garewicz 1979; Gorleé 1990; Tursman 1987; and in particular, Merrell 1995, for the notion of sign generation and de-generation by 'upward' and 'downward' recursive processes).

12 The concept of *tacit knowledge* is primarily derivative of the work of Michael Polanyi (1958). See also Merrell (1995), for more details on *embedment/de-embedment*, and *automatization/de-automatization*.

13 See, for example, Gregory (1981) and Rock (1983), and for the notion of 'unconscious inference,' Helmholtz (1876), Popper (1972, 1974); also relevant is Polanyi's (1958) concept of *tacit knowing*.

14 If figure 3 appears strikingly comparable to Eigen's hypercycles (Eigen and Schuster 1979), it is not exactly by design, nor is it mere coincidence. I have argued that recursive cycles, whether consisting of Peirce's three sign components or his basic ten signs, is essential to his general concept of the sign (Merrell 1995).

15 Talk of sign valency is deemed appropriate, for, after all, Peirce was by profession a chemist (see Tursman 1987).

16 For Peirce's 'objective idealism,' see Almeder (1980); also Merrell (1991b, 1995).

17 This formulation evinces similarity with what in logic is known as the 'Grelling paradox' (DeLong 1970:246).

18 According to the Gaia hypothesis, everything is organism, including the entire earth itself; it is alive. Each biological organism in this sense is a sort of microcosm of the whole. Moreover, according to the 'nootemporal' concept – to be discussed below – biological evolution recapitulates the experience of an entire phylum effective in the present, a concept that quite effectively anticipates Rupert Sheldrake's (1988b) hypothesis of 'morphic fields' allowing for projection into the future for the purpose of developing subsequent action.

19 For the biological counterpart to this nature of semiosis, to be discussed further in chapters 8 and 9, see Wicken (1987:121–30).

20 For a discussion of time- and space-binding, the first entailing processes, either from multiple past configurations to some definite future configuration or from past configurations to multiple possible future configurations, and the second entailing the simultaneity of all possible configurations bound into one package, a rhizomic plenum, see Jantsch (1980). (I briefly address this topic in chapter 4).

Chapter 2: As Ongoing Semiosis

1 For the 'pragmatic maxim,' see Peirce (*CP*:2.402, 427, 5.18; *MS* 327); also Almeder (1980), Merrell (1995), and Nesher (1983, 1990).

2 The *enfolded-unfolded* image is also a metaphor of physicist David Bohm's (1980) 'holomovement,' described and related to the concept of semiosis in Merrell (1991b, 1992).

3 Regarding the 1/10 sec. time lapse between stimuli and consciousness *of* them, Norbert Wiener compares brain activity to an oscillator, in a passage that I believe merits full citation:

It is important to observe that if the frequency of an oscillator can be changed by impulses of a different frequency, the mechanism must be non-linear. A linear mechanism acting on an oscillation of a given frequency can produce only oscillation of the same frequency, generally with some change of phase and amplitude. This is not true for non-linear mechanisms, which may produce oscillations of frequencies which are the sum and differences of different orders, of the frequency of the oscillatory and the frequency of the imposed disturbance. It is quite possible for such a mechanism to displace a frequency; and in the case which we have considered, this displacement will be of the nature of an attraction. It is not too improbable that this attraction will be a long-time or secular phenomenon, and that for short times this system will remain approximately linear.

Consider the possibility that the brain contains a number of oscillators of frequencies of nearly 10 per second, and that within limitations these frequencies can be attracted to one another. Under such circumstances, the frequencies are likely to be pulled together into one or more little clumps, at least in certain regions of the spectrum. The frequencies that are pulled into these clumps will have to be pulled away from somewhere, thus causing gaps in the spectrum, where the power is lower than that which we should otherwise expect. That such a phenomenon may actually take place in the generation of brain waves for the individual

... is suggested by the sharp drop in the power for frequencies above 9.0 cycles per second (1948:199).

See also Pöppel [1972, 1988] for a well-developed argument and a liberal dose of citations regarding this phenomenon.

4 See Savan (1987–8; also Merrell 1995) for further on the types of interpretants.

5 The term 'negentropy' has been used by many cyberneticists as a swim against the current in terms of order somewhat miraculously arising out of disorder. Prigogine, however, adds a corollary: negentropy does not occur without the system itself exporting massive quantities of entropy. As I pointed out in chapter 1, you can't get something from nothing, but only something at the expense of something else.

6 In Merrell (1995:chap. 6) I attempt to illustrate how this process occurs by means of a 'nonlinear, orthocomplemented logic' as a variation of 'quantum logic,' to which I refer briefly at the end of chapter 5 of this enquiry.

7 For further on Peirce's enigmatic 'Man ≈ Sign' equation, Burks (1980), Fairbanks (1976), Merrell (1991b, 1995), Sebeok (1977b), Peirce (*CP*:5.268, 5.313, 6.332); also related to this theme is Bohm (1987), on meaning in scientific, and for that matter all, discourse.

8 In other words, Peirce's *vagueness* is always *inconsistent* in a finite world, for contradictions are duty bound to persevere; and *generality* is always *incomplete* in a finite world, for, given Hempel's (1946) 'paradox of induction,' no generality can hold absolutely nor can it be absolutely certain.

9 See Merrell (1991b, 1995) for further discussion of Wheeler and his relevance to Peircean semiotics.

10 I do not use the term 'hierarchy' according to its traditional meaning, against which poststructuralists, deconstructors, and postmodernists enjoy ranting. 'Hierarchies,' as conceived here, are not of the binary sort, with priority on one pole of the opposition. Rather, I use the term much in the manner of its use in biology, especially as revealed in the work of Pattee: a complementary relationship between distinct levels of organization, rather than pushes and shoves between opposing forces existing at the same level (see also Argyros 1991).

11 In this vein, the 'emergentist' Roger Sperry (1966) interprets consciousness as:

a direct emergent property of cerebral activity [which] is conceived to be an integral component of the brain process that functions as an essential constituent of the action and exerts a directive holistic form of control over the flow pattern of cerebral excitation ... Although the mental properties in brain activity, as here conceived, do not directly intervene in neuronal physiology, they do *supervene* ... The individual nerve impulses and associated elemental excitory events are obliged to operate within larger circuit-system configurations of which they as individuals are only a part. These larger functional entities have their own dynamics in cerebral activity with their own qualities and properties. They interact causally with one another at their own level as entities. It is the emergent dynamic properties of certain of these higher specialized cerebral processes that are interpreted to be the substance of consciousness. (Dewan 1976:184)

12 Admittedly, some scholars, among them Charles Morris (1938), have rather unfortunately given a behaviourist interpretation to Peirce (but see Almeder 1980 and Rochberg-Halton 1986 for a contrary view).

13 In general, when Schrödinger's *differentials* associated with consciousness are brought to the level of awareness, then the subject can potentially effectuate changes in her behaviour as well as her conception and perception of her world. The ontogeny of the subject is not merely located in the brain, but rather, in the entire individual – and by extension, collective – soma. It is the entrenched repetition of a string of events that have taken place in much the same fashion thousands of times in the past. It brings about actions and reactions on the part of the individual without her having any longer to 'think about' them.

Chapter 3: The Time of the Mind-Sign

1 The intrinsic-extrinsic perspectives in relation to the work of Spencer-Brown (1979) is an outgrowth of Maturana-Varela's (1980, 1987; Varela 1979) interpretation of him, as I have developed the topic elsewhere (Merrell 1982, 1983, 1985, 1991b, 1995).

2 Cf. note 8 of chapter 1. I have discussed the terms *vague* and *general*, in conjunction with *inconsistency* and *incompleteness*, in previous enquiries (Merrell 1991b, 1995), following initial suggestions by Rescher and Brandom (1979), and refer to them, with brief commentary, in the remaining chapters of this volume.

3 See Dozoretz's (1979) treatment of such a 'middle ground' regarding Peirce's distinction between the mathematically 'real,' the 'real,' and the fictitious. I also refer briefly to this topic in chapter 9.

4 For more detail, Merrell (1985a, 1985b, 1991b, 1995).

5 Significantly enough, a variant of this idea had already been developed by Eddington (1946) in his attempt to account for the existence of the observer in an extradimensional domain.

6 It bears mentioning that process philosopher Henri Bergson (1911), somewhat comparable to Peirce, argues that there is much more to consciousness than discontinuous shifts from one state to another. Consciousness is for him a continuous movement in 'real time.' He insists on the distinction between 'real time' (duration of 'being') and what I have here dubbed imaginary, complex, or abstract time (the atemporality of 'nonbeing'), and on an indisoluble link between 'real time' as duration and evolution as a process of life (a topic to be taken up in chapters 8 and 9).

7 For illuminating work on the nature and problem of dispositions, with occasional reference to Peirce, I recommend Hacking (1975, 1990).

8 Eddington coins the term 'arrow of time' to qualify the indomitable irreversibility as illustrated by a stone dropped in a placid pond causing ripples to move outward in concentric circles. What is virtually unthinkable is a situation in which the ripples reverse themselves and converge to a central point, somehow sucking in energy as they do so: a 'negentropic' move.

9 We have a remarkable image of the distinction between the two orders in question in Jorge Luis Borges' (1962) 'Library of Babel,' organized in the order of the B-series, and the inhabitants, each with his/her minuscule mind playing out of his/her individual A-series, while trying to find some semblance of order in the nightmarish system (more on this in chapter 9).

10 This phenomenon has been subjected, by Goodman (1978), to a radical constructivist philosophy, which is quite in line with the chapters that follow in this volume.

11 Interestingly enough, and in conjunction with note 3 of chapter 2, the duration of the experiential moment of consciousness has been variously estimated by Buddhists to be approximately 1/75 second, or about 13 milliseconds, which agrees quite closely with the results of experimental psychology (Conze 1970; Whitrow 1980). According to Buddhist thought, these durations merge in natural, automatic, causal processes, abiding momentarily and then separating again in constant turmoil, to produce, given our persistence of vision, the appearance of the world as we know it (Hayward 1987).

12 It bears mentioning at this point that neither Wheeler, Prigogine, nor Peirce advocates any form or fashion of idealism whereby the universe of becoming is dependent on the mind's making it so. To cite Popper (1974:160), that indefatigable realist, theories of the classical sort brand 'unidirectional change as an illusion. This makes the catastrophe of Hiroshima an illusion. Thus it makes our world an illusion, and with it all our attempts to find out more and more about our world. It is therefore self-defeating (like every idealism).' With a favourable nod to Popper – at least in this respect – and in line with Wheeler, Prigogine, and Peirce, the universe is there, for sure, as a 'real' entity. Bits and pieces of it have become mind-dependent 'semiotically real' phenomena for some agent or other and *put to use* according to particular interpretations of them. Yet the 'real' continues to exist, independently of any and all semiotic agents.

13 For further discussion on this topic with respect to time, see Whitrow (1980:314–52), Smart (1964), Capek (1965), Grünbaum (1963).

Chapter 4: A Pluralist Semiotic Universe

1 I write 'semiotic units' in reference to signs of various types and degrees of complexity so as to differentiate them from 'semiotic objects,' which are a necessary component of the signs.

2 A look at Bunn's (1981) treatment of 'four-dimensional semiotic objects' – unfortunately, limitations of time and space do not permit their full discussion here – might be helpful in conjunction with my own remarks on this topic.

3 See also Merrell (1991b) on Fraser from within a different semiotic context.

4 As a brief aside, Layzer (1975) puts forth the radical hypothesis that even if a Laplacean Superobserver could exist, total information about the universe at the molecular scale would still be impossible. He concludes:

> The order is unknowable even in principle. Imagine an unbounded stack of playing cards, topless and bottomless, deck piled on deck without limit. Information about the order of the cards in one section of the stack is of no help, because any given sequence is repeated an infinite number of times elsewhere, in the same way that patterns of stars and galaxies are repeated throughout the universe. It is meaningless to say that you are at such and such a place in the stack, even when you have full information about the order of the cards and that place. You still don't know whereabouts you are in the stack, any more than the typical observer knows whereabouts he is in the cosmos. The Cosmological Principle says he doesn't know and he can't know. (in Campbell 1982:89)

This stack of cards is indeed a counterpart to Borges' Library, as I have observed elsewhere (Merrell 1991a).

5 It bears pointing out that within the *eotemporal* realm there is dual recognition of time: (1) chronometric – clock time with which to measure which events come before and which after, from a given frame of reference – whose nature is in the order of symmetry, reversibility, mirror reflexivity, and (2) entropic – an instrument, such as a thermometer, for measuring dissipation of energy and establishing a before and an after. Both of these times are in essence of the B-series variety. A-series time, in contrast, is transitive; its perception pertains most properly to the *biotemporal*, and especially in the human subjective sense, to the *nootemporal* sphere.

6 The problematics of whether irreversibility is real or a construct of the mind is most forcibly foregrounded here. In one form or another, Wigner, cited above, and others (Herbert 1985; Sarfatti 1974; Walker 1970; Wolf 1986) attempt to integrate consciousness into the quantum theoretical equation. One of the most ambitious attempts to do so – though he and Wigner would lock horns – and quite in line with Peircean semiotics as herein presented, is that of Wheeler's (1980a, 1980b) 'self-excited' universe. Past, present, and future depend on conscious (semiotic) agents as *participatory*, bringing them into existence and pushing the entire universe toward its completion (see also Skolimowski 1987, for the metaphysical ramifications of Wheeler's view).

7 See also Jakobson (1984). However, more in line with the tenets of the present study, Einstein's work should be brought into relation with the work of Benjamin L. Whorf's linguistic relativity, a topic perceptively developed by Heynick (1983).

8 Of course, it might also be contended that these a prioris are culture-bound and language-bound, stemming from the work of Benjamin L. Whorf and those who have followed him – but for a critique of this view, see Rosch (1974, 1975, 1977).

9 Admittedly, the table contains binaries. But saving grace is to be had, I would submit, in so far as the processes of sign generacy and de-generacy are a fact of life, thus serving to fuse all virgules between otherwise dichotomous terms, which, I expect, will become apparent as the following chapters unfold.

10 Without being able to do just service to this intriguing problem here, I refer the reader to Michael Lockwood's (1991) ruminations on quantum theory in his attempt to come to grips with the place of mind and consciousness in the universe (also Zohar 1990).

11 This facet of Peirce's thought is cited often in conjunction with his notion of *abduction* (*CP*:1.121, 5.591, 5.604, 7.39, 7.220; also Fann 1970).

12 See Gregory (1988) for an excellent argument to the effect that physics is about language (signs) more than about hard-nosed data and the physical objects of the world.

13 In Merrell (1995:chap. 7), I offer a more detailed account of the semiosic process transpiring in Macbeth's brain-mind as he became aware of the dagger-figment before him.

14 For example, see Kauffman (1986), Kauffman and Varela (1980), Spencer-Brown (1979).

Chapter 5: Space-Time, and the Place of the Sign

1 However, to reiterate, there is no immediacy of sensations directly available to the conscious mind. Relative immediacy of sensations as the phrase is used here alludes to tacit inferences, nonconscious perceptual judgments, which downplay the role of intellection and control (yielding primary qualities) and highlight surface appearances (of secondary qualities).

2 Piaget (1971:221–3) refers to McCulloch and Pitts' 'neural nets' edified upon the 16 functions of the bivalent logic of propositons (McCulloch 1965:205).

3 The 'holism' presented here is more attuned to Glaserfeld than Quine. That is to say, it is of 'semiotically real' worlds as *Umwelt*-dependent, rather than the radically 'linguicentric' Quinean view (but for variations on and moderations of this 'linguicentrism,' see Davidson 1984; Fodor and Lepore 1992; Evnine 1991; Putnam 1990).

4 See Varela (1984b) and von Foerster (1984), for experiments and thought experiments in neurophysiology and psychology that substantiate this phenomenon.

5 Interestingly enough, studies have demonstrated that children spontaneously tend to produce drawings comparable to Klee, Miró, and Picasso, which adds support

to Heelan's contention that the non-Euclidean perspective is 'deeper' than the Euclidean one (Campbell 1986; see also *CP*:5.145).

6 In Merrell (1985a) I outline points of contact between Peirce and Derrida, and in Merrell (1991b) I briefly write on Deleuze (and Guattari) and Peirce.

7 I should point out at this juncture that Piaget labels his interpretation of structuralism 'genetic structuralism,' though actually, in light of the view being unfolded here it should be dubbed 'de-generate' in the sense that the tendency is toward equilibrium, symmetry, and homeostasis, with a minimum of conflict and tension.

8 In this respect, paramorphic models are also comparable to Mary Hesse's (1966) 'analogical models' in science (see also Leatherdale 1974).

9 The reader will have undoubtedly found my relating metaphors to paramorphic rather than homeomorphic models strange. Yet the interactionist theory of metaphor (Black 1962) evinces striking parallels with Peirce's diagrams (constituting a type of *hypoicon*, along with images and metaphors). Both involve relations between parts (attributes) of two entities, as schemata, such interaction arising, most properly speaking, as Seconds.

10 For example, see Eliade (1959) and Jung (1964) on the heterogeneous space of myth, ritual, and subjectivity in general, in contrast to the space of Cartesian-Newtonian space.

11 This view of time, by the way, is reminiscent of the Mathematician's imaginary time as a series of point-instants, in light of the disquisition in chapter 3 – though Bergson (1911) argues to the contrary.

12 The 'semiotic logic' or 'logic of semiosis' I refer to is a 'nonlinear orthocomplemented logic' of the most general sort which includes classical orthodox linear logic within local domains (see Merrell 1995).

Chapter 6: Assembly-Line Signs, and Beyond

1 As mentioned in the preface of this volume, I have written on postmodernism and its relation to Peircean semiotics in *Semiosis in the Postmodern Age* (1995). Here, however, I attempt to boot the postmodern theme to a higher level, ultimately relating it to the 'Life ≈ Signs' equation.

2 Consequently, it might appear that upon attempting to qualify our present *mise en scène*, this maelstrom of enigmatically organized complexity, I can do no more than dwell on surface features, on the radical foregrounding of 'information' to the exclusion of form and of any sort of putative 'deep meaning.' This is actually quite in keeping with our postmodern world, concerned as it is with surface appearances. Nothing of import, no difference that really makes a difference, should lie occult, to be disinterred by anointed – or self-appointed – priests and priestesses of analytical methods at considerable cost of time and effort. Whatever requires

undue expenditure of labour is usually not supposed to be worth the risk anyway, for all signs must offer themselves up for our consumption in terms simply of what they are, or appear to be – or at least that is the tale we are often told. Needless to say, while on the one hand I defer somewhat to the postmodern attitude, on the other, I differ from it. I have, throughout the three volumes making up this study, attempted to strike a balance between description and explanation-understanding, analysis and synthesis, explicitness and implicitness, and cognition and intuitive sensibilities.

3 Regarding the 'mode of information' in postmodern society, see, in addition to Poster, Agger (1990), Harvey (1989), Huyssen (1986), Jameson (1992), Kellner (1989), Wakefield (1990), Wellmer (1976, 1985).

4 Along comparable lines, and in addition to Baudrillard, for example, Houston (1984), Marchland (1985), Poster (1990).

5 However, it bears pointing out that Charles Jencks (1977) would label Jameson's conception and terminology part and parcel of late-modernism rather than postmodernism.

6 Baudrillard is influenced in developing his three orders of simulacra and the transitions between them by Foucault's 'epistemic shifts,' via Gaston Bachelard. His conception of simulacra is also somewhat comparable to Charles Morris' (1946:23) 'pure' iconic signs, which consist of duplicity, reproduction, replication. The problem is that, as we shall note, Baudrillard's lead-headed masses do not conceive simulacra as such. To all appearances they take them in as de-generate signs, but as if they were Peirce's 'pure' icons, which – contra Morris – are mere quality, and unrelated to anything else as such.

7 In fact, Baudrillard argues, even the most adverse of antagonisms – capitalism and socialism – are annulled by the natural dependence of one upon the other. Consequently, they are free to open themselves up to cooperation and collaboration. But if this should occur, the dyad could run the risk of melting entirely, as we have witnessed over the past couple of years.

8 I write 'bordering on Secondness,' since the signs as mere atoms enjoy hardly any relation to the realm of Firstness from which they emerged or to that of Thirdness into which they are in the process of passing away. And, with no more than a bare suggestion of their object, or even of their surrounding neighbours, they are only a pale reflection of genuine Secondness.

9 Significantly, in this regard, Derrida in 'The Ends of Man,' while attempting to seek out and destroy the remnants of humanism in Western thought, offers a comparable statement: 'His [Zarathustra's] laughter then will burst out, directed toward a return which no longer will have the form of the metaphysical repetition of humanism, nor, doubtless, 'beyond' metaphysics, the form of a memorial or a guarding of the meaning of Being, the form of the house and of the truth of Being. He will

dance, outside the house, the *aktive Vergesslichkeit*, the 'active forgetting,' and the cruel (*grausam*) feast of which the *Genealogy of Morals* speaks' (1982:136).

10 Lyotard (1984) offers diatribes against the Enlightenment dreams of modernity, in line with the general postmodernist posture, and against Habermas (1979, 1984, 1987). From a comparable neopragmatist antimodernist perspective, see Bernstein (1983, 1992), Rajchman and West (1985) and Rorty (1991), and for the debate on Habermas, Bernstein (1985), and Kolb (1990).

11 Such neutral discourse would be tantamount, we must suppose, to Barthes's (1964) 'degree zero' language and that of Group μ (1981) by the same name. But if such discourse were actually to exist, it would be antithetical to the truly scientific mode (Merrell 1995:chap. 7).

12 As I maintained in note 12, chapter 5, I have elsewhere developed a logic of 'orthocomplementarity' as a model of semiosis.

Chapter 7: Rhetoric, Syncopation, and Signs of Three

1 At the outset I will be charged once again with artificially erecting a couple of towers of hierarchical, binary oppositions. I hope to illustrate, however, that the system is as a whole dynamic, ongoing, and ever-changing, given its myriad complexity.

2 In this regard see Merrell (1985b), for what I have termed 'semantic lag,' the hysteresic or lagging effect of language (representation, semiotic objects) behind the meanings (thought, interpretants) intended.

3 I repeat my reference to Tursman (1987) and to my own observations on this topic (Merrell 1995).

Chapter 8: Knowing Signs, Living Knowledge

1 But see a critique of this view in Hesse (1980) and Hacking (1983); also Merrell (1991b, 1995).

2 Nor do we find any answer in the humanities. Derrida's now notorious view – and Rorty's (1979) from among other vantages – that we cannot step outside our metaphysics is a point well taken (also Baynes et al. 1987; Bernstein 1986; de Gramont 1990; Harvey 1986; O'Hara 1985; Sacks 1989). Furthermore, the complementary notion that we cannot step outside our ethnocentrism has become prevalent over the past years in the social sciences (Hollis and Lukes 1982; Jarvie 1984; Keesing 1987; Krausz 1989; Marcus and Fischer 1986; Tyler 1987).

3 Peirce maintained faith in the 'reality' of types, though he argued time and again that we can never know that 'reality' in all its plenitude. In this sense, pragmatism is actually more hopeful than the stock interpretations of poststructuralism, deconstruction, and postmodernism. Yet it is not exactly 'realist,' but 'objectively

idealistic' in so far as we might as well forget the unrelenting dreams of reason, truth, and the good life for all, and simply do the best we can (also Rorty 1982, though he is critical of Peirce on other points). And it is not 'idealist,' strictly speaking, for the 'real' does exist, though we, as a mere bundle of energy, material, and information, cannot know the world as it is; we can only become aware of what we thought we knew but did not.

4 Regarding this controversy, see Eco (1986), Ransdell (1979, 1986), Pignatari (1983), Sebeok (1976b).

5 See also Escher's 'Print Gallery,' for comparable Möbius-strip folds (and discussion in Merrell 1995).

6 I refer the reader also to Hofstadter's (1979) masterful discussion of Escher's 'Hands.'

Chapter 9: Chance and Legacy

1 Indeed, the legacy of Saussurean semiology is Darwinian through and through. Tim Ingold (1986:chap. 4) offers an excellent commentary on semiology in relation to the mechanistic view of evolution, though, to my way of thinking, he does not go far enough.

2 Sebeok's (1979:xii) observation is unfortunately still part and parcel of the mechanical model, and I suspect he would modify it somewhat in light of recent findings.

3 See Lewontin, Rose, and Kamin (1984), and Ingold (1986), for an elaborate argument against determinism either of the biological or cultural variety, or any combination thereof.

4 Though he is vague on this issue, Hassan has – most likely unwittingly – fallen into this trap. More recently, Poster (1989), and even Jameson (1992), Kroker (1992), and Lasch (1977), place undue emphasis on the signifier/signified breach and binarism. Granted, they focus on larger, exceedingly more complex issues. But by and large they unfortunately reduce these issues to aleatoric, atomistic comings and goings of *minutiae*. These moves are a counterpart to Eco (1976, 1979) in his effort to wed Peirce and Saussure – strange bedfellows – upon drawing on AI models and cybernetic concepts and terminology, which are, I would suggest, actually quite alien to Peirce, not to mention Saussure.

5 In anthropology, the *meme* has been taken to be the cultural analogue of the *gene*. It is extrasomatic in terms of its being an elemental structure, and endosomatic in so far as it is centred within the individual. It can be conceived as 'implicit culture,' embedded semiosic behaviour (Gerard, Kluckhohn, and Rapoport 1956:10), or more technically, as a 'mnemotype' (Blum 1963). I here use the meme-gene pair

of terms much as does Ingold (1986), and, in addition, interject it into the general semiosic process.

Chapter 10: For a Critique of the Autonomy of the Sign

1 Regarding Wittgenstein's remarks on such series, which bear on his philosophy of mathematics, see Kripke (1982; for comments on, Merrell 1992:ch. 5).
2 I also touch on this theme in the final chapter of *Signs Becoming Signs* (Merrell 1991b).
3 Peirce's *breadth* and *depth* are qualified as *extension-denotation* and *comprehension-connotation* (though care must be exercised here, for the concepts are not to be related either to the Fregean tradition or analytic philosophy). He further subdivides his pair of terms into (1) *essential* breadth and depth, (2) *substantial* breadth and depth, and (3) *informed* breadth and depth corresponding to Firstness, Secondness, and Thirdness respectively. The first is a condition of factual ignorance but of the possibility for future actuals, the second is the realm of existents, and the third is mediated by language (for additional, see Goudge 1952; Liszka 1989; Merrell 1995).
4 The underscored terms are Spinoza's, taken up by Bohm (1980) and Deleuze (1990); see also Merrell (1991b, 1995).
5 In *Pararealities* (1983) I discuss the consequences of this fourth category, following Spencer-Brown's elegant calculus outlined in his *Laws of Form* (1979).
6 It is reminiscent of what I have elsewhere hyperbolically called the 'octopus model,' a universe of point-signs each of which is an 'octopus-body' whose 'tentacles' are the infinite number of lines emanating from that point ready and waiting to suck in one or more of all the other point-signs (Merrell 1986).
7 In fact, Foucault's focus during his earlier years on 'archaeology' in *The Order of Things* (1970) reveals an important facet of the alternating climate in our so-called postmodern world regarding signs, their genesis, life, and ultimately, death.
8 An even more extreme case is found in Nesher (1983, 1990) whom I have briefly taken to task elsewhere (Merrell 1991b).
9 Worthy of note are key entries in the *Encyclopedic Dictionary of Semiotics* (Sebeok et al. 1986; also see Nöth 1990). Regarding recent extensive work on Peircean semiotics and literature, see especially Finlay (1990), Johansen (1992), Sheriff (1989), and, of course, Eco (1991).
10 This is the essence, as I have suggested throughout this trilogy, of Wheeler's 'meaning physics,' which is radically semiotic in nature (see Sebeok 1991).

References

Agger, Ben (1990). *The Decline of Discourse: Reading, Writing and Resistance in Postmodern Capitalism*. New York: Falmer.

Almeder, Robert (1980). *The Philosophy of Charles S. Peirce: A Critical Introduction*. Totowa, NJ: Rowman and Littlefield.

Argyros, Alexander J. (1991). *A Blessed Rage for Order: Deconstruction, Evolution, and Chaos*. Ann Arbor: University of Michigan Press.

Arnheim, Rudolf (1954). *Art and Visual Perception*. Berkeley: University of California Press.

Baer, Eugen (1988). *Medical Semiotics*. Lanham: University Press of America.

Barth, John (1968). *Lost in the Funhouse: Fictions for Print, Type, Live Voice*. Garden City, NY: Doubleday.

Barthes, Roland (1964). *Writing Degree Zero*. Boston: Beacon.

– (1972). *Mythologies*, trans. A. Lavers. New York: Hill and Wang.

Bateson, Gregory (1972). *Steps to an Ecology of Mind*. New York: Chandler.

Baudrillard, Jean (1975). *The Mirror of Production*, trans. M. Poster. St Louis: Telos.

– (1981). *For a Critique of the Political Economy of the Sign*, trans. C. Levin. St Louis: Telos.

– (1983a). *Simulations*. New York: Semiotext(e).

– (1983b). *In the Shadow of the Silent Majorities*, trans. P. Foss, J. Johnston, and P. Patton. New York: Semiotext(e).

– (1988). *The Ecstasy of Communication*, trans. B. Schutze and C. Schutze. New York: Semiotext(e).

Baynes, Kenneth, James Bohman, and Thomas McCarthy, eds. (1987). *After Philosophy: End or Transformation?* Cambridge: MIT.

Beadle, George and Muriel Beadle (1966). *The Language of Life*. Garden City, NY: Doubleday.

Beckett, Samuel (1955). *Molloy, Malone Dies, The Unnamable*. New York: Grove Press.

Bellone, Enrico (1982). *A World on Paper: Studies on the Second Scientific Revolution.* Cambridge: MIT.

Benardete, José A. (1964). *Infinity: An Essay in Metaphysics.* Oxford: Clarendon Press.

Benveniste, Emile (1971). *Problems in General Linguistics*, trans. M. Meek. Coral Gables: University of Florida Press.

Bergson, Henri (1911). *Creative Evolution.* New York: Modern Library.

– (1935). *The Two Sources of Morality and Religion.* New York: Holt.

Berlinski, David (1986). 'The Language of Life.' *In Complexity, Language, and Life: Mathematical Approaches*, ed. J.L. Casti and A. Karlqvist, 331–67. Berlin: Springer-Verlag.

Bernal, John Desmond (1967). *The Origins of Life.* Cleveland: World.

Bernstein, Richard J. (1983). *Beyond Objectivism and Relativism: Science, Hermeneutics, and Praxis.* Philadelphia: University of Pennsylvania Press.

– (1986). *Philosophical Profiles: Essays in a Pragmatic Mode.* Pittsburgh: University of Pennsylvania Press.

– (1992). *The New Constellation: The Ethical-Political Horizons of Modernity/Postmodernity.* Cambridge: MIT.

– ed. (1985). *Habermas and Modernity.* Cambridge: MIT.

Berry, George D.W. (1952). 'Peirce's Contribution to the Logic of Statements and Quantifiers.' In *Studies in the Philosophy of Charles Sanders Peirce*, ed. P.P. Wiener and F.H. Young, 143–52. Cambridge: Harvard University Press.

Bertalanffy, Ludwig von (1968). *General Systems Theory.* New York: Braziller.

Black, Max (1962). *Models and Metaphors.* Ithaca, NY: Cornell University Press.

Blum, H.F. (1963). 'On the Origin and Evolution of Human Culture.' *American Scientist* 51, 32–47.

Bohm, David (1957). *Causality and Chance in Modern Physics.* Philadelphia: University of Pennsylvania Press.

– (1965). *The Special Theory of Relativity.* New York: Benjamin.

– (1980). *Wholeness and the Implicate Order.* London: Routledge and Kegan Paul.

– (1987). *Unfolding Meaning.* London: ARK.

Bohr, Niels (1958). *Atomic Physics and Human Knowledge.* New York: Wiley.

Borges, Jorge Luis (1962). *Labyrinths: Selected Stories and Other Writings*, ed. D.A. Yates and J.E. Irby. New York: New Directions.

Bouissac, Paul, et al, eds. (1986). *Iconicity: Essays on the Nature of Culture.* Tübingen: Stauffenburg Verlag.

Bridgman, Percy W. (1959). *The Way Things Are.* Cambridge: Harvard University Press.

Brillouin, L. (1949). 'Life, Thermodynamics and Cybernetics.' *American Scientist* 37, 554–68.

Brooks, Daniel R. and E.O. Wiley (1986). *Evolution as Entropy: Toward a Unified Theory.* Chicago: University of Chicago Press.

Bruner, Jerome (1957). 'Going Beyond the Information Given.' In *Contemporary Approaches in Cognition* (Symposium held at the University of Colorado), 41–69. Cambridge: Harvard University Press.

Buchler, Justus (1955). *Nature and Judgment*. New York: Grosset and Dunlap.

Buczynska-Garewicz, Hanna (1979). 'The Degenerate Sign.' In *Semiotics Unfolding* (Proceedings of the Second Congress of the International Association for Semiotic Studies) vol. 1, ed. T. Borbé, 43–50. Berlin: Mouton de Gruyter.

Bunch, Bryan (1989). *Reality's Mirror: Exploring the Mathematics of Symmetry*. New York: Wiley.

Bunn, James H. (1981). *The Dimensionality of Signs, Tools, and Models*. Bloomington: Indiana University Press.

Burks, Arthur W. (1980). 'Man: Sign or Algorithm? A Rhetorical Analysis of Peirce's Semiotics.' *Transactions of the Charles S. Peirce Society* 16 (4), 279–92.

Cairns-Smith, A.G. (1982). *Genetic Takeover and the Mineral Origins of Life*. Cambridge: Cambridge University Press.

Campbell, Donald T. (1974a). 'Unjustified Variation and Selective Retention in Sociocultural Evolution.' In *Studies in the Philosophy of Biology*, ed. F.J. Ayala and T. Dobzhansky, 139–61. Berkeley: University of California Press.

– (1974b). 'Evolutionary Epistemology.' In *The Philosophy of Karl Popper*, ed. P.A. Schilpp, 413–63. LaSalle, IL: Open Court.

Campbell, Jeremy (1982). *Grammatical Man: Information, Entropy, Language, and Life*. New York: Simon and Schuster.

– (1986). *Winston Churchill's Afternoon Nap: A Wide-Awake Inquiry into the Human Nature of Time*. New York: Simon and Schuster.

Capek, Milic (1961). *The Philosophical Impact of Contemporary Physics*. New York: American Book.

– (1965). 'The Myth of the Frozen Passage: The Status of Becoming in the Physical World.' In *Boston Studies in the Philosophy of Science*, vol. 2, ed. R.S. Cohen and M.W. Wartofsky, 441–61. Dordrecht, Holland: D. Reidel.

– (1972). 'The Fiction of Instants.' In *The Study of Time*, ed. J.T. Fraser, F.C. Huber, and G.H. Miller, 332–44. Berlin: Springer-Verlag.

Cassirer, Ernst (1944). *An Essay on Man: An Introduction to a Philosophy of Human Culture*. New Haven: Yale University Press.

Casti, John L. and A. Karlqvist, eds. (1986). *Complexity, Language, and Life: Mathematical Approaches*. Berlin: Springer-Verlag.

Charon, Jean E. (1987). 'The Real and the Imaginary in Complex Relativity.' In *The Real and the Imaginary: A New Approach to Physics*, ed. J.E. Charon, 47–68. New York: Paragon House.

Cherry, Colin (1953). 'Some Experiments upon the Recognition of Speech, with One and with Two Ears.' *Journal of the Acoustic Society of America* 25, 975–9.

– (1954). 'Some Further Experiments upon the Recognition of Speech, with One and with Two Ears.' *Journal of the Acoustic Society of America* 26, 554–9.

– (1968). *On Human Communication*. Cambridge: MIT.

Colapietro, Vincent (1986). 'Peirce's Various Attempts to Define Semiosis.' *Semiotics 1986*, ed. J. Deely, 350–61. Lanham, MD: University Press of America.

– (1989). *Peirce's Approach to the Self: A Semiotic Perspective on Human Subjectivity*. Albany: State University of New York Press.

Comfort, Alex (1984). *Reality and Empathy: Physics, Mind, and Science in the 21st Century*. Albany: State University of New York Press.

Conze, Edward (1970). *Buddhist Thought in India*. Ann Arbor: University of Michigan Press.

Cornford, F. (1936). 'The Invention of Space.' In *Essays in Honour of Gilbert Murray*, ed. H.A.L. Fisher, et al, 215–35. London: Allen and Unwin.

Culler, Jonathan (1981). *The Pursuit of Signs: Semiotics, Literature, Deconstruction*. Ithaca, NY: Cornell University Press.

Dantzig, Tobias (1930). *Number: The Language of Science*, 4th ed. New York: Free Press.

Davidson, Donald (1984). *Inquiries into Truth and Interpretation*. Oxford: Clarendon Press.

Davies, Paul (1988). *The Cosmic Blueprint*. New York: Simon and Schuster.

Davis, Joel (1991). *Mapping the Code: The Human Genome Project and the Choices of Modern Science*. New York: Wiley.

Dawkins, Richard (1986). *The Blind Watchmakers*. New York: Norton.

Deleuze, Gilles (1968). *Différence et répétition*. Paris: PUF.

– (1990a). *The Logic of Sense*. New York: Columbia University Press.

– (1990b). *Expressionism in Philosophy: Spinoza*. New York: Zone Books.

Deleuze, Gilles and Félix Guattari (1983). *Anti-Oedipus: Capitalism and Schizophrenia, I*. Minneapolis: University of Minnesota Press.

– (1986). *Kafka: Toward a Minor Literature*, trans. D. Polan (Theory and History of Literature, 30). Minneapolis: University of Minnesota Press.

– (1987). *A Thousand Plateaus: Capitalism and Schizophrenia, II*, trans. B. Massumi. Minneapolis: University of Minnesota Press.

DeLong, Howard (1970). *A Profile of Mathematical Logic*. New York: Addison-Wesley.

Denbigh, Kenneth G. (1975). *An Inventive Universe*. London: Hutchinson.

Denbigh, K.G. and J.S. Denbigh (1985). *Entropy in Relation to Incomplete Knowledge*. Cambridge: Cambridge University Press.

Derrida, Jacques (1972). *Positions*. Paris: Editions de Minuit.

– (1973). *Speech and Phenomena, And Other Essays on Husserl's Theory of Signs*, trans. D.B. Allison. Evanston, IL: Northwestern University Press.

– (1978). *Writing and Difference*, trans. A. Bass. Chicago: University of Chicago Press.

– (1982). *Margins of Philosophy*, trans. A. Bass. Chicago: University of Chicago Press.

Dewan, E.M. (1976). 'Consciousness as an Emergent Causal Agent in the Context of Control System Theory.' In *Consciousness and the Brain: A Scientific and Philosophical Inquiry*, ed. G.G. Globus, G. Maxwell, and I. Savodnik, 181–98. New York: Plenum.

Dewey, John (1946). 'Peirce's Theory of Linguistic Signs, Thought, and Meaning.' *Journal of Philosophy* 43 (4), 85–95.

De Witt, Bryce, and Neill Graham, eds. (1973). *The Many-Worlds Interpretation of Quantum Mechanics*. Princeton, NJ: Princeton University Press.

Dobbs, H.A.C. (1971). 'The Dimensions of the Sensible Present.' *Studium Generale* 24, 108–26.

Dobzhansky, Theodosius G. (1962). *Mankind Evolving: The Evolution of the Human Species*. New Haven: Yale University Press.

– (1974). 'Chance and Creativity in Evolution.' In *Studies in the Philosophy of Biology*, ed. F.J. Ayala and T. Dobzhansky, 307–37. Berkeley: University of California Press.

Dozoretz, Jerry (1979). 'The Internally Real, the Fictitious, and the Indubitable.' In *Studies in Peirce's Semiotic, 1*, ed. J.E. Brock, et al, 77–87. Lubbock, TX: Institute for Studies in Pragmaticism.

Dreyfus, Huber L. and Paul Rabinow (1982). *Michel Foucault: Beyond Structuralism and Hermeneutics*. Chicago: University of Chicago Press.

Dunne, J.W. (1934). *The Serial Universe*. London: Faber and Faber.

Eco, Umberto (1976). *A Theory of Semiotics*. Bloomington: Indiana University Press.

– (1979). *The Role of the Reader: Explorations in the Semiotics of Texts*. Bloomington: Indiana University Press.

– (1984). *Semiotics and the Philosophy of Language*. Bloomington: Indiana University Press.

– (1986). 'Mirrors.' In *Iconicity: Essays on the Nature of Culture*, ed. P. Bouissac et al, 215–38. Tübingen: Stauffenburg Verlag.

– (1991). *The Limits of Interpretation*. Bloomington: Indiana University Press.

Eco, Umberto, and Thomas A. Sebeok, eds. (1983). *The Sign of Three: Dupin, Holmes, Peirce*. Bloomington: Indiana University Press.

Eddington, Arthur S. (1946). *Fundamental Theory*. Cambridge: Cambridge University Press.

– (1958a). *The Nature of the Physical World*. Ann Arbor: University of Michigan Press.

– (1958b). *The Philosophy of Physical Science*. Ann Arbor: University of Michigan Press.

– (1959). *Space, Time and Gravitation: An Outline of the General Relativity Theory*. New York: Harper and Row.

Edgerton, S.Y., Jr. (1976). *The Renaissance Rediscovery of Linear Perspective*. New York: Harper and Row.

Eigen, Manfred (1971). 'Self-Organization of Matter and the Evolution of Biological Macromolecules.' *Naturwissenschaften* 58, 465–523.

Eigen, Manfred, and Peter Schuster (1977). 'The Hypercycle: A Principle of Self-Organization. Part A: Emergence of the Hypercycle.' *Naturwissenschaften* 64, 541–65.

– (1978a). 'The Hypercycle: A Principle of Self-Organization. Part B: The Abstract Hypercycle.' *Naturwissenschaften* 65, 7–41.

– (1978b). 'The Hypercycle: A Principle of Self-Organization. Part C: The Realistic Hypercycle.' *Naturwissenschaften* 65, 347–69.

– (1979). *The Hypercycle: A Principle of Natural Self-Organization.* New York: Springer-Verlag. (Contains most of 1977, 1978a, 1978b.)

Eliade, Mircea (1959). *The Sacred and the Profane,* trans. W.R. Trask. New York: Harcourt, Brace and World.

Evnine, Simon (1991). *Donald Davidson.* Stanford, CA: Stanford University Press.

Fadiman, Clifton, ed. (1958). *Fantasia Mathematica.* New York: Simon and Schuster.

Fairbanks, Matthew J. (1976). 'Peirce on Man as a Language: A Textual Interpretation.' *Transactions of the Charles S. Peirce Society* 12 (1), 18–32.

Fann, K.T. (1970). *Peirce's Theory of Abduction.* The Hague: Martinus Nijhoff.

Feyerabend, Paul K. (1975). *Against Method.* London: NLB.

– (1987). *Farewell to Reason.* London: Verso.

Finlay, Marike (1990). *The Potential of Modern Discourse: Musil, Peirce, and Perturbation.* Bloomington: Indiana University Press.

Fisch, Max (1986). *Peirce, Semeiotic, and Pragmatism.* Bloomington: Indiana University Press.

Fitzgerald, John J. (1966). *Peirce's Theory of Signs as Foundation for Pragmatism.* The Hague: Mouton.

Flaubert, Gustave (1954). *Bouvard and Pecuchet,* trans. T.W. Earp and G.W. Stonier. Norfolk, CN: J. Laughlin.

Fodor, Jerry A. (1987). *Psychosemantics: The Problem of Meaning in the Philosophy of Mind.* Cambridge: MIT.

Fodor, Jerry A., and Ernest Lepore, eds. (1992). *Holism: A Shopper's Guide.* London: Blackwell.

Foerster, Heinz von (1984). 'On Constructing a Reality.' In *The Invented Reality,* ed. P. Watzlawick, 41–61. New York: Norton.

Foucault, Michel (1970). *The Order of Things.* New York: Pantheon.

– (1977). *Discipline and Punish: The Birth of the Prison.* New York: Pantheon.

– (1980). *Power/Knowledge: Selected Interviews and Other Writings 1972–1977,* ed. and trans. C. Gordon. New York: Pantheon.

Francastel, P. (1977). *Peinture et société.* Paris: DeNöel/Gonthier.

Franz, Marie Luise von (1974). *Number and Time,* trans. A. Dykes. Evanston, IL: Northwestern University Press.

Fraser, J.T. (1979). *Time as Conflict: A Scientific and Humanistic Study*. Basel: Birkhäuser.

– (1982). *The Genesis and Evolution of Time: A Critique of Interpretation in Physics*. Amherst: University of Massachusetts Press.

Gaggi, Silvio (1989). *Modern/Postmodern: A Study of Twentieth-Century Art and Ideas*. Philadelphia: University of Pennsylvania Press.

Gamow, George (1947). *One, Two, Three ... Infinity*. New York: Viking.

Gardner, Martin (1964). *The Ambidextrous Universe: Mirror Asymmetry and the Time-Reversed Worlds*. New York: Scribner's.

Geertz, Clifford (1975). *The Interpretation of Culture*. New York: Basic.

Gerard, R.W., C. Kluckhohn, and A. Rapoport (1956). 'Biological and Cultural Evolution: Some Analogies and Explorations.' *Behavioral Science* 1, 6–34.

Gibson, J.J. (1966). *The Senses Considered as Perceptual Systems*. Boston: Houghton-Mifflin.

Glaserfeld, Ernst von (1974). 'Piaget and the Radical Constructivist Epistemology.' In *Epistemology and Education (Report 14)*, ed. C.D. Smock and E. von Glaserfeld. Athens, GA: Mathemagenic Activities Program.

– (1979a). 'Cybernetics, Experience, and the Concept of Self.' In *A Cybernetics Approach to the Assessment of Children: Toward a More Humane Use of Human Beings*, ed. M.N. Ozer. Boulder, CO: Westview Press.

– (1979b). 'Radical Constructivism and Piaget's Concept of Knowledge.' In *The Impact of Piagetian Theory*, ed. R.B. Murry, 109–24. Baltimore: University Park Press.

– (1984). 'An Introduction to Radical Constructivism.' In *The Invented Reality*, ed. P. Watzlawick, 5–19. New York: Norton.

Gleick, James (1987). *Chaos: Making a New Science*. New York: Viking.

Globus, Gordon (1976). 'Mind, Structure, and Contradiction.' In *Consciousness and the Brain: A Scientific and Philosophical Inquiry*, ed. G.G. Globus, G. Maxwell, and I. Savodnik, 271–93. New York: Plenum.

Gombrich, Ernst H. (1960). *Art and Illusion*. Princeton, NJ: Princeton University Press.

– (1979). *The Sense of Order: A Study in the Psychology of Decorative Art*. Ithaca, NY: Cornell University Press.

Goodman, Nelson (1978). *Ways of Worldmaking*. Indianapolis: Hackett.

Gorlée, Dinda L. (1990). 'Degeneracy: A Reading of Peirce's Writing.' *Semiotica* 81 (1/2), 71–92.

Goudge, Thomas A. (1952). 'Peirce's Theory of Abstraction.' In *Studies in the Philosophy of Charles Sanders Peirce*, ed. P.P. Wiener and F.H. Young, 121–32. Cambridge: Harvard University Press.

Gramont, Patrick de (1990). *Language and the Distortion of Meaning*. New York: New York University Press.

Granet, Marcel (1968). *La Pensée chinoise*. Paris: Albin Michel.

Greenlee, Douglas (1973). *Peirce's Concept of Sign*. The Hague: Mouton.

Gregory, Bruce (1988). *Inventing Reality: Physics as Language.* New York: Wiley.

Gregory, Richard L. (1981). *Mind in Science: A History of Explanations in Psychology and Physics.* Cambridge: Cambridge University Press.

Gregory, Richard L. and Ernst Gombrich, eds. (1973). *Illusion in Nature and Art.* New York: Scribner's.

Greimas, A.J. (1966). 'Eléments pour une théorie de l'interprétation du récit mythique.' *Communications* 8, 28–59.

– (1970). 'Sémantique, Sémiotique et sémiologies.' In *Sign, Language, Culture*, ed. C.H. Schooneveld, 13–27. The Hague: Mouton.

Griffin, David Ray, ed. (1988). *The Reenchantment of Science: Post-modern Proposals.* Albany: State University of New York Press.

Groupe μ (1981). *A General Rhetoric*, trans. P.B. Burrell and E.M. Slotkin. Baltimore MD: Johns Hopkins University Press.

Grünbaum, Adolph (1963). *Philosophical Problems of Space and Time.* New York: Knopf.

– (1967). *Modern Science and Zeno's Paradoxes.* Middletown, CN: Wesleyan University Press.

Habermas, Jurgen (1979). *Communication and the Evolution of Society.* Boston: Beacon.

– (1984). *The Theory of Communicative Action*, vol. 1. Boston: Beacon.

– (1987). *The Philosophical Discourse of Modernity.* Cambridge: MIT.

Hacking, Ian (1975). *The Emergence of Probability.* Cambridge: Cambridge University Press.

– (1983). *Representing and Intervening: Introductory Topics in the Philosophy of Natural Science.* Cambridge: Cambridge University Press.

– (1990). *The Taming of Chance.* Cambridge: Cambridge University Press.

Hanson, Norwood R. (1958). *Patterns of Discovery.* Cambridge: Cambridge University Press.

– (1969). *Perception and Discovery.* San Francisco: Freeman, Cooper.

Harré, Rom (1970). *The Principles of Scientific Thinking.* New York: Macmillan.

– (1981). 'The Evolutionary Analogy in Social Explanation.' In *The Philosophy of Evolution*, ed. U.J. Jensen and R. Harré, 161–75. Brighton: Harvester Press.

Hartshorne, Charles (1970). *Creative Synthesis and Philosophic Method.* LaSalle, IL: Open Court.

Harvey, David (1989). *The Condition of Postmodernity: An Enquiry into the Origins of Cultural Change.* Cambridge, MA: Blackwell.

Harvey, Irene E. (1986). *Derrida and the Economy of 'Différance.'* Bloomington: Indiana University Press.

Hassan, Ihab (1980). *The Right Promethean Fire: Imagination, Science, and Cultural Change.* Urbana: University of Illinois Press.

– (1987). *The Postmodern Turn: Essays in Postmodern Theory and Culture.* Columbus: Ohio State University Press.

Hawkins, David (1964). *The Language of Life: An Essay in the Philosophy of Science*. San Francisco: Freeman.

Hayward, Jeremy W. (1987). *Shifting Worlds, Changing Minds*. Boston: Shambhala.

Hebb, Donald O. (1949). *The Organization of Behavior*. New York: Wiley.

Heelan, Patrick (1983). *Space-Perception and the Philosophy of Science*. Berkeley: University of California Press.

Heisenberg, Werner (1958). *Physics and Philosophy*. Cambridge: Cambridge University Press.

Helmholtz, H. von (1876). 'The Origin and Meaning of Geometrical Axioms.' *Mind* 1, 301–21.

Hempel, Carl G. (1946). 'A Note on the Paradoxes of Confirmation.' *Mind* 55, 79–82.

Herbert, Nick (1985). *Quantum Reality: Beyond the New Physics*. Garden City, NY: Anchor.

Hesse, Mary B. (1966). *Models and Analogies in Science*. Notre Dame: University of Notre Dame Press.

– (1980). *Revolutions and Reconstructions in the Philosophy of Science*. Bloomington: Indiana University Press.

Heynick, Frank (1983). 'From Einstein to Whorf: Space, Time, Matter, and Reference Frames to Physical and Linguistic Relativity.' *Semiotica* 45 (1/2), 35–64.

Hinton, C. Howard (1887). *What Is the Fourth Dimension?* London: Sonnenschein.

– (1888). *The New Era of Thought*. London: Sonnenschein.

Hoffmeyer, Jesper, and Claus Emmeche (1991). 'Code-Duality and the Semiotics of Nature.' In *On Semiotic Modeling*, ed. M. Anderson and F. Merrell, 117–66. Berlin: Mouton de Gruyter.

Hofstadter, Douglas R. (1979). *Gödel, Escher, Bach: An Eternal Golden Braid*. New York: Basic.

Hollis, Martin, and Steven Lukes, eds. (1982). *Rationality and Relativism*. Cambridge: MIT.

Houston, Beverle (1984). 'Viewing Television: The Metapsychology of Endless Consumption.' *Quarterly Review of Film Studies* 9 (3), 183–95.

Husserl, Edmund (1913; 1970). *Logical Investigations*. New York: Humanities Press.

Hutcheon, Linda (1988). *A Poetics of Postmodernism: History, Theory, Fiction*. New York: Routledge.

Hutten, Ernest H. (1962). *The Origins of Science: An Inquiry into the Foundations of Western Thought*. London: Allen and Unwin.

Huyssen, Andreas (1986). *After the Great Divide: Modernism, Mass Culture, Postmodernism*. Bloomington: Indiana University Press.

Ingold, Tim (1986). *Evolution and Social Life*. Cambridge: Cambridge University Press.

Irigaray, Luce (1980). 'When Our Lips Speak Together,' trans. and with intro. by C. Burke. *Signs: Journal of Women in Culture and Society* 6 (1), 66–79.

– (1985). *This Sex Which Is Not One*, trans. C. Porter and C. Burke. Ithaca, NY: Cornell University Press.

Ittelson, W.H., and F.P. Kilpatrick (1952). 'Experiments in Perception.' *Scientific American* 185, 50–5.

Ivins, William J., Jr. (1973). *On the Rationalization of Sight*. New York: DaCapo.

Jacob, François (1982). *The Logic of Life: A History of Heredity*. New York: Pantheon.

Jakobson, Roman (1964). 'Principes de phonologie historique.' In N.S. Troubetskoy, *Principes de phonologie*, trans. J. Cantineau, 315–36. Paris: Klincksieck.

– (1972). 'Verbal Communication.' In *Communication: A Scientific American Book*, 39–42. San Francisco: W.H.Freeman.

– (1973). *Main Trends in the Science of Language*. London: Allen and Unwin.

Jameson, Fredric (1979). 'Reification and Utopia in Mass Culture.' *Social Text* 1, 130–48.

– (1981). *The Political Unconsciousness: Narrative as a Socially Symbolic Act*. Ithaca, NY: Cornell University Press.

– (1983). 'Postmodernism and Consumerist Society.' In *The Anti-Aesthetic: Essays on Postmodern Culture*, ed. H. Foster, 111–25. Port Townsend, WA: Bay Press.

– (1984). 'Postmodernism, or, The Cultural Logic of Late Capitalism.' *New Left Review* 146, 59–92.

– (1992). *Postmodernism, or, The Cultural Logic of Late Capitalism*. Durham, NC: Duke University Press.

Jantsch, Erich (1980). *The Self-Organizing Universe: Scientific and Human Implications of the Emerging Paradigm of Evolution*. Oxford: Pergamon.

– ed. (1981). *The Evolutionary Vision*. Boulder, CO: Westview.

Jarvie, I.C. (1984). *Rationality and Relativism: In Search of a Philosophy and History of Anthropology*. London: Routledge and Kegan Paul.

Jencks, Charles (1977). *The Language of Postmodern Architecture*. New York: Rizzoli.

Jenny, Hans (1967). *Cymatics: The Structural Dynamics of Waves and Vibrations*. Basel: Basilius.

Johansen, Jørgen Dines (1992). *Dialogic Semiosis*. Bloomington: Indiana University Press.

Jung, Carl G. (1964). *The Collected Works of C.G. Jung: Civilization in Transition*, vol. 10, trans. R.F.C. Hull. (Bollingen Series, 20). Princeton, NJ: Princeton University Press.

Kauffman, Louis H. (1986). 'Self Reference and Recursive Forms.' *Journal of Social Biological Structure* 9, 1-21.

Kauffman, Louis H. and Francisco J. Varela (1980). 'Form Dynamics.' *Journal of Social Biological Structure* 3, 171–216.

Keesing, Roger M. (1987). 'Anthropology as Interpretive Quest.' *Current Anthropology* 28 (2), 161–76.

Kellner, Douglas (1989). *Jean Baudrillard: From Marxism to Postmodernism and Beyond*. Stanford, CA: Stanford University Press.

Kevles, Daniel J., and Leroy Hood, eds. (1992). *The Code of Codes: Scientific and Social Issues in the Human Genome Project*. Cambridge: Harvard University Press.

Klenk, V.H. (1976). *Wittgenstein's Philosophy of Mathematics*. The Hague: Martinus Nijhoff.

Kline, Morris (1980). *Mathematics: The Loss of Certainty*. Oxford: Oxford University Press.

Kolers, Paul (1972). *Aspects of Motion Perception*. Oxford: Pergamon.

Koyré, Alexandre (1957). *From the Closed World to the Infinite Universe*. Baltimore, MD: Johns Hopkins University Press.

– (1968). *Metaphysics and Measurement: Essays in Scientific Revolutions*. London: Chapman and Hall.

– (1978). *Galileo Studies*, trans. J. Pepham. Atlantic Highlands, NJ: Humanities Press.

Krausz, Michael, ed. (1989). *Relativism: Interpretation and Confrontation*. Notre Dame: Notre Dame University Press.

Kripke, Saul A. (1982). *Wittgenstein on Rules and Private Language*. Cambridge: Harvard University Press.

Kristeva, Julia (1969). *Semiotiké: Recherches pour une sémanalyse*. Paris: Seuil.

– (1984). *Desire in Language: A Semiotic Approach to Literature and Art*, trans. T.S. Gora, A. Jardine, and L.S. Roudiez. Oxford: Blackwell.

Kroker, Arthur (1992). *The Possessed Individual: Technology and New French Theory*. New York: St Martin.

Kuhn, Thomas S. (1970). *The Structure of Scientific Revolutions*. Chicago: University of Chicago Press.

– (1977). *The Essential Tension*. Chicago: University of Chicago Press.

Lacan, Jacques (1966). *Ecrits*. Paris: Seuil.

– (1975). *Le Séminaire, Livre XX: Encore*. Paris: Seuil.

– (1982). *Feminine Sexuality*, trans. J. Rose. New York: Norton.

Laclau, E. (1985). *Hegemony and Socialist Strategy*. London: Verso.

Laing, R.D. (1970). *Knots*. New York: Random House.

Lasch, Christopher (1977). *Haven in a Heartless World: The Family Besieged*. New York: Basic.

Laszlo, Ervin (1987). *Evolution: The Grand Synthesis*. Boston: Shambhala.

Layzer, David (1972). 'Cosmology and the Arrow of Time.' In *Vistas in Astronomy*, ed. A. Beer, 279–87. New York: Pergamon.

– (1975). 'The Arrow of Time.' *Scientific American* 233 (6), 56–69.

Leach, Edmund (1961). *Rethinking Anthropology*. London: Athlone.

– (1964). 'Anthropological Aspects of Language: Animal Categories and Verbal Abuse,' in *New Directions in the Study of Language*, ed. E.H. Lenneberg, 23–63. Cambridge: MIT.

Leatherdale, W.H. (1974). *The Role of Analogy, Model and Metaphor in Science*. Amsterdam: North-Holland.

Lecercle, Jean-Jacques (1985). *Philosophy through the Looking-Glass: Language, Nonsense, Desire.* LaSalle, IL: Open Court.

Lee, H.N. (1965). 'Are Zeno's Paradoxes Based on a Mistake?' *Mind* 74 (296), 563–70.

Lefebvre, Henri (1971). *Everyday Life in the Modern World*, trans. S. Rabinovitch. New York: Harper and Row.

Lehmann, Hugh (1979). *Introduction to the Philosophy of Mathematics.* Totowa, NJ: Rowman and Littlefield.

Leighton, T., and W.F. Loomis (1980). 'Introduction.' In *The Molecular Genetics of Development*, ed. T. Leighton and W.F. Loomis, xiii–xxiii. New York: Academic Press.

Lewontin, R.C. (1992). 'The Dream of the Human Genome.' *The New York Review of Books* May 28, 31–40.

Lewontin, R.C., Steven Rose, and Leon J. Kamin (1984). *Not in Our Genes: Biology, Ideology, and Human Nature.* New York: Random House.

Liszka, James Jakób (1989). *The Semiotic of Myth: A Critical Study of the Symbol.* Bloomington: Indiana University Press.

Lockwood, Michael (1991). *Mind, Brain, and the Quantum: The Compound 'I.'* London: Blackwell.

Löfgren, Lars (1978). 'Some Foundational Views on General Systems and the Hempel Paradox.' *International Journal of General Systems* 4, 243–53.

– (1981a). 'Knowledge of Evolution and Evolution of Knowledge.' In *The Evolutionary Vision*, ed. E. Jantsch, 129–51. Boulder, CO: Westview.

– (1981b). 'Life as an Autolinguistic Phenomenon.' In *Autopoiesis: A Theory Of Living Organization*, ed. M. Zeleny, 236–49. New York: North-Holland.

– (1984). 'Autology of Time.' *International Journal of General Systems* 10, 5–14.

Lovelock, J.E. (1979). *Gaia: A New Look at Life on Earth.* Oxford: Oxford University Press.

Lumsden, Charles J. (1986). 'The Gene and the Sign: Giving Structure to Postmodernity.' *Semiotica* 62 (3/4), 191–206.

Lumsden, C.J. and E. O Wilson (1981). *Genes, Mind and Culture.* Cambridge: Harvard University Press.

Lyotard, Jean-François (1984). *The Postmodern Condition: A Report on Knowledge*, trans. G. Bennington and B. Massumi. Minneapolis: University of Minnesota Press.

– (1988). *The Differend: Phrases in Dispute*, trans. G.V. D. Abbeele (Theory and History of Literature 46). Minneapolis: University of Minnesota Press.

McCulloch, Warren Sturgis (1965). *Embodiments of Mind.* Cambridge: MIT.

MacDermott, David (1974). *Meta Metaphor.* Boston: Beacon.

McTaggart, J.M.E. (1927). *The Nature of Existence*, vol. 2. Cambridge: Cambridge University Press.

Marchand, Roland (1985). *Advertising and the American Dream: Making Way for Modernity, 1920–1940.* Berkeley: University of California Press.

Marcus, G.E., and Michael M.J. Fischer, eds. (1986). *Anthropology as Cultural Critique: An Experimental Moment in the Human Sciences*. Chicago: University of Chicago Press.

Marvin, Carolyn (1988). *When Old Technologies Were New: Thinking about Electric Communication in the Late Nineteenth Century*. New York: Oxford University Press.

Masters, Roger D. (1970). 'Genes, Language, and Evolution.' *Semiotica* 2 (4), 295–320.

Matte Blanco, Ignacio (1975). *The Unconscious as Infinite Sets: An Essay in Bi-Logic*. London: Duckworth.

Maturana, Humberto and Francisco Varela (1980). *Autopoiesis and Cognition: The Realization of the Living*. Dordrecht, Holland: D. Reidel.

– (1987). *The Tree of Knowledge: The Biological Roots of Human Understanding*. Boston: Shambhala.

Mays, W. (1953). 'An Elementary Introduction to Piaget's Logic.' In *Logic and Psychology*, by J. Piaget, ix–xvi. Manchester: Manchester University Press.

Mellor, D.H. (1981). *Real Time*. Cambridge: Cambridge University Press.

Merleau-Ponty, Maurice (1962). *Phenomenology of Perception*, trans. C. Smith. New York: Humanities Press.

Merrell, Floyd (1975). 'Structuralism and Beyond: A Critique of Presuppositions.' *Diogenes* 92, 67–103.

– (1983). *Pararealities: The Nature of Our Fictions and How We Know Them*. Amsterdam: John Benjamins.

– (1985a). *Deconstruction Reframed*. West Lafayette, IN: Purdue University Press.

– (1985b). *A Semiotic Theory of Texts*. Berlin: Mouton de Gruyter.

– (1986). 'An Uncertain Semiotic.' In *The Current in Criticism*, ed. V. Lokke and C. Koelb, 243–64. West Lafayette, IN: Purdue University Press.

– (1991a). *Unthinking Thinking: Jorge Luis Borges, Mathematics, and the 'New Physics.'* West Lafayette, IN: Purdue University Press.

– (1991b). *Signs Becoming Signs: Our Perfusive, Pervasive Universe*. Bloomington: Indiana University Press.

– (1992). *Sign, Textuality, World*. Bloomington: Indiana University Press.

– (1995). *Semiosis in the Postmodernist Age*. W. Lafayette, IN: Purdue University Press.

Monod, Jacques (1971). *Chance and Necessity*, trans. A. Wainhouse. New York: Random House.

Morin, Edgar (1987). 'What Could Be a Mind Able to Conceive a Brain Able to Produce a Mind?' In *The Real and the Imaginary: A New Approach to Physics*, ed. J.E. Charon, 1–14. New York: Paragon House.

Morris, Charles (1938). *Foundations of the Theory of Signs*. Chicago: University of Chicago Press.

– (1946). *Signs, Language, and Behavior*. New York: Prentice-Hall.

Murphey, Murray G. (1961). *The Development of Peirce's Philosophy*. Cambridge: Harvard University Press.

Nadin, Mihai (1982). 'Consistency, Completeness and the Meaning of Sign Theories.' *American Journal of Semiotics* 1 (3), 79–98.

– (1983). 'The Logic of Vagueness and the Category of Synechism.' In *The Relevance of Charles Peirce*, ed. E. Freeman, 154–66. LaSalle, IL: Monist Library of Philosophy.

Nesher, Dan (1983). 'A Pragmatic Theory of Meaning: A Note on Peirce's "Last" Formulation of the Pragmatic Maxim and its Interpretation.' *Semiotica* 44 (3/4), 203–57.

– (1990). 'Understanding Sign Semiosis as Cognition and as Self-Conscious Process: A Reconstruction of Some Basic Concepts of Peirce's Semiotics.' *Semiotica* 79 (1/2), 1–49.

Neumann, Erich (1954). *The Origins and History of Consciousness*, trans. R.F.C. Hull (Bollingen Series, 42). New York: Pantheon.

Neuwirth, Lee Paul (1979). *Knots, Groups, and 3-Manifolds*. Princeton, NJ: Princeton University Press.

Newton-Smith, W.H. (1981). *The Rationality of Science*. London: Routledge and Kegan Paul.

Nicolis, Grégoire and Ilya Prigogine (1989). *Exploring Complexity: An Introduction*. New York: Freeman.

Noble, G.B. (1969). *Applied Linear Algebra*. Englewood Cliffs, NJ: Prentice-Hall.

Nodine, C.F., and D.F. Fisher, eds. (1979). *Perception and Pictorial Representation*. New York: Praeger.

Nöth, Winifred (1990). *Handbook of Semiotics*. Bloomington: Indiana University Press.

O'Hara, Daniel T., ed. (1985). *Why Nietzsche Now?* Bloomington: Indiana University Press.

Ortega y Gasset, José (1948). *The Dehumanization of Art, and Notes on the Novel*. Princeton, NJ: Princeton University Press.

Oyama, Susan (1985). *The Ontogeny of Information: Developmental Systems and Evolution*. Cambridge: Cambridge University Press.

Pagels, Heinz (1985). *Perfect Symmetry: The Search for the Beginning of Time*. New York: Simon and Schuster.

Pais, Abraham (1991). *Neils Bohr's Times, in Physics, Philosophy, and Polity*. New York: Oxford University Press.

Panofsky, E. (1960). *Renaissance and Renascences in Western Art*. Stockholm: Almqvist and Wiksell.

Park, David (1980). *The Image of Eternity: Roots of Time in the Physical World*. New York: New American Library.

Parker, DeWitt (1941). *Experience and Substance*. Ann Arbor: University of Michigan Press.

Pattee, Howard H. (1969). 'How Does a Molecule Become a Message?' *Developmental Biology*, Supplement 3, 227–33.

– (1970). 'The Problem of Biological Hierarchy.' In *Towards a Theoretical Biology, 3*, ed. C.H. Waddington, 117–36. Chicago: Aldine.

– (1972). 'Laws and Constraints, Symbols and Languages.' In *Towards a Theoretical Biology, 4*, ed. C.H. Waddington, 248–58. Edinburgh: University of Edinburgh Press.

– (1977). 'Dynamic and Linguistic Modes of Complex Systems.' *International Journal of General Systems* 3, 259–66.

– (1979). 'Robert Rosen, Howard Hunt Pattee, and Raymond L. Somorja: A Symposium in Theoretical Biology.' In *A Question of Physics: Conversations in Physics and Biology*, ed. P. Buckley and F.D. Peat, 84–123. Toronto: University of Toronto Press.

– (1986). 'Universal Principles of Measurement and Language Functions in Evolving Systems.' In *Complexity, Language, and Life: Mathematical Approaches*, ed. J.L. Casti and A. Karlqvist, 268–81. Berlin: Springer-Verlag.

Penrose, Roger (1989). *The New Emperor's Mind: Concerning Computers, Minds, and the Laws of Physics*. Oxford: Oxford University Press.

Piaget, Jean (1953). *Logic and Psychology*. Manchester: Manchester University Press.

– (1965). *The Moral Judgment of the Child*. New York: Free Press.

– (1968). *Logical Thinking in Children*, ed. I.E. Sigel and F.H. Hooper. New York: Holt, Rinehart and Winston.

– (1970). *Structuralism*, trans. C. Maschler. New York: Basic Books.

– (1971a). *Biology and Knowledge*, trans. B. Walsh. Chicago: University of Chicago Press.

– (1971b). *Psychology and Epistemology: Towards a Theory of Knowledge*. New York: Viking Press.

– (1977). *The Development of Thought: Equilibration of Cognitive Structures*, trans. A. Rosin. New York: Viking.

Piaget, Jean and Barbel Inhelder (1956). *The Child's Conception of Space*, trans. F.J. Langdon and J.L. Lunzer. London: Routledge and Kegan Paul.

Pignatari, Decio (1978). 'The Contiguity Illusion.' In *Sight, Sound, and Sense*, ed. T.A. Sebeok, 84–97. Bloomington: Indiana University Press.

Poincaré, Henri (1952). *Science and Hypothesis*, trans. F. Maitland. New York: Dover.

– (1963). *Mathematics and Science: Last Essays*, trans. J.W. Bolduc. New York: Dover.

Polanyi, Michael (1958). *Personal Knowledge*. Chicago: University of Chicago Press.

Pöppel, Ernst (1972). 'Oscillators as Possible Basis for Time Perception.' In *The Study of Time*, ed. J.T. Fraser, F.C. Haber, and G.H. Miller, 219–41. New York: Springer-Verlag.

– (1988). *Mindworks: Time and Conscious Experience*. Boston: Harcourt, Brace, Jovanovich.

Popper, Karl R. (1972). *Objective Knowledge*. Oxford: Oxford University Press.

– (1974). *Unended Quest: An Intellectual Autobiography*. LaSalle, IL: Open Court.

Poster, Mark, ed. (1988). *Jean Baudrillard: Selected Writings.* Stanford, CA: Stanford University Press.

– ed. (1989). *Critical Theory and Poststructuralism: In Search of a Context.* Ithaca, NY: Cornell University Press.

– (1990). *The Mode of Information: Poststructuralism and Social Context.* Chicago: University of Chicago Press.

Pribram, Karl H. (1971). *Languages of the Brain: Experimental Paradoxes and Principles of Neuropsychology.* Englewood Cliffs, NJ: Prentice-Hall.

– (1981). 'The Distributed Nature of the Memory Store and the Localization of Linguistic Competencies.' In *The Neurological Basis of Signs in Communicational Processes,* ed. P. Perron (Toronto Semiotic Circle Monographs, Working Papers and Prepublications, 2–3), 127–82. Toronto: Victoria College.

– (1991). *Brain and Perception: Holonomy and Structure in Figural Processing.* Hillsdale, NJ: Lawrence Erlbaum.

Prigogine, Ilya (1980). *From Being to Becoming: Time and Complexity in the Physical Sciences.* San Francisco: Freeman.

– (1983). '¿Tan sólo una ilusión?' In *¿Tan sólo una ilusión? Una exploración del caos al orden,* ed. J. Wagensberg. Barcelona: Tusquets Editores.

– (1985). 'Forward.' In *Atoms of the Living Flame,* by George Prescott Scott, ix–x. Lanham, MD: University Press of America.

Prigogine, Ilya and Isabelle Stengers (1984). *Order out of Chaos: Man's New Dialogue with Nature.* New York: Bantam.

Putnam, Hilary (1990). *Realism with a Human Face,* ed. J. Conant. Cambridge: Harvard University Press.

Quine, Willard van Orman (1953). *From a Logical Point of View.* New York: Harper and Row.

– (1969). *Ontological Relativity and Other Essays.* New York: Columbia University Press.

Radnitsky, Gerald, and W.W. Bartley, III, eds. (1987). *Evolutionary Epistemology, Rationalism, and the Sociology of Knowledge.* LaSalle, IL: Open Court.

Rajchman, John, and Cornel West, eds. (1985). *Post-Analytic Philosophy.* New York: Columbia University Press.

Ransdell, Joseph (1979). 'The Epistemic Function of Iconicity in Perception.' In *Studies in Peirce's Semiotic, 1,* ed. J.E. Brock, et al., 51–66. Lubbock, TX: Institute for Studies in Pragmaticism.

– (1986). 'On Peirce's Conception of the Iconic Sign.' In *Iconicity: Essays on the Nature of Culture,* ed. P. Bouissac, et al, 51–74. Tübingen: Stauffenburg Verlag.

Rauch, Irmengard (1984). '"Symbols Grow": Creation, Compulsion, Change.' *American Journal of Semiotics* 3 (1), 1-23.

Reichenbach, Hans (1956). *The Philosophy of Space and Time,* trans. M. Reichenbach. New York: Dover.

Rescher, Nicholas (1978). *Peirce's Philosophy of Science*. Notre Dame: University of Notre Dame Press.

Rescher, Nicholas and Robert Brandom (1979). *The Logic of Inconsistency: A Study of Non-Standard Possible World Semantics and Ontology*. Totowa, NJ: Rowman and Littlefield.

Révész, Géza (1957). 'Optik und Haptik.' *Studium Generale* 6, 374–9.

Richards, J.L. (1979). 'The Reception of Mathematical Theory: Non-Euclidean Geometry in England, 1868–1883.' In *Natural Order: Historical Studies of Scientific Culture*, ed. B. Barnes and S. Shapin, 143–63. London: Sage.

Roberts, Don (1973). *The Existential Graphs of Charles S. Peirce*. The Hague: Mouton.

Rochberg-Halton, Eugene (1986). *Meaning and Modernity: Social Theory in the Pragmatic Attitude*. Chicago: University of Chicago Press.

Rock, I. (1983). *The Logic of Perception*. Cambridge: MIT.

Romanyshyn, Robert D. (1989). *Technology as Symptom and Dream*. London: Routledge.

Rorty, Richard (1979). *Philosophy and the Mirror of Nature*. Princeton, NJ: Princeton University Press.

– (1982). *Consequences of Pragmatism*. Minneapolis: University of Minnesota Press.

– (1991). *Objectivity, Relativism, and Truth, Philosophical Papers Volume 1*. Cambridge: Cambridge University Press.

Rosch, Eleanor (1974). 'Linguistic Relativity.' In *Human Communication: Theoretical Explorations*, ed. A. Silverstein, 95–121. New York: Halsted Press.

– (1975). 'Universals and Cultural Specifics in Human Categorization.' In *Cross-Cultural Perspectives on Learning*, ed. R. Brislin, S. Bochner, and W. Lonner, 177–206. New York: Halsted Press.

– (1977). 'Human Categorization.' In *Studies in Cross-Cultural Psychology*, vol. 1, ed. N. Warren, 3–49. London: Academic Press.

Rucker, Rudy (1984). *The Fourth Dimension: Toward a Geometry of Higher Reality*. Boston: Houghton-Mifflin.

Sacks, Mark (1989). *The World We Found: The Limits of Ontological Talk*. LaSalle, IL: Open Court.

Salmon, Wesley C. (1970). *Zeno's Paradoxes*. Indianapolis: Bobbs-Merrill.

Salthe, Stanley N. (1985). *Evolving Hierarchical Systems: Their Structure and Representation*. New York: Columbia University Press.

– (1992). *Complexity and Change in Biology: Development and Evolution*. Cambridge: MIT.

Sarfatti, Jack (1974). 'Implications of Meta-Physics for Psychoenergetics Systems.' *Psychoenergetics Systems*, vol. 1, 3–10. London: Gordon and Breach.

Saussure, Ferdinand de (1966). *Course in General Linguistics*, trans. W. Baskin. New York: McGraw-Hill.

Savan, David (1987–88). *An Introduction to C.S. Peirce's Full System of Semeiotic* (Monograph Series of the Toronto Semiotic Circle, 1). Toronto: Victoria College.

Schechner, Richard (1982). *The End of Humanism: Writings on Performance*. New York: Performing Arts Journal Publications.

Schrödinger, Erwin (1954). *Nature and the Greeks*. Cambridge: Cambridge University Press.

– (1967). *What Is Life?* and *Matter and Mind*. Cambridge: Cambridge University Press.

Searle, John (1977). 'Reiterating the Differences.' *Glyph* (Johns Hopkins Textual Studies, 1), 198–208. Baltimore, MD: Johns Hopkins University Press.

Sebeok, Thomas A. (1976a). *Contributions to the Doctrine of Signs*. Bloomington: Indiana University Press.

– (1976b). 'Iconicity.' *Modern Language Notes* 91, 1427–56.

– (1977a). 'Ecumenicalism in Semiotics.' In *A Perfusion of Signs*, ed. T.A. Sebeok, 180–206. Bloomington: Indiana University Press.

– (1977b). *How Animals Communicate*. Bloomington: Indiana University Press.

– (1979). *The Sign and Its Masters*. Austin: University of Texas Press.

– (1983). 'On the History of Semiotics.' In *Semiotics Unfolding* (Proceedings of the Second Congress of the International Association for Semiotic Studies, 1979), vol. 1, ed. T. Borbé, 353–4. Berlin: Mouton de Gruyter.

– (1986). *I Think I Am a Verb*. New York: Plenum.

– et al, eds. (1986) *Encyclopedic Dictionary of Semiotics*, 3 vols. Berlin: Mouton de Gruyter.

– (1991). *Semiotics in the United States*. Bloomington: Indiana University Press.

Sebeok, Thomas A., and R. Rosenthall, eds. (1981). *The Clever Hans Phenomena: Communication with Horses, Whales, Apes, and People*. New York: New York Academy of Sciences.

Sellars, Wilfrid (1963). *Science, Perception, and Reality*. New York: Humanities Press.

Shanker, Stuart (1987). *Wittgenstein and the Turning-Point in the Philosophy of Mathematics*. Albany: State University of New York Press.

Sheffer, Henry M. (1913). 'A Set of Five Independent Postulates of Boolean Algebra.' *Transactions of the American Mathematical Society* 14, 481–8.

Sheldrake, Rupert (1988a). 'The Laws of Nature as Habits: A Post-modern Basis for Science.' In *The Reenchantment of Science: Post-modern Proposals*, ed. D.R. Griffin, 79–86. Albany: State University of New York Press.

– (1988b). *The Presence of the Past: Morphic Resonance and the Habits of Nature*. New York: Random House.

Sheriff, John K. (1989). *The Fate of Meaning: Charles Peirce, Structuralism, and Literature*. Princeton, NJ: Princeton University Press.

Short, Tom L. (1981). 'Peirce's Concept of Final Causation.' *Transactions of the Charles S. Peirce Society* 17 (4), 369–82.

– (1982). 'Life among the Legisigns.' *Transactions of the Charles S. Peirce Society* 18 (4), 285–310.

Singer, Beth (1983). *Ordinal Naturalism*. Lewisburg, PA: Bucknell University Press.

Singh, Jagjit (1966). *Great Ideas in Information Theory, Language and Cybernetics*. New York: Dover.

Skolimowski, Henryk (1986). 'Quine, Adjukiewicz, and the Predicament of 20th Century Philosophy.' In *The Philosophy of W.V. Quine*, ed. L.E. Hahn and P.A. Schilpp, 463–90. LaSalle, IL: Open Court.

– (1987). 'The Interactive Mind in the Participatory Universe.' In *The Real and the Imaginary: A New Approach to Physics*, ed. J.E. Charon, 69–94. New York: Paragon House.

Slaatte, H.A. (1968). *The Pertinence of the Paradox*. New York: Humanities Press.

Smart, Barry (1991). *Modern Conditions, Postmodern Controversies*. London: Routledge.

Smart, J.J.C (1964). *Problems of Space and Time*. New York: Macmillan.

Snyder, Joel (1980). 'Picturing Vision.' *Critical Inquiry* 6 (3), 499–526.

Spencer-Brown, G. (1979). *Laws of Form*. New York: Dutton.

Sperry, Roger W. (1966). 'Brain Bisection and Consciousness.' In *Brain and Conscious Experience*, ed. J.C. Eccles, 298–313. New York: Springer.

Stewart, Ian (1989). *Does God Play Dice? The Mathematics of Chaos*. London: Blackwell.

Suzuki, David, and Peter Knudston (1990). *Genethics: The Clash between the New Genetics and Human Values*. Cambridge: Harvard University Press.

Sypher, Wylie (1962). *Loss of the Self in Modern Literature and Art*. New York: Random House.

Szamosi, Géza (1986). *The Twin-Dimensions: Inventing Time and Space*. New York: McGraw-Hill.

Terdiman, Richard (1985). *Discourse/Counter-Discourse: The Theory and Practice of Symbolic Resistance in Nineteenth-Century France*. Ithaca, NY: Cornell University Press.

Thompson, Manley (1953). *The Pragmatic Philosophy of C.S. Peirce*. Chicago: University of Chicago Press.

Thorpe, W.H. (1956). *Learning and Instinct in Animals*. London: Methuen.

Toulmin, Stephen (1972). *Human Understanding I*. Oxford: Clarendon.

Turkle, Sherry (1978). *Psychoanalytic Politics: Freud's French Revolution*. New York: Basic Books.

Turley, Peter T. (1977). *Peirce's Cosmology*. New York: Philosophical Library.

Tursman, Richard (1987). *Peirce's Theory of Scientific Discovery: A System of Logic Conceived as Semiotic*. Bloomington: Indiana University Press.

Tyler, Stephen (1987). *The Unspeakable: Discourse, Dialogue, and Rhetoric in the Postmodern World*. Madison: University of Wisconsin Press.

Uexküll, Jakob von (1957). 'A Stroll through the Worlds of Animals and Men: A Picture Book of Invisible Worlds.' In *Instinctive Behavior: The Development of a Modern Concept*, ed. C.H. Scholler, 5–80. New York: International Universities Press.

– (1982). 'The Theory of Meaning.' *Semiotica* 42 (1), 25–82.

Uexküll, Thure von (1982). 'Introduction: Meaning and Science in Jakob von Uexküll's Concept of Biology.' *Semiotica* 42 (1), 1–24.

Ulmer, Gregory L. (1985). *Applied Grammatology: Post(e)-Pedagogy from Jacques Derrida to Joseph Beuys*. Baltimore, MD: Johns Hopkins University Press.

Ushenko, Andrew (1946). 'Zeno's Paradoxes.' *Mind* 55, 131–43.

Valéry, Paul (1947). *Monsieur Teste*, trans. J. Mathews. New York: McGraw-Hill.

Varela, Francisco J. (1979). *Principles of Biological Autonomy*. Amsterdam: North-Holland.

– (1984a). 'The Creative Circle: Sketches on the Natural History of Circularity.' In *The Invented Reality*, ed. P. Watzlawick, 309–23. New York: Norton.

– (1984b). 'Living Ways of Sense-Making: A Middle Path for Neuroscience.' In *Disorder and Order* (Proceedings of the Stanford International Symposium, Sept. 1981), ed. P. Livingston, 208–24. Saratoga, CA: Anma Libri.

Waddington, Conrad H. (1957). *The Strategy of the Genes*. London: Allen and Unwin.

– (1977). *Tools for Thought*. St Albans: Paladin.

Wakefield, Neville (1990). *Postmodernism: The Twilight of the Real*. London: Pluto Press.

Walker, Evan Harris (1970). 'The Nature of Consciousness.' *Mathematical Biosciences* 7, 138–78.

Wartofsky, Marx (1980). 'Art History and Perception.' In *Perceiving Artworks*, ed. J. Fisher, 23–41. Philadelphia: Temple University Press.

– (1979). *Models: Representation and Scientific Understanding* (Boston Studies in the Philosophy of Science, 48). Dordrecht, Holland: D. Reidel.

Wellmer, Albrecht (1974). 'Communication and Emancipation: Reflections on the Linguistic Turn in Critical Theory.' In *On Critical Theory*, ed. J. O'Neill, 231–63. New York: Seabury Press.

– (1985). 'On the Dialectic of Modernism and Postmodernism.' *Praxis International* 4 (4), 337–62.

Weyl, Hermann (1949). *Philosophy of Mathematics and Natural Science*. New York: Atheneum.

Wheeler, John Archibald (1980a). 'Beyond the Black Hole.' In *Some Strangeness in the Proportion: A Centennial Symposium to Celebrate the Achievement of Albert Einstein*, ed. H. Woolf, 341–75. Reading, MA: Addison-Wesley.

– (1980b). 'Law without Law.' In *Structure in Science and Art*, ed. P. Medawar and J.H. Shelley, 132–68. Amsterdam: Excerpta Medica.

– (1984). 'Bits, Quanta, Meaning.' In *Theoretical Physics Meeting*, 121–34. Napoli: Edizioni Scientifiche Italiane.

Whitehead, Alfred North (1925). *Science and the Modern World*. New York: Macmillan.

– (1938). *Modes of Thought*. New York: Macmillan.

Whitehead, Alfred North, and Bertrand Russell (1927). *Principia Mathematica*, 2nd ed. Cambridge: Cambridge University Press.

Whitrow, G.J. (1980). *The Natural Philosophy of Time.* Oxford: Clarendon.

Wicken, J.S. (1979). 'The Generation of Complexity in Evolution: A Thermodynamic and Information-Theoretical Discussion.' *Journal of Theoretical Biology* 77, 349–65.

– (1980). 'A Thermodynamic Theory of Evolution.' *Journal of Theoretical Biology* 87, 9–23.

– (1987). *Evolution, Thermodynamics, and Information: Extending the Darwinian Program.* Oxford: Oxford University Press.

Wiener, Norbert (1948). *Cybernetics: Or, Control and Communication in Animals and the Machine.* Cambridge: MIT.

Wigner, Eugene (1967). *Symmetries and Reflections, Scientific Essays.* Bloomington: Indiana University Press.

– (1969). 'The Unreasonable Effectiveness of Mathematics in the Natural Sciences.' In *The Spirit and the Uses of the Mathematical Sciences,* ed. T.L. Saaty and F.J. Weyl, 123–40. New York: McGraw-Hill.

Wilhelm, Richard (1967). *The I Ching: Or, Book of Changes.* Princeton, NJ: Princeton University Press.

Wilkins, John (1968). *An Essay towards a Real Character, and a Philosophical Language.* Menstan: Scolar Press Facsimile (reprint of London: Gellibrand, 1668).

Wilkins, M.H.F. (1987). 'Complementarity and the Union of Opposites.' In *Quantum Implications: Essays in Honour of David Bohm,* ed. B.J. Hiley and F.D. Peat, 338–60. London: Routledge and Kegan Paul.

Winfree, Arthur T. (1972). 'Spiral Waves of Chemical Activity.' *Science* 175, 634–6.

– (1987). *When Time Breaks Down: The Three-Dimensional Dynamics of Electrochemical Waves and Cardiac Arrhythmias.* Princeton, NJ: Princeton University Press.

Wittgenstein, Ludwig (1953). *Philosophical Investigations,* trans. G.E.M. Anscombe. New York: Macmillan.

– (1961). *Tractatus Logico-Philosophicus,* trans. D.F. Pears and B.F. McGuinness. London: Routledge and Kegan Paul.

Wolf, Fred (1986). *Star Wave: Mind, Consciousness, and Quantum Physics.* New York: Macmillan.

Young, Arthur (1976). *The Geometry of Meaning.* San Francisco: Delacorte Press.

Young, John Z. (1978). *Programs of the Brain.* Oxford: Oxford University Press.

Yourgrau, Wolfgang (1966). 'Language, Spatial Concepts and Physics.' In *Mind, Matter, and Method,* ed. P.K. Feyerabend and G. Maxwell, 496–9. Minneapolis: University of Minnesota Press.

Zavarzadeh, Mas'ud, and Donald Morton (1991). *Theory, (Post)Modernity, Opposition: An 'Other' Introduction to Literary and Cultural Theory.* Washington, DC: Maisonneuve.

Zohar, Danah (1990). *The Quantum Self: A Revolutionary View of Human Nature and Consciousness Rooted in the New Physics.* New York: Morrow.

Index

Definitions of key terms can be found in the glossary.